UNDERSTANDING GOD'S HEART *for* Children

TOWARD A BIBLICAL FRAMEWORK

EDITED BY
DOUGLAS MCCONNELL, JENNIFER ORONA, PAUL STOCKLEY

Originally published in 2007 by Authentic, in partnership with World Vision

2019 Reprint with permission by
Mind the Millstone
c/o Dave Scott
Fuller Theological Seminary
135 N Oakland Ave
Pasadena, CA 91101

Understanding God's Heart for Children
ISBN-13: 978-1-793037-30-5

Copyright © 2007 by Douglas McConnell, Jennifer Orona, and Paul Stockley

All rights reserved. No part of this book may be reproduced in any form without permission in writing from the publisher, except in the case of brief quotations embodied in critical articles or reviews.

Scripture quotations marked AMP are taken from the *Amplified Bible*, Copright © 1943, 1958, 1962, 1964, 1965, 1987 by The Lockman Foundation. Used by permission.

Scripture quotations marked NAS are taken from the NEW AMERICAN STANDARD BIBLE ®, Copyright © 1960, 1962, 1963, 1968, 1971, 1972, 1973, 1975, 1977, 1995 by Th Lockman Foundation. Used by permission.

Scripture quotations marked NRSV are taken from the New Revised Standard Version Bible, copyright 1989, Division of Christian Education of the National Council of the Churches of Christ in the United States of America. Used by permission. All rights reserved.

Scripture quotations marked NIV are taken from the *Holy Bible, New International Version®*, NIV®, Copyright © 1973, 1978, 1984 by International Bible Society. Used by permission of Zondervan. All rights reserved.

Scripture quotations marked MSG are taken from THE MESSAGE. Copyright © 1993, 1994, 1995, 1996, 2000, 2001, 2002. Used by permission of NavPress Publishing Group.

Cover design: Paul Lewis
Interior design: Angela Lewis
Editorial team: Megan Kassebaum
Minor revisions for 2019 reprint: Dave H. Scott

ACKNOWLEDGEMENTS

It is with great joy that we acknowledge the efforts of the many, many people who allowed this project to come together.

To the staff of Viva Network in Oxford and around the world, thank you for convening the original meetings that developed the concept of "Understanding God's Heart for Children" and for helping caregivers around the world realize the need for a biblical framework. Special thanks to Louie Cadaing and Arlynn Contreras of Lifestream; Patrick McDonald, Martin Hull, Katy Miles, Ian Smith, and the international team of Viva; Isobel Booth-Clibborn, Lorenzo Davids, Ian and Katharine deVilliers, Susan Greener, Helen Manley, Alfredo Mora, Janna McConnell, and the others who gave input for the draft biblical framework at Childswickham in 2004; and the presenters, practitioners, and participants that helped to develop the concepts more fully at the international Cutting Edge Conference in 2005.

To Karissa Glanville, Nelli Kärkkäinen, Bryant Myers, the Tyndale Foundation, and the Children at Risk Team of Fuller Theological Seminary, thank you for the input and practical assistance in completing this project. We would also like to thank the authors who willingly contributed their time and effort to provide this resource for caregivers around the world, along with the staff of Authentic Media and World Vision, especially Volney James, Angela Lewis, Milana McLead, and Jojo Palmer.

To Janna McConnell, Paul Orona, and other friends and family members who supported and encouraged us as we undertook this project, thank you for your patience, generosity, and encouragement. This book would not be here without you.

Finally, we are grateful to God for his provision and protection, for caring deeply for children, and for teaching us to follow his example.

Doug McConnell, Jennifer Orona, and Paul Stockley
May 2007

CONTENTS

Foreword ... vii
BY PATRICK MCDONALD, CHIEF EXECUTIVE, VIVA NETWORK

An Introduction to *Understanding God's Heart for Children* ... 1
BY DOUGLAS MCCONNELL

    DISCUSSION QUESTIONS ... 8

Chapter 1: Created with Dignity ... 9

    BIBLICAL REFLECTION ... 11
    God Creates Every Unique Person as a Child with Dignity
    BY DOUGLAS MCCONNELL

    CRITICAL ISSUES ... 20
    Theological Dignity And Human Rights For Children
    BY DAVE SCOTT

    PRACTITIONER'S RESPONSE ... 27
    Recognizing Uniqueness and Dignity
    BY PERRY G. DOWNS

    CASE STUDY ... 30
    PEPE: A Mission Preschool Program, Opening Doors for Children in Deprived Communities
    BY GEORGIE AND STUART CHRISTINE

    PRACTICAL IMPLICATIONS ... 37
    Holistic Ministry to Child Addicts
    BY PREMILA PAVAMANI WITH JENNIFER ORONA

    DISCUSSION QUESTIONS ... 42

Chapter 2: Placed in Families ... 43

    BIBLICAL REFLECTION ... 45
    The Vocation of Parenting: A Biblically and Theologically-Informed Perspective
    BY MARCIA J. BUNGE

    CRITICAL ISSUES ... 57
    Children's Needs for Parental Love in a Systemically Broken World
    BY KATHARINE MEESE PUTMAN

    PRACTITIONER'S RESPONSE ... 65
    Nurturing and Restoring *Shalom:* Parents and their Children, a Response to Marcia Bunge and Kathy Putman
    W. MEREDITH LONG

CASE STUDY 69
Street-Living and Working Children
BY GREG W. BURCH

PRACTICAL IMPLICATIONS 74
Children Seeking Family In War And Sexual Exploitation
BY MICHAEL MCGILL

DISCUSSION QUESTIONS 80

Chapter 3: Caring in Community 81
BIBLICAL REFLECTION 83
The Roles and Responsibilities of Children and Their Communities
BY JENNIFER ORONA

CRITICAL ISSUES 93
God Intends for Children to Thrive in Stable and Loving Relationships
BY JUDITH ENNEW

PRACTITIONER'S RESPONSE 102
From a Child's Words
BY JONI L. MIDDLETON

CASE STUDY 106
Child Sponsorship Projects: A Breakthrough for Children at Risk in the Indian Context
BY THOMAS SWAROOP WITH JENNIFER ORONA

PRACTICAL IMPLICATIONS 110
Building Communities for Jesus: Literacy, Civics, Evangelism
BY BESA SHAPLLO WITH JENNIFER ORONA

DISCUSSION QUESTIONS 114

Chapter 4: Well-being in Society 115
BIBLICAL REFLECTION 117
Let Love be Genuine and Relational
BY WENDY SANDERS,
WITH SUPPLEMENTARY MATERIAL BY TRI BUDIARDJO
ADAPTED BY PAUL STOCKLEY

CRITICAL ISSUES 131
Society Has a God-Given Responsibility for the Well-Being of Children and Families
BY RAVI JAYAKARAN WITH PAUL STOCKLEY

PRACTITIONER'S RESPONSE 137
Caring in Society
BY GLENN MILES

CASE STUDY 142
Advocacy: A Challenging Issue?
BY JOANNA WATSON

PRACTICAL IMPLICATIONS 148
Human Trafficking: Children and the Sex Trade
BY CHRISTA FOSTER CRAWFORD AND MARK CRAWFORD

DISCUSSION QUESTIONS 154
APPENDIX 4.1 155
Serious Deprivation Across the Globe in Relation to Basic Services
APPENDIX 4.2 156
Access to Basic Social Welfare Facilties: A Comparative Profile
APPENDIX 4.3 157
Profiles

Chapter 5: A Hope for the Generations 161
BIBLICAL REFLECTION 163
Children are a Promise of Hope
BY STEPHEN TOLLESTRUP

CRITICAL ISSUES 173
Hope for Every Generation
BY LINDA WAGENER

PRACTITIONER'S RESPONSE 180
A Child Spells Hope in the Wake of the Tsunami
BY KEITH J. WHITE

CASE STUDY 184
Generation 2 Generation
BY DAPHNE KIRK WITH PAUL STOCKLEY

PRACTICAL IMPLICATIONS 188
HIV and AIDS: Care for Orphans and Vulnerable Children
BY PAUL STEPHENSON, BARD SUIPPOLD, MARK LOREY, ET. AL.

DISCUSSION QUESTIONS 196

Chapter 6: Members in God's Church 197
BIBLICAL REFLECTION 199
God Welcomes Children Fully into the Family of Faith
BY KARA POWELL

CRITICAL ISSUES 209
Nurture and the Family of Faith
BY NDABA MAZABANE WITH DOUGLAS MCCONNELL

PRACTITIONER'S RESPONSE 216
Being the Family of Faith
BY DOUGLAS MCCONNELL

CASE STUDY 221
Faith-Based Organizations and Evangelical Churches in Romania: Partership, Theology, and Children at Risk
BY BILL PREVETTE WITH JENNIFER ORONA

PRACTICAL IMPLICATIONS Back to Basics: Care for Children Affected by HIV and AIDS BY SUSIE HOWE WITH JENNIFER ORONA	224
DISCUSSION QUESTIONS	228

Chapter 7: Participants in God's Mission — 229

BIBLICAL REFLECTION — 231
Children and God's Mission
BY GUSTAVO CROCKER WITH KARISSA GLANVILLE

CRITICAL ISSUES — 240
Raising Kids of Mission in the 21st Century
BY KARISSA GLANVILLE

PRACTITIONER'S RESPONSE — 248
We Have Forgotten That We Belong to Each Other
BY JUDE TIERSMA WATSON

CASE STUDY — 252
King's Kids
BY BARBARA RUEGGER WITH PAUL STOCKLEY

PRACTICAL IMPLICATIONS — 257
Understanding God's Heart for Chidlren
BY CATHRYN BAKER

DISCUSSION QUESTIONS — 261

Conclusion — 262
BY PAUL STOCKLEY

Bibliography — 268

For Further Reading — 289

About the Editors — 290

About the Authors — 291

FOREWORD

By Patrick McDonald, Chief Executive, Viva Network

We often miss the obvious.

Understanding God's Heart for Children draws us back to basics. As some of the world's foremost missionary leaders, seminarians, teachers, and practitioners point out, if we miss the centrality of children in everything we do—we have missed it.

Children create sanity in a mad world. They draw us back from our self-destructive habits of overwork, abuse, neglect, and callousness, and instead they bring tenderness, joy, and play.

Yet so very often we miss it. We don't give children the time of day. We ignore them in our strategies, we fail them in our budgets, we don't consider them in our forecasts. Jesus once mentioned millstones and deep seas and I doubt he was being ambiguous or trying to make a joke—he reminded us, you and me—of a future and of choices made, by us now, and him then.

Despite that, we find today across our nations children suffering in ways words fail to describe. In a world that has more, knows more, and can do more, these 'little ones' are denied even just a cup of cold water. It is a scandal. Outrageous. Contrary to any and every convention of civility, dignity, and compassion.

But friends, it is not just 'out there'. We miss it, don't we . . . the obvious I mean:

If as parents we don't give children the time and attention they need, if we don't raise them as we should, then something is profoundly wrong.

If as churches we fail to raise children as priceless individuals committed to a common cause, then something is profoundly wrong.

If as communities we fail to reach out to children on the edges, under bridges, and in brothels, then something is profoundly wrong.

Understanding God's Heart for Children points a way forward. Through a simple, easy to follow biblical framework, this book places children back where they should be. Not higher or lower. Not as Barbie dolls to be worshipped but as an integral part of the human experience.

Understanding God's Heart for Children points out that the way to engage children is not to try and soup up our programs to compete with MTV, but to give them the cause that stands knocking at their hearts' door, to point out that they have got responsibilities, that we are counting on them, and that they have something vital, important, essential to do. Some people call that child participation—we call it understanding the heart of God.

Written by practitioners, teachers, and theologians, this significant volume points out that the mission of the church has only a little to do with airplane tickets and foreign lands, and a lot to do with what happens in our living rooms, on our doorsteps, in our churches, and from that platform 'to the ends of the earth.' Some people call that authenticity. We call it understanding God's heart.

Understanding God's Heart for Children lays down the tenets of a revolutionary message. If we were to absorb what it states, our lives, our churches, our seminaries, and our communities would be very different.

As would indeed our children. Oh God—so be it!

March 2007

AN INTRODUCTION TO
UNDERSTANDING GOD'S HEART FOR CHILDREN

By Douglas McConnell
Fuller Theological Seminary

The eyes of a little boy peered out from behind the legs of his grandfather. The old man welcomed us to the house of his son in a town in southern Uganda. "Do you love my Jesus?" he asked with strong conviction. Not used to such a forthright greeting, we paused before responding, "Yes, we love your Jesus." Inside was his son Joseph, a well-educated accountant who formerly held a position in Kampala. Joseph, in his early thirties and himself a father, was wasting away from AIDS. Infected in the city from one of his many indiscretions, Joseph brought the disease home to his faithful wife, who in turn was infected. She had died only months earlier. Faced with the awful reality that his son would soon join the ranks of the millions of orphans and vulnerable children, Joseph not only was suffering the ravages of the disease, but was also brokenhearted. In his death, he took comfort knowing that his godly father was there to care for his young son.

Joseph died just days after our visit. Sadly, stories like his touched an estimated 8,493 families per day in 2004 alone.[1] As of December 2004, 39.4 million people were living with HIV; 2.2 million of them were children.[2] The AIDS pandemic has already taken one or both parents from over 14 million children worldwide, and most estimates indicate that this figure will rise to 25 million within the next five years. In June 2002, religious leaders from Africa lamented the impact on HIV and AIDS on children today. "Children . . . are being crushed by HIV/AIDS. . . . Many are sick, suffering cruel deprivations, and are frightened and alone in a world where no one seems to care. Worse, there is yet another burden. These children are stigmatized, made to feel ashamed by the source of their suffering, HIV/AIDS."[3]

Our assessment of the plight of children must not stop with the AIDS pandemic. Between 1960 and 2001, the human population doubled from 3 billion to 6.1 billion. The pace continues unchecked, with nearly a billion people added to the earth's population in the last decade.[4] In their analysis of the demographic impact of this growth, Himes and Olmo point out that "almost a third of the population is below age 15 in both Asia and Latin America, 30 and 32 percent respectively. Africa, with 43 percent of the population

---

[1] UNAIDS, 79, This figure is based on estimates that 3.1 million people died of AIDS in 2004.
[2] UNAIDS/WHO, 2004, 1.
[3] From the Final Declaration of the African Religious Leaders Assembly on Children and HIV/AIDS, Nairobi, Kenya, June 2002, cited in UNAIDS, 2003, 30. *What Religious Leaders Can Do About HIV/AIDS: Action for Children and Young People.*
[4] Ibiblio, "World Population," www.ibiblio.org/lunarbin/worldpop/index.html (accessed October 15, 2005).

or 338 million young people under the age of 15, continues to be the youngest region."[5] The distribution of children, poverty, and the ratio of children to adults are critical variables in our analysis.

The HIV and AIDS pandemic, the plight of street children, the commercial sexual exploitation of children, child soldiers, and many other global threats are major risks facing children in the twenty-first century. While concern for children at risk is not new for Christians, the recent population trends and a growing awareness of the situations facing so many of the world's children have rendered them among the most significant challenges facing churches and missions today.

In the midst of these staggering problems there is a growing movement among God's people that has taken up the challenge to serve Christ among the least of these, children on the margins of society. Initially, groups like World Vision, World Relief, Tear Fund, and a range of other non-profit organizations were the leaders among evangelicals. However, as population growth continued, missions and churches began to wake up to the need to engage with a holistic approach. At the same time, new initiatives emerged that were committed to work with children as their primary calling.

A Biblical Conversation is Needed

Viva Network is a wonderful example of the growth of the Christian response, particularly among evangelicals who in the 20th century were more reluctant to engage on a broad scale. From its humble beginnings in the mid-1990s, the network has grown among the Christian childcare community, embracing like-minded people from the largest non-profit organizations like World Vision International, to small ministries whose work is focused on a specific location or group of children. Today, "Viva Network is a global movement of Christians with 81 network initiatives in 48 countries, helping 1.2 million children."[6]

As Viva Network matured, so has the need to better articulate the foundations that shape the response within the network. As is the case with many new initiatives among Christians, the Bible becomes the common denominator for our work together. Not surprisingly, biblical texts that speak directly about children are the first to be used as support for the mission of the individual or group. Among the most often used is the statement by Jesus to the disciples about allowing little children to come to him (Matt. 19:14, Mark 10:14-15). Other biblical passages are also significant, but none as much as this statement.

Among the workers associated with Viva Network, an important concern to go beyond the motivational aspects of Jesus' call to the children arose over the past few years. It became evident that the rest of Jesus' statement, "To such as these [children] that the kingdom of God belongs" (Mark 10:14), demanded a greater understanding of the biblical

---

[5] Judith Himes and Angelique Olmo, "Executive Summary: International Youth," 2002, www.prcdc.org/summaries/intlyouth/intlyouth.html (accessed April 20, 2004).
[6] See http://www.viva.org/.

mandate. The result was a widely felt need to explore the Bible to gain a better understanding of the mission of God to children.

Impetus for this conversation rode on the momentum provided by the Cutting Edge biennial symposia sponsored by Viva Network.[7] This is a forum in which a broad consortium of (primarily evangelical) Christian agencies have been represented, all of whom are working with children in especially difficult circumstances or in high risk environments—those who have more loosely been termed as "children at risk".

During 1999 to 2002, Louie Cadaing and Arlynn Contreras of Lifestream (in the Philippines) shared experiences of a radical initiative which included children in all their planning and decision processes. They allowed their idea to be used and adapted to help workers explore Scripture and use their insights to reflect on their own childcare practices. So "Understanding God's Heart for Children" was born, and a toolkit published and shared with the network members. This has since been used in many contexts, and some of the outcomes fed into regional symposia in Latin America, Asia, and Africa.

Helping this process along, Keith White (of Mill Grove, UK) presented a paper in 2001 entitled: "a Little Child will Lead Them" encouraging us to dig deeper, and presenting a Christological framework for thinking about children and childhood.[8] Participants in the symposium shared how they used specific Scripture references as a motivating source, and expressed the many problematic and unanswered questions they face as Christians in ministry to children.

By 2002, Keith White and some colleagues launched the Child Theology Movement. The primary goal was to explore strands of the conversation, with special focus on the concept of "the child in the midst": how the child becomes the language of God to us. This movement established an important initiative for exploring theological issues; not as a new sub-discipline of systematic theology, but as a more inclusive way to think theologically. The work of the Child Theology Movement is bringing new insights into our traditional understandings of the Church, the work of Christ, the nature of the Kingdom of God, and the mission of God.

In 2004 at Childswickham in Oxfordshire, UK, after months of identifying potential approaches, several members of the network and participants in the symposia met together to draft the "Understanding God's Heart for Children" framework. The intent of the framers was to identify a number of statements that would provide a starting point for a broader discussion of a biblical basis for our mission to children at risk.

The framework became the focus of the fifth International Cutting Edge Conference, in September 2005. Entries in this volume were either delivered as plenary papers and responses or were prepared at the request of the editors to fill out sections which required additional material.

Beginning with Children and the Kingdom

---

[7] Materials from the Cutting Edge 2005 conference are available online at www.asia.viva.org/ce2005/.
[8] See http://www.viva.org/en/articles/gods_heart/child_lead.pdf.

The initial work identified seven key phrases that provide an overview of a kingdom approach to our responsibility to and for children.[9] An important premise of the framework is that creation and redemption flow through the Scriptures and guide our understanding of God's plan. Beginning with the creation account in Genesis, the statements follow the broad flow of redemption history, specifically trying to identify how children fit into the story. The role of family, while filled with ambiguities in Scripture, is also critical to our understanding as a central unit of society and foundational to the biblical framework.[10] The statements must be seen as an integrated whole, not as independent variables. The seven statements that follow represent the beginnings of our conversation on issues of biblical and missiological significance.[11]

1) *God creates every unique person as a child with dignity.* By virtue of creation, humankind is male and female (Gen. 1:27). As such, human beings are interdependent upon one another. The command "be fruitful and multiply" (Gen. 1:28) is a natural consequence of this relational interdependence. It follows that every child born of human parents carries the image of God, independent of any decision of the will or privilege of birth.

2) *Children need parental love in a broken world.* The account of the Fall introduces a constant in our missiological reflection. The presence of evil in all its manifestations not only impacts the context for mission to children at risk but permeates all of our responses. Our mission to children at risk therefore recognizes that parents (either biological or adoptive) or other primary caregivers need help in the form of empowerment in order to more fully supply the parental love that each child needs.

3) *God gives children as a gift to welcome and nurture.* Often, Scripture reminds us that children are a gift. The best example comes from Jesus: he placed a child before the disciples, then called on them to welcome children (Matt. 18:5) and nurture them as part of living as the people of God (Deut. 4:9; 6:7; 11:19).

4) *Society has a God-given responsibility for the well-being of children and families.* The manner in which true transformation must be pursued is part of the revelation of the plan for the people of God. Given the deep love of God for the orphan and

---

[9] An expanded discussion of the framework is available in C. Douglas McConnell, "Children and the Kingdom: Missiological Reflections on Children at Risk," in *Changing Our Response: Mission in the Era of HIV/AIDS*, edited by Jonathan J. Bonk, 20-26. Additionally, some of the material in this section appeared in C. Douglas McConnell, "A Missional Response to Children at Risk," *Theology News and Notes*, no. 3 (2005): 8–10 (used by permission), www.fuller.edu/news/pubs/tnn/2005_fall/index.htm.
[10] For a helpful discussion of the role of the family, see Christopher J. H. Wright, *Old Testament Ethics for the People of God*, 327–62.
[11] The seven italicized statements are taken directly from the Viva Network's *Understanding God's Heart Biblical Framework* (working paper, Oxford, 2004).

widow and all those who are marginalized, an important indicator of the well-being of our worship and of our society is seen in the well-being of the vulnerable.[12]

5) *Children are a promise of hope for every generation.* Although in Christ alone is our hope for salvation (1 Peter 1:19-21), there is also a deep sense of hope and fulfillment that is born in each new generation. Given this picture of the hope found in children, we affirm that there are important generational responsibilities for the nurture of children.

6) *God welcomes children fully into the family of faith.* Children are essential to the life and ministry of the church, bringing spiritual gifts and abilities and fulfilling definite roles. The church needs to be a place where children may dynamically connect with God and engage in meaningful participation; discipled, equipped and empowered for life and ministry. As members of the family of God, children are to be cared for as sons and daughters and are part of the admonition to love and serve one another.[13]

7) *Children are essential to the mission of God.* Christ made it clear that children are able to receive the kingdom of God (Mark 10:14) and are therefore able to be an active part of the kingdom community. One implication is that they are able and (not surprisingly) often willing to embrace the Great Commission. An important corollary is the imperative that churches and missions must embrace a radical commitment in mission to children at risk.

Launching the Broad Conversation

This volume brings a contribution to a new level of opportunity before us within the movement of Christians committed to children at risk. Each chapter has been organized to include a reflection on one of the seven statements followed by responses to the main presentation and then examples of how the statement is working itself out in various contexts. The authors represent both practitioners and scholars who are concerned about a strong basis for understanding God's heart for children.

In preparing the volume for publication, our editorial team recognized that we are still at the beginning of the conversation. There is a great need to deepen the biblical studies as well as the missiological reflections. However, in any new field of study, the earliest works serve to initiate the conversation rather than make the definitive contribution. It appears that the primary value of the framework will be its ability to broaden the parameters of the issues covered, while also giving some benchmarks for current practices on each point.

---

[12] The link between the well-being of the vulnerable and the well-being of our worship and of society was made in a presentation by Bryant Myers at the annual missiology lectures at Fuller Seminary, November 8, 2006.
[13] This explanatory elaboration of statement 6 is taken from the *Understanding God's Heart Biblical Framework*.

While this compendium acts as an introduction to the current state of the global conversation within Viva Network, there is also a very helpful series of books edited by Marcia Bunge, a contributor in this volume. The first book in the series, *The Child in Christian Thought*,[14] introduced an invaluable resource for thoughtful practitioners and scholars alike. The next volume will focus on the child in the Bible with contributors covering key texts in the Old and New Testaments. Additionally, Keith White, also a contributor in this volume, continues to lead the Child Theology Movement, which has produced a number of helpful publications.

We are grateful to each of the contributors in this volume for their willingness to work together in the preparation of the manuscript. The author of each article gave their time and energies with a goal of furthering the discussion for the sake of children. In that sense, this book represents another attempt to be a voice for the voiceless.

Our Mission to Children at Risk

As we have begun to understand, the nature of our missional response depends heavily on the efforts of local churches, responding to the needs of children in a manner that reflects the values and the presence of the Kingdom of God. Beyond strategies and methods is a consistent realization that God has local custodians of the Gospel of the Kingdom with the capacity and the responsibility to impact the world in the name of Christ Jesus our Lord. During a walk on the coast of southern Wales in 1998, Patrick McDonald, the founder of Viva Network, related his concern over the sheer magnitude of the problem. As we talked, we realized this amazing plan of God to use his Church to impact the world of children. It has ever been so, but for the two of us it came as a profound new truth. The Church in the world is the ideal structure, at least humanly speaking, to tackle globally the issues facing the more than 1.5 billion children at risk and to do so with any hope of sustainability. From that day until this, we have continued to keep our focus on awakening the Church to its responsibilities for the children.[15]

If churches and missions are to engage seriously on a global scale in a missional response to children at risk, some radical changes must take place. The picture of what those changes entail and how we are going to achieve them is in part the subject of this book. While there are many hopeful signs, the scale of the problems has outpaced all of our efforts. Many of the issues we face are global in nature and have already found a place on the agendas we are pursuing. One thing is certain, based on the patterns and mandates of Scripture, local churches must rise up as extended families prepared to accept children into their midst.

Children as children are able to receive the Kingdom. They are also the largest population bloc of human beings. Churches and missions must not only see them as precious in the sight of God, but also must view them with a love that demands advocacy for justice and invitation for belonging. As has been said, children are human beings, not

---

14 See Marcia J. Bunge.
15 Some of this material appears in McConnell, "A Missional Response to Children at Risk," 10.

human becomings. A sensitive response that engages the whole Church on behalf of those who are targeted by evil and by emissaries of the worst kinds of depravity is the least that we can do. The call to the Church today is a call to wake up to this God-given responsibility before it is too late. In the words of Jesus, "Whoever welcomes this child in my name welcomes me" (Luke 9:48).

INTRODUCTION
DISCUSSION QUESTIONS

Each affirmation is followed by some questions to provoke interaction and dialogue about the framework, the issues and challenges arising. Some questions are focus questions, which help in understanding the affirmation. Others questions are application questions, which provide a stimulus to action.

Here are useful generic questions to have in mind as you read through the affirmations and responses in the chapters that follow.

1) How do we understand this affirmation in our own context? What issues does it raise, and what challenges does it highlight?

2) How are the values and principles expressed by this affirmation being put into action in our work? . . . in our family, community, church, organization, network?

3) What are we doing to exemplify or embody God's intent and to further God's desire for children in this particular aspect?

4) In respect to this affirmation, what are some of the obstacles that we are facing as a family, community, church, etc?

5) How can we overcome the obstacles and meet the challenge of God's purpose?

6) Who else can help us in working together to achieve this?

CHAPTER 1
CREATED WITH DIGNITY

God creates every unique person as a child with dignity.

We all begin life as children, created in the image of God. Children are born fully human, with identity and purpose. The journey of childhood is part of God's plan. All people reflect God's image through living in loving community with him and one another. Children most fully express their God-given dignity in glorifying Him.

God intends that no one prevent a child's life from fulfilling His purpose. Respecting the image of God in every child demands a Christ-like response to nurture them throughout childhood.

"For it was you who formed my inward parts;
you knit me together in my mother's womb.
I praise you, for I am fearfully and wonderfully made.
Wonderful are your works;
that I know very well.
My frame was not hidden from you,
when I was being made in secret,
intricately woven in the depths of the earth.
Your eyes beheld my unformed substance.
In your book were written all the days that were formed for me,
when none of them as yet existed."

—Psalm 139:13-16 NRSV

"Dignity is not about capability, giftedness, culture, social conditions, or economic status. It is God-given. Accepting human dignity is recognizing and honoring God the Creator and Redeemer, as well as Jesus Christ, who came as a child to save us. The incarnation of the Lord Jesus Christ is proof of human dignity. He was born as a child and grew up with uniqueness as an individual person to o the will of his Father. Affirming and celebrating the uniqueness of individuals is acknowledging God's purpose and destiny for them, determined by God, for the praise of his name."[1]

—Alemu Beeftu

---

[1] Alemu Beeftu, "Biblical Basis for Recognizing Uniqueness and Dignity," (Cirencester, UK: Cutting Edge V Conference, September 29-30, 2005).

BIBLICAL REFLECTION

GOD CREATES EVERY UNIQUE PERSON AS A CHILD WITH DIGNITY

By Douglas McConnell
Fuller Theological Seminary

The sidewalk café outside the restaurant was crowded as I moved toward the door. Before I could enter, a familiar voice called out, "Grandpa you're late! I've already eaten." I looked up to see Emma sitting at a table with her family. In her mind, my presence was not only appreciated, it was expected. As I paused to greet my daughter's family, I realized that to five-year-old Emma, the only reason Grandpa would be there was to spend time with her. While that would have been my preference, I was late to another dinner with my colleagues.

In her innocence, Emma reminds us of an important theme in Scripture. Relationships help to define who we are and why we exist. In the story of creation, human beings hold a special position in the created order.

> *Then God said, "Let us make humankind in our image, according to our likeness; and let them have dominion over the fish of the sea, and over the birds of the air, and over the cattle, and over all the wild animals of the earth, and over every creeping thing that creeps upon the earth." So God created humankind in his image, in the image of God he created them; male and female he created them. God blessed them, and God said to them, "Be fruitful and multiply, and fill the earth and subdue it; and have dominion over the fish of the sea and over the birds of the air and over every living thing that moves on the earth" (Gen. 1:26-28 NRSV).*

The Genesis account provides the beginning point from which to understand the uniqueness of humankind. Our concern for children in high risk situations flows out of the fact that God cares for all creation. This is particularly true of human beings, who alone among creation are made in the image and likeness of God. As we will demonstrate in this article, every human being enters the world as a child bearing the dignity uniquely set in the creation of humankind. Of all the characteristics attributed to human beings created in the divine image, being in relationship to God, to one another, and having responsibility for all creation helps us to view children in the context

> Every human being enters the world as a child bearing the dignity uniquely set in the creation of humankind.

of God's care. To better understand the image of God, we must look at these relationships and their implications individually.[1]

In Relationship to God

We understand the being of God as existing in three persons: Father, Son, and Holy Spirit. The use of the plural verb form in Genesis 1:26, "Let us make humankind . . ." is not intended to articulate the Trinity, but does suggest God as a being in fellowship. It is in the New Testament that God as the Triune being is fully developed. At the crown of the entire creation which was declared as "very good" (Gen. 1:31), God created humankind distinct from the rest of creation, in God's image (Gen. 1:27).[2] A closer look at the words *image* and *likeness* indicate that humankind "is a representation of God who is like God in certain respects."[3]

Human beings were created to be in relationship to God. The Westminster Assembly in 1647 stated this clearly in the form of a question and answer. "Question 1. What is the chief end of man? Answer. Man's chief end is to glorify God, and to enjoy him forever."[4] The term "man" here is used to mean all human beings, not simply individuals. In their attempt to state the purpose for our collective being, the authors of the Westminster Catechism portrayed a human being's relationship with God as enjoyment. Such an emphasis is often missing in much of our teaching and preaching, yet it is a very important perspective to those who choose to work with children.

The idea of enjoyment is not such a difficult thing to grasp. Children are often examples of pure enjoyment in the simplest of things. For example, it seems that no matter how difficult the circumstances of life, wherever there are children, there will be creative play. In a garbage dump, I saw children making a game of salvaging items to sell for survival. They happened upon a discarded ball that became the center of a makeshift game of soccer. Piles of trash were converted into goal posts and boundary lines. Laughter was heard in the hot sun. And little laborers were converted into champions of their own imagination, transported from hell to heaven in a matter of moments.

---

[1] Originally published in summary form in *Restore: Pursuing God's Standards for Children* 1 (2005): 6-8. Reprinted by permission of the author and the publisher.
[2] Although there are often attempts to differentiate between the terms *image* and *likeness* (Gen. 1:26), the distinctions are not convincing since they appear to be used interchangeably in Genesis 1:27 and Genesis 9:6 (image) and Genesis 5:1 (likeness). In the context of Genesis 1:26, we see the image and likeness as components of the concept we most often refer to as "the image of God" (*imago Dei* in Latin). A more fruitful discussion for our purposes is found in an examination of those characteristics that are attributed to humankind as a result of being created in the image of God. In this paper only three of these attributes will be explored: relationship to God, relationship to one another, and responsibility for creation. For a further discussion, see C.E. Gunton, *The Triune Creator*, 193-211; Vigen Guroian, "The Ecclesial Family," 66-69; A.A. Hoekema, *Created in God's Image*.
[3] Hoekema, 13.
[4] Westminster Assembly, "The Westminster Shorter Catechism, 1647," http://www.reformed.org/documents/wsc/index.html (accessed June 4, 2005).

Our understanding of God as the Creator who desires us to "enjoy him forever" draws us nearer to the loving relationship God intended. We are in danger of making this concept too lofty and out of reach for people. If we remember that God is the creator and sustainer of all creation, we can find enjoyment of God's presence in every sphere of life. It is vital that in serving children we embrace our relationship to God in ways that will impact our actions and response to children. Over the years, I have noticed that those who are most successful in working with children are able to engage in the playtime as much as the other parts of ministry. As we embrace God's presence along with embracing the children, a burden is lifted that can be a real blessing to everyone involved.

When we consider the ideal of creation, we are left with the important realization that life in relationship to God was intended to be full of care and protection.[5] The problem with this idyllic scenario is that our experience with children living in risky environments mocks the ideals of God's created order. While we see glimpses of real joy in the makeshift soccer game, our focus is inevitably pulled to the garbage dump. Given this stark contrast, what do we offer children who suffer the cruelties of poverty, abandonment, and abuse? As those who are called to serve the Kingdom of God standing beside children, we must respond to these questions with an appropriate amount of humility and caution.

Promises made (especially of divine intervention) in the lives of our young friends must be backed by the faithfulness of God's people. Perhaps the most challenging aspect of such a promise is the commitment to longevity that must accompany our service to children. It is not hard to imagine that in the mind of an AIDS orphan each night is a question for the caregiver, "Will you be here in the morning?"

Despite this stern warning, at the heart of mission to children at risk is the promise of God's eternal love and care. When Jesus spoke of life abundantly (John 10:10), he referred to the love of God that transforms the existence of humankind so radically that he had to introduce the concept of rebirth (e.g. John 3:3). With anything less than the offer of God's direct intervention, our efforts are limited to the human plans and institutions that have in most cases failed to provide real transformation. To adequately deal with the implications of our promise, we need to consider not only the ideal of creation, but also our experience of redemption in Christ.

Another challenge that we face is that although being created in the image of God means being in relationship to God, humankind lives in a fallen world where nature is cursed.[6] Humans are separated from God by the universal presence of sin. Looking, as we must, at the despicable actions of the sex trafficker or the oppressive hand of a corrupt political leader, we are aghast at the thought that they too are created in the image of God. Is it not right to hate them as somehow less human than we are and certainly as less in need of care than the children we commit our lives to serving?[7]

---

[5] Although beyond the scope of this paper, the concept of protection as related to the imagery of the Good Shepherd in John 10 is a fruitful study as it relates to the role of the Church in caring for those who are marginalized and vulnerable.

[6] For a helpful discussion of the theological and ethical implications of this concept, see C.J.H. Wright, *Old Testament Ethics for the People of God*, 129-144.

[7] The important discussion of the corruption of the image of God experienced in and through the Fall (Gen. 3) will be dealt with in the second affirmation found in the next section of this volume. For a discussion of the

> One of the biggest challenges for all who serve children at risk is to maintain perspective in the midst of crisis. To do so, we must identify with the source of the dignity. It is not in the creature, but in the Creator.

Gunton provides some relief to the dilemma: "At the very least, the human being, simply as created, is of the kind of *being* that a certain radical moral respect is due to every human person, however sunk in villainy and depravity."[8] One of the biggest challenges for all who serve children at risk is to maintain perspective in the midst of crisis. To do so, we must identify with the source of the dignity. It is not in the creature, but in the Creator. As Grogan noted, "The infinite value of each person rests on the divine image."[9]

The image of God is both incomplete and corrupt in every human being. It is only in the saving work of Christ on the cross that redemption can be understood. Those who are in Christ, redeemed by the finished work on the cross, are a new creation and in Christ are reconciled to God (2 Cor. 5:16-17). So it follows that our mission, like that of the Apostles, is to be ambassadors for Christ, appealing to those whom we serve to be reconciled to God (2 Cor. 5:18-20).

We, therefore, face the stern warning against inflated promises with a deep and lasting faith that God does not show favoritism in offering the gift of salvation, "For, 'Everyone who calls on the name of the Lord shall be saved'" (Rom. 10:13; cf. Eph. 2:8-9). Historically, we have understood that redemption, which is begun through faith, will be perfected as part of a future promise. That hope for the future is stated in one of the oldest and most ecumenical of the Christian Creeds: "We look for the resurrection of the dead, and the life of the world to come. Amen."[10] Although evangelizing children raises some serious concerns since they are susceptible to manipulation and a desire to please adults, it remains an irrevocable element of the mission of God.

In Jesus, we are introduced to an amazing new dimension of the dignity of the divine image. When Jesus came to earth in the incarnation, God became human in order to reconcile humankind to himself. Our uniqueness as human beings in the created order, therefore, is based on the image of God, on the event of the incarnation of God to reconcile the world, and the promise of his coming Kingdom, thereby bringing together all of human history.[11]

---

different ways that the presence of sin in children and the approach to salvation has been expressed historically, see Marcia J. Bunge, ed., *The Child in Christian Thought*.

[8] Gunton, 204.
[9] G.W. Grogan, *New Dictionary of Christian Ethics and Pastoral Theology*, 476.
[10] "The Nicene Creed," http://www.creeds.net/ancient/nicene.htm (accessed July 24, 2006). The Nicene Creed, initiated by the Emperor Constantine in 325 C.E., was finally adopted in 381 C.E.
[11] Jürgen Moltmann, *On Human Dignity: Political Theology and Ethics*, 20; see Karl Barth, *Church Dogmatics*, 183-187.

In Relationship to Humankind

In addition to our relationship to God, human beings are in relationship to one another. From the beginning, humankind was created as both male and female (Gen. 1:27). As created persons dependent upon God, human beings are also interdependent on one another. This is clearly seen in the fulfillment of the command to "Be fruitful and multiply" (Gen. 1:28). God chose to multiply humankind through the physical bond between the male and female. As Gunton put it, "To be in the image of God is therefore to be in necessary relation to others so made."[12]

At the time of birth that observation is particularly relevant. At birth, the baby is inescapably dependent upon caregivers. From feeding and security to more subtle aspects of human development, early childhood is a time in which relationships with other humans are most formative. From these early stages, the child undergoes biological changes, forms cognitive responses to the world, and learns to form attachments to others.[13]

In the creation of humankind, the ability to procreate carries the image of God from generation to generation.[14] This act of divine design has important consequences for what it means to be human. Each child born is linked irrevocably through procreation to God, the first two human beings, and every other person.[15] The dignity we share as persons, therefore, is not based on privilege or decision, but rather on God's plan for creation. Gunton clarifies the point well: "Just as to be God is not to be an individual but three persons inextricably interrelated as being in communion, so to be . . . [humankind], as male and female, is to be created for life in community."[16]

Our interdependence is based upon the premise that at the heart of our existence is a call to love God and to love our neighbor (Matt. 22:37-40). While this is not our experience in a fallen world, it is not intended to be ignored.

Accepting our interdependence within the Christian community is foundational to our witness in the fallen and hurting world. Jesus stated this clearly to his disciples, "Just as I have loved you, you also should love one another. By this everyone will know that you are my disciples, if you have love for one another" (John 13:34-35). As those called to be followers of Christ, our testimony is carried in our love for one another. The most practical level of love is serving one another. Jesus consistently demonstrated his claim that he came to serve (Mark 10:45), through his actions toward others and in fulfilling the ultimate sacrifice of service, his death on the cross.

---

[12] Gunton, 208.

[13] For an in-depth discussion of human development based on a theological understanding of the image of God and its relational implications, see J.O. Balswick, P.E. King, and K.S. Reimer, *The Reciprocating Self: Human Development in Theological Perspective*.

[14] The generational aspects of our understanding of humankind with specific reference to children will be covered in the section dealing with affirmation five in this volume.

[15] This link will be explored in greater depth in the second affirmation in this volume.

[16] Gunton, 208.

Similarly, as those who serve children, particularly children who face life-threatening risks, we must view our service in relation to their needs.[17] Consider the following case: On a busy street under the expressway, a woman in her early twenties walked from car to car begging with two small children. At first sight, it appeared that this poor mother was a victim of the endless cycle of poverty so common in her Southeast Asian city. Based on this assumption, the missional response would naturally focus on housing, vocational training, the schooling needs for the children, and the sharing of the redemptive power of the Gospel. Upon further investigation, a leading missiologist living in the city revealed that the young woman was taken from her rural family with the promise of work in the city. The children were actually hired on a daily basis from a poor family, transported by car to join the young woman to bolster her appearance as a needy beggar. The whole deceptive industry was controlled by an unscrupulous businessman who trades in the exploitation of the poor.

In such a complex case, the missional response is much broader than simply an intervention to provide for the immediate needs (safe shelter and protection from reprisals by the businessman, for example) of the three beggars. Practical needs such as sustainable care, a safe community, schooling, and long-term vocational assistance must be part of the response.[18] On another level, however, there are deeper issues of human trafficking and exploitation that require expertise in advocacy and the legal channels to break the cycle and prevent continued exploitation. Although the issues appear to be limitless, it is important to also engage in an attempt to bring reconciliation to the families involved. The anger and animosity that grows from being subjected to exploitation by one's family, even if the arrangement was based on deceit, must be dealt with before healthy relationships can be restored.

In this case, there are many levels in which the people involved are interdependent. Obviously, the perpetrators of such crimes of exploitation and abuse are dependent upon the supply of vulnerable persons to exploit. Sadly, the poor are too dependent upon any possible sources of income for their very survival. There must also be those who will patronize the exploiter and the exploited, known in economic terms as the demand.

> As those who serve children, particularly children who face life-threatening risks, we must view our service in relation to their needs.

The demand can vary from the need for cheap labor to commercial sexual exploitation and human slavery. In this case, the force driving the demand can even be the caring people who make contributions to the beggars and yet seemingly tolerate such exploitation through inaction or even apathy. On the missional response side, those who are able to make contact with people on the street are dependent upon the additional assistance and support provided by others in their ministry. And beyond direct involvement, to initiate significant long-term

---

[17] For a more complete discussion of community in the theology of the Apostle Paul, see R. Banks, *Paul's Idea of Community*.
[18] For a further discussion, please see the articles in affirmation four of this volume.

ministries that will work toward prevention, a network of people is necessary to truly impact such systemic evil.[19]

Our understanding of humankind created in the image of God means that we must see other human beings as we see ourselves. Too often, our categories for viewing others range from loved one or friend to stranger or enemy. Yet we are inextricably linked to every other human being on earth. The prophet Jeremiah received a message from God that brought this truth to light in a very specific context. Jeremiah was to tell the exiles living in captivity in Babylon, "But seek the welfare of the city where I have sent you into exile, and pray to the Lord on its behalf, for in its welfare you will find your welfare" (Jer. 29:7). How hard it must have been to hear that those exploited and held captive by a foreign tyrant were to seek the welfare of their oppressors, because ultimately the welfare of the captives was bound up in the welfare of the captors.

As we consider the implications of our interdependence, we do so with the assurance that we serve the living God. Our relationship to God is that of both children and servants; this brings with it the assurance of God's presence in all that we do. Seeing children in especially difficult circumstances through the lens of God's loving presence helps to place all the extremes and complexities into proper relief. If we also consider the truth that we belong to the community of believers who have been redeemed by the Lord Jesus Christ, we begin to realize the resources that accompany our call to serve God among the children of the world.

In Relationship to Creation

Along with the dignity shared by all human beings created in the image of God, there is a God-given responsibility to care for creation. One important result of the command to populate the earth is that we would, "subdue it; and have dominion over [the earth]" (Gen. 1:28). In contemporary usage, the concept that relates most closely to "subdue" and "dominion" is that we must be stewards of the planet that is our home. This means that we must care for the earth. It does not belong to us, but to God who gave us the responsibility. Our relationship to God requires that we recognize his ownership of creation. In the goodness of God, we see not only his ownership but also our own dependence on the creation. The bountiful earth provides the home on which we may be fruitful and multiply.

The psalmist captured the extent of God's possession of the earth: "The earth is the Lord's and all that is in it, the world, and those who live in it; for he has founded it on the seas, and established it on the rivers" (Ps. 24:1-2). The home provided to humankind, in all its richness and in every location, belongs to God. In Psalm 8, the majesty and wonder of God may be seen in the creation, "O Lord, our Sovereign, how majestic is your name in all the earth! You have set your glory above the heavens . . . O Lord, our Sovereign, how majestic is your name in all the earth!" (Ps. 8:1, 9). And by way of affirming the stewardship of the earth we see in the creation account (Gen. 1:28), the psalmist expresses

---

[19] See the article by Greg Burch in this volume.

it to God in the words, "You have given . . . [human beings] dominion over the works of your hands; you have put all things under their feet" (Ps. 8:6).

It is quite remarkable to consider the extent of this responsibility as stewards of creation. In rural areas where the land is seen not as real estate but as fertile ground for growing food, this sense of stewardship makes sense. For example, women in the Southern Highlands of Papua New Guinea carefully prepare their gardens for planting sweet potatoes, mounding the soil so that the constant rains will not rot the plants in the ground. They dig trenches around the gardens to act as a fence to keep out stray pigs and to clearly demarcate their respective garden plots. When the time comes to dig the potatoes they remove the plants to gather the maximum crop and to allow the ground to sit fallow before replanting the next crop. The connection between these hardworking women and the land is part of the cycle of life in rural Papua New Guinea.

Interdependency extends beyond the relationships between human beings to that of humankind and creation. The health and well-being of humans is inextricably linked to the health and well-being of the earth. Given this connection, consider again our missional response to the children whose lives are dependent on the income generated by scavengers of garbage dumps. The Smokey Mountain United Methodist Church planted in 1985 continues to provide weekly worship services, Bible studies, a kindergarten, vocational skills training, literacy programs, and sponsorships for children to attend schools.[20] The holistic approach of this outreach to children and their families is a good example of a front-line missional response.

When taken in the broader context, the stewardship of creation must go beyond even direct missional responses to more comprehensive attempts to address the issues. Initiatives that seek to transform the lives of people and raise them out of the dump in the literal sense such as the Smokey Mountain United Methodist Church are essential.[21] Beyond local initiatives, serious attempts to engage in transformational development on a broader scale require action that will address the systemic problems such as political and economic factors that perpetuate the conditions facing poor communities like Smokey Mountain and Payatas. The magnitude of such a challenge is overwhelming and points again to the wisdom of mobilizing the broadest possible base of resources. At the individual level, it is wise to remember words that have been attributed to Mother Teresa, whose life and mission impacted the entire world: "If you can't feed a hundred people, then feed just one."[22]

Our relationship to creation goes beyond simple usage of the bounty of the earth for our purposes. It requires effort at every level of society to care for the environment with the recognition that part of the role of humankind in creation is to be stewards of that which belongs to the Creator God. It follows that as we care for our world, it in turn cares and provides life support for us. If we narrow our focus, our ministries and projects for children

---

[20] P. Jeffrey, "The Gospel on Smokey Mountain: A United Methodist Congregation in Ministry," *New World Outlook*, September/October 2005, http://gbgm-umc.org/global_news/full_article.cfm?articleid=3470 (accessed July 28, 2006).

[21] For an in-depth discussion of transformational development, see Bryant Myers, *Walking With The Poor: Principles and Practices of Transformational Development*.

[22] Mother Teresa, http://www.brainyquote.com/quotes/authors/m/mother_teresa.html (accessed November 22, 2006).

must take into account the condition of the environment in which they live, making appropriate responses to improve the condition in which the children are found. For instance, providing educational opportunities without cleaning up water supplies does little for children suffering from water born diseases.

Based on our relationship to God, to other persons, and to creation, we can now more fully understand the dignity of personhood. Every person is created in the image of God, with dignity and the unique capacity to impact our existence.[23]

Serving with Dignity

Through creation, every human being begins the journey of life as a child with dignity. Every child is of infinite value to the Creator simply because they are created in God's image. Their worth is not primarily found in their potential, but in their being as a child. Through the birth of Jesus as a child, God became a human, thereby revealing the true value of all human life. Jesus became a baby and grew to adulthood (Luke 2:7, 52), signifying the uniqueness and dignity of humanity in all of creation. To be a child is to be fully human. And reciprocally to experience childhood is a necessary part of being fully human. As it is so often stated, children are human beings, not human becomings. We therefore affirm that childhood is an integral part of God's plan for human beings. We must also affirm that every human being is a unique person created by God as a child with dignity.

Beyond this affirmation, we recognize that as bearers of not only the image of God but also the message of redemption in Christ, our service is not limited to children living in risky environments only. If we are to embrace the transformation that God desires, the mission is to seek the welfare of the children, their families, their communities, and even the ones who put them at risk. As we recognize the overwhelming scope of our mission, we must also recognize that God is calling us to serve together with other followers of Christ.

---

[23] It is here that anyone who works with children at risk must stop and ask about the reality of sin. Please see the next section for a further discussion on this topic.

CRITICAL ISSUES

THEOLOGICAL DIGNITY AND HUMAN RIGHTS FOR CHILDREN

By Dave Scott
Fuller Theological Seminary

The rights of children are a ticklish topic for many Christians. Among some parts of the Church, the mere mention of children's rights is enough to end a conversation, especially the sort of theological dialogue we are attempting to have in this book. Furthermore, rights language and its accompanying rights-based paradigm for ministry are sometimes considered to be incompatible with any Christian foundation for ministry. So, given that many of the articles in this book make use of rights and rights language in their discussion of the various points of the Understanding God's Heart for Children biblical framework, it seems necessary at this point to clarify our intent.

It is not our purpose to argue for a rights-based paradigm for ministry, as opposed to any other kind of paradigm (needs-based or otherwise). Rather, the position of this book (and the particular task of this article) is to clip away at some of this hairy problem by suggesting that the use of rights language and the leverage that comes with it can be very helpful in ensuring God's purposes in children's lives are achieved, and that governments and institutions of society provide an environment in which children are not denied this opportunity. In other words, even if we do not agree with the entirety of the human rights agenda at the international level, we believe that many Christian ministries can justifiably use rights language as one tool for accomplishing what God has called us to do in the lives of children.

> The Understanding God's Heart for Children Biblical Framework can help to provide a more specific basis for systematic critique of and dialogue with the UN Convention on the Rights of the Child and other human rights documents.

Furthermore, this article also hopes to show that the Understanding God's Heart for Children framework can help to provide a more specific basis for systematic critique of and dialogue with the UN Convention on the Rights of the Child and other human rights documents. If we are interested in using rights in our work, having a framework such as this one upon which to base our engagement would seem to be a crucial tool for us as Christians. It is in one or both of these ways that the other articles in this volume will be discussing children's rights.

However, before this can happen, it is important to address one of the concerns that has been expressed about children's rights—namely, that rights language and rights-based work are necessarily secular. In the following section, we hope to disprove this by showing that, at least in its original intent, the rights dialogue was begun only on the presupposition that rights are *not* a secular construct, but that they were chosen because so many different religious and philosophical systems of thought could all agree on their importance.

The Philosophical Foundations of Human Rights in International Dialogue

It was 1947, and the UN committee charged with drafting the original Declaration of Human Rights was at a stalemate.[1] Their specific task was the challenge of identifying the single philosophical or theological foundation for the planned Declaration, which was in turn intended to provide the basis for international dialogue regarding concern for all peoples. It was to be the lynchpin of all international cooperation—giving a universal basis for accountability and concern across national and cultural borders. But despite their grand intentions, they were unable to progress beyond their individual positions.[2]

What they found was that whether or not a tradition included the specific term or concept of rights, there were at least very similar ideas in every major religious and philosophical tradition that was represented in the committee. Furthermore, each delegate in turn seemed completely convinced of the superiority of their understanding of rights, and that their position deserved the privileged role of providing the ultimate foundation. Hindu, Confucian, Buddhist, Christian, Secular, Jewish, and Muslim perspectives all clashed and, rather than moving closer towards agreement, the delegates seemed to become ever more polarized as the discussions proceeded. As time wore on, the reality dawned that no single superior foundation was going to emerge from that debate. But rather than being disheartened by this, the committee proposed a better solution. They reasoned that, instead of trying to force consensus in an otherwise fractured debate, since all groups agreed that rights were important, perhaps they could move ahead on that basis alone. So, in the words of Jacques Maritain, "Yes, we agree about the rights, but on the condition that no one asks us why." He maintained that agreement was only possible, "not on the basis of common speculative ideas, but on common practical ideas, not on the affirmation of one and the same conception of the world, of man, and of knowledge, but upon the affirmation of a single body of beliefs for guidance on action."[3]

It is notable that this agreement and the ensuing discussions were not based in support that was somehow abstracted from the various views represented. Nor was it a secular process. Rather, each person was encouraged to hold and express their particular viewpoint, as long as they did not require others to agree with anything beyond their choice of final action. This understanding supports Glen Stassen's claim that, "The ethic of human rights can be a universal ethic, not because its *source* is a common philosophy believed by all people but because its *intention and application* affirm the rights of all persons."[4]

---

[1] This document was originally titled the Universal Declaration of the Rights of Man, but English language usage since that time has required the revision of its title.
[2] Paul Brink, "Debating International Human Rights: The 'Middle Ground' for Religious Participants," *The Brandywine Review of Faith and International Affairs*, Fall (2003).
[3] Jacques Maritain, "Introduction."
[4] Glen H. Stassen, *Just Peacemaking: Transforming Initiatives for Justice and Peace*.

There are several key ideas we can gather from these events. First, we can be encouraged that, at least in their inception, rights were not intended to be a secular construct. They are not necessarily grounded in Rousseau's contract between people or any other Enlightenment concept, as some have claimed. Instead, anyone can participate in discussing, debating, and defending rights, no matter what their perspective is, as long as their perspective recognizes the validity and importance of rights.

Second, the fact that there was Christian involvement in this discussion should encourage us as we think through these matters that, at least in 1947, it was believed that rights and Christian theology were not mutually incompatible. Rather, they believed that there was a Christian theological foundation for rights.

Third, it is important to emphasize that commitment to the potential of rights language is different from commitment to any of the human rights documents. We can believe in the philosophical validity of rights as Christians and still legitimately question the ways in which certain legal documents deal with rights in light of our beliefs. Speaking from a Christian standpoint, (and perhaps aided by the Understanding God's Heart framework) we can justifiably consider both the specific rights that are enumerated in these documents, as well as the ways that they stipulate those rights are to be respected.

Points of Continuity

So, how does the Understanding God's Heart for Children framework view children's rights, and specifically the UN Convention on the Rights of the Child (CRC)? Fundamentally, the first affirmation of the framework lays a relatively strong foundation for children's rights when it claims that, "God creates every unique person as a child with dignity." The theological idea of dignity, as resulting from the *imago dei* that God bestowed upon humanity (as Dr. McConnell has explained in the previous article), bears strong similarity to the idea of rights as used in international parlance. The CRC justifies protection, provision and participation for children on the basis that all human beings (and hence, all children) bear rights. Correspondingly, the first affirmation of the Biblical Framework states that every child deserves "respect" and "nurture".

But these connections go much further than merely foundational issues. For example, each of the guiding principles of the Convention on the Rights of the Child find analogs in the "Understanding God's Heart for Children framework."

UNCRC	UGHFC
Article 2: Non-discrimination	Affirmation 1
Article 3: Best Interests of the Child	All
Article 6: Survival and Development	All
Article 5: Parental Guidance and the Child's Evolving Capacities	Affirmations 2 & 3
Article 12: Participation	Affirmations 6 & 7

Article two of the Convention stresses the critical importance that the rights of the child be extended to all children, regardless of race, religious background, or disability. All children have the same rights. This is mirrored in affirmation 1 of the framework which, by grounding dignity in the *imago dei*, extends that dignity to every child no matter their background or abilities, since the image of God is shared by every human being.

The third article of the Convention speaks of the need to ensure that in any action taken concerning children, "the best interests of the child shall be a primary consideration." Although this same sentiment is not explicitly stated in the framework, support for it would seem to come from each of the first four affirmations, since each one identifies (perhaps even more clearly than the Convention) what those best interests are: to be respected and nurtured (affirmation 1), to be raised by at least one loving, committed adult (affirmation 2), to thrive in stable and loving relationships (affirmation 3), and to flourish in a just society (affirmation 4). Indeed, an argument could be made that the last three affirmations add even more to that understanding of best interests: to receive faith and be seen as central to God's purposes (affirmation 5), to be full members of the family of faith (affirmation 6), and to be part of the mission of God (affirmation 7).

Similarly, each of the affirmations draws connections with article six of the convention: the right to life, survival, and development. The right to life is best referenced in affirmation 1, but each of the other affirmations also addresses different dimensions of survival and development.

The guiding principle of parental guidance is another point of strong similarity between the two documents. The second affirmation of the biblical framework provides strong theological support for the role of parents and families in the growth and nurturing of children, while still recognizing that these relationships can too often be broken. Therefore, the framework allows for the possibility that for whatever reason, parents may struggle to fulfill their intended role as primary caretakers of children. It is in this situation that the framework recommends that others should take over care, both for parents and children. Similarly, the Convention stresses not just the important role that parents play in the raising of children, it does this by affirming both parents' responsibility to care for their children as well as how states' parties should endeavor to restore families whenever they are broken. The central statement on parental guidance is found in article five, where the rights and responsibilities of parents to provide appropriate guidance and support to their children is preserved. However, this should be appreciated in the larger context of the CRC's concern for families, which begins in paragraph five of the Preamble by asserting the critical importance of assisting and protecting families as the fundamental group of society and the natural environment for the growth of children. Components of the CRC's strong commitment to family are further fleshed out in articles 9, 10, 11, 18, 19, 20, 21 and 27.

With regards to participation, the Convention stresses in article 12 that children must be granted the right to express their views and have those views receive due weight in accordance with their developmental capacities in any decisions that affect them. Although the Understanding God's Heart for Children affirmations do not lay out such a grand statement regarding participation, the importance of participation is clearly laid out in affirmation six. In this affirmation, the Church is identified as a place where children should be fully welcomed and encouraged to participate as members of the family of God. It is this affirmation, along with the recognition of the full dignity of children in affirmation one, that creates a context quite amenable to the understanding of participation as espoused in the CRC.

The Convention on the Rights of the Child (CRC) works with our "Understanding God's Heart for Children Biblical Framework:"

- Uniqueness of every part of the creation in the Bible (Genesis 1:27-31; 2:19-20): The man gives names to all of the animals. Naming gives them identity based on their unique characteristics.
- Uniqueness and naming in the CRC: The CRC affirms the uniqueness and dignity of a child through child rights. To give a child a name is one form of acknowledgment of the basic rights of a child. The CRC specifically mentions that a child has the right to a legal name (Articles 7 and 8).

Example: The simple act of giving a name to a child speaks so loudly in a country like Indonesia where 55 percent of children do not have a legal identity.[1] Globally, around 48 million children each year are not registered at birth, depriving them of a nationality and a legal name.[2] Without a legal name, these children simply do not legally exist. The first and basic child protection issue is legal identity. The first and most basic element of dignity is a name.

God taught humans to give names even to the animal world. How much more must we name a child to discern that child's uniqueness and to declare them as unique.

—*Tri Budiardjo*

---

1. UNICEF, "At a Glance: Indonesia," http://www.unicef.org/infobycountry/indonesia.html (accessed June 20, 2006).
2. UNICEF, "Child Protection from Violence, Exploitation, and Abuse,"

Points of Discontinuity

Of course, when comparing these two documents, a number of key points of marked discontinuity also emerge.

Responsibilities—Not Rights (Per Se)

First and foremost, the Understanding God's Heart for Children framework, like the Bible, does not couch its injunctions about care for children in terms of rights *per se*. Rather, besides making a clear statement about human dignity in the first affirmation, it follows the Biblical pattern of speaking about the needs of children and the responsibilities adults and societies have towards them. Only once (in Psalm 140:12) does the Bible ever speak of "rights" in the sense that we talk about them today, and this is only in a handful of modern translations. Moreover, these translations only cloud the issue, since the idea of "rights" in the modern sense did not exist in the time the Psalmist was writing. This is a significant difference between the two documents, since it means that the framework is more consistent with its Biblical source, and ensures that it is not promoting just one paradigm for ministry.

The Impact of the Fall

Secondly, the Convention on the Rights of the Child tends to downplay the significance of sin, whereas the Biblical Framework recognizes sin as the major factor that must be addressed (affirmation 2). This is not to say that the framers of the Convention believed that if every states' party fulfilled all of the requirements set out in the CRC we would usher in a utopian age of universal care and concern for children. Rather, even if all people's rights were upheld, we would provide only a minimal basis for peace and justice.[5] Yet even this seems remarkably unrealistic to Christians who are convinced of the truth of original sin and complete depravity. We cannot deny that every human initiative is tainted with the stain of sin, and that our only chance to achieve anything worthwhile for children or for God himself is through his acts of sovereign grace. Yet this is a reality that is not actually addressed in any significant way in the Convention.

The Centrality of Self-Sacrifice

Affirmation six says that, "children . . . are part of the admonition to love and serve one another." Let us take note that the kind of love to which this affirmation refers is no less than the love of Christ. "I command you to love each other in the same way that I love you. And here is how to measure it—the greatest love is shown when people lay down their lives for their friends" (John 15:11, NLV). A definition of love like this clearly goes beyond any command laid out in the Convention.

Furthermore, this love is intended to be doled out in a mutual fashion, as exemplified in the New Testament's many "one another" passages. This approach goes beyond the potentially selfish attitude that can be displayed by those who would assert their "rights." This self-giving love is central to the Christian walk and exists on a different moral plane than the idea of rights.

---

[5] Judith Ennew and Paul Stephenson, eds., *Questioning the Basis of our Work: Christianity, Children's Rights, and Development*, 17.

Spirituality as the Core

It begins with an idea of dignity that directs us back to God himself in the *imago dei*. As a result, it is clear that God is not only the reason that we serve, but also that the things that most concern him are the areas which need to take primacy in our work with children. What this means is that a view of holism derived from the Understanding God's Heart framework may include the same variety of concerns that are addressed in the Convention (or any other human rights document), but at the core of all of these concerns we are convinced that the spiritual issues must be addressed in a significant way. If we truly believe that children's existence is only dignified as a result of being endowed by God with his own image, we will be convicted to ensure that children have the opportunity to be introduced to that same God in a way that is appropriate for them.

> We have every reason to engage with rights as a tool for accomplishing God's purposes in the world.

Conclusion

Rather than rejecting rights wholly, as Christians working with children around the world, we should feel that we have every reason to engage with rights as a tool for accomplishing God's purposes in that world. Although rights language and the rights-based paradigm can seem like forbidding terrain, we should feel encouraged that a range of different ways to interact with this landscape are possible. We can also be encouraged by the substantial overlap in the specific issues that are addressed in both the biblical framework and documents like the Convention on the Rights of the Child. Furthermore, by using the Understanding God's Heart for Children theological framework carefully, we may find ways to not only relate to rights language and the power it can sometimes leverage—we can also discover the basis and opportunity to critique those rights and become even more effective advocates for children.

PRACTITIONER'S RESPONSE

RECOGNIZING UNIQUENESS AND DIGNITY

By Perry G. Downs
Trinity Evangelical Divinity School

Clearly, God values all persons, and because of the *imago Dei*, it is incumbent upon us, as followers of the Lord Jesus, to affirm the dignity and worth of all persons. It is precisely because of the doctrine of creation that all people have value and worth.

For the past twenty years, my wife and I have cared for a severely handicapped African American woman. Her name is Angel. Angel came into our home as a foster child when she was three years old. She has cerebral palsy, a condition that resulted from trauma at birth. Her brain was injured, and as a result she has profound limitations. She cannot care for herself in any way. She cannot walk, stand, sit up, or even roll over by herself. We feed, bathe, dress, and diaper her every day, having done so for over twenty years. She is one of thirty foster children we have taken into our home over the years.

Our lives are scheduled around Angel and her needs. Many times people wonder why we would limit our lives in this way; to care for someone who is so limited in ability, of a different race, and not our own child. I often ask my students at Trinity Evangelical Divinity School why it makes sense for us to do this ministry. Of course the answer is the *imago Dei*.

> Imago Dei:
> image of God

Angel deserves the care that we provide because she is a human being, made in the image of God. Human dignity does not reside in ability, potential, image (as advertising would have us believe), wealth, nationality, or gender. Dignity resides in origin and destiny. The issue is not what we have, what we can do, or who we know. The matter of dignity is rooted first and foremost in origin. From where did we come?

Modern science argues that humankind is simply the next rung up the evolutionary ladder. It argues that the origin of human life, and indeed all life, is a result of cosmic chance and nothing more. All human life could therefore be expendable because there would be no more value to human beings than to animals. Just as a horse that is deemed defective or unproductive can be destroyed, so people like Angel could be destroyed if they were equal to animals.

Biblically speaking, however, we see that humankind is the unique creation of God. We are made in God's image and, therefore, we reflect back God's glory. While I fundamentally agree, there are two issues I believe need to be raised and clarified.

The first issue has to do with the image of God and the Fall. The creation narrative of Genesis 3 moves directly into the story of the Fall. When Adam and Eve sinned, all of creation was affected. Angel's condition of cerebral palsy is a direct result of that sin, because through that sin evil was introduced into the created order and things are no longer the way they ought to be. Nonetheless, all people still carry within them the *imago Dei*. Certainly the Fall has marred the image, but it has not erased it. Whether people come to Christ for forgiveness or not, they still have great worth and dignity because they still have the image of God within them. The poorest, most sinful, and most profoundly handicapped people still carry within them the image of God. When we bring ministry to people, it is not to restore human dignity; rather it is to affirm it. It is because people are made in God's image that they matter. By bringing food, clothing, shelter, education, and of course, the message of the Gospel, we are demonstrating that all people have dignity, and all are worthy of our best efforts because of that dignity, which is inherent within them by virtue of God's act of creation.

My second response is rooted in the creation narrative of Genesis 1. Here I am not disagreeing at all, but rather I am adding what I believe to be a critical point. The text reads: "So God created humankind in his image, in the image of God he created them; male and female he created them" (Gen. 1:27).

The text raises the issue of gender, indicating that humankind is both male and female. Just as there is a tri-unity in the Godhead (Father, Son, and Holy Spirit), there is a bi-unity in humankind, namely male and female. Part of being in God's image is that we are created male and female. This bi-unity is a reflection of the tri-unity of God.

The implications of this doctrine are profound. As a male, I *need* female presence in my life to fully reflect the image of God. I must be in relationship with women to have the full image of God being expressed in my life. Likewise, women must be in relationship with men to have the image of God fully reflected in them. This does not only imply marriage or sexual relationships, but also cultural and social relationships where men and women work together for common goals and a common good. Mutual respect and value of one another are essential.[1]

Sadly, many cultures tend to devalue women, seeing them as somehow less significant than men. At times, women are treated as second-class citizens, or worse, as property to be used or passed on. But the doctrine of creation insists that women and men are of equal value because it is in the two genders that the image of God is fully reflected. Therefore, any perspective or practice that discriminates against women or girls, or devalues females in any way, is at profound odds with the doctrine of creation. Because we call ourselves "Christian," it is incumbent upon us to value all persons equally. To put it more directly, the doctrine of creation and the doctrine of *imago Dei* require that we treat girls with the same degree of respect that we have for boys.

Dignity:
- Based on the image of God
- Affected by the fall
- To be affirmed through ministry

An understanding of uniqueness is also important. Different cultures express it differently. In the United States, we emphasize individuality and uniqueness above everything else. People from other cultures who come to live in the United States must understand the centrality of individualism in the American mindset to make sense of our crazy culture. It is difficult for many Americans to understand that we actually have more

---

[1] For a further discussion on this topic, see the article by Doug McConnell in this volume.

commonalities than differences with other people. Our over-emphasis on individualism in the west can even cause extremes in adolescent behavior and fashion, and we see that many western teenagers go further and further to find ways to express their individuality. It is not hard to see how an over-emphasis on uniqueness can lead to self-centeredness and a contradiction of all cultural restraints, all in the name of personal freedom and individuality. As we speak of uniqueness, we must do so within the context of the importance of community and the commonalities we have with all people everywhere At the end of the day, there is more that makes us alike, than makes us different.

Failure to recognize uniqueness, however, can also bring about negative results. As my field is in education, I will speak to this issue in relation to educational practices. In some contexts, students are treated as if they were nothing more than empty containers, whose heads must be filled with information to be memorized. Students are not expected to be able to think for themselves and may even be punished if they do attempt to think. I have had doctoral students who have confessed that it was not until their studies for their Ph.D. degree, that they were ever taught to think for themselves. If all we do as educators is expect learners to memorize and give back 'the right answer,' we do great violence to the truth of *imago Dei* and the truth that, because of God's image within us, we all have something unique to bring into this world.

In our role as foster parents, my wife and I take children, many times infants, into our home and provide temporary shelter and care until they can be adopted or returned to their family of origin. One of the most delightful aspects of this ministry is to create a context where the individual personality of each child can emerge. We always watch with a certain degree of wonderment at the unique personality that we begin to see. We have never forced our children to become something they are not; rather, we have always respected the individuality and uniqueness that God has placed in us all.

It seems to me that because every person is unique, we, as child specialists, need to find ways to affirm that uniqueness without going to the extreme of unbridled individualism. I believe that a good place to begin would be in affirming educational practices that allow for some degree of creativity, personal expression, and personal thought. We must help children learn to think and to reason, not simply to memorize. The doctrine of creation demands this.

> Uniqueness:
> - In the context of interdependence
> - To be valued in relationships

Our responsibility is to look at all people, especially children, through eyes that see them for who they are—persons of great worth and great dignity, uniquely made in God's image. It is because God has made all persons, male and female, in his own image that we, as followers of God, must work for the good of all people, especially children.

CASE STUDY

PEPE: A MISSION PRESCHOOL PROGRAM, OPENING DOORS FOR CHILDREN IN DEPRIVED COMMUNITIES

BY GEORGIE AND STUART CHRISTINE
BMS WORLD MISSION, BRAZIL

The PEPE Story: A Brief Historical Review[1]

Georgie Christine, a teacher, and her husband Stuart, missionaries with the British Baptist Missionary agency, BMS World Mission, had already seen the crisis faced by the preschool-aged children that swarmed everywhere in the *favela* of Jardim Olinda, São Paulo. Without books in their shacks, with parents often unable to read or write, with little sense of discipline or structure to their day, few social skills, and little opportunity to develop fine motor coordination skills by participating in artistic activities at home, they were going to have a hard time when they started school alongside more advantaged kids.

So in August of 1992, the first 12 five- and six-year-olds were gathered into the broken down space cheerfully called a classroom and the PEPE—*Programa de Educação Pré-Escolar* or Program of Preschool Education, was born.

And what an impact it had in the community!

> "Before you came, Jardim Olinda had no hope. Now we have hope.!"
> —a young mother

The doors and the hearts of the community opened wide and the church was born together with the PEPE! PEPE quickly became a model that other churches wanted to adopt. By 2006, over six thousand children were in PEPEs in more than eleven different countries. From city slums to arid rural interiors, from tropical African forests to Andean mountain villages, the PEPEs are proving an extraordinarily versatile and effective program for the transformation of children, their families, and their communities through local church mission.

---

[1] See www.PEPE-Network.org.

FIGURE 1.2 The PEPE Network

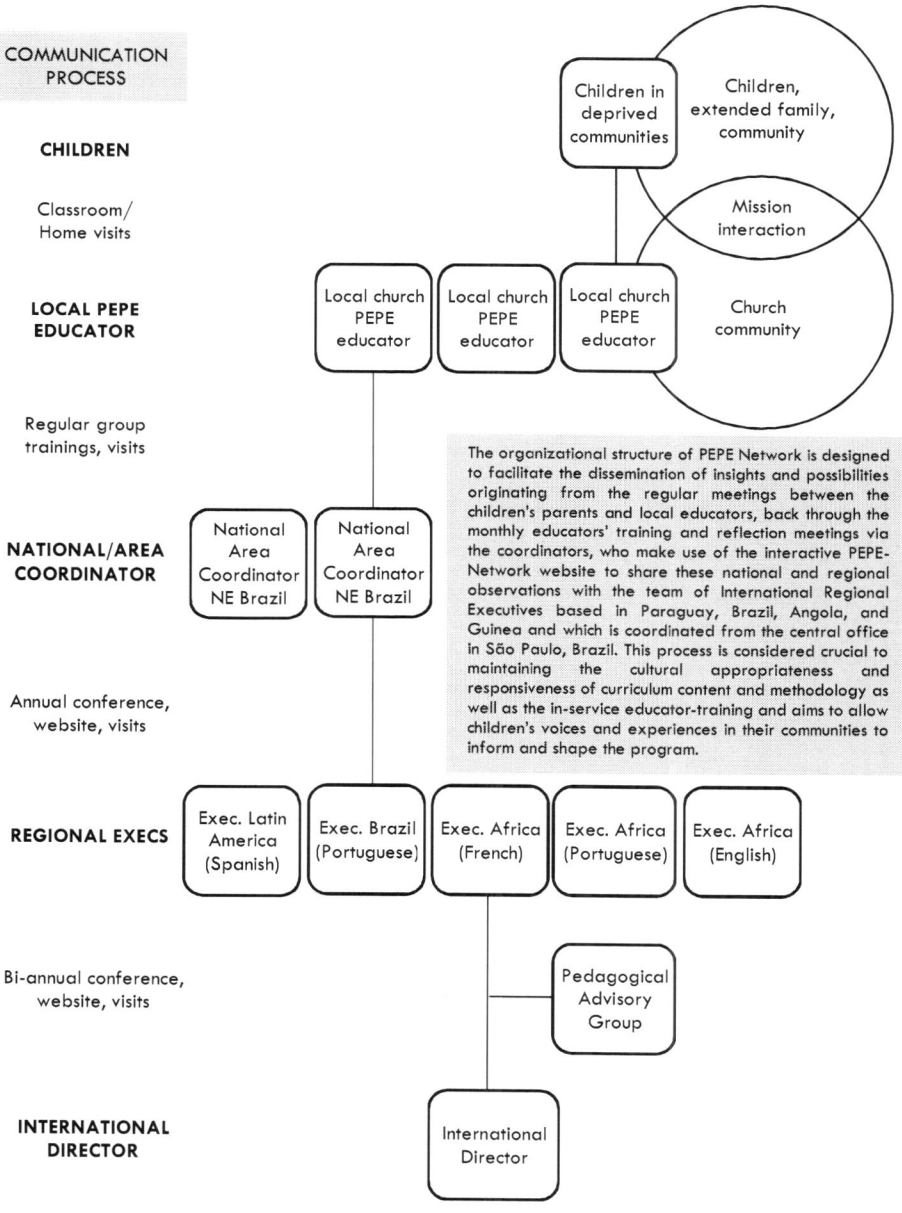

PEPE: A MISSION PRESCHOOL PROGRAM

Alice's Story: A Dream Come True

Her first day of school . . . Alice filed in to the PEPE classroom with the other five-year-olds. Whilst they ran and banged and chattered, she stood rooted to the floor, taking in the cracked but colorfully painted walls, the pictures and charts, the thirdhand chairs and desks. I was just able to hear her murmur: This is all I have ever dreamed of!

Social Deprivation and the Preschool-Aged Child

There are two main situations of social deprivation undermining the dignity and freedom of development of children in Brazil. One is the endemic poverty of northeastern Brazil, characterized by drought, social exploitation, and national neglect. At the other extreme are the children being brought up in the slums or *favelas* of the megacities, often with precarious housing, damp and unhealthy conditions, and violence all around.

A study published in October 1999 in the *Exame* journal, a sort of Brazilian "Time" magazine, revealed that nationally, 36 percent of poor children stay in school for less than one year. Only 27 percent complete eight years, 9 percent the full state school program up to twelve years, and less than one-half of 1 percent actually go on to tertiary education.[2] The consequences of these social and educational disadvantages in the early years are profound. They can also be life-determining, especially in cities where employment is conditioned by the demands of global markets, requiring near first world standards of education. In this setting, hundreds of thousands of virtually uneducated and unemployable young people live out a reality of social and economic marginalization that breeds frustration, disillusionment and resentment.

Josiana's Story

She is seven and often comes to the PEPE crying and irritable because she has had nothing to eat since the day before. At home, her father and mother are under the influence of drugs again. The little money there was has been spent on drugs and food has been forgotten.

In the PEPEs, children like Josiana are loved and cuddled not to satisfy an adult need for emotional release, but because they are recognized as, and helped to understand themselves as, full of worth and loveliness due to God's commitment to them.

Whatever you did for one of the least of these . . . [3]

The PEPE program has enabled many churches to make a meaningful and significant response and also to be there for the children in their suffering.

---

[2] "A Pobreza do Debate," *Exame*, October 6, 1999, http://portalexame.abril.com.br/busca/resultado/index.html?d1=938764800&d2=941443140&qu=escolar&ao=0&dia1=1&mes1=10&ano1=1999&dia2=31&mes2=10&ano2=1999&rd=1&num=10&x=29&y=8 (accessed August 22, 2006).

[3] See Matthew 25:40.

Why is Preschool Input So Effective, and Hence So Important, for Deprived Children?

- It intervenes in children's life experience at a moment when God has made them keen to learn.

- Their world is defined primarily by the home and extended family, which are God's special provision for a child's development.

- There is still relatively little negative peer group pressure.

- The slum community is most sensitive to its God-ordained communal responsibility for its young and vulnerable members.

- Preschool occurs before the child has been psychologically hindered by being sinfully labeled as a 'failure' in society's first great testing system, school.

- Families (which constitute the child's main sphere of life experience during the preschool years) can experience contact with Kingdom values through the active involvement of the local church in preschool programs.

The Educator's Story

An educator describes her experiences: *"After only three months of work, we are able to see positive results, especially in the way the children get on with one another. In the beginning they were very aggressive, but as time has passed there has been a terrific change in the way they have behaved together. They no longer cling to the teacher. They play and help one another."*

It is not likely that the restoration of the personal and social dimensions of a child's God-given humanity will be as easy again! Church-based preschool intervention creates a unique opportunity for breaking the miserable, God-denying cycle of poverty and indignity into which these children are born.

Areas of Development

PEPEs address five significant areas of early childhood deprivation, providing opportunities for educational, physical, psychological, social, and spiritual development.

Educational

Due to the lack of educational preparation, the project-based, interdisciplinary, and clearly structured PEPE curriculum and routine help to prepare the child and the parent (who are often unused to an organized schedule at home) for the demands of school organization and discipline.

Physical

Children come to us with a range of physical problems: physical and sexual abuse, malnutrition, and chronic medical conditions, to name a few. Some children suffer from more severe physical or mental disorders such as deafness, visual deficiencies, Down's syndrome, and more. The preschool forms a base for identifying and beginning to deal with these problems. When possible, the PEPEs provide a simple meal, toothbrushes, lessons about personal hygiene, a chance for daily brushing of teeth, and occasional visits from health professionals both at school and in the home. Children with physical and mental disabilities can be integrated into the class as they begin to discover their potential.

Psychological

The child will often have witnessed traumatic scenes of violence and disorder either in the home or community. Threats, shouting, and verbal abuse are common. Drunkenness and drug abuse often control family life. This environment produces fear, aggressiveness, introversion, and lack of self-esteem and confidence. The preschool helps by providing a context where alternative and constructive values are encouraged, including patience, prayer, positive forms of self-expression, positive attitudes toward adults, self-respect, and confidence.

Gisele's Story

The leaders of a new, small PEPE had a difficult decision to make. Gisele was a problem child . . . even her mother said so. She was a very sad little girl who hardly ate, didn't take part in activities with other children and from time to time suffered convulsions. Should they take her on?

With love and attention, prayer and care, Gisele was transformed. Today, her mother is thrilled by the changes. The lethargy and convulsions are gone and Gisele is developing the skills she will use in primary school. She plays and laughs with the other children to the delight and admiration of the whole community. God's presence is felt in the favela as his image is affirmed in Gisele's life.

Social

Due to the need to go out to work, single parents will sometimes lock the child in the shack during the day or simply leave the child to their own devices in the community. The preschool provides opportunities to develop the children's social abilities in ways that will allow them to integrate more successfully into society, created by God for life in community with others and with him.

Spiritual

In a community characterized by severe material necessity and lack of human opportunity, there is a marked tendency to seek supernatural help of any kind. The preschool offers an orderly and loving environment in which the children and their parents can experience Christian truth and values both in word and deed. Prayer at meals and in groups encourages children to share their faith and their needs. Bible stories, Christian music, and relationships with Christian peers and adults also help the children to form relationships with Christ. The child not only becomes an *object* of blessing but learns to understand that they can become an *agent* of blessing themselves—a participant in the story that God is writing in this world.[4]

The Goals of the Preschool Program

For the children: To enter primary school enthusiastically, with good self-esteem, and the social and educational skills and the spiritual experience to fulfill their God-given potential.

For the parents: To share in their child's experience of educational and spiritual enrichment.

For the community: To appreciate the educational and spiritual value of the PEPE and to pursue other beneficial community programs; to see the church as their ally.

For the missionary educators: To develop their personal spirituality and teaching capacity.

For the church: To mobilize the gifts of its members to express their faith in word and deed for the benefit of the local community.

Our Mission Statement

To enable Christian churches to express their faith and love in action by providing excellent preschool education for children of all religions in deprived communities around the world.

The Pastor's Story

In 2001 we began a church planting project in a very poor community where adult illiteracy is very high. We desired to meet some of this social need and share the message of Jesus. The PEPE with its educational emphasis has been brilliant. Many children, parents, and educators have become Christians, discovering God's love and developing a new understanding of their worth as individuals created and loved by God.

---

[4] See the article by Gustavo Crocker in this volume.

The impact that it has had on the life of the church in the community has been extraordinary. Credibility is the key word! The church is really respected, like Acts 2:42 in action. Even though the surrounding area is very violent, I am able to walk around quite freely day or night. One of the most exciting things is that we are seeing the first of the converted parents training to become teachers in the PEPE themselves!

The program is proving to be an excellent vehicle for taking the churches with even the most meager human and material resources out of their buildings to discover the power and life-changing potential of the Gospel in the poverty-stricken communities around them.

> "They devoted themselves to the apostles' teaching, to fellowship, to the breaking of bread and to prayer."
>
> —Acts 2:42

PRACTICAL IMPLICATIONS
HOLISTIC MINISTRY TO CHILD ADDICTS

By Premila Pavamani with Jennifer Orona
Emmanuel Ministries Calcutta

Anandaloy

Every child is made in the image of God, with intrinsic value and worth. Children are a heritage from the Lord (Ps. 127:3), but they are in dire distress. They are oppressed, voiceless, poor, and lost. At Emmanuel Ministries, our goals are to look for and find these children, remove hindrances, and introduce them to the Lord Jesus.

Most of the children in our ministry come from the city's railway platforms. Being abandoned, running away from dysfunctional families, becoming lost during mega festivals or natural calamities, or traveling to look for odd jobs can all lead children to the railway stations. These children are at high risk for exploitation, crime, addiction, physical and sexual abuse, and sexually transmitted diseases. A recent survey conducted by the Calcutta Samaritans showed that more and more, street children were resorting to drugs—petrol, glue, tobacco, crude heroin (called "brown sugar"), synthetic drugs, and illicit liquor.

In response to these challenges, Emmanuel Ministries established a home called "Anandaloy," or "Home of Joy." Established in 2001 as a night shelter for street children who were abusing drugs and alcohol, Anandaloy eventually developed into a residential facility for male child addicts. The Anandaloy home is a sanctuary for traumatized street and railway platform children who are driven to drugs and alcohol. After a drug-free period at a detoxification center, they are welcomed into the home and gradually weaned away from earlier habits through a customized recovery program, non-formal and formal schooling, and family-style community living.

Ministry and Activities

We believe that every child, regardless of their personal situation, has intrinsic worth, value, purpose, intelligence, and competence. No child should be marginalized. Instead, they must be helped to understand their identity and purpose in life. They must be nurtured with opportunities and resources to realize their full potential.

Currently, the Anandaloy residential facility is home to twenty-six boys between 12 and 18 years of age.[1] Fourteen of the boys are in the drug rehabilitation program.[2] Most children remain with us for around seven months, but some stay for three or even four years.[3] We encourage each boy to take leadership responsibilities within the home.

Our goal is to show respect no matter what condition we find the children in. The nonjudgmental approach that we take does not let children off the hook, though—our 70 percent recovery rate (with follow up) demonstrates that our methods help to remove barriers from the children's lives while encouraging them to make better choices. We try to always be available and open, regardless of the children's responses. Children need to know that they are important to us and that we care enough to go the second, third, and even the tenth mile with them.

> Jesus said to them, "Allow the children to come to Me—do not forbid or prevent them—for to such belongs the kingdom of God. Truly I tell you, whoever does not receive and accept and welcome the kingdom of God like a little child positively shall not enter it at all."
>
> —Mark 10:14-15 AMP

Children, especially abused, hurt, and addicted children, cannot be advised or motivated until they can trust us. For this reason, we emphasize consistency in routines, attitudes, and spiritual life. Persistence in prayer is essential. We choose to never give up and to keep trusting in God for miracles despite every adversity.

Structure and Strategies

Some current conservative estimates state that at least 18 million children are currently living on the streets of India.[4] Kolkata has the largest number, estimated to be between 100,000 and 125,000.[5] These children are largely unprotected, wide open to abuse and exploitation, and at very high risk for HIV and AIDS.

---

[1] Although we do not currently have younger children, we do accept them into the program. The youngest child to have been detoxified was 6½ years old.

[2] There are also 12 non-addict boys at Anandaloy. We believe that integration is a key element in recovery from addiction. However, this paper deals exclusively with the addicted children.

[3] Those who stay for long periods (beyond one year), do so either because their families cannot be traced, or because their families do not wish them to return. Although we make every effort to reintegrate them with their families, it does not always work out.

[4] Human Rights Watch, "Police Abuse and Killings of Street Children in India," http://www.hrw.org/reports/1996/India4.htm (accessed May 26, 2006). Unfortunately, accurate and current statistics are very difficult to find. This estimate comes from a 1991 Census in India, and demonstrates a significant increase from the Operations Research Group-Baroda's 1983 estimate of 11 million street children. In 2004, UNICEF estimated that over 304 million people now lived in India's urban centers. See http://www.unicef.org/infobycountry/india_india_statistics.html.

[5] Consortium for Street Children, "India," http://www.streetchildren.org.uk/resources/details/?type=country&country=64 (accessed May 26, 2006). This number is a conservative estimate from 1994, and is likely to have increased since then due to natural disasters (including the 2004 tsunami), increased urbanization, and other on-going risks.

At Emmanuel Ministries Calcutta, our vision is to see an empowered and transformed community of children in terms of rights, privileges and resources with the promise of hope and a future. We aim to affirm the worth and dignity of child addicts, enabling and empowering them through a "whole person recovery" program. We also seek to intervene, rescue, treat and rehabilitate children, implementing the rights of the child and preventing abuse, exploitation, HIV and AIDS.

> Our vision is to see an empowered and transformed community of children in terms of their rights, privileges and resources with the promise of hope and a future.

Our mission is to develop a movement for children at risk addicted to mood altering substances. We hope to empower child addicts through an affirming home environment, spiritual formation, literacy, medical assistance, and vocational training.

The Program at Anandaloy

The first day, straight from the streets, railway station, or detoxification center, is spent helping the child to become familiar with the home, the boys, and the expectations for personal hygiene and health. Each new boy is treated as an honored guest on their first day.

Our daily schedule is fairly full and structured. After washing up in the morning, the boys participate in an exercise activity such as football or karate. They are also encouraged to play indoor and outdoor games at other times throughout the day. In addition, they are given opportunities to learn through formal and non-formal education, times of sharing about health and hygiene, and extra tutoring according to their individual interests. The entire group helps to keep the house clean, and meals are provided three times each day. To help with spiritual and psychological development, the boys participate in morning and evening devotions, input sessions on whole person recovery, and group and individual counseling sessions.

Sometimes, the boys are taken out for special excursions. They worship and participate in youth events at a local church. They also take part in extracurricular activities which are aimed at encouraging the whole person toward recovery.

Strategies

"Children are born fully human, with identity and purpose." We help the children to recognize their significance by giving them a sense of belonging, showing attention and affection, providing therapy, encouraging responsibility, and working together.

Give children a sense of belonging. A child's first need is to belong. It is normal for addicts to feel that somehow, "we are different." Children take pride when given responsibility through the program, and they feel accepted because most of our caregivers and motivators have broken free from similar backgrounds.

Pay attention. The attention of peers, seniors and especially caregivers lets them know that they are made in the image of God, and thus worthy of love, trust, attention and compassion. Affection is a must.

Provide therapy. Therapy can help the children recover some of the hopes and joys of childhood. Recreation, games, good tasty food, outings, and storytelling can help the children to learn trust, security, hope, and love.

Disciplined freedom is an essential element of the program. For example, they can go out to the market, play with the local youth club members, participate in local cultural functions, and so on, but never alone, always in a group. The boys are also responsible for all matters of housekeeping, including security, cooking, cleaning, and maintenance.

Work as a community. We help the boys to develop a sense of community by empowering them to share their thoughts and ideas with the entire group. The boys decide what should be done in a case of indiscipline or in a crisis, and the caregivers respect their decisions within reason.[6] In addition, we help them to learn the value of possessions by encouraging them to share, and providing material goods only when they are needed.

Examples of Ministry to Children

Raja Das

Raja Das is so excited about working with the lost, runaway, addicted, and abandoned children at a drop-in center near one of Kolkata's main railway station platforms. He recalls that this same platform had been his home for many years after he was thrown out of his family as a child.

Soon, he was made painfully aware of the dynamics that operate on the platform among the various groups of people, the stranded boys, the gangs, and the police. Survival dictated that he join a gang, and as the newest recruit, he was often exploited. Crime thrived, and in the company of criminals he soon got hooked on alcohol, marijuana, glue sniffing, and synthetic drugs. The threat of death by police violence and rival gang members constantly haunted him. In his five years there, the police booked him often. His longest stay in prison was nine months. During this crisis period in his life, God intervened when a community worker from the Emmanuel Ministries Calcutta befriended Raja. Through this friendship, he was motivated to go for detoxification and was later welcomed into Anandaloy.

The acceptance and affection he received, along with the recovery program he participated in, brought about a transformation. To learn that God loved him enough to die for him was the beginning of the process. He soon completed his non-formal education courses and has remained clean for five years. Through hard work and perseverance, he has become a leader. He is now a strong role model for newcomers, encouraging them to lead a life free of crime and drugs.

---

[6] See the article by Judith Ennew in this volume.

Since our aim is always to reunite children with their families, we encouraged him to visit his home. Although his family rejected him once again, this resilient young man did not let their rejection adversely affect him. He has happily embraced family life back at Anandaloy, where he freely shares with many other children the hope of a new life in Christ and the promise for a future that he himself received and now enjoys.

Sukumar

Abandoned at the age of four, Sukumar grew up with two beggars who begged in distant towns, and was offered incentives to consume small quantities of liquor by laborers in a local kiln. By age six, he was addicted.

A nearby storeowner silently observed what was happening to Sukumar. A recovering addict himself, he tried to befriend Sukumar. Later, God in his providence planned for this same storeowner to visit Kolkata on business. He was surprised to see Sukumar loitering in one of the railway stations. Sukumar told him that he had no idea how he got to Kolkata.

The storeowner contacted Emmanuel Ministries Calcutta, and Sukumar was immediately allowed to enter the detoxification program. From there, he moved to Anandaloy. He has been promoted to Class 2 of the Calcutta Emmanuel School and is even securing high ranks in his class. Anandaloy provided him with a loving family environment, giving him back his childhood and showing him how much God loves him.

Conclusion

God's desire is for children to fulfill his purposes in their lives. He intends for them to be protected, loved, affirmed, and nurtured to attain their full potential. In our broken world of dysfunctional families where children have become dispensable, the restoration of an extended family structure that accepts and affirms the child addict gives the Holy Spirit an opportunity to heal, restore and renew them so that they recognize their true identity as members of the family of God and responsible citizens of our country.

CHAPTER 1
DISCUSSION QUESTIONS

1) What do we understand by people being made "in the image of God"? If children are made in God's image, what does this say to us (theologically or otherwise) about the character and nature of God? What does it say to us about children and childhood?

2) In our work with children, how can we recognize, affirm, and restore the expression of dignity in their lives?

CHAPTER 2
PLACED IN FAMILIES

Children need parental love in a broken world.

God's design is for each child to be born, vulnerable and dependent, to loving parents within the covenant of marriage. God's desire is for each child to grow in this secure, caring environment. In a fallen world, people and relationships can be damaged. When parents struggle to fulfill their intended role, others must provide dedicated care for them and their children.

God intends for all children to be raised by at least one loving, committed adult.

"If asked, "How do you nurture the faith of your children?" many parents might answer, 'We pray at meals and at bedtime, read the Bible together, and go to church.' Although these are significant experiences for children, relationships with parents and other significant adults provide the most formative influences for children."[1]

—Scottie May, et al

"I bow my knees before the Father, from whom every family in heaven and on earth takes its name."

—Ephesians 3:14-15 NRSV

"The value and significance of children is related to the fall. They are not just a blessing to the family and a heritage from God, they are God's instruments to make his salvation realized and his redemption plan accomplished."

—Tri Budiardjo

---

[1] Scottie May et al., *Children Matter: Celebrating Their Place in the Church, Family, and Community*, 152.

BIBLICAL REFLECTION

THE VOCATION OF PARENTING: A BIBLICALLY AND THEOLOGICALLY INFORMED PERSPECTIVE

BY MARCIA J. BUNGE
VALPARAISO UNIVERSITY

We all realize that one of the most important ways to help children is by supporting their parents or primary caregivers. Supporting parents is especially important because the family has the most potential of any institution for providing for children's basic needs and for shaping their spiritual and moral lives.[1] Even though children are influenced by many other factors, parents are often still the primary shaping force (whether negative or positive) in a child's development.

Even though we recognize this, support for children and parents is undermined in a number of ways both in contemporary cultures and even within the Church. For example, poverty, minimum paying jobs, or tight working schedules often do not allow parents to provide for their children's basic needs let alone to spend enough time with them.

Although the Church certainly upholds the importance of parenting and does offer a variety of programs for families, there are also elements in the Church that undermine support for children and parents. For example, the Church does not have strong teachings about parenting or children. The Church basically says that parents are to teach children the faith and that children should obey their parents. Beyond this, little is said about the nature of children, about a child's spiritual life, or about our precise obligations and duties toward children.

Furthermore, children's ministry and religious education programs are often not only theologically weak and under-funded but also neglect to keep in mind the importance of parents in the faith development of children. Religious education programs tend to operate in isolation from the home, not as an extension of the home. Thus many parents within the Church are neglecting to speak with their children about moral and spiritual matters. They also neglect to integrate practices into their everyday lives that nurture faith.

---

[1] Merton Strommen, "A Family's Faith, A Child's Faith," in *Dialog* (Summer 1998): 177-178. Merton Strommen, founder of both the Search Institute and the Youth and Family Institute, claims that the family is still "the most powerful institution in promoting faith in children and youth." He admits that children are influenced by their family, congregation, community and culture. Each level of influence makes a significant impact (positive or negative) in shaping the characteristics of children. He believes, however, that the "primary force in the life of a person is the family." Thus, families, not the church, must be seen as the backbone of spiritual and moral formation of children. For an excellent resource that emphasizes the role of the family in faith formation see Merton P. Strommen and Richard Hardel, *Passing on the Faith: A Radical New Model for Youth and Family Ministry*. See also Don Browning et al., *From Culture Wars to Common Ground: Religion and the American Family Debate*, 308.

Because of this, we need to find ways to support parents and help them take up their role as the primary agents of a child's moral and spiritual formation more seriously and urgently. We also need to ensure that all children, even those without parents or families, are given the kind of parental love they need.

One way to support both parents and children is by articulating sound theologically and biblically informed understandings of parenting. My hope is that this section begins to take up that task and stimulate further theological reflection.

> Because parenting is undermined, we need to find ways to support parents and help them take up their role as the primary agents of a child's moral and spiritual formation more seriously and urgently. We also need to ensure that all children, even those without parents or families, are given the kind of parental love they need.

Part I: The Sacred Task of Parenting

Certainly a biblically and theologically informed view of parenting emphasizes that parents are to love their children. There are numerous stories in the Bible of parents who love their children. Many analogies are also made between parental love and the love of God (see Hos. 11:1-8).

Parental love is, of course, multi-faceted. It involves not only feelings but also particular attitudes, actions, and responsibilities. Following, are four dimensions of a biblical and theological understanding of the primary purpose and task of parenting. By no means exhaustive, they draw attention to some important themes. Moreover, each element of this view of parenting corresponds to a particular view of children, and the list as a whole reminds us that a strong theological understanding of parenting can only be articulated by cultivating a vibrant and complex theological understanding of children themselves.[2]

First, and perhaps most simply, parents are to provide for their children's basic needs of food, shelter, and affection. When parents are unable to take up this task or if they have died, then others in the community must help. Numerous biblical passages explicitly command us to care and provide for our own children and for poor children and orphans—among the most vulnerable in society.[3] God is also depicted as the "father of orphans and protector of widows" (Ps. 68:5). They too are "neighbors" in our midst. Thus, caring for children, like caring for adults, is part of seeking justice and loving our neighbor.

The responsibility to care for the basic needs of not only our own children but also those of orphans and the poor is built, in part, on the biblical notion that all children, like all adults, are fully human and made in the image of God (Genesis 1:27). Although parents nurture them, they are made not only in the image of their parents, but in the greater image

---

[2] For a fuller discussion of the central elements of a theological understanding of children on which this chapter builds, see Marcia J. Bunge, "The Dignity and Complexity of Children: Constructing Christian Theologies of Childhood," 53-68; "A More Vibrant Theology of Children," *Christian Reflection: A Series in Faith and Ethics* (Summer 2003): 11-19; and "Retrieving a Biblically Informed View of Children: Implications for Religious Education, a Theology of Childhood, and Social Justice," *Lutheran Education* 139, (Winter 2003): 72-87.

[3] See, for example, Exodus 22:22-24; Deuteronomy 10:17-18; and 14:28-29.

of God.[4] It follows that children, like adults, possess the fullness of humanity. Regardless of race, gender, or class, they have intrinsic value.

Second, and perhaps less emphasized, is that the Bible also indicates that parents are to respect, to enjoy, and to be thankful for their children. Sarah rejoiced at the birth of her son, Isaac (Gen. 21:6-7).[5] Parents cultivate attitudes of respect, joy, and gratitude, in part, by viewing children as gifts of God. Many passages in the Bible speak of children as gifts of God or signs of God's blessing. For example, Leah, Jacob's first wife, speaks of her sixth son as a dowry, or wedding gift, presented by God (Gen. 30:20).[6]

> Parents are to . . .
> 1) provide for their children's basic needs
> 2) respect, enjoy, and be grateful for their children
> 3) nurture their children's faith and help them use their gifts to love and serve others
> 4) listen to children and learn from them

A third dimension of the sacred task of parenting is that parents are to nurture their children's faith and help them use their gifts and talents to love and serve others and contribute to the common good. Parents and other caring adults are to nurture, teach, and guide children, helping them to develop intellectually, morally, emotionally, and spiritually. Several biblical passages speak about these responsibilities of parents. For example, adults are to "train children in the right way" (Prov. 22:6) and bring up children "in the discipline and instruction of the Lord" (Eph. 6:4).[7]

Connected to this understanding of parenting is a view of children as developing beings and moral agents in need of instruction and guidance. Although they are made in the image of God and fully human, they also need the help of adults to teach and to direct them. More specifically, children need to learn how to read and study God's Word, how to worship and pray, how to live out their faith, and how to develop their gifts and talents so that they can better use them to love and serve others.

Fourth, the sacred task of parenting also involves listening to children and learning from them. As followers of Christ, Christian parents have this responsibility. This includes taking their questions and concerns seriously, and paying attention to the lessons that children can teach them.

This fourth element of a sacred view of parenting is built on a biblical understanding of children as models of faith for adults and representatives of Jesus. Many gospel passages turn upside-down the common assumption held in Jesus' time and our own: that children are to be seen but not heard and that the primary role of children is to learn from and obey adults. In contrast, the New Testament depicts children in striking and even radical ways as moral witnesses, models of faith for adults, sources or vehicles of revelation,

---

[4] See the article by Doug McConnell in this volume.
[5] See, for more examples, Jeremiah 20:15; Luke 1:14; and John 16:20-21.
[6] See, for more examples, Genesis 30:22; 1 Samuel 1:11,19; Genesis 30:11; and Psalm 127:3. Also see article by Jennifer Orona in this volume.
[7] See, for more examples, Isaiah 38:19; Psalm 78:4b; Deuteronomy 6:5; 11:18-19; 31:12-13; Genesis 18:19; and Proverbs 2:9.

representatives of Jesus, and even paradigms for entering the reign of God (Matt. 18:2-5; 19:14).

Viewing children as models for adults or vehicles of revelation does not mean that they are creatures who are "near angels," "closer to God," or "more spiritual" than adults. However, these passages and others do challenge adults to honor children's questions and insights, and to recognize that children can positively influence the community and the moral and spiritual lives of adults.

These four elements provide only a brief sketch of a biblically and theologically informed view of parenting, yet even these four aspects alone remind us that one can build a strong view of parenting only by cultivating, at the same time, a vibrant and complex theological understanding of children and childhood. The Bible gives us a richer view of both parenting and children.

There are many ways that Christian theologians in the past have understood the complex and sacred task of parenting, incorporating these four and other elements. Here are just three examples, but there are many others. Christians from all denominations and backgrounds can search their traditions for other meaningful ways to speak about the task of parenting that better reflect a biblically informed understanding of it.

For example, John Chrysostom, an important figure in the 4th century Church and for Eastern Orthodox communities of faith today, spoke about the family as a "sacred community" or a "little church."[8] For him, this means that parents should read the Bible to their children, pray with them, and be good examples. Being a little church also means that the family reaches out to the poor and needy in the community. Chrysostom ranks the neglect of children among the greatest evils and injustices. For him, neglect of children includes inordinate concern for your own needs and affairs above those of your children. He also believes that we neglect children when we focus on secular standards of success, such as wealth or fame, or when we are preoccupied with accumulating possessions.

Like Chrysostom, Horace Bushnell, a leading Congregationalist pastor and scholar of the 19th century, also speaks of the family as a "little church."[9] Although he sees the important role of the Church in the faith development of children, he believes that the primary agent of grace is the family, not the Church. "Religion never thoroughly penetrates life," he said, "until it becomes domestic."[10] His popular book, *Christian Nurture*, envisions spiritual formation as a natural process that takes place not merely by reading the Bible and teaching children aspects of the faith but rather through everyday practices and routines and the examples of adults. Thus, he stresses the heroic importance of "small things" and claims that "it requires less piety . . . to be a martyr for Christ than it does to . . . maintain a perfect and guileless integrity in the common transactions of life."[11] He also

---

[8] For a full discussion of Chrysostom, see Vigen Guroian, "The Ecclesial Family: John Chrysostom on Parenthood and Children," 61-77.
[9] For a full discussion of Bushnell, see Margaret Bendroth, "Horace Bushnell's Christian Nurture," 350-364.
[10] Horace Bushnell, *Christian Nurture*, 63.
[11] Horace Bushnell, "Living to God in Small Things," 291-292.

encourages parents to interweave lessons about the faith with play and a variety of fun activities. [12]

Another way theologians have emphasized the importance of parenting is by speaking of it as a divine calling or vocation. Martin Luther, the 16th century Reformer, for example, reflected deeply on the central tasks and responsibilities of parenting, and he incorporated parenting into his view of vocation or calling as a whole. Martin Luther emphasizes that all believers are called to love God and to love and serve their neighbors, especially those in need.[13]

Although Luther claims all believers share this common Christian calling, he also emphasizes that they honorably carry it out in a wide variety of specific "vocations"—in specific "stations" or "places of responsibility" in which they serve the well-being of others, whether at home, at work, at church, or in civic life. Thus, even children and students have a calling here and now. They already have certain responsibilities that benefit the family and the community.

Given his view of vocation, Luther speaks meaningfully about the sacred task and calling of parents. Luther believes parenting is a serious and divine calling that is "adorned with divine approval as with the costliest gold and jewels."[14] In one often quoted passage, he says the following:

Now you tell me, when a father goes ahead and washes diapers or performs some other mean task for his child, and someone ridicules him as an effeminate fool . . . . God, with all his angels and creatures, is smiling—not because that father is washing diapers, but because he is doing so in Christian faith.[15]

Luther further underscores the importance of parenting by saying that parents are apostles, bishops, and priests to their children.[16] According to Luther, as priests and bishops to their children, parents have a twofold task: to nurture the faith of their children; and to help them develop their gifts to serve others. He also helped parents in this task by

---

[12] As Bendroth explains, Bushnell, like Chrysostom, also has high expectations for parental influence. He believes that it would be almost impossible for a child who had been properly nurtured to reject the Christian faith. In the face of criticism by several of his contemporaries who claim that godly parents sometimes produce ungodly children for no apparent reason, Bushnell responds that there are so many ways to account for the failure of childrearing that doubts about his argument are unwarranted. He also claims that parents who neglect the spiritual well-being of their children will be judged by God. See "Horace Bushnell's Christian Nurture."
[13] See Mark 12:28-24; Mt 22:34-40; Lk 10:25-28. This sense of calling is built on Jesus' command to his followers to "love the Lord your God with all your heart, and with all your soul, and with all your mind, and with all your strength" and to "love your neighbor as yourself."
[14] LW 45: 39.
[15] LW 45: 40-41.
[16] For a full discussion of Luther's views on parenting, see, for example, Jane E. Strohl, "The Child in Luther's Theology: 'For What Purpose Do We Older Folks Exist, Other Than to Care for . . . the Young,'" 134-159; William Lazareth, *Luther on the Christian Home: An Application of the Social Ethics of the Reformation;* and Gerald Strauss, *Luther's House of Learning: Indoctrination of the Young in the German Reformation.*

preaching about parenting and by writing "The Small Catechism," which was intended for use in the home.[17]

Part II: Ten "Best Practices" for Nurturing the Moral and Spiritual Lives of Children

In addition to speaking about the home as a "little church" or parenting as a "vocation or calling," these and other Christian theologians offer highly practical advice about how parents and other caring adults can teach and pass on the faith, and help children to use their gifts and talents to love and serve others. As we examine the work of theologians and the Bible itself, we find that they emphasize ten "best practices" for nurturing the moral and spiritual lives of children. Though not a guarantee, these practices have been used across traditions to foster the moral and spiritual formation of children.

Recent sociological and psychological studies on moral or spiritual development also confirm the value of these kinds of activities. These are ten valuable ways of creating a space for the Holy Spirit to work in the lives of children and adults. These practices can be carried out both by parents and other caring adults.[18]

1) Reading and Discussing the Bible and Interpretations with Children

Augustine, Luther, Calvin, Schleiermacher, and many other theologians have emphasized the importance of this practice. Regardless of our view of biblical authority or biblical interpretation, so-called conservative and liberal Christians today would all agree that the Bible is the central text for the Christian church and contains truths and stories that parents or caring adults need to tell and to teach children. Adults will read different Bible stories to children in different ways, but no matter what their approach, they should cultivate in children the sense that the Bible is worth reading and re-reading. It is a vast and abundant gold mine of wisdom that can never be fully excavated.[19]

---

[17] For discussions of Luther and Calvin, see Jane E. Strohl, "The Child in Luther's Theology," and Barbara Pitkin, "'The Heritage of the Lord': Children in the Theology of John Calvin," 134-193. The German Lutheran Pietist, August Hermann Francke, also spoke meaningfully about the sacred task of parenting. He claimed that the primary goal of parents is to help children live out their vocation. They are to help children grow in faith, empowering them to use their gifts and talents to love and serve God and the neighbor and to contribute to the common good. See Marcia Bunge, "Education and the Child in Eighteenth-Century German Pietism: Perspectives from the Work of A. H. Francke," 247-278.

[18] The first four practices have been creatively emphasized in the work of the Youth and Family Institute.

[19] See Paul Griffiths, *Religious Reading: The Place of Reading in the Practice of Religion*. Here we can learn from the contemporary thinker, Paul Griffiths, who makes a distinction between "religious reading" (which is done slowly, repeatedly, and with the aim of gaining wisdom for life from the text) and "consumerist reading" (which is done quickly and with the aim of getting information).

2) Worshipping With a Community and Carrying Out Family Rituals of Worship and Prayer

Parents should worship regularly with their children. Many sociological studies have also shown the importance of building family identity and sense of connection simply by going to church together and keeping the Sabbath. Rituals of worship and prayer at home are also important. Here, we can learn much from the Jewish tradition about worshipping and praying together as a family in the home. Sociological studies also show the importance of family rituals to help create family identity and connectedness. These rituals can be as simple as saying prayers before meals or carrying out annual family traditions during Lent or Advent.

3) Introducing Children to Good Examples, Mentors, and Stories of Service and Compassion

We all recognize the importance of good examples in the lives of children. Within the Church or other religious communities, being a good example means that we should be believers ourselves and should strive to live out our faith in our everyday lives. My own college students tell me not only about how important their parents have been to them but also teachers or coaches or other adults who cared for them and took an interest in them.

4) Serving Together and (what is connected to service) Teaching Financial Responsibility

Parents and other caring adults teach children much about their faith and values when they find ways to carry out service projects together with children. This can be done in formal or informal ways, such as helping a neighbor, serving food to the poor, or participating in a Habitat for Humanity project. The value of this kind of mutual service was underscored in a survey that found that "involvement in service proved to be a better predictor of faith maturity than participation in Sunday school, Bible study, or worship services."[20]

Connected to service is teaching financial responsibility. The United States today is a country in which children are daily bombarded with advertisements and where we have more shopping malls than schools. The favorite activity of 95 percent of high school girls is shopping, and the number one reason that students must drop out of college is credit card debt. Although we live in a highly consumerist culture, most of my college students admit that they have never spoken to their parents about money and finances. Christian parents must realize that financial responsibility goes along with service to others: knowing how to spend money wisely and to use it to help others.

---

[20] Strommen and Hardel, 95.

5) Singing Together and Exposing Children to the Spiritual Gifts of Music and the Arts

The arts, especially music, have always been an important vehicle of moral and spiritual formation in the Christian tradition. Martin Luther, for example, believed that music was not simply an ornament for worship services but rather a vital element of human existence, an instrument of the Holy Spirit, and a powerful vehicle for spreading the Gospel. He emphasized the value of music in these bold words, "Next to the Word of God, music deserves the highest praise."[21] Because of the vital role of music and the arts in spiritual life, he specifically encouraged Christians to sing with children and to train them in music and the arts.[22]

6) Appreciating the Natural World and Cultivating a Reverence for Creation

There are many examples within the Christian tradition of how close contact with the natural world has been a source of spiritual growth and inspiration. Many biblical passages emphasize the beauty and goodness of creation and the importance of going to the wilderness for spiritual renewal, cleansing, or insight. Early in the Christian tradition, monks retreated to the wilderness to meditate. They wrote eloquently about the insights they gained about God's creation and their place in it. The important relationship between the spiritual life and the natural world is also found in the works of Celtic Christians, medieval mystics, St. Francis, and many contemporary Christian writers today, such as Leonardo Boff and Wendell Berry. Many of my students echo this long tradition when they tell me of wilderness trips with their families or their life-changing experiences at Bible Camps, church camps, or wilderness retreat centers.

7) Educating Children and Helping Them Discern their Vocations

Many theologians, such as Martin Luther and August Hermann Francke, an 18th century German Lutheran, would add that we nurture faith in children by helping them discern their gifts and talents and by providing them with a good liberal arts education so that they can use their gifts to love and to serve others. Both believe a strong liberal arts program will help children develop their God-given gifts and talents, enabling them to serve both church and society.[23] In other words, they believe that nurturing faith is

---

[21] Forward to Georg Rhau's *Symphoniae iuconudae* in LW 53: 323.

[22] In one passage Luther claims, "I would like to see all the arts, especially music, used in the service of him who gave and made them. I therefore pray that every pious Christian would be pleased with this [the use of music in the service of the gospel] and lend his help if God has given him like or greater gifts. As it is, the world is too lax and indifferent about teaching and training the young for us to abet this trend." "Preface to the Wittenberg Hymnal" (1524) in LW 53: 316.

[23] For Luther's ideas on education, see, for example, his "Sermon on Keeping Children in School" (1530) and his "To the Councilmen of All Cities in Germany That They Establish and Maintain Christian Schools" (1524). In his letter to the councilmen, he underscores the importance of education by saying: "Now the welfare of a city does not consist solely in accumulating vast treasure, building mighty walls and magnificent buildings and producing a goodly supply of guns and armor. Indeed, where such things are plentiful, and reckless fools get control of them, it is so much the worse and the city suffers even greater loss. A city's best and greatest welfare,

connected to nurturing a child's capacity to love and serve others. Parents and caring adults are to help children find their vocation: not just help them see what is fulfilling or makes the most money, but how they can best use their talents to make a difference in the world and to contribute to the common good. Given their views of education and vocation, both Luther in the 16th century and Francke in the 17th century (in contrast to many in their time) were advocates of excellent schools and education for all children (including girls and the poor). They prompted real educational reforms that continue to influence German schools today.

8) Fostering Life-Giving Attitudes toward the Body, Sexuality, and Marriage

Although the Christian tradition has a somewhat ambivalent legacy regarding the body, the Jewish and Christian traditions both affirm the goodness of our bodies and our sexuality and the goodness of the natural world in general. Adults should therefore help children understand from an early age that taking care of their bodies is part of honoring God and God's gifts to us. They should also help children understand the proper context for the expression of sexuality and speak to them about Christian understandings and expectations of marriage and sexual activity. I am always shocked when most of my college students tell me that they have never had conversations with either their parents or their pastors about sexuality, even though their lives are inundated by the media with messages about their bodies and sexuality.

9) Listening To and Learning from Children

Adults also cultivate faith in children by listening to their questions, insights, and concerns. In this way, faith can be taken to heart and appropriated. Furthermore, as the gospels and our own experiences teach us, children also nurture, deepen, and challenge our own faith.

10) Taking Up a Christ-Centered Approach to Discipline, Authority, and Obedience; and Recognizing that, in the Tradition, Parental Authority is Always Limited

Given the view of parenting described in the first part of this section, we can see why, from a Christian perspective, adults must take up a Christ-centered approach to discipline, authority, and obedience. Disciplining children, from a Christian perspective, should never be equated to physically punishing them.[24] True discipline has much more to do with being followers and disciples of Christ.

Furthermore, we must realize that although parents and other adults do have authority over children, this authority is never absolute. The Bible emphasizes not only that children

---

safety, and strength consist rather in its having many able, learned, wise, honorable, and well-educated citizens." Martin Luther, *Martin Luther's Basic Theological Writings*, 712-713. For Francke's view of education, see Bunge, "Education and the Child in Eighteenth-Century German Pietism."

[24] See the article by Joni Middleton in this volume.

should obey their parents, but also that parents should not provoke their children to anger (Col. 3:21). The book of Proverbs, which some Christians use to justify use of the "rod," speaks primarily about instructing children in wisdom and warns parents, "Do not set your heart on [your children's] destruction" (Prov. 19:18).[25] Furthermore, the Bible and the tradition recognize that when parents are sinful or unjust, children need to disobey their parents. In the end, a child's final loyalty is to God and not to parents. Thus, parents *do* have authority over their children, but this authority is limited. It must be centered in Christ-like love, and it is never an excuse for treating children unjustly or unkindly.

Part III: The Messiness and Complexity of Family Life

Although children best thrive when they are raised by two loving parents within the covenant of marriage and who carry out these and other "best practices," in a fallen world, people and relationships can be damaged. Single-parent and even two-parent families are broken and struggling in various ways. There are also many children who have no parents at all or their parents cannot care for them. Some of them get help from neighbors, relatives, and the community. However, others do not. In this case, children themselves often become the primary caregivers. They are forced to abandon their own education, go to work, and raise their younger siblings. Indeed, the number of child-headed households or children being raised by grandparents is rising all around the world. Other parents have abused or neglected their children. Still other parents and their relatives have died in wars or because of disease. Whether in refugee camps, foster care homes, or orphanages, the care of orphans in many countries around the world is uneven and substandard. Sometimes their situation is even life-threatening.

> A child's final loyalty is to God and not to parents. Thus, parents do have authority over their children, but this authority is limited. It must be centered in Christ-like love, and it is never an excuse for treating children unjustly or unkindly.

Part IV: Implications and Potential Strategies

Although children around the world face these and other challenges, the Church must find ways to help all children by supporting parents or primary caregivers in the sacred task of parenting and by ensuring that all children receive the love and care that they need. Several potential strategies follow from a Christian view of the sacred task of parenting.

For example, the Church, State, and international organizations could aim to help parents in these seven specific ways, many of which overlap with several goals of international initiatives, such as the World Fit For Children, the Convention on the Rights of the Child, and the Millennium Development Goals:

---

[25] See the article by William J. Brown on Proverbs and the notion of discipline in the forthcoming book, *Biblical Perspectives on Children and Childhood*.

1) Provide all children and families with safe drinking water, proper nutrition, and adequate health care.

2) Help reduce poverty and help all families reach an adequate standard of living.

3) Achieve free and universal education; help all children have access to excellent schools and ways to explore and to sharpen their gifts and talents to serve others.

4) Safeguard the natural environment and the diversity of life for the sake of children's quality of life and spiritual growth.

5) Protect children from abuse, neglect, and physical punishment.

6) Help reduce infant mortality and the number of orphans, especially by combating diseases such as HIV and AIDS and malaria.

7) Strengthen foster care programs, improve orphanages, and accelerate the process of adoption for children in need.

The Church itself can also support parents, primary caregivers, and children in these six additional ways:

1) Emphasize the sacred task of parenting in the Church, and preach and teach on the subject.

2) Offer programs that prevent divorce and support all families.

3) Create excellent religious educational materials and programs that are theologically sound, honor the questions and insights of children themselves, and emphasize the importance of parents and primary caregivers in faith development.

4) Provide parents and primary caregivers with ideas and resources for nurturing faith at home.

5) Listen more attentively to children and learn from them; recognize the importance of children in the faith journey and spiritual maturation of adults.

6) Strengthen theologies of childhood and child theologies.

Regarding the last point: On the one hand, the Church should develop "theologies of childhood" that primarily provide sophisticated theological understandings of children and our obligations to them. On the other hand, it should develop "child theologies" that reexamine not only conceptions of children and obligations to them but also rethink fundamental doctrines and practices of the Church as a whole. Drawing on insights from a variety of other theologies, child theologies have as their task not only to strengthen the Church's commitment to and understanding of a group that has often been voiceless, marginalized, or oppressed—children—but also to reinterpret the Church's theology and practice as a whole.[26]

Conclusion: Our Common Task in Nurturing Children

We share a common task in caring for children and nurturing their moral and spiritual lives. It is clearly an important and complex task that requires a cooperative effort among parents, relatives, friends, religious communities, schools, the state, and international organizations. All of us, whether or not we are parents ourselves, need to work diligently on many levels and in many ways to protect and to nurture children.

---

[26] The term, "Child Theology," has been coined by Keith J. White, Haddon Willmer, and John Collier, leaders of the Child Theology Movement. The Child Theology Movement is a not-for-profit limited company registered in London, England. For more information about the Movement, send an e-mail to: info@childtheology.org or see the website: www.childtheology.org. White and Willmer are currently writing a book with the working title, *Child Theology—The Child in the Midst.* For more about the distinction between and the significance of theologies of childhood and child theologies, see my article on religious understandings of children, "The Child, Religion, and the Academy: Developing Robust Theological and Religious Understandings of Children and Childhood," *Journal of Religion* 86, no. 4 (2006): 549.

CRITICAL ISSUES

CHILDREN'S NEEDS FOR PARENTAL LOVE IN A SYSTEMICALLY BROKEN WORLD

BY KATHARINE MEESE PUTMAN
FULLER THEOLOGICAL SEMINARY

So many vultures circled overhead, the blue sky appeared overcast. I made my way through mounds of garbage with trucks roaring by as they brought yet more. The stench was unbearable, and I had to cover my mouth and nose with a cloth to breathe. My eyes were stinging shut from the dust, which the wind whipped incessantly.
Children live here!
I couldn't stop thinking this, as I watched even the littlest ones sort through refuse and glass to find bits to recycle. All of us had to jump out of the way when a new truck dumped garbage. I'm told some of the children at times don't make it, and are maimed or killed by the tons of garbage filled with sharp, heavy objects poured daily into the Guatemala City Dump. If they aren't hurt by the garbage, they are damaged by the community violence, drugs, rampant abuse, and constant necessary labor to help their families earn enough money for food each day.
I was touring the dump while visiting a Christian ministry's school there, where I regularly offer workshops. Before lunch at the school, I stood by a sink to help the five-year-olds from the dump community wash their hands before the meal. One little boy smiled shyly and lingered, wanting me to continue running the warm water over his hands. I tried to suppress my surprise when I saw that he had lost a few fingers. I wasn't successful. His face filled with shame, he whipped his hands away, shoved them in his pockets and ran. My heart cried out in anguish. Wasn't it tragic enough that this boy lived in the midst of refuse, fear, hunger, violence, and abuse surrounded by a community that called him a "Scavenger"? His shame at being maimed by his environment prevented him from accepting compassion offered in Christ's name.
The effects of the Fall so often create mistrust that destroys the chance for relationships within families and communities to help restore God's image and order. Those of us who work with children are likely very aware that the Fall was systemic (affected all levels of society) and cyclical in nature (problems on one level of society cause problems in other levels, which worsen problems in the first level). One doesn't have to be a family systems psychologist to see this. We see the effects of sin on families and the difficulty they experience in parenting and in carrying out the ten parental "best practices" that Marcia Bunge describes in her section.[1] In his letter to the Romans, Paul states "Against its will, everything on earth was subjected to God's curse" (Rom. 8:20). Collectively, we face the

---

[1] See the article by Marcia Bunge in this volume.

challenges to parents and families: pain, suffering, broken relationships, civil conflict, chronic poverty, and disease, because all of God's creation has been impacted by Adam's sin. It is important to understand the multiple ways the Fall has impacted children's lives and environment in order to develop comprehensive interventions that will help restore God's order and plan for their optimal development.

Impact of Original Sin on Relationships

We were created in God's image to be in unbroken, harmonious relationship and yet retain our unique selves, as exemplified in the Trinity. The first sin of humankind began with a breach in Adam and Eve's relationship with God. Adam and Eve mistrusted God's guidance for them and listened to the serpent instead.[2] This mistrust in their hearts created the path for the first sin, and continues to be a major consequence of original sin that cyclically creates consequences and environments that breed further mistrust and separation from God. This downward spiral of mistrust and sin in Adam and Eve's own family is reflected in the first recorded act of family violence in the Bible when Cain killed Abel (Gen. 4:8). The consequences of the Fall undermine our intimate relationships and ultimately damage our ability to be in family and community. Since children are born entirely dependent on their parents and their communities, they are the most vulnerable to the consequences of sin's destruction of relationships.

> Since children are born entirely dependent on their parents and their communities, they are the most vulnerable to the consequences of sin's destruction of relationships.

From a theological point of view, the goal of child development is for the child to become a unique being who is in relationship with both God and other human beings.[3] Parental love is nurturing, caring, stable, and attentive to children's needs and can come from parents, teachers, mentors, the church community, and neighborhoods. Marcia Bunge's work illustrates Christ's value for children and the kinds of nurturing that children need to grow developmentally and in their faith. This kind of love models Christ's love for children and builds the foundation for children to develop a relationship with God. When children are born into a home with two loving parents and a nurturing community who know God, they are more likely to trust God, themselves, and others. The ten parental tasks that Marcia Bunge outlines are more likely to happen within the family and the community. With this foundation, children have help in the restoration of God's image in them and they are ahead in the journey of spiritual, psychological, and emotional development.[4] This chapter will present the consequences of the Fall in the lives of marginalized children and families to better understand their needs. It will then investigate the ways that God longs to meet

> *Shalom*: fullness of life; peace

---

[2] Stanley J. Grenz, *Theology for the Community of God*, 190.
[3] Jack O. Balswick, Pamela E. King, and Kevin S. Reimer, *The Reciprocating Self: Human Development in Theological Perspective*, 40. See also the article by Doug McConnell in this volume.
[4] Marcia J. Bunge, *The Child in Christian Thought*, 21.

these needs in order to restore the *shalom* and blessing that Meredith Long describes in his response. Finally, the chapter will provide illustrations of a Christian program in the Guatemala dump that works toward restoring this *shalom*.

Impact of Sin on Children's Relationships and Development

The impact of the Fall presents risks in children's families and environments that systemically undermine the network of relationships on which they depend. Their relationships are impacted at all levels: parent, family, and community. In certain environments (such as the dump community and many global urban environments), children face poverty, malnutrition, unsuitable housing, inferior medical care, inadequate schools, family disruption, family and community violence, child labor, and sexual exploitation.[5] The AIDS pandemic has left 12 million children in sub-Saharan Africa without one or both parents, and globally, the fabric of communities in areas such as these has been completely devastated by the disease.[6]

At the parental and familial levels, parents in chronically stressed environments are often overwhelmed, distressed, and fearful, which can make it difficult for them to establish a secure relationship and bond with young children. Additionally, poor mothers, who are often single and are isolated by lack of support or fear of community violence, are more likely to be abusive than non-poor mothers.[7] Cycles of abuse and violence can start in families where children learn that the only way to get what they want in relationships is through coercion and intimidation. Fathers who have learned this kind of cycle can also perpetrate domestic violence within the family. Witnessing domestic violence is another form of abuse for children and has similar adverse effects on children's development.[8] Furthermore, the aid organization mentioned in the visit above, asked for consultation because they told us that rates of sexual abuse are extremely high in the dump community.

In addition to abuse in the home, children from communities where there are high levels of poverty and broken families are often at higher risk for exposure to community violence.[9] In a survey we conducted with workers at the ministry organization in the Guatemala City Dump, we asked workers to report the kinds of community violence to which the children with whom they work are exposed. They reported that over 50 percent of the children they work with are exposed to the following top five types of trauma: 1) being sexually assaulted or raped; 2) having known someone who was killed by another person; 3) having been so sick they could have died; 4) being slapped or hit by someone who is not a family member; 5) being beaten up or mugged.[10] Exposure to community

---

[5] James Garbarino et al., *Children in Danger: Coping with the Consequences of Community Violence*, 52; and Karl Dorning, *Crying Out: Children and Communities Speak On Abuse and Neglect*, 2.
[6] UNAIDS, *2004 Report on the Global AIDS Epidemic*, 5.
[7] Richard J. Gelles and Claire Pedrick Cornell, *Intimate Violence in Families*, 107.
[8] William Arroyo and Spencer Eth, "Assessment Following Violence-Witnessing Trauma," 29.
[9] For a further discussion on the community consequences of sin and suggestions for ministry, see the third affirmation in this volume.
[10] Katharine Meese Putman, "Report to the Christian Ministry in the Dump Community," 16.

violence can also have detrimental effects on children's ability to develop trusting relationships with parents and other positive adults in the community.

Parents who grew up in communities where there were high levels of violence and trauma and where there are few economic opportunities often do not have a means of processing that trauma. They can become depressed and isolated and turn to alcohol and substance abuse for relief from their symptoms. Drugs and alcohol are also readily available for children, who often use these as a means for escape and numbing their feelings, because they frequently do not have other sources of hope. Substance abuse within families often further breaks down relationships, undermines trusts, and makes physical and sexual abuse of children more likely.[11]

The undermining of parental love can impact children in many ways. The absence of a secure, warm, and stable parent-infant attachment during a child's early life, whether because a parent is overly stressed or absent, makes it difficult for children to form intimate, lasting relationships later in life,[12] including a relationship with God. In addition to impairment in relationships to primary caregivers, children living in chronic stress, violence, and abuse can have difficulty concentrating and sleeping. Additionally, their social relations with peers are often impacted in that they form aggressive or sexualized play, begin to act in an uncaring way from experiencing pain and loss, and can have severe restriction in their play for fear of re-experiencing a traumatic event.[13] Furthermore, these children are more at risk for psychological disorders, such as depression and post-traumatic stress disorder, and can have impaired intellectual and moral development. As discussed above, they can also turn to substance abuse for relief and escape from the situation, which also adversely impacts their psychological, physical, and spiritual development.

> The absence of a secure, warm, and stable parent-infant attachment during a child's early life makes it difficult for children to form intimate, lasting relationships later in life, including a relationship with God.

The entire relationship network for children is impacted by consequences of the Fall at all levels. Community networks that might serve to fill in the gaps are more stressed than in communities with more resources. Teachers in high-risk communities are often working in conditions of high demand and few resources, making it difficult for them to consistently be available for children emotionally. Communities ravaged by AIDS, civil conflict, and violence also offer few resources in terms of mentoring or positive networks for children. The cyclical and systemic nature of the Fall is reflected in that children's developmental challenges combined with the lack of relational networks makes it much more difficult for children to form stable, positive relationships or to be in community, where God's image is expressed most profoundly.[14]

---

[11] Jeanette L. Johnson and Michelle Leff, "Children of Substance Abusers: Overview of Research Findings," *Pediatrics* 103 (1999): 1085-1099.
[12] Urie Bronfenbrenner, *The Ecology of Human Development: Experiments by Nature and Design,* 135-136.
[13] Garbarino, Dubrow, and Pardo, 56.
[14] Grenz, 177.

God's Care through Parental Love

Thankfully, God specializes in restoring that which is broken. "In his kindness God called you to his eternal glory by means of Jesus Christ. After you have suffered a little while, he will restore, support, and strengthen you, and he will place you on a firm foundation." (I Pet. 5:10). God longs to restore the *shalom* that Meredith Long describes[15] and to pass "the blessing" through families to children instead of the legacy of the Fall. The work of the ministry at the dump with whom I consult in Guatemala City will be used to illustrate practical ways that the community can either directly provide or support parents in providing many ways of loving children that mirror the "ten best practices" for demonstrating God's parental love that Marcia Bunge suggests.

1) Reading and Discussing the Bible and Interpretations of It with Children

This ministry at the Guatemala City Dump provides daily Bible studies for children in the school. As the children become older, the ministry puts them in charge of educating smaller children to help them understand the significance of reading and teaching Scripture to younger children in the community. Since many of the parents cannot read, the ministry also offers a "parent school" where they teach parents to read and also read Scripture to them.

2) Worshipping With a Community and Carrying Out Family Rituals of Worship and Prayer

Children regularly worship together and pray at the school. In the parent school and at regular parent meetings, the ministry staff worship and pray with parents from the community as well. They encourage families to participate in prayer together at home and to join one of the Christian churches in the dump community.

3) Introducing Children to Good Examples, Mentors, and Stories of Service and Compassion

This Christian ministry incorporates volunteers from the dump community who have either gone through the school or become Christians to serve as community support volunteers. Several of their teachers and staff are also from the dump community. In this way, children can see people from their own community who have a relationship with God and have chosen to follow God's path. They become empowered to show God's love to other members of their community and in this way to see that they have strength and value.

In environments where there is abuse and community violence, it is important to help children find ways to talk about their traumatic experiences in a safe place. Having a consistent, caring individual in their lives who listens, validates them, and reinforces that

---

[15] See the article by Meredith Long in this volume.

abuse is wrong goes a long way toward improving mental health and reinforcing life-giving ways of relating to others, themselves, and God.

A vital aspect of demonstrating parental love is supporting community members who are providing parental love for children. Teachers, who are so often the most consistent adults for children, need support and encouragement as well. Many of our ongoing workshops are designed to support the teachers at the ministry's school. These teachers often need care themselves to be able to express God's love to children on a consistent basis and in the face of the behavior difficulties that so often accompany at-risk children.

Another way to provide an example is to help children experience an environment that is "safe." The school creates this kind of "safe" culture in that no child is allowed to bully or intimidate another child. This kind of environment plants the seed that there is a way to live without violence and abuse and also creates the value that everyone has a voice from God that needs to be protected and cultivated.

4) Serving Together and (what is connected to service) Teaching Financial Responsibility

The children are often given service opportunities to younger children in the school. They can also participate in outreach projects to the community. When Hurricane Katrina hit the Gulf Coast of the United States, the entire school and children of all ages spent an extended period of time on their knees in prayer for this area of the United States.

Additionally, this ministry program has a micro-enterprise program where they teach families about finances and business and give them small business loans. This can help families to become more economically viable and can demonstrate opportunities and possibilities to children for a life outside the dump.

5) Singing Together and Exposing Children to the Spiritual Gifts of Music and the Arts

Jesus highly values children and says we are to approach God as they do. For both children and adults, play and rest are necessary for our emotional health. Through these, we open ourselves to experience joy and transcendence that can bring us closer to God.[16] In communities like the dump with their continual work needs for survival, there is often no time for children to play. In our workshop for parents, we gave parents the opportunity to spend time playing themselves, so they can learn how valuable it is and how good it feels. They loved to play games! We then encouraged them to give their children at least 10 minutes each day free from work to play.

This ministry organization also has a stage. They give children of all ages the opportunity to create singing and worship-related "shows" that they put on for the community and for visitors. The children create artwork for the shows, which they display in their classroom and the ministry organization and give to visitors.

---

[16] Robert K. Johnston, *The Christian at Play*, 81.

6) Appreciating the Natural World and Cultivating a Reverence for Creation

Many of the children and their parents have never been outside the dump community and don't know much about God's natural world. The ministry at the dump takes children to a camp in the mountains every year so they can see and appreciate the goodness of God's creation.

7) Educating Children and Helping Them Discern their Vocations

The ministry at the dump provides basic education and Bible study for children. It also trains them in skills (such as computer skills) to help them to be able to obtain jobs after school. Again, many of their families have been in the dump community for generations, and they are not aware of possibilities for life outside the dump community. They have had children go to university within Guatemala and with scholarships in the United States. Part of helping them learn their vocation from God is helping them to be open to the possibility that there are other vocations that are possible for them outside the dump.

The ministry also offers a school for parents to help them learn the value of education. Many of them never went to school themselves or have had negative experiences with institutions that marginalize them. This school validates parents' desire to learn and reinforces the importance of education within their families.

8) Fostering Life-Giving Attitudes toward the Body, Sexuality, and Marriage

The children in the dump grow up in a community that marginalizes them, calls them "Scavengers" and gives them the message that they are not valuable. The Christian ministry staff at the Guatemala City dump provides parental love directly to children by always calling them "treasures" to let them know they are made in God's image and are highly valuable. They also provide models of ways to relate (such as caring, healthy marriages) and encouragement to abstain from sexual activity until marriage.

Children internalize the message that they are not valuable when there is abuse within the family or community. Because sexual abuse is a large problem, the ministry tries to find creative ways of protecting children in a context where laws against abuse are not enforced. One creative way they have protected children is by building bunk beds for people in the community so that a predatory older sibling will have less access to younger children than when all siblings share one bed.

9) Listening To and Learning from Children

In the community at the Guatemala City dump, the primary emphasis is on survival. School is considered a luxury, and parents have to give up the children's potential income in order to let them attend. There are situations where children come home from school and then have to work until midnight washing bits that the family has collected from the dump to prepare them to exchange for money. The idea of taking time to listen to children or learn from them is often a foreign concept. Parents themselves may not have had the opportunity to feel valued, be listened to, or feel they have something that others can learn from them. I led a workshop for parents from the dump community in which we spent half of the allowed time listening to their concerns, giving them validation for their sacrifice in allowing children to come to school, and asking us to teach them about their community. We were modeling the skills of listening, validation, and praise, and the parents responded very positively.

Additionally, we and the ministry staff consistently emphasize the value of expressing affection for children, calling them positive names and not negative, and hugging them. Parents in chronically stressed environments often have difficulty expressing emotion and need to be encouraged to demonstrate their love for their children and to be open to learning from them.

10) Taking up a Christ-Centered Approach to Discipline, Authority, and Obedience; and Recognizing that, in the Tradition, Parental Authority is Always Limited

A Christ-centered approach to discipline means providing consequences in a way that reflects Christ's love and value for children. I have consulted with teachers in the school about how to discipline children while understanding the contexts that create challenging behavior in children. The teachers at the school do everything they can to not yell and certainly do not hit children. They model for them how to discipline in a loving way.

Also, the ministry offers workshops for parents on how to discipline children in a positive way. We put on a workshop that had several role plays in which we portrayed different ways of responding to children. We demonstrated that showing children affection and care while disciplining them is actually more effective in the long run at managing difficult behavior. We also emphasized God's plan for peace and harmony in families and how negative treatment of children does not foster long-term peace.

This Christian ministry at the dump has been very creative in finding ways to implement the "best practices" for showing God's love for children. For children without parents, like AIDS orphans, we need to be more creative about how the community can support foster parents and/or support orphan-headed households so that children have parental love from many sources.

These kinds of systemic interventions to express and support parental love can stop the cycle of broken relationships that the Fall created. It can help to reaffirm God's image in children and their communities.

PRACTITIONER'S RESPONSE

NURTURING AND RESTORING *SHALOM*: PARENTS AND THEIR CHILDREN, A RESPONSE TO MARCIA BUNGE AND KATHY PUTMAN

By W. Meredith Long
World Relief

> *The Lord said to Moses, "Tell Aaron and his sons, 'This is how you are to bless the Israelites. Say to them:*
> *" 'The Lord bless you and keep you;*
> *the Lord make his face shine upon you and be gracious to you;*
> *the Lord turn his face toward you and give you peace.' "*
> *"So they will put my name on the Israelites, and I will bless them."*
> —(Num. 6:22-27 NIV)

The Israelites who received this blessing recognized that it was rooted in their relationship to God. God turned graciously toward them and gave them his name and favor. Peace with their Lord brought fullness of life, of peace, of *shalom* in every area of living. *Shalom* is rooted in a right relationship to God. We also experience *shalom* only in right relationship with one another.

Our individual well-being is intimately tied with the well-being of our communities and families. We experience *shalom* only in a right relationship to the environment. When through poverty and injustice we are no longer able to provide basic needs or exercise any control over our situation, we cannot experience *shalom*.[99] Finally, we experience *shalom* only in a right relationship with ourselves. We must be able to give and receive love.

Dimensions of *Shalom*
1) Relationship to God
2) Relationship to Ourselves
3) Relationships to Others
4) Relationship to the Environment

Marcia Bunge, in her paper, presents a biblical model of parents as the nurturers of *shalom* within their families. She presents four dimensions of a biblical understanding of parenting (see table 2.1) that relate to the four relational dimensions of *shalom*. Her ten central parental tasks demonstrate how parents nurture *shalom*. It is only within this context of peace that children are fully able to experience fullness of life at every stage of their development.

---

[99] W. Meredith Long, *Health, Healing and God's Kingdom*, 14-15.

When sin entered the world, *shalom* was destroyed. The community of adults and children who built their lives around the city's refuse in the dump of Guatemala City graphically reflected the destruction of *shalom*. Every relationship—with God, others, themselves, and their environment was marred. Healing is the restoration of *shalom*. The Hebrew word for healing most often used in the Old Testament connotes restoration of something that is broken or sick to its original state of wholeness. The Greek word most often used in the New Testament for healing is sometimes translated "healing" and other times "salvation."

> It is only within the context of peace that children are fully able to experience fullness of life at every stage of their development.

In Luke 8:43-48, Dr. Luke makes this distinction very clear in his account of the woman who had suffered bleeding for twelve years. Though the woman had been to many doctors, none had been able to heal her. The words used here express the idea that she had not received any effective therapy (v. 43). When she pushed her way through the crowd and touched Jesus, she was immediately healed. Here, Luke uses a second word meaning to be cured of a disease. When Jesus turned and said to her, "Daughter, your faith has healed you. Go in peace" (v.48), he used a third word that in other places is translated "to save" or "to make whole again." When Jesus saved the woman, he restored her to relationship with the broader community and to God. According to the Jewish law, she was unclean because of her bleeding. She was not permitted to touch another without also making them unclean. She was also barred from worship in the temple. Jesus restored her to fullness.

In Kathy Putman's account, she presents how sin destroys the peace and well-being of children in the four dimensions of *shalom* and the importance of parents and of the extended family of God in restoring relationships and bringing fullness once more (see table 2.1).

Framing the two papers in the context of *shalom* and healing does more than provide an integrative biblical framework. It can also inform interventions that are directed toward parents and children.

In the following table, I intentionally grouped the interventions together rather than assigning them to a single cell. Reading and discussing the Bible, for instance, is normally framed within the context of nurturing or restoring a relationship to God. But it also shapes children's attitudes toward their parents and themselves. The nature of the parents' interaction with the Bible and with their children also shapes the child's relationship with others and themselves. Parents who use the Bible chiefly to identify and punish evil in their children and others often rear children who are insecure and judgmental of others.

Table 2.1

Parents and the Family of God Nurture and Restore *Shalom*

Relation-ship to:	Nurturing (Bunge)		Restoring (Putman)	
	Four dimensions of biblical parenting	Parental tasks	Effects of sin upon children	Restoring children to fullness of life
God	Nurturing and recognizing them as models of faith.	Read and discuss Bible. Worship in community and family. Introduce children to good examples. Participate in service. Sing and develop love for music and the arts. Appreciate nature and revere creation. Educate and help discern vocation. Foster life-giving attitudes to the body, sexuality and marriage. Listen to and learn from children. Rightly discipline children within a Christ-centered perspective.	Inability to conceive of a loving God or to build intimacy to him.	Directly provide parental love to children within the family of God. Develop safe environments of love, growth and play. Provide for basic needs. Equip parents to better love their children. To practice and to enable parents to practice the four dimensions of parenting and the ten parental tasks.
Our-selves	Responding to them as gifts of God made in his image and sources of joy.		Parental inability to bond, inability of child to give or receive love or intimacy, warped views of sex and sexuality.	
Others	Use gifts and talents to love and serve others.		Use of coercion and intimidation to shape relationships.	
Environ-ment	Provide for basic needs of food, shelter, and affection.		Poverty, malnutrition, unsuitable housing, lack of access to health and medical care.	

Parental action toward children, then, touches every area of relationship. We must therefore examine our programs from multiple perspectives. Programs to empower children and youth as leaders may lead to exploitation unless they are also shaped by concern for others. Likewise, programs to shape and change patterns of sexual behavior among youth often fail unless the young men and women also receive instruction in social and negotiation skills.

Sin also touches every key relationship. Kathy Putman traces how children who have never experienced a secure, warm, and loving parental relationship act out that loss within themselves, with others, and with God. If we address the behavioral problems of children without building a secure, consistent, and loving relationship toward them, we will most often fail.

Above all else, our failures drive us back to God as we realize that he is the only true healer. Little children who have suffered from the sin of others in many dimensions of life retain their God-given intuition to recognize and respond to true goodness and love. As those who nurture the children God has given us to parent or who minister healing to children whose lives have been marred by adults who betray that trust, we recognize that such powerful goodness and love must come from God, who indwells us.

CASE STUDY

STREET-LIVING AND WORKING CHILDREN

BY GREG W. BURCH
NIÑOS DE LA LUZ

A View from Latin America

While orienting two newly arrived boys at a home outside of Caracas, Venezuela, I caught glimpses of their story between the breakdancing lessons they gave me. Both boys came from very poor households with many siblings and eventually came to live on the street through a common progression of events; from begging, to selling flowers and candy, to working longer and longer nights as the nightclubs let out. As time went on, they dropped out of school. They were forced to spend some nights on the street and were soon introduced to drugs and the inhaling of shoe glue that many street-living children practice.

The two boys had grown tired of sleeping and working on the streets of Caracas, so they "turned themselves in." Even the city social worker recognized that the government detention center was not going to be able to provide what they wanted and needed,[1] so the boys were brought to us.

> The Impact of Evil:
> • Cosmological Level
> • Structural Level
> • Personal Level
>
> The Church's Response:
> • Prayerful Intercession
> • Incarnational Ministry
> • Vigilant Advocacy

While not definitive, this story is representative of some of the experiences of children living on the streets today in Latin America and other parts of the world. Both Daniel and José are victims of an all-out assault by the enemy to destroy the lives of young people.

To fully understand the complexities involved in the lives of these children, the issues of structural and personal sin must be taken into account. Basically, the impact of evil in our world can be described on three levels: cosmologically, structurally, and personally.[2] The damage done by sin and evil prove the Church's need for prayerful intercession, incarnational ministry, and vigilant advocacy in order to be effective in ministry with street children.

---

[1] Sadly, the opposite is often true. Government workers and others often believe that detention centers and prisons are the best places for children who live on the streets.
[2] Jude Tiersma Watson, "Faces of Evil in the City," 1.

The "Powers"

"For our struggle is not against flesh and blood, but against the rulers, against the authorities, against the powers of this dark world and against the spiritual forces of evil in the heavenly realms" Ephesians 6:12. [3]

Whether spiritual realities that we face every day, [4] evil personal spiritual beings manifested as territorial spirits, [5] manifestations of inner and outer aspects of power in society,[6] or primarily societal systems with "a Power that is at work behind the powers . . . [with] spiritual forces committed to evil that are infiltrating and using systems and structures"[7] most traditions believe that the powers are active today, and represent a going astray from God's original intent. We can be assured that both individuals and society are affected by these principalities and powers that the apostle Paul and others refer to. We can also be assured that our response as believers should be in harmony with the Bible's admonition to confront the powers that have created aspects of injustice in society.

> "We can see the cosmic struggle, the spiritual battle that rages around children. Children are critical for God to accomplish his plans, so the Enemy fiercely attacks them, seeking their destruction."
> —Tri Budiardjo

Cosmological Level

In 2005, twenty-five delegates representing more than a dozen organizations from around the world came together to work toward the formation of a Global Strategy with Street Children.[8] *180 Degrees—United Global Action with Street Children* coalition is committed to serving street-living and working children and to promote helpful resources and accountability among NGOs and churches focused on street children worldwide.

Scripture reminds us that *"the devil prowls around like a roaring lion looking for someone to devour"* (1 Peter 5:8). The coalition of *180 Degrees* recognizes this, and is seeking to help believers engage with street-living and working children on a level that encourages the protection of all children. Part of this protection includes recognizing that on a cosmological level, we have an enemy that seeks to destroy the lives of God's precious children. *"The weapons we fight with are not the weapons of the world. On the contrary,*

---

[3] All Scripture quotations are taken from the New International Version.
[4] Hendrik Berkhof, *Christ and the Powers*, 18.
[5] This is the case in the third wave or spiritual warfare tradition. See C. Peter Wagner, "Territorial Spirits and World Missions," *Evangelical Missions Quarterly* 25, no. 3 (1989): 278.
[6] See, for example, Walter Wink, *Naming the Powers: The Language of Power in the New Testament*, 5.
[7] Robert C. Linthicum, *Empowering the Poor*, 19.
[8] A familiar term to describe both street-living and working children is "street children." Other terms are also possible. In the book *Community Children* I discuss why I feel that "street children" is *not* the most appropriate term. Due to the use of this term in academic literature and its common recognition, however, I will on occasion use it as well.

they have divine power to demolish strongholds" (2 Cor. 10:4) and free those that have been taken captive.

The enemy of *all* children is the devil. In many ways, the cosmological understanding is best represented by the spiritual warfare concept that has been promoted in recent years by such people as Peter Wagner, John Dawson and Ed Silvoso, but the idea of a cosmic war is much older than them.

Since Adam and Eve, the earth and human beings have been caught up in a cosmic fight that takes no prisoners. If we fail to recognize this cosmic battle, the consequences will result in a less than proper understanding of the contributing issues that have led to the disempowerment and marginalization of the children we seek to reach.

Structural Level

Since my first exposure to ministry among street-living children in 1992, I have heard over and over again, "I was beaten by the police last night." Sadly, this is not just a figment of the child's imagination. Why is it that those who are called to serve and protect can do so much harm?

Social structures (i.e. religious, political, and economic systems) which God has meant for good have at some point become corrupted.[9] Yet we know that God desires to restore all things unto himself, including worldly structures. Like Paulo Freire,[10] John Friedmann calls upon development workers to encourage the poor to understand the issues in their lives that contribute to their poverty. Friedmann guides us to see "poverty as a form of social and political disempowerment and access to the bases of social power."[11]

Generally speaking, children at risk do not have access to bases of social power. Social power includes and excludes. Poor children such as street children are excluded from participating in society and deemed ignorant and unworthy of such great responsibility. This leads to protectionism and paternalism.[12]

The systems that God has given us for organization and for maintaining some justice in our world have at some point seemingly been corrupted. They impact the lives of street-living and working children on a global scale.

Religious bodies and systems have not been spared the hideous effects of the fallen powers. Recently a missionary told me their mission was considering starting up an

---

[9] Linthicum, 14.

[10] Paulo Freire, *Pedagogy of the Oppressed*, 35. Freire is best known for his revolutionary pedagogy which calls for a *concientização* (conscientization or consciousness-raising) paradigm that encourages the poor and oppressed to engage in the political process.

[11] John Friedmann, *Empowerment: The Politics of Alternative Development*, 8.
Alternative Development is a term that arose in response to the outcomes of the Third System Project (A result of the 1976 "International Foundation for Development Alternatives" conference). The Third System Project not only recognized the place of the state and the market, but the role of the people themselves, that is, their social power and self-determinism.

[12] As a dad with two young children I certainly understand the need to protect children in a healthy way. If I protect them in a way that never allows for their personal agency, their sense of self-determination, and choice, however, I crush their God-given sense of dignity as human beings. Protectionism steals away personal agency.

orphanage for children because it would be looked upon favorably by the government where they were based. I was taken aback by the thought that this well-known mission organization would use orphaned boys and girls as political pawns!

Religious structures certainly play an important role in our societies as structural backbones to our communities that can either work for or against God's purposes.[13] *180 Degrees—United Global Action with Street Children* coalition is seeking to develop an accreditation system that endorses best practices among organizations and churches that minister to street and working children.

Personal Level

Children living on the street are not just sinned against, but also sinners. Coming out of a theater with some colleagues in Caracas, Venezuela, we were taken aback by the loud exploding glass bottle at our feet and screams near the exit of the theater. Immediately, I recognized two of the boys. They stood on opposite sides of the street, throwing glass bottles at each other.

As a result of the Fall and our rebellious nature, we have turned our backs on God and have sought to "do it our way." Moltmann comments on this dilemma saying that "we have to speak about human beings as God's image and as sinners at the same time."[14] Sin should be understood as corrupting our relationship with God and our fellow human beings.[15] Children who one minute are protecting one another from those outside their peer groups (a view of the "goodness") turn on each other with a violent assault in the next minute (a view of the "sinner").

Because of our sinful state, relationships are broken and in need of restoration.[16] We also know that restoration will only come as a result of God's healing power in the lives of individuals and society. God has called us to bring about reconciliation, with his help, between his creation, in both the vertical (human to God) and horizontal (human to human and other created being) senses. To encourage the street-living and working child toward the Father of the fatherless is our supreme task and one that will only take place as we kneel down low in prayer and conversation with the homeless and working child God has called us to reach.

In Response

The Church of Jesus Christ is called to respond to sin on the cosmic, structural, and personal levels. Certainly, we must begin with prayer. God is calling his people to intercede for destitute children in both prayer and in changing societies' attitudes toward children.

---

[13] See Linthicum, 11.
[14] Jürgen Moltmann, *God in Creation*, 229.
[15] See the articles by Katharine Meese Putman and Meredith Long in this volume.
[16] See Romans 8:22

Our first desire is to gain God's perspective and to receive God's heart for neglected young people in our cities. It is through intercessory prayer that we enter into the actual context.

Secondly, we can respond through incarnational ministry. In John 1:14a we are told, "The Word became flesh and made his dwelling among us." God did not cease to be God, but he chose to communicate his love to us by becoming one of us. So too can we bring a relevant and hope-filled contextualized Gospel to the children we are called to reach. We, too, must learn from the people to whom we are called to minister. When we become learners and servants, we will then be in a better position to communicate the love of God through a contextual message to these children, and to deal with the sin that entangles these young lives.

A third response to sin is found through vigilant advocacy. This means to be willing to stand up for children by confronting the powers, and at times, the very people that seek to destroy these young lives. God himself takes offense when those who are vulnerable are mistreated.[17] If the Church does not stand up and defend homeless children and youth, then who will? Advocacy is an important means to provide protection for the homeless child and a way that points towards reconciliation.[18]

It is my prayer that the millions of street-living and working children who are caught up in this cosmic-earthly battle around the world will one day claim the Lord Jesus Christ as their Redeemer and Savior. Despite the cosmological, structural, and personal sin that opposes such a reconciliation, we know that we serve a God that actively seeks the restoration of his creation and rejoices over children turning to him.

---

[17] See Exodus 22:21-23

[18] For a further discussion on advocacy, see the article by Joanna Watson in this volume.

PRACTICAL IMPLICATIONS

CHILDREN SEEKING FAMILY IN WAR AND SEXUAL EXPLOITATION[1]

By Michael McGill
Fuller Theological Seminary

It is clear that children should be valued, nurtured and protected within a family structure by loving parents.[2] It is also clear that the concept and practice of family and family roles vary greatly throughout the world without there being one right image of family. Another question we must ask is, "How does a child satisfy the need for family when their family is missing or abusive?"

Much of what children need is universal. How these needs are met is not. They are satisfied in different cultures, contexts and families through different means. Psychological and sociological research point to the reality that if these very right longings are not met, the loss will lead to patterns that are destructive to self and others, until the loss can be properly grieved.

> **ABBREVIATIONS**
> LRA: Lord's Resistance Army
> LTTE: Liberation Tigers of Tamil Eelam
> MODEL: Movement for Democracy in Liberia

Children in extreme contexts lacking healthy parental support often get very creative and desperate in finding ways to satisfy longings unmet by "traditional" or biological parents. We should be aware of the complexity of ambivalent emotions tied to experiencing good things in bad places. Understanding children's desires and how they are partially met in contexts of exploitation, is an important part of developing programs that better meet children's needs within contexts such as Internally Displaced Persons camps, or after they are removed from such contexts as an army or brothel. If children's needs, and in particular familial needs, are not met outside of the patterns or contexts from which they are removed, they will be more likely to return to the same exploitive patterns or contexts.

The Question of Choice

Those seeking to exploit children for war, sex, or other purposes will often look for children who are more vulnerable, particularly children whose families have not met their need for protection, education, value and community. Researcher Jessica Schafer highlights that in the civil war in Mozambique, "as part of their mobilization strategy, the military leadership of both government and RENAMO forces took advantage of the

---

[1] All Scripture quotations are taken from the New International Version unless otherwise noted.
[2] See the article by Marcia Bunge in this volume.

recruits' psychological need for a substitute family."[3] It is also well documented that people recruiting children for sexual exploitation will often use the child's unmet familial longings in order to manipulate the child into prostituting.[4]

Children are often violently forced to join and remain with brothels or armies who exploit and abuse them. However, this is not always the case. There are many cases where children exercise some level of choice in being prostituted or joining a military force, or choosing to remain after abduction despite ample opportunity for escape.[5] They do so because within their perception of the limited options available, it satisfies some of their desires.

> "But if anyone causes one of these little ones who believe in me to sin . . .'
> —Matthew 18:6

Between 60 and 90 percent of women in prostitution were sexually abused as children by male relatives or acquaintances.[6] This high percentage does not even include those children who were sexually abused only by people they did not know. The following is a simplification of commonly accepted reasoning for such a significant correlation.

Virtually anyone who is regularly abused begins looking desperately for a way to have control in life. If a woman (or man) cannot gain control in the area of her life where she is being abused, she will look for other areas to gain control. A girl who is regularly abused will typically begin to discover a way to have choice or power in the matter. By selling her body she can have some level of control over when she is abused, how she is abused, and she may even receive some resource benefit from the abuse. Surely, she should not have to make this sort of choice, but when she is forced to do so by people who use their power to exploit her vulnerability, it is understandable that she would prefer the limited benefits of prostitution rather than continual abuse with no choice or benefit.

Emily's description of her experience concisely reflects the dynamic outlined above and is fairly stereotypical:

> *Prostitution was my boyfriend's idea. He thought it would be an easy way for 'us' to make money. I started when I was twenty-one or twenty-two. Prostitution was a continuation of the sexual abuse I endured as a child.*[7]

Child soldiers may have to make a similar sort of "choice", and their logic sometimes looks like this:

---

[3] Boyden and de Berry, 88.

[4] Caution with terminology must always be used when speaking of sexually exploited children, especially with the term "prostitution." "Prostitution" often implies an empowered choice, and this is very rarely the case with sexually exploited children. In a given context, it may be appropriate to note that some level of "choice" is being exercised, but it is never a true or full choice. An alternative phrase is "children engaged in prostitution," referring to an act rather than a state of being.

[5] Chen Reis, *Children in Combat,* edited by Lois Whitman and Michael McClintock, vol.8, no.1 (G) (New York: Human Right's Watch, 1996), 8.

[6] Division for Gender Equality, *Prostitution and Trafficking in Human Beings: Fact Sheet*, 2.

[7] Nonna M. Hughes and Claire Roche, eds., *Making the Harm Visible: Global Sexual Exploitation of Women and Girls, Speaking Out and Providing Services*, 296.

I could lay down my gun and leave the army, and again be powerless and vulnerable—able to be exploited at the whim of abusers. Or, I can keep my gun and have some power over how and when I am exploited.

Power is not good or bad. What holds moral value is how one chooses to use, or desires to use that power.

Several consistent desires of children have become evident after a review of interviews of children involved in armed conflict and sexual exploitation in Uganda[8] and around the world.[9] Some of children's reasons for participation in armed violence and prostitution reveal God-given desires that a loving family is meant to satisfy. It is important to understand these God-given desires in order to develop programs that address them through more healthy and constructive means.

> Exploiters will often look for lonely, isolated children and use their unmet familial longings as a tool for manipulation.

Protection, education, a sense of value, and community are four needs the Bible calls families to help lovingly satisfy for their children. The following sections look at how children feel that these familial desires are partially met through military involvement.

Protection

One of the most common reasons that children "willingly" join or continue in military service is because they have the good desire to protect others or themselves when they are not sufficiently protected by their family or community. This good desire should be recognized as such, even when an exhibited means of satisfying the desire is a perversion of what God intended.

---

[8] See, for example, Patrick J. Bracken and Celia Petty, *Rethinking the Trauma of War*; Annette Weber, *Uganda, Abducted and Abused: Renewed Conflict in Northern Uganda (Human Rights Watch)*; Jo Becker, *Uganda, Stolen Children: Abduction and Recruitment in Northern Uganda*, vol.15, no. 7 (A) (Human Rights Watch, 2003); Alex Moorehead et al., *Uganda: Uprooted and Forgotten: Impunity and Human Rights Abuses in Northern Uganda*, vol. 17, no. 12 (A) (Human Rights Watch, 2005).

[9] See, for example, Tony Tate, *How to Fight, How to Kill: Child Soldiers in Liberia,* edited by Lois Whitman, 16, no.2 (A) (New York: Human Rights Watch, 2003); Boyden and de Berry; Jo Becker and Tejshree Thapa, *Sri Lanka: Living in Fear, Child Soldiers and the Tamil Tigers in Sri Lanka*, vol. 16, no. 13 (C) (Human Rights Watch, 2004); Sara Rakita, *Forgotten Children of War: Sierra Leonean Refugee Children in Guinea*, vol. 11, no. 5 (5) (Human Rights Watch, 1999); Duncan Green, *Hidden Lives: Voices of Children in Latin America and the Caribbean*; Karen Emmons, *Adult Wars, Child Soldiers: Voices of Children Involved in Armed Conflict in East Asia and Pacific Region*, trans. M. McGill - mac (Bangkok: UNICEF, 2002); Kevin Heppner and Jo Becker, *My Gun Was as Tall as Me: Child Soldiers in Burma*.

Protecting Others

> *Government militia members would beat my uncle and force him to carry cooking oil long distances. Myself, I was made to tote large bags of cassava to distant military positions. Finally, I decided . . . Better to join them, so they would not continue to disturb my people.*[10]

God did not intend for children to sacrifice themselves on behalf of their parents. Still, many children feel that this is their only choice. In the case of children engaged in prostitution, there are some children who realize what their parents are doing and comply with their parents' wishes, only to become slaves to the sex industry.[11]

This is certainly not God's intent; it is a perversion of the care and support that parents are to extend toward their children.[12]

> "But we are ready to arm ourselves and go ahead of the Israelites until we have brought them to their place. Meanwhile our women and children will live in fortified cities, for protection from the inhabitants of the land."
> —Numbers 32:17

Protection of Self

One girl who came from a physically abusive home was convinced that the LTTE was her only option for a better life.[13] Stephen was ten years old and fought with the LRA in north Uganda. "I was shown how to load, assemble, and clean the gun . . . I never used the gun in battle, but carried it for an adult soldier. It felt nice to have the gun. I felt safe."[14]

The desire to protect one's self is good and right. Children should be given opportunities to help protect self and others in ways that are developmentally appropriate and do not put them unreasonably at risk, as does military service. Most importantly, family should provide protection for children so that they are not forced to protect themselves against foes that are too great for them.[15]

Education

HRW's 2004 report on child soldiers in Liberia noted that, "The vast majority of the children interviewed for this report highlighted their desire for education in the future and

---

[10] Tate, 12.
[11] Phyllis Kilbourn and Marjorie McDermid, *Sexually Exploited Children: Working to Protect and Heal*, 19.
[12] See the article by Douglas McConnell in this volume.
[13] Becker and Thapa, 22.
[14] Becker, 13.
[15] The king's edict granted the Jews in every city the right to assemble and protect themselves; to destroy, kill and annihilate any armed force of any nationality or province that might attack them and their women and children; and to plunder the property of their enemies (Est. 8:11).

their wish to return to or to begin school. They stressed the need for education to make something of their lives and put their past behind them."[16]

The Bible demonstrates the need for education, along with God's desire that families fulfill this need. Educating children was the plan for moving the nation away from the path of their stubborn and rebellious forefathers, and onto a path of faithfulness.[17]

Fourteen-year-old Mia from Northern Thailand writes:

> *the occupation that most people know in Mae Sai is prostitution, because it is well known in Mae Sai . . . The girls in this profession come into it on their own free will because their own countries are not that developed . . . The girls have not studied thus this is their main profession to gain money.*[18]

It is tragic to hear the language of this child who has been deceived into believing that children freely choose to have their bodies exploited sexually by men (primarily) who use their greater power and resources to prey on the vulnerable. In the midst of this all, little Mia believes education would have changed everything for her and the other children.

Value

When children do not feel highly valued by their family, they are drawn toward places in which they feel valued. Our true and unshakable value is that which is given to us by God.

The Ugandan government actively recruits and uses former LRA abductees in combat. "Boys, some of whom had spent years with the LRA undergoing the hardships detailed above, were tempted with promises of respect, money, new uniforms, and a better life."[19]

God makes people in his image,[20] and they have a right desire to have their innate value respected rather than denied.[21]

---

[16] Tate, 40.
[17] "Only be careful, and watch yourselves closely so that you do not forget the things your eyes have seen or let them slip from your heart as long as you live. Teach them to your children and to their children after them. Remember the day you stood before the LORD your God at Horeb, when he said to me, Assemble the people before me to hear my words so that they may learn to revere me as long as they live in the land and may teach them to their children" (Deut. 4:9-10). "Teach them to your children, talking about them when you sit at home and when you walk along the road, when you lie down and when you get up" (Deut. 11:19). See also Psalm 78:5-7
[18] Siroj Sorajjakool, *Child Prostitution in Thailand: Listening to Rahab*, 18.
[19] Becker, 21.
[20] "God said, 'Let Us make man in Our image, according to Our likeness'" (Gen. 1:26). For a further discussion on this topic, see the article by Doug McConnell in this volume.
[21] See 1 Peter 2:17.

Community

God has made humanity to live and thrive in community.[22] To be truly ourselves, we must be connected with others. In Matthew 18:5 Christ encourages us to receive all children, not just our own. In this way, we provide a loving community for children who are not finding such communion from their own families.

Young teens are at a stage of development when group connection is extremely important. The loss of a family or community can be one of the deepest pains a person experiences. Sometimes, exploiters use a child's need for family and group connection in an open and direct strategy for manipulation and control.

In fact, for the young fighters studied by Schafer, violence was not even the most devastating aspect of war; many of them found separation from family far more painful. Appropriating Shona patriarchal imagery and casting the troops as children and the leaders as fathers, the RENAMO forces filled this void and ensured filial loyalty and discipline through a system of 're-socialisation' using concepts of substitute kinship.[23]

> "And whoever welcomes a little child like this in my name welcomes me."
> —Matthew 18:5

"Substitute kinship" and community can also be partially satisfied amidst child sexual exploitation. Ruby had been exploited by many men before moving into a Christian boarding school when she was fifteen years old. For a few weeks she was very happy and grateful to be in a clean, safe place where people would encourage and pray for her. Nevertheless, she soon became depressed. In tears she told a counselor "I'm lonely. I like it here, but I'm so lonely."[24] After only three months at the school, Ruby returned to a life of sexual exploitation. Ruby felt that somehow her right longing for intimacy in community was satisfied to a greater extent in her prior context of abuse. This is not uncommon. Exploiters will often look for lonely, isolated children and use their unmet familial longings as a tool for manipulation.

Conclusions

If children's needs are not satisfied to the degree they should be satisfied by family, a child or young person will look to have their desires satisfied through other, potentially destructive means. Thus, sometimes children's reasons for participation in armed violence and prostitution reveal God-given desires that a loving family has not satisfied. It is critical that Biblical children at risk programs meet children's need for protection, education, value, and community to a much greater degree than does prostitution or military involvement.

---

[22] See also chapter 3 in this volume.
[23] Boyden and de Berry, xxii.
[24] Kilbourn and McDermid, 255.

CHAPTER 2
DISCUSSION QUESTIONS

1) In a broken world what can we truly aspire to in terms of providing parental love to every child? It takes more than one (or even two) adults to raise a child, so how can this aspiration realistically be met for abandoned children, or for child–headed households?

2) How is parenting understood in my context? What impact does culture have on that understanding? How would I act if I really believed that parenting is a sacred trust given me by God?

CHAPTER 3
CARING IN COMMUNITY

God gives children as a gift to welcome and nurture.

It is a privilege to join with children in celebrating their uniqueness, valuing childhood as formative for all of life. Family, friends, church and the local community are responsible for creating an environment that promotes children's well-being.

God intends for children to thrive in stable and loving relationships.

"I cannot live authentically without welcoming the others... For I am created to reflect the personality of the Triune God."[1]
—Judith Gundry-Volf and Miroslav Volf

"At that time the disciples came to Jesus and asked, 'Who is the greatest in the Kingdom of heaven?' He called a child, whom he put among them, and said, 'Truly I tell you, unless you change and become like children, you will never enter the Kingdom of heaven. Whoever becomes humble like this child is the greatest in the Kingdom of heaven. Whoever welcomes one such child in my name welcomes me.'"
—Matthew 18:1-5 NRSV

---

[1] Judith Gundry-Volf and Miroslav Volf, *A Spacious Heart: Essays on Identity and Belonging*, 59.

BIBLICAL REFLECTION

THE ROLES AND RESPONSIBILITIES OF CHILDREN AND THEIR COMMUNITIES

BY JENNIFER ORONA
FULLER THEOLOGICAL SEMINARY

It Takes a Village

"It takes a village to raise a child." This well-known adage is often quoted at baby dedication services, opening ceremonies for children's programs, and other formal events. Sadly, its implications are not often understood, and even less often followed. Is this statement true? What about children whose life circumstances provide more challenge and danger than nurture and care? Furthermore, are the roles of children limited to being subjects and recipients of care, and nothing more? Should children have responsibilities in the life of the community as well? In biblical, historical, and contemporary theological perspectives, children and their communities have related to one another in a variety of different ways. In the present day, Christians must learn from these perspectives to understand their implications for ministry to children, especially children at risk.

A Theological Understanding of Community

A community is more than a neighborhood, more than a group of people who live near each other. It is a theological concept, and it relates to God's intentions for the world. In the New Testament, the concept of *oikos* went beyond the nuclear family to include all members of the household, consisting of servants, extended family members, and often, members of multiple generations. Acts 18:8, for example, makes use of this word in describing the situation when a synagogue official named Crispus "became a believer in the Lord, together with all his household (*oikos*)." The entire household learned about Christ together. It was a communal activity.[1]

1 Timothy 3 builds on this concept by relating it to the community of faith:

> *I am writing these instructions to you so that, if I am delayed, you may know how one ought to behave in the household (oikos) of God, which is the church of the living God, the pillar and bulwark of truth (1 Tim. 3:14-15).*

---

[1] The word 'household' in Acts 11:14; 16:15, 31; and Romans 16:5 also comes from the Greek word *oikos*.

While children may not have been considered the most important members of the household, they were nevertheless included in the concept of *oikos*. The first Christians "organized their world with the community in mind, a community that was not an end in itself but that tried to be open and welcoming. Salvation of the city was to come about through the conversion of the house."[2]

Humans remain incomplete as individuals, relying on support from others. According to Jürgen Moltmann, the *imago Dei* is a relational concept: "Only in human fellowship with other people is the human person truly an image of God (Gen. 1:28)."[3] On the other hand, sin causes "the destruction of community" because of its outward-rippling consequences.[4]

God lives in community in the Trinity, and his essence of love is fully realized in relationships between the members of the Trinity.[5] As a relational Being, God created humanity to be relational as well. God created the world to live in community with him and others.[6] With this in mind, let us examine what the Bible says about the relationships between children and their communities.

Biblical Perspectives

What does the Bible have to say about the idea that "God gives children as a gift to welcome and nurture"? The Word of God presents an interesting juxtaposition of ideas when it comes to children and their communities.

Gifts and Blessings

Children are a gift to the entire community. They are called "olive shoots" (Ps. 128:3), a "heritage from the Lord" (Ps. 127:3), and "arrows" in a quiver (Ps. 127:4-5). Children serve as living testimonies to God's faithfulness and blessing. Their lives demonstrate the hope of the future in the life of the community. Parents are to welcome each child as a gift, a blessing, and a responsibility.

---

[2] Francois Bovon, "Family and Community in the New Testament," *Sewanee Theological Review* 45, no. 2 (2002): 127-134.
[3] Jürgen Moltmann, *On Human Dignity: Political Theology and Ethics*, 25. See Stanley J. Grenz, *Theology for the Community of God*, 179. See also the article by Doug McConnell in this volume.
[4] Stanley J. Grenz, *Theology for the Community of God*, 181.
[5] For more on this concept, see Ray S. Anderson, *On Being Human: Essays in Theological Anthropology*, 73.
[6] Various opinions exist on the concept of the social Trinity. Colin Brown, for example, views the relationships between the members of the Trinity as more of a hierarchy, focusing more on the distinctions between the roles of each member than on the unity of the entire Godhead (Colin Brown, *That You May Believe: Miracles and Faith Then and Now*, 170-174). Other theologians speak of the differentiation between the members of the Godhead, but include the concepts of relationship and reciprocity (See Anderson, 76, 85, 114). Others describe a hierarchical structure within the Trinity, but emphasize unity within the diversity, distinct roles in the midst of a common purpose for the world. (See Robert Banks, *Paul's Idea of Community*, 186). Still others see each member of the Trinity as an equal participant in mutually reciprocal relationships with the others, creating a unity within the social Trinity (Grenz, 112-115).

In fact, the Bible contains examples of parents who were so grateful for God's gift of children that they gave the children to serve the entire community by giving them back to the Lord.[7] For those who remained faithful, God promised over and over again to bless them with many children.[8]

As noted previously, God's gift of the *imago Dei* grants inherent dignity to each human being, but the ravages of sin have marred this image and dignity. In God's redemptive plan, however, Jesus Christ serves as the ultimate image of God that makes possible abundant life both in heaven and on earth. This life is not limited to individual achievement and self-fulfillment. Indeed, Jürgen Moltmann claims that Christians living in *community* with God and people is the fulfillment of the human destiny.[9]

> The Christ-child serves as God's ultimate gift to communities—to all the communities of the world!

The Christ-child serves as God's ultimate gift to communities—to all the communities of the world! God gave his Son, Jesus, as a child to promote justice and righteousness throughout the world.[10] This is why "life in the Christian community is based on the reality of God's becoming human."[11] Just as Jesus blessed the world by entering it, children bless their families and communities through their very existence.

Children are gifts and examples for their communities, and communities are responsible to protect and teach them as well. The commands of Deuteronomy 6 to love God and pass his instructions on to children were addressed to the entire people of Israel, not just to individual parents or families:

Now this is the commandment . . . that the Lord your God charged me to teach you . . . so that you and your children and your children's children may fear the Lord your God all the days of your life, and keep all his decrees and his commandments that I am commanding you, so that your days may be long. Hear, therefore, O Israel, and observe them diligently . . . (Deut. 6:1-3).

While parents have the primary responsibility for training children, the entire community should be involved as witnesses, teachers, and role models.

Welcoming and Service

Jesus took this point even further by teaching his followers to welcome children as welcoming God. "Whoever welcomes one of these little children in my name welcomes me; and whoever welcomes me does not welcome me but the one who sent me," he declared (Mark 9:37). Just as the women of Naomi's town welcomed Ruth's new son (Ruth

---

[7] See, for example, 1 Samuel 1:21-28.
[8] See Genesis 12:2; 13:16; 15:5; 17:5-7.
[9] Moltmann, 16.
[10] See Isaiah 9:6-7; Luke 2:10-12; John 3:16.
[11] Moltmann, 89.

4:16-17), and just as all firstborn males were to be consecrated to the Lord by being presented to him at the temple in the presence of the community (Luke 2:22-23), the community of faith is to welcome children into its presence as well.

1 Timothy 4:12 reminds us that the young can serve as examples to all.[12] They deserve to be welcomed and respected just like everyone else. Jesus treated children with respect for their importance in God's eyes:

> *People were bringing little children to Jesus to have him touch them, but the disciples rebuked them. When Jesus saw this, he was indignant. He said to them, "Let the little children come to me, and do not hinder them, for the Kingdom of God belongs to such as these. I tell you the truth, anyone who will not receive the Kingdom of God like a little child will never enter it." And he took the children in his arms, put his hands on them and blessed them (Mark 10:13-16).*

> "I cannot live authentically without welcoming the others. For I am created to reflect the personality of the Triune God."
> —Judith Gundry-Volf and Miroslav Volf, *A Spacious Heart: Essays on Identity and Belonging*

Although the disciples tried to keep the children away from Jesus because they did not consider them to be important people in his ministry, Jesus "rebuked them," making the children models for the disciples instead. He allowed the children access to his presence, taking them in his arms and blessing them. Jesus welcomed children as participants in the Kingdom of God and ministered to them as willingly as he ministered to adults. He did not despise or reject them because of their childlikeness, but blessed them, used them as examples, and allowed them to praise him openly.[13]

Historical Perspectives in Theology

"It takes a village to raise a child," but how should the village view the child? What are the child's responsibilities within the village? No uniform view of children throughout history exists. In fact, scholars often disagreed on the nature of children, much as they do today. Some modern-day students of history have attempted to explain their views as a historical progression of thought with regard to children, but a less rigid perspective may be required, as a variety of different views have been evident during all of the time periods in question. Rather than viewing history as gradually progressing to the advanced state of the present time, let us take an overview of several common themes in history instead.

Children as Weak and Subordinate Members of the Community

---

[12] "Let no one despise your youth, but set the believers an example in speech and conduct, in love, in faith, in purity" (1 Tim. 4:12).

[13] For a further discussion on children in the church and in mission, see the sixth and seventh affirmations of this volume.

In the logic-driven perspective of the Aristotelian mindset, a number of thinkers (much like many people today) have viewed children as weaker than their adult counterparts, lesser beings in every way and lower in status than their more logical and experienced elders. This condescending view, in turn, has implications for the treatment of children within their communities.

Thomas Aquinas, a thirteenth century Christian theologian, believed that children were "immature and simpleminded," but that their basic tendencies, needs, and desires were not evil.[14] They grow and change, developing new skills and the ability to think in more complex ways. Like contemporary stage and developmental theories, however, this mindset is likely to lead to the view of children as less than human, as human 'becomings' instead of human beings. Because their ability to reason is not at an adult level, Aquinas and others believed that children were subordinate members of the community.[15] Therefore, the community had a responsibility to teach and train the children to develop adult abilities.

In the 1400s and 1500s, Martin Luther continued this emphasis on education to push children along toward adulthood.[16] Although he valued children for their potential and emphasized the community's responsibilities toward children, Luther viewed children as lesser members of the community because of what he considered to be their "deficiencies."

It is true that communities have a responsibility to train children. It is also true that children should develop more advanced skills of reasoning and thinking as they grow older. This does not, however, mean that children are any less human or do not have the ability to give back to their communities. Children are created in the image of God, and their communities must respect them as valuable in and of themselves.[17]

Children as Mini-Adults

At the other end of the spectrum, some have viewed children as miniature adults. In his controversial work, *Centuries of Childhood*, Philippe Aries claimed that until the modern period of history, most adults in France viewed children as smaller versions of themselves.[18] This allowed children to relate freely with adults in work, play, and worship, but it also meant that children were required to take on adult responsibilities at a very early age.

While some have questioned Aries' work, the view of children as miniature adults is still evident today. It led adults to believe that original sin corrupted even infants and very young children, and that they would be eternally condemned if they were not baptized. At around age seven, they were considered to be just as morally responsible as adults, and they were in danger of going to hell if they died before they accepted the mindset and practices of the Church in their time. Karl Rahner and others have argued against this view,

---

[14] Cristina L.H. Traina, "A Person in the Making," 106.
[15] Traina, 111.
[16] Jane E. Strohl, "The Child in Luther's Theology," 134.
[17] See the article by Doug McConnell in this volume.
[18] Philippe Aries, *Centuries of Childhood: A Social History of Family Life*. See also Richard R. Osmer, "The Christian Education of Children in the Protestant Tradition," *Theology Today* 56, no. 4 (2000): 507.

claiming that "God is operative at *every* stage of human growth and development, childhood being no exception."[19]

Several centuries after Christ, Augustine viewed children in a similar way. He did not see children as guilty in the sense that they sinned even in infancy, but he believed that infants and young children demonstrated sinful tendencies and simply did not possess the power to act on them. This perspective of "non-innocence" led him to advocate for the practice of infant baptism.[20] Augustine saw the humility of children as an example to be emulated, but he viewed accountability and responsibility to their communities almost as a repayment for the many sins that they committed during childhood.[21] Martha Stortz would argue that Augustine did not perceive children as mini-adults, but rather, that he "portrayed adults as grown-up children—only more complex."[22] Augustine's beliefs in the sinfulness and evil tendencies of children, however, demonstrate that he judged children from an adult point of view, treating them as he would treat adults, and showing little understanding of their vulnerability and distinct childlike qualities.

Children as Vulnerable and Worthy of Care

Children are just as valuable as adults, but they are distinct from adults in many ways. When we regard children as vulnerable and worthy of care, we demonstrate our understanding that they are gifts to be protected and blessings to be welcomed and cared for. They are fully human, but they have different needs than people of other ages. They may be physically weaker and logically not as advanced, but their spiritual state should not be judged by their physiological and developmental characteristics.[23]

In the eighteenth century, John Wesley recognized this and saw ministry to children as a worthy activity. He started "charity schools" for children of all classes.[24] While they were run on strict schedules and did not believe in the value of play, they were open to girls and boys, poor and rich."[25] He understood that children needed to be nurtured and trained, but his great respect for their inherent value helped him to treat them in more humane and considerate ways than many of his contemporaries. Indeed, children and adolescents "were often at the core of local revivals,"[26] a fact that demonstrated his willingness to learn from the young. Pamela Couture expands on this view: "Caring with children and others who are afflicted, including those who suffer innocently, in the Wesleyan view, is a means of grace, a means of religious experience through which we find God."[27]

---

[19] Mary Ann Hinsdale, "Infinite Openness to the Infinite," 421.
[20] Martha Ellen Stortz, "'Where or When Was Your Servant Innocent?,'" 82.
[21] Stortz, 84, 87.
[22] Stortz, 101.
[23] See Galatians 3:26, 28; 4:6-7
[24] Richard P. Heitzenrater, "John Wesley and Children," 287.
[25] Pamela D. Couture, *Seeing Children, Seeing God: A Practical Theology of Children and Poverty*, 54.
[26] Heitzenrater, 295.
[27] Couture, 48.

Contemporary Perspectives in Theology

"It takes a village to raise a child," but does the child play a role? If so, what does this role look like? Like the historical perspectives discussed above, contemporary perspectives on children and communities vary, too. Echoes of the past are evident in many of the views, but modern changes such as urbanization, capitalism, popular psychology, and globalization affect these views in different ways.

Children as Burdens and Commodities

One all-too-common view of children and their communities applies the capitalistic mindset of producers and consumers to children in the context of their families and communities. This perspective of market economics is more often implicit than explicit, but it is apparent nevertheless. The individualism, discovery, and "self-expression" of modern times, for example, lead to a much more sinister view of children than is obvious at first.[28] They are consumers of goods. They use up resources. They do not produce anything of value to pay for their own keep. Although most people would not verbalize these sentiments, articles written in the United States about the rising cost of raising children, selective abortion techniques, and the emphasis on the "return on the investment" of education demonstrate that "late modernity . . . is a period of declining appreciation of childhood."[29]

> "In a two-tiered world that separates those who can produce and consume from those who cannot, children, especially poor children, have a stark disadvantage."
> —Bonnie J. Miller-McLemore

This perspective is visible in many different contexts. For many wealthy families, David Elkind's concept of the "hurried child" typifies this view. Middle class children are rushed from one activity to the next, creating a "poverty of tenuous connections."[30] Their broad network of surface relationships does not supply the sense of community that they need, and the focus turns to achievement and "success" instead of healthy relationships and giving back to the community. In other contexts with less material wealth, children are also viewed as commodities. Child labor, bonded labor, sexual trafficking, and other forms of exploitation of children demonstrate that in many places, children continue to be viewed as commodities, to be bought and sold, used to repay debts, and abused for adult purposes.

Bonnie J. Miller-McLemore notes, "In a two-tiered world that separates those who can produce and consume from those who cannot, children, especially poor children, have a stark disadvantage."[31] A child, brutalized by police because of age, poverty, or culture; a child soldier, injured or killed by war or genocide; a street child, murdered by a "death squad" for not attending school and having "no future;" a child sex worker, "purchased"

---

[28] Richard R. Osmer, "The Christian Education of Children in the Protestant Tradition," *Theology Today* 56, no. 4 (2000): 513.
[29] Osmer, 516.
[30] Couture, 29. See David Elkind, *The Hurried Child: Growing Up Too Fast Too Soon.*
[31] Bonnie J. Miller-McLemore, *Let the Children Come: Reimagining Childhood from a Christian Perspective*, 91.

for an illicit experience at the expense of a child's hopes, spirit, and even life:[32] all of these children and more suffer from views within their communities that they are somehow less than human, to be used and discarded when no longer needed, useful, or desired.

Bryant Myers contrasts this perspective with an exhortation to the Church: "Could [Christians] take a lead in modeling Christ's admonition to welcome the children by creating a place and a voice for children and youth to speak for themselves?"[33] In other words, Christians can take the lead in changing the view of children as burdens and commodities by welcoming children fully and encouraging them to participate as members within the community of Christ.[34]

Children as Victims

Partially in reaction to the treatment of children only as burdens and commodities, many liberation theologians and others have taken the view of children as victims. While this is a necessary corrective to the previous mindsets, it may be an overcorrection from a biblical perspective.

Douglas Sturm, for example, views children as the victims of market-driven economics and modern-day perspectives. He places emphasis on the rights of children, labeling any "deprivation" or lack as "suffering."[35] "The anguish of suffering must not blind us from the mandate for emancipation," he declares.[36] Many children around the world suffer, and Christians are called to care for children. Treating children primarily as victims, however, may not be the best way to minister to them. A victim mentality is often a mentality of helplessness, and if children perceive themselves as helpless, they will not be as empowered to participate in ministry, advocate for themselves, and take a stand against injustice.

It is true that children need love,[37] but focusing solely on their individual rights without respect to their roles and responsibilities in the context of their communities does them a disservice. If they accept this thought pattern, they will grow up focusing only on themselves and their own needs, not willing to contribute to the greater good of the community.[38]

Sometimes, children *are* victims. They are victims of poverty, of economic, political, and cultural discrimination, of abuse, neglect and abandonment. Sturm understands this well, and presents a more well-rounded perspective of children around the world than

---

[32] See Gary A. Haugen, *Good News About Injustice: A Witness of Courage in a Hurting World*, 24-27, 121; Amnesty International in Tobias Hecht, *At Home in the Street: Street Children of Northeast Brazil*, 119; Glenn Miles and Josephine-Joy Wright, *Celebrating Children!*, 384.

[33] Bryant L. Myers, "Strategic Trends Affecting Children," 114.

[34] For more on this topic, see the sixth and seventh affirmations in this volume.

[35] Douglas Sturm, "On the Suffering and Rights of Children: Toward a Theology of Childhood Liberation," *Cross Currents* 42, no. 2 (1992): 149, 158.

[36] Sturm, 150.

[37] Sturm, 157.

[38] See Fred Van Geest, "Deepening and Broadening Christian Citizenship: Going Beyond the Basics without Succumbing to Liberal and Communitarian Ideals," *Christian Scholar's Review* 34, no. 1 (2004): 91-118. See also Iain Byrne, *The Human Rights of Street and Working Children*, 4.

many.[39] His concept of "deprivation," however, is not as simple as he makes it seem. This point of view laments the fact that in modern times, children are excluded from workplaces, worship services, and other activities and locations that they formerly had access to. While this is true, the best interests of the child must also be considered. Do children really need to be exposed to all aspects of life from an early age? This is not to say that they should be summarily excluded from all 'adult' realms, but neither should they experience all of the evil elements of their societies simply for the purpose of 'equality.' The complexities of these issues must be considered with wisdom and discretion.

The problems of viewing children solely as victims are better understood by Bonnie J. Miller-McLemore. She notes that children are sometimes "victims of narcissistically needy parents," sometimes "victims of a punitive Christianity," and often victims of adverse life circumstances.[40] Nevertheless, she tempers her perspective by placing the popular psychological perspective of children as victims in dialogue with the biblical ideals of empathy, forgiveness, and gentle correction.[41] Adults do not exist exclusively to care for children, but rather, both children and adults should have mutually reciprocal relationships of responsibility and care that are appropriate to their ages and abilities.

Children as Intrinsically Valuable

A more biblically accurate view reminds us that children have inherent worth. They are intrinsically valuable in the eyes of God, and they should have the same value as every other person. Like the perspectives of Wesley and others, this point of view emphasizes the image of God as the foundation and motivation for ministry to children.

> Recognizing the intrinsic worth of children causes adults to welcome children. This, in turn, helps adults to become "childlike" in their attitudes, developing the humility that Christ calls for in his people.

In this view, the powerful are not demonized, but the marginalized are not dehumanized, either. Children are neither idolized nor ignored. They are not treated with paternalistic condescension, nor are they freed from all responsibility as victims. Instead, they are welcomed as participating members with different abilities and different gifts to contribute to the community. In fact, Jesus used some of the most marginalized members of society as examples for the powerful of his day: "In the gospels . . . children, sinners, eunuchs, and prostitutes serve paradoxically as role models in a society led by men sure of their own rights."[42]

According to Judith Gundry-Volf, the inherent value of all people leads to mutual relationships and blessings.[43] Recognizing the intrinsic worth of children causes adults to welcome children. This, in turn, helps adults to become "childlike" in their attitudes,

---

[39] See Sturm, 149-150, 159-160.
[40] Bonnie J. Miller-Mclemore, 30, 36.
[41] Bonnie J. Miller McLemore, 38, 46, 48-49.
[42] Bovon, "Family and Community in the New Testament."
[43] Judith Gundry-Volf, "To Such as These Belongs the Reign of God: Jesus and Children," *Theology Today* 56, no. 4 (2000): 469.

developing the humility that Christ calls for in his people.[44] As discussed previously, Jesus exhorts his followers to seek these childlike qualities in relationship with children. In turn, this act of welcoming children can help the followers of Christ to enter the Kingdom of God.

Children are so valuable that they also have important functions within their communities. They are not excluded from participation because of their age. In fact, they are increasingly being viewed as "subjects of their own development, as potential agents of transformation."[45]

Implications

"It takes a village to raise a child"—but what about the children who do not have a positive system of support? What about the children whose villages have been destroyed by war, earthquakes, famine, disease, and poverty? What implications do our understandings of children in community have for children living in high-risk situations?

What Type of Village?

Perhaps the adage should be reframed to a more accurate representation of God's intent for his people in community, something like, "It takes a village of mutually reciprocating members that appreciate the intrinsic value of each person and that serve, welcome, nurture, teach, and learn from one another with the love of God." This may not be as pithy, but hopefully, it is a step in the direction of discovering what God intends. After all, Christ did not limit his statement to either children or adults when he described God's commandments for ideal relationships:

> "Hear, O Israel, the Lord our God, the Lord is one. Love the Lord your God with all your heart and with all your soul and with all your mind and with all your strength . . . Love your neighbor as yourself." There is no commandment greater than these (Mark 12:29-31).

As followers of Christ, we must seek to make this ideal a reality in our attitudes, actions, and our very lives.

---

[44] See Matthew 18:1-5.
[45] Myers, 108, 114.

CRITICAL ISSUES

GOD INTENDS FOR CHILDREN TO THRIVE IN STABLE AND LOVING RELATIONSHIPS

By Judith Ennew
Centre for Family Research, University of Cambridge

The idea that children are gifts from God and at the core of family life raises questions not only about relationships between adults and children, but also about relationships between adults and God. In addition, it appears to contain assumptions about the kind of family life children experience. Although God's intention may be for families to be stable and loving, reality can be very different, as those of us who work with vulnerable children know only too well. Many childhoods seem to lack both stability and love most, if not all, of the time. We are constantly challenged in this broken world by how far we are from fulfilling God's intent for human childhoods.

The phrase "God intends" implies the existence of an overall plan for children and childhood, which I would argue is part of what Vaughan Roberts has called a storyline that can be traced throughout Scripture.[1] This implies far more than the cosy objective that children should live in two-parent, one-wage-earning Christian families. It also has more import than the arguments of twentieth century historians, such as Philippe Ariès, that childhood was "discovered" around the time of the industrial revolution.[2] Although social scientists now research childhood as a special stage in human existence, Scripture shows that it belongs to all historical epochs rather than being a newly-discovered social concept. In the New Testament, childhood is explicitly distinguished from adulthood, in a more dramatic sense than its recent discovery by academics: for without deliberately changing and becoming like little children, adults will never enter the Kingdom of heaven (Matt. 18:3).[3]

In this broader context, I want to examine the implications of the words "gift", "welcome," and "nurture", as well as what it means to claim that "God intends for children to *thrive* in stable and loving relationships." If children are truly a gift from God (and what else could they be?) this is valid for all children—desired or unwished-for, talented or less able, alone or in families.

So let me begin with the idea of gift. An association between children and God's generosity is vitally important, not because of a simple reciprocal relationship between grateful parents and a generous God, but because the core of Christian faith is the gift of grace.

---

[1] Vaughan Roberts, *God's Big Picture: Tracing the Story-line of the Bible.*
[2] Philippe Ariès, *Centuries of Childhood: A Social History of Family Life.*
[3] All Scripture quotations are taken from the New International Version unless otherwise noted.

In human societies, the essence of giving, as the anthropologist Marcel Mauss pointed out, is reciprocity.[4] A gift always has to be repaid in some form of accountable equivalence. God's generosity, on the other hand, cannot be fully repaid, although the potential for reciprocity always exists. On the one side, by far the greater gift and at the heart of his covenant, God constantly offers the lavish gift of grace. The lesser gift is (or should be) our recognition of his grace and our gratitude, expressed through praise and thanks. Reciprocity also implies acceptance on each side: God's undeserved acceptance of mercy, compassion, and forgiveness, and our need to accept his forgiveness. Thus, God's practical gifts and blessings (children, homes, food) cannot be thought of as exactly equivalent to gifts given between human beings. The rules God employs for giving are more lavish, more generous, and also more difficult for us to comprehend, much less follow, especially if a particular gift is not exactly what we wished for but we must accept it gracefully.

> **Reciprocal Gifts of Grace**
> 1) God's merciful and generous gift of grace to us
> 2) Our recognition of his grace and our gratitude

Superficially, the gift of a child is easy to accept with joy and gratitude. Yet, what does it mean in our lives and ministries:

- If a child is longed for and prayed for, but not given?

- If the child we are given has a disability?

- If the gift is received and loved and then taken away?

With respect to the first of these questions, a large proportion of the Biblical narratives related to women concern women who long for a child. Mary's dutiful acceptance of the sudden and unrequested gift of motherhood is an exception to this pattern (Luke 1:38); Hannah's misery about her inability to bear a child is a more usual tale (1 Sam. 1). The reciprocal relationship through which this woman's prayers for motherhood were answered is recorded at some length: the Lord was "gracious" to Hannah and she bore a son whom she returned, as promised, to the God who granted her prayer. Even though Hannah and her husband enjoyed further children, this reciprocal act of returning her firstborn child is acknowledged to entail enduring pain, even though it is paralleled by Hannah's second gift—her song of exaltation (1 Sam. 2).

Many women (and men) desperately desire to have children yet remain childless, even if they are in a position to take advantage of modern reproductive technology. Such scientific interventions have somewhat unsubtly changed the perception of children from being gifts to being thought of as rights or possessions. Reproductive technology has now reached such a degree of sophistication that, for wealthy parents, a child can appear to be less a gift from God than a designer toy, a lifestyle addition. This tends to obscure God's role in the process, reducing his intent for children to human intentions to have children.

---

[4] Marcel Mauss, *The Gift: The Form and Reason for Exchange in Archaic Societies*.

> The desires of barren women might be argued to be the most enduring of all motifs of femininity in the Bible.

Within the community of believers, inability to have children can be a challenge to faith and ministry. Many disappointed couples take Psalm 27 literally to mean that, if children are a reward from God, their own inability to have children indicates that they are being subjected to divine punishment. The richness of God's love cannot be reduced to apportioning children as rewards. Grace, rather than any child however welcome, is the gift that matters.

Reproductive technology has resulted in potential for choice that brings into sharp focus social attitudes that make some children more welcome than others. Girls and boys are valued differently, for example, and desired for different reasons and at varied times in the domestic cycle.

Reproductive technology has also produced a tendency—especially in developed countries—towards "normalization", by which I mean the selection of children with certain characteristics, of which sex is only one possible preference. Gifted children—beautiful, intelligent, talented—are desired gifts, not only by parents but also by the social values and imperatives of medicine.

This brings me to considering my second question, "What if the child we are given has a disability?" Human beings with "genetic disorders" are often seen as unwelcome gifts, and that the correct approach to reproduction is the selective abortion of "faulty", or "abnormal" fetuses. Sometimes parents are pressurized by medical professionals to eliminate a child, if a pregnancy scan or test has shown a defined "defect." My own family includes a child with Downs, who is a great joy to all who know her. Yet her parents were greatly distressed throughout a subsequent pregnancy by the assumption that they would submit to an amniocentesis in the expectation that they would automatically abort a fetus that tested positive for Downs. Their decision to refuse amniocentesis, on the grounds that they would not contemplate fetus elimination was based not on any religious affiliation but rather on their professional dedication to children's rights. Both their daughters were referred to in the womb as "our little bearer of rights", which implied commitment to the provision of rights for children with disabilities in Article 23 of the 1989 United Nations Convention on the Rights of the Child.[5]

Medical pressure on these parents turned rapidly to attempts to interfere with their decision and comments that were close to verbal abuse. The mildest form consisted of comments that a child with a disability is a "burden"—not the most effective argument to use with parents whose Downs Syndrome daughter is a joy. Nor is this denigrating attitude in line with the current euphemism "special" applied to such children. This is not to deny that caring for a child with severe disability can be both physically and emotionally draining. Yet a friend of mine with a much-loved, brain-damaged son stopped going to church after years of listening to prayers from the congregation for him to be "cured." She had already been given the grace to love and welcome her son and love him as he was given to her. If she needed prayers it was for the physical and emotional strength (as well

---

[5] United Nations, *Convention on the Rights of the Child,* "Article 23."

as practical help from neighbors and others) to continue to care for him as he grew older and taxed her strength still further. Eventually, it became unbearable for her to have to feel the constant lack of welcome for him from within her social world.

All children are acceptable to God and loved by him: "For you love all things that exist, and detest none of the things that you have made, for you would not have made anything if you had hated it." (Wisdom of Solomon 11:24).[6] All children have a place in the world, which we need the grace to discover. I learned this lesson myself in a very practical way. When I first went to work in Jamaica in 1979, I was not in good shape emotionally. It felt as if my world had collapsed, but I could not describe my misery to strangers, and did not expect sympathy. More than anything else I needed hugs, but lacked the capacity to show this or to express my need—except unconsciously to one twelve-year-old, brain-damaged boy. He was doubly-incontinent, barely able to walk and incapable of speech. Yet he took one look at me and saw what the university-educated adults around us failed to see. Breaking away from his mother's grasp he struggled over to me, dragged himself onto my lap and proceeded to smother me with hugs and kisses. He did this every time he saw me during my six months in Jamaica, and this unconditional love went a long way towards healing my pain. When I finally admitted this to his mother she wept because, she told me, someone else besides her and her husband had finally seen a purpose in their beloved son's existence.

In all these cases, parents had to come to terms with the difference between the child of their imagination and the child of God's gift. I once attended a seminar reporting research in Germany with young people who had been born with no limbs or attenuated limbs as the result of their mothers taking the drug thalidomide during pregnancy. The researchers commented that these young people did not visualize the lack of limbs as a loss. Despite the difficulty of some aspects of their lives they could not sense the loss of something they had never experienced. It was their parents who experienced the loss of the "complete child" they had imagined during pregnancy, along with anticipating the difficulties both they and their children would face in a world that comes close to denying their humanity.

Children with disabilities are not just bearers of rights, they are made in God's image,[7] and God's imagination encompasses far greater variety than we can envisage. The crucial aspect is for parents—indeed, the whole community—to welcome each and every child as a unique, special human being, gifted as the image of God.

Cultural definitions of "disability" vary considerably. In the Southeast and East Asian region where I live and work, children with relatively minor birth defects are often abandoned, considered to be completely outside society. One case in point is children born with cleft palates, or "hare lips", who are frequently rejected at birth. According to doctrines of repeated reincarnation there is no merit in caring for such children, because such a person has been born with a disability, and become an orphan, as the direct result of improper behavior in the immediate past existence.

---

[6] "The Wisdom of Solomon: New Revised Standard Version," http://www.anova.org/sev/htm/ap/04_wisdomofsolomon.htm (accessed August 17, 2006).

[7] See the first affirmation in this volume.

> Parents have to come to terms with the difference between the child of their imagination and the child of God's gift.

My third question also relates to our complete dependence on God: What if the gift is received and loved and then taken away? This can also be perceived by parents as punishment, with the same yearning for answers to the questions "Why?", "Why me?", "What have I done to deserve this?" It is easy to repeat liturgical formulae such as "The Lord gave, and the Lord has taken away; blessed be the name of the Lord" (Job 1:21) in church services, but when parents are faced with the loss of children who have been received and loved, their pain is almost unbearable.

Grief is not always confined to individual loss, and it can be even more difficult to find ways of thinking about and reacting to the communal loss of many children in disasters and conflicts. This is caught very well in Scripture in the metaphorical image provided by Matthew (quoting Jeremiah) to describe communal pain after the slaughter of young children in Bethlehem by King Herod:

A voice is heard in Ramah,
weeping and great mourning,
Rachel weeping for her children
And refusing to be comforted,
Because they are no more (Matt. 2:18).

Living in Thailand, I became particularly conscious of this after the massive loss of life in the tsunami at the end of 2004. I learned much through the personal challenge of finding sensitive ways of listening to and talking with people who might have lost not only a spouse but also all their children. I found that I could only respond to their brokenness in any way that made sense to me—and, I hope, to them—through a new awareness of my total dependence on God. I also found parents who could accept their loss, without question and without bitterness.

The social science record also shows examples of children who use their own spiritual strengths as a gift to their parents.[8] Robert Coles, in a study focusing on children's moral intelligence, found that a terminally ill child can be non-egocentric and prayerfully empathetic. Coles discusses his work with a boy named David who was dying from leukemia. David had been asking the doctors and nurses if they prayed for their patients, including him, and told them that he prayed for them. Baffled, the doctors and nurses called on Coles, as a psychologist, to "assess what was troubling David." Taking the same approach, that there was something wrong with David for which he required counselling, Coles assumed the prayers were to ask God for a cure. On the contrary, David explained,

---

[8] See the sixth and seventh affirmations of this volume.

I ask God to be nice to them, so they don't feel too bad if us kids go to meet Him. . . When I meet God I'll put in a good word for the people [who work] in this hospital.

In response, Coles admits that he was "finally beginning to realize . . . how important [David's] religion was to him."[9]

This leads me to my final consideration of what it means to nurture the children we are given. There is no template for childrearing in Scripture, indeed there is an apparent contradiction. The frequently misquoted "proverb", "Spare the rod and spoil the child"[10] contrasts with the tender simile of children's development as a climbing plant: "Train a child in the way he should go and when he is old he will not turn from it" (Prov. 22:6). The latter appears to be closer to God's heart. Samuel Martin reminds us that English translations that appear to prescribe beating children as the best form of discipline do not take into account that the original Hebrew term translated as "child" refers to young men rather than to small children, and not at all to girls.[11]

It would be wonderful if we could base our childrearing on the methods used by Zechariah and Elizabeth to raise John the Baptist so that "the child grew and became strong in spirit" (Luke 1:80). But the Bible is silent on this. We have only one clue, although it is important. In the matter of the child's name they followed the command of God and not the pressures from family and friends (Luke 1:59-64).

A further implication of this brief passage is the reference to growing "strong in spirit." Nurture is of course intended to ensure that children thrive (which I take to mean grow as God intends they should) physically, emotionally, and spiritually, or as Luke puts it with respect to the adolescence of Jesus, "in wisdom and stature, and in favor with God and men" (Luke 2:52). Yet Jesus was the firstborn son in a complete family, in a permanent community in which his father was gainfully employed. What are the implications for our attempts to fulfill God's plan for children if their right and need to thrive in stable and loving relationships is threatened by:

- Abusive parents?

- Domestic violence?

- "Irregular" family structures?

- Parental illness and death?

- Parents' inability to cope?

---

[9] Robert Coles, *The Moral Intelligence of Children*, 177.
[10] See Proverbs 13:24.
[11] Samuel Martin, *Thy Rod Does Not Comfort Me: Christians and the Spanking Dilemma*.

- Natural disaster and armed conflict?

This list is itself a clear reminder of how far this sinful world is from God's plan for children. Not all parents want their children, not all children feel wanted, many children wish they were dead or had never been born. They may live in dysfunctional families, or be abandoned, or orphans, or children infected or affected by HIV, or street children, or children with disabilities. We tend to deal with these groups under specific labels, with programs for each category. But such children are crying out for their uniqueness to be recognized; they are not just categories. They are all born in the image of God.[12]

In her recent book, *From the Ground Up*, Kathryn Copsey argues that from the day a child is gifted in the image of God, that image is progressively marred by sin, tarnished by the world, and scratched by experiences.[13] The challenge for those working with vulnerable children is to reverse these processes, nurture children's awareness of others, appreciation of values and ability to make moral choices. In addition, although it is not possible to legislate so that all children are loved and wanted, it is possible to help parents and communities to accept and gratefully nurture all children in their care. Despite the fact that international legislation repeatedly refers to the right of children to "grow up in a family environment, in an atmosphere of happiness, love and understanding"[14] it is not possible to legislate for loving relationships. But it may be possible to provide support for children to develop through education in homes, families, and communities, as well as in schools.

Unfortunately, international (and national) plans for education do not include spiritual nurture. The international community's commitment to "Education for All" sets the goal of "education" for majority-world children as low as five years of poor-quality schooling.[15] Education is thus reduced to enrollment in schools and basic literacy and numeracy, without taking into account the rights outlined in Article 29 of the United Nations Convention on the Rights of the Child. These refer to education that prepares children "for responsible life in a free society, in the spirit of understanding, peace, tolerance, equality of sexes, and friendship among all peoples, ethnic, national and religious groups and persons of indigenous origin."[16] Education for All also fails to take into account the important role that can be played by families and communities. This leaves a vast field of unmet needs. How can we provide spiritual nurture for children outside family care, children with severe disabilities, children of other faiths, bereaved children, severely ill and dying children, abused and exploited children?

Working out how we go about nurturing children's spirituality entails recognizing that this aspect of the gift that God gives in each new human being is something pre-existing and eternal. This is based on the clear message from Jesus that children's spirituality is something that adults can and must learn from.

---

[12] See the article by Doug McConnell in this volume.
[13] Kathryn Copsey, *From the Ground Up: Understanding the Spiritual World of the Child*.
[14] United Nations, *Convention on the Rights of the Child*, "Preamble."
[15] See, for example, http://www.unesco.org/education/efa/ed_for_all/background/background_documents.shtml.
[16] United Nations, *Convention on the Rights of the Child*, "Article 29."

In *The Spirit of the Child,* David Hay and Rebecca Nye report that, through talking to children, they identified a 'relational consciousness', which they describe as the potential for spirituality in every human being. They admit discovering "relational consciousness" through conversations with six- to eleven-year-olds, despite having been blind to this idea when designing their research. This awareness of other people not only underpins all religious experience, they suggest, but is also vital for both individuals and communities to grow and thrive. It is a human universal that cannot be claimed by any one belief system. Thus, they argue, the nurture of spirituality should be the bedrock of all childrearing and education. It cannot be quarantined in religious education or Sunday School, but is essential to education in the broadest sense, for individuals and for the persistence of human communities. This relational spirituality cannot be taught like a series of facts and rules. Throughout their childhood and by a variety of adult and child agents, children can be encouraged to become more aware of their spiritual potential, to listen to their imagination and creativity.[17]

Even from a non-religious perspective, Richard Coles observed that "children very much need a sense of purpose and direction in life, a set of values, grounded in moral introspection."[18]

Children are not only gifts but also responsibilities, because they are a poignant reminder of the humanity of Christ who, like all of us, experienced "childhood." The fact that all adult interactions with children are flawed can be salvaged only if and when we acknowledge God's supremacy and accept responsibility for our mistakes. The extent of the damage inflicted on children in this fallen world can barely be grasped—the numbers of children at risk or in need of rescue and rehabilitation are overwhelming. We have a huge responsibility to respond to children's needs for welcome and nurture, to recognize their spiritual strength and learn from it, to treat each and every one of them with respect as a unique gift in the image of God, rather than a member of a category or an item in a program. It is not possible to begin such work unless we recognize that we, too, are children crying out from the nightmares of our world, trusting in our Father and relying fully on him:

The cry to God as "Father"
in the New Testament
is not a calm acknowledgment
of a universal truth about
God's abstract fatherhood.
It is the child's cry
out of a nightmare.

It is the cry of outrage,
fear, shrinking away,
when faced with the horror

---

[17] David Hay and Rebecca Nye, *The Spirit of the Child.*
[18] Coles, 177.

*of "the world"—
yet not simply or exclusively—
protest, but trust as well.*

*"Abba Father"
all things are possible
to Thee . . .* [19]

---

[19] Rowan Williams, quoted in *Celtic Daily Prayer: A Northumbrian Office*, 27.

PRACTITIONER'S RESPONSE

FROM A CHILD'S WORDS

BY JONI L. MIDDLETON
DEEPIKA SOCIAL WELFARE SOCIETY, PROJECT RESCUE, INDIA

Introduction

Children are at risk all around us. Whether they're latchkey kids, day laborers, heads of orphaned households, abused, child soldiers or living in gang infested neighborhoods. Those of us who work with children at risk would see each of these children as gifts, but do the children themselves see that they are gifts? How do we instill within children the sense that they are gifts from God? What does it mean for them to be a gift? What does "welcoming and nurturing" a child look like?

> When a child faces so many obstacles to survive each day, how can we create and sustain opportunities for them to thrive as a welcomed and nurtured gift of God?

These questions often overwhelm me as I sit at my computer trying to create training modules to help our staff, or when I sit on the floor playing "Uno" with girls born and raised in a red-light district.[1] Yet, those same girls have given me glimpses of the answers when I think about how they have welcomed and nurtured me. In Calcutta, we have 19 young girls who have adopted me as their "Joni Auntie."

Each of them has her own story of pain, neglect, and insecurity. Some of them struggle with behaviors which shock and bewilder our staff. Some of them believe lies about their home life because they or their mothers feel the truth is too painful to bear. Yet, these same girls have been my teachers, prayer partners, cooking assistants, storytellers, play pals, and huggers. In the midst of their trauma and painful memories, I have seen them find ways to laugh, to encourage one another, to initiate hugs, and to speak their thoughts. They have welcomed me and nurtured me in calling me "Auntie," learning from me, asserting themselves, stepping out of their pain and embracing me, and in their forbidding me to travel to those faraway places to speak and teach. They own me in ways I still can't explain.

But how did they get to that place where they could begin to embrace their healing? What did we do in our work to help them feel like a gift instead of an "occupational hazard" of their mother's exploitation? I have struggled to find the right words and thoughts to suggest how we had worked this out in Calcutta. I even wondered if the children really believed they were gifts from God. So, out of the desperation of writer's block, I took the statement to the girls with whom I work. Their responses to the statement far surpass what

---

[1] A red-light district is a place where prostituted individuals work and live.

could have been my potentially smug and pedantic expressions. They seem to have stated the obvious, but I continue to marvel at the depth of their comments.

The girls began shyly sharing how they thought "God gives children as gifts to welcome and nurture." The youngest was the first to speak up, but seemed to give the most profound response, "Children are gifts from God because he loves us." Other children began giving their reasons about how welcomed they believed themselves to be, and how adults could show that welcome. One girl said, "Children should be loved." Another admonished, "Parents must correct us." An older girl said, "Adults should understand us, even what's in our hearts." And finally, one girl said, "Adults must have the right behavior." Although each of these girls have struggled with the difficulties Ennew addresses, their five statements all reflect the perception of children who believe they are gifts and should be welcomed and nurtured.

"Children are Gifts Because He Loves Us."

I look for the theology and the Scriptures, but Neelam, only four years old, simply states the obvious. God in his great love gave us children. They are more than just "the hope of the next generation" or "our future" or the progeny of marriage. Jesus elevated their status from reproductions for some future state to role models of what the Kingdom of God is all about.[2] They do not have to grow up to teach us adults how to live in the Kingdom. Several years ago when Keith White talked about the child in the midst of us, he described the Kingdom of God in a less adult and more childlike way. He said, "The Kingdom is in fact not like an earthly kingdom at all! It's the opposite in every way. Upside down! Inside-out! The best way of describing it is not as a place or territory at all, but as 'God's way of doing things'".[3]

When Jesus directed the crowd's eyes and minds to a child standing before them and said, "Unless you change and become like little children, you will never enter the Kingdom of heaven" (Matthew 18:3 NIV), he challenged the adult world and turned maturity on its head. He redirected the crowd's adult eyes and ways of measuring and evaluating the Kingdom to children and their ways. He reminded us that those little reproductions of ourselves are indeed his great love-gifts to us.

> God in his great love gave us children. They are more than just "the hope of the next generation" or "our future" or the progeny of marriage.

---

[2] See also Orona's comments about Jesus praising "their childlike qualities" in this volume and Judith Ennew, *Questioning the Basis of our Work*, 69.
[3] Keith White, "A Little Child Will Lead Them: Rediscovering Children at the Heart of Mission," http://www.viva.org/?page_id=296 (accessed May 31, 2006).

"Children Should be Loved" and "Parents Must Correct Us."

Punishment
- Done out of anger
- To deal with frustrations of caregiver
- Corrects the child's behavior to match the adult's expectations
- Adult-centered

Correction
- Done with love
- To help the child learn right and wrong
- Recognizes the child's own gifts and abilities
- Considers "the best interests of the child".

When I asked the girls how parents and adults show that they love children, the girls said, "Mom corrects me." I was surprised. But, when Goma explained her statement, she described correction more than punishment. She said that her mother loved her so much that she would tell her a different way to do something. Pushpa added that people who love children help them to understand right and wrong.

Love and correction. What an astonishing combination! Isn't this an illustration of that upside-down nature of the Kingdom? Most of us would say that we do the work we do because we love children. But doesn't much of our work revolve around correction? We see children's rights being plundered, so we raise awareness. We see problems for children, and we set out to correct those problems. In essence, our programs are corrective measures. Goma and Pushpa would say that we love them.

"Adults Should Understand Us, Even What's in our Hearts."

Each time I visit the girls in the home, I feel welcomed. Usually, the minute I step into the room, nineteen girls jump to their feet and surround me, waiting to give me greetings and hugs. Most of us have experienced this same response from children. Once they become familiar with us or begin to heal from their trauma, the welcome they give us is overwhelming and extraordinary. That challenges me to make sure I look into their hearts. I can learn all I can about how sexual exploitation, neglect, abandonment, post-traumatic stress disorder, and other challenges have affected these girls, but can I sense what is in their hearts? Can I help them to identify their frustrations and weaknesses along with their dreams and aspirations?

We believe we should listen to children and encourage them to participate in our programs, and yet, I only asked the girls with whom I work for their thoughts about this subject when I could not think of anything to say. We face the dilemma in knowing the balance between participation and direction for a child. How can we understand what's in the heart of a child who is faced prematurely with the responsibilities of parenthood while they are still learning how to grieve the loss of their parents? To what extent should child soldiers decide how to play with children when they have both witnessed and been party to the deaths and abuses of other children and adults? Our organizations work to understand their child's heart. They are not adults. They are children. Let us always provide a safe place where we can encourage and expect them to be children.

"Adults Should Have the Right Behavior."

So much of welcoming and nurturing children involves appropriate adult behavior. We create child protection policies, screening procedures, and codes of conduct to ensure that adults behave appropriately with children. We train our children about how adults should act with them and how they should act with other children. Much of the Bible revolves around appropriate behavior because we live in a sin-centered world. In our fallen state, we forget how to act in Kingdom ways. Many of our children come from homes and communities where they have seen more dysfunctional behavior than any of us would like to imagine.

Our programs with children and their communities must reflect our belief that they are gifts to be welcomed and nurtured. We must celebrate them as gifts and welcome them with open hearts and wide arms. At times, we will lovingly correct them, their families, and their communities. We should work to enable parents to be better nurturers of their own children. When we face the many challenges of working with children—limited funds and resources, not enough staff, power cuts and water shortages, bombs, corruption, and poverty—we show that God has a purpose and plan for every child. When we welcome children as gifts, we can listen to their stories, watch them play with abandon, and walk away genuinely blessed because they let us step into their world from time to time.

CASE STUDY

CHILD SPONSORSHIP PROJECTS: A BREAKTHROUGH FOR CHILDREN AT RISK IN THE INDIAN CONTEXT BUILDING COMMUNITIES

BY THOMAS SWAROOP WITH JENNIFER ORONA
COMPASSION INTERNATIONAL–INDIA

Description and History

At Compassion International, we believe that all children should have the right to be free from physical, sexual, emotional and other forms of exploitation.[1] Our mission is to "partner with churches to help them provide Indian children with the opportunity to rise above their circumstances and become all God has created them to be."[2] Our long-term objective is to enable children to complete basic education, along with either higher education or vocational training that can help them to become responsible and fulfilled Christian adults.

Since 1968, Compassion International has partnered with local churches in India to provide a variety of services to children in high risk situations. Currently in India, more than 52,000 children are involved in sponsorship programs in 230 projects.

Ministry and Activities

This ministry is Christ centered, child focused, church based, and committed to integrity.[3] We seek to empower local churches to minister to the children in their communities. Compassion provides on-going training and orientation to members of the church.

Our work takes place at three different levels:

3) Child Survival Program (0-3 years)

---

[1] United Nations, *Convention on the Rights of the Child*.
[2] Compassion International, "India," http://www.compassion.com/about/where/india.htm (accessed February 21, 2006).
[3] Compassion International, "How We Work," http://www.compassion.com/about/how/default.htm (accessed May 23, 2006).

4) Child Sponsorship Program (3-21 years)

5) Leadership Development Program (for outstanding graduates)

Local church ownership and committed partnership are crucial. In order to work at all three levels, Compassion and the local church partner together to create a Child Development Center (CDC) with the objective of enrolling children who live in risky environments and provide them with opportunities for holistic development.

Of course, a program cannot truly welcome and nurture children "in stable and loving relationships" unless it has caring adults. Project staff are always available for the children. They are trained in child psychology, childcare, and counseling. Sometimes there are the challenges of low qualifications, high turnover, and lack of adequate infrastructure, however, when CDCs are run well, children benefit immensely and develop in numerous ways.

Holistic development implies balanced attention to all aspects of a child's growth and nurture. For this reason, the CDCs focus on four main areas of development: physical (through supplementary nutrition, health screenings, and training), cognitive (by providing education and resource centers), social/emotional (by providing opportunities for appropriate interactions with peers, caregivers, and other members of the community through music, arts, crafts, camps, career trainings, and other programs), and spiritual growth(through emphasis in all programs, especially Vacation Bible Schools, retreats, and spiritual camps). All programs are age-graded or appropriately coincided with children's developmental timeframes.

> In all our programs, spiritual truths are integrated with activities, lessons, and relationships to help the children grow in their faith and learn about all that God intends for them.

Structure and Strategies

Compassion's decision to partner with local churches is a strategic one, as our website explains: "We believe local congregations are catalysts for community change and optimize the mutual respect, resources and common purpose that are critical in caring for children. When this kind of relationship takes hold, it's amazing how children come alive."[4]

Compassion International advocates for children in need by helping the Church to reach impoverished children through sponsorship. Compassion partners with churches because churches are God's instruments of change in society. Each new CDC must be initiated by a local partner church. This ensures that the local church will be committed to the program. The local partner takes responsibility to provide the facilities and appoint the required administrative staff.

Compassion International provides regular support for program development, training for the project staff, and facilitation for the caregivers and workers who are involved in

---

[4] Compassion International, "Church Partnership,"
http://www.compassion.com/about/how/churchpartnership.htm (accessed May 23, 2006).

direct interaction with children. Project staff are also oriented to culturally appropriate Child Development principles. Nevertheless, issues in the local culture and community can threaten the peaceful functioning of the projects, and the migration of families can affect the children's attendance.

Despite these challenges, ministry can still occur. The long-term commitment that we are able to make through sponsorship allows the children to develop an emotional attachment to their sponsors. It also changes the lives of sponsors as they see the effects of sponsorship support in the lives of the children. In addition, the children know that the stability and love they experience through this long-term commitment allows them to plan for the future, including family, career, and life.

Child, Parent, and Community Participation

Compassion International's CDCs give children a voice, empowering them to participate in their own development. Caregivers at the CDCs spend quality time with children and empower them to reach for their full potential. Older children are even encouraged to take up volunteer responsibilities at the center, nurturing their leadership development.

Parents are always welcome at the CDCs. Staff members at the centers understand that the project truly belongs to the community, and acknowledge the important role that they play in the lives of their children by expecting parents to be deeply involved in "all aspects of their child's development, including:

- Planning daily activities.

- Helping to make project decisions.

- Ensuring that money is spent wisely and only for the purpose that it was given."[5]

> Parents are empowered to make good decisions that affect their families and the entire community in positive ways.

Compassion recognizes that a safe and permanent home with family members is the best place for children to grow up.[6] To this end, projects build on the family's decision-making capacities by engaging them in the planning of new programs. Regular meetings help to equip parents with the skills required for nurturing children, and often increase the family's income as well. As a result of the positive relationships between staff and parents, the parents often seek guidance from the project staff. In turn, children become more safe, healthy, and strong as each CDC works to support and strengthen their entire family.

---

[5] Compassion International, "Child's Family," http://www.compassion.com/about/how/childsfamily.htm (accessed May 23, 2006).
[6] For a further discussion of the role of parents and families, see the second affirmation in this volume.

The community and the staff of the CDC share in one another's lives by visiting, caring, and sharing resources in order to build bridges with the children's families. Through this, they remain aware of the family's condition and needs. Care extends beyond the boundaries of the church and center as the ministry branches out into homes within the community. In turn, the community develops a sense of ownership of the project as they begin to understand the church's genuine concerns. The informal interactions between staff, caregivers, families, and community members also lead to strong relationships. The center utilizes resources from other groups and builds networks for sharing and learning within the community. The use of local resources is encouraged as a sign of the community's willingness to promote child development.

Conclusion

Throughout its 38 year history, Compassion International–India has sought to empower children, families, and communities to "thrive in stable and loving relationships." Child Development Centers, family participation, and community development programs are just a few of the ways that we address the holistic needs of our sponsored children in India. Through all of our experiences, both positive and challenging, we have learned that children truly are "a gift to welcome and nurture," and that it really is "a privilege to join with children in celebrating their uniqueness, valuing childhood as formative for all of life."

PRACTICAL IMPLICATIONS

BUILDING COMMUNITIES FOR JESUS: LITERACY, CIVICS, EVANGELISM

BY BESA SHAPLLO WITH JENNIFER ORONA
MISSION POSSIBLE ALBANIA

Mission Possible Albania

After the communist leadership had proclaimed Albania totally atheist in 1967, they sealed the country off from the rest of the world for two decades (1971–1991). As an English teacher in Albania at the time, I never thought that one day I would find myself serving as the director of a Christian organization there.

The Albanian government enforced atheism and the majority of its population had little or no open opportunity to experience the love of God and to learn how to build faith in him. Many parents had not heard or experienced faith in the Lord during their lifetimes. When we started the *Miracle* magazine, we wanted to focus on the new generation of Albania, the children who would have a natural inclination towards God. We hoped that our *Miracle* magazine would do a real miracle: children would teach faith to their parents.

In 1998, I met Rev. Robert Rice of Literacy Ministries International and the Bible League. Bob shared his interest in a literacy project for Albania. He wanted to develop a primer, and his prayers were guiding him towards Mission Possible. I, on the other hand, saw the primer and a literacy program as tools to make *Miracle* even more effective.

The spread of blood feuds—a central topic of one special edition of *Miracle*—had closed many children into their houses. Others were closed out of schools and they had to sell cigarettes or other things in the streets in order to support themselves and their families. Consequently, a significant number of teenagers had grown up completely illiterate. No one had yet thought of preparing a primer especially for the teenagers and adults.

In 1999, together with the Bible League, we began working on the Bible content primer. In 2002, after almost a year of hard work in the extremely poor region of Bathore located in the suburbs of the Albanian capital, Tirana, thirteen students from the pilot program received certificates of completion. We continued the program in a children's home in Tirana with a group of gipsy children. Finally, we knew that the situation had ripened for a bigger challenge. We would use literacy to enter Bathore, this poverty-stricken, underdeveloped area, with the Word of God. Our purpose was quite simple: *to initiate a process of transformation that would open these people up to God.*

From 2004 to 2005, we used the Bible content primer to teach 240 people of Muslim background to read and write and with over 200 children and adults who attended our Bible clubs for twenty weeks. When we finished the courses, we realized that a transformation had occurred. The children and adults gained more than just literacy; they gained a new sense of confidence and a new feeling of community.

Challenges, Problems, and Opportunities

We hoped to reach the people of Bathore and decided to follow the pattern that Jesus modelled for us. He worked miracles and provided for the needy in order to help the people know their Father. As we worked with the people of Bathore, we understood the importance of relationships more and more. Our teachers did more than teach. "God intends for children to thrive in stable and loving relationships," and our teachers experienced this as they showed love and built relationships with the students. The students began to realize it was out of love that the teachers were there. So, they began to comprehend the love of Jesus and the hope he offered to them and their families.

The primer not only helped illiterate people learn to read and write faster than it would take in the normal educational system, but its content was put together in a way that would gently introduce the students to Jesus and his works and thus, help them find the road to hope and salvation. Therefore, in the first phase of the project we sowed the seeds, which we expected to bear fruit in the second phase that followed: that of the Bible Study.

> "Therefore be imitators of God, as beloved children, and live in love, as Christ loved us and gave himself up for us, a fragrant offering and sacrifice to God."
>
> —*Ephesians 5:1-2* NRSV

The literacy effort helped the children both directly and indirectly. Parents learned about God's Word along the way. Love and correction work hand in hand to help children develop into healthy citizens of their communities,[1] and the parents learned how to lovingly correct their children through the Word of God. They also gained access to written materials about parenting.

We had to face the challenge of changing the community at large. Mission Possible did not work alone in this ministry. Organizations like Literacy Ministries International, Bible League, Geneva Global, Blythswood, Eurovangelism, the national churches of different denominations, various NGOs, and teachers inside and outside the community came together. We could feel God's invisible hand, greater than us, regulating the whole effort.

The people in Bathore lived in misery, poverty and hopelessness, but they were still a proud people who clung to their traditions. We did not try to impose our thoughts on them, but we let them understand that our love was genuine and that Jesus loves each one of us regardless of our culture or background. This process was a gradual step-by-step process:

1) Teaching writing and reading

2) Teaching God's Word

---

[1] See the article by Joni Middleton in this volume.

3) Planting churches

Our project included *only* the first two steps. As for the third, we would say: *prayerfully a church will be planted eventually.* We thought that planting a church might be too early in a community like Bathore because of the religious background, traditions, and other challenges. But God works miracles and the church in Bathore is one of them.

Faith is very important in every step of our lives. We were learning this lesson little by little in the process of working in Bathore. Our teachers needed faith to overcome all the difficulties and barriers that they faced. When we taught through a Bible content primer, we also taught faith—and people began to open up. Through prayers and dedication, one can develop projects and find the money to sustain them, but love moves things and makes people believe.

Building Communities for Jesus

While it is true that the religious background of these people is Muslim, it is also true that it is *tradition* that they are most afraid to break away from, and tradition as the only thing that keeps them together. By building a system of faith, as well as educating them with the basic principles of citizenship, we hope to make them better believers altogether. The organization and development of a Christian Community Center that will be a place to hold literacy classes, Bible studies, and courses related to citizenship seems to be the most effective solution to the needs of the Bathore community at this time.

The Process
1) Literacy and Introductory Bible Courses
2) Civics and Bible Courses
3) Vocational Skills and Bible Courses

The Plan-
1) Teaching Writing and Reading
2) Teaching God's Word
3) Planting Churches

We at Mission Possible see ourselves planting the seeds for future believers. This is a process that does not take place overnight, but requires time and persistence. We envision a three-step transformation process. 1) Literacy and introductory Bible courses. 2) Civics and Bible courses, as described above. 3) Basic vocational skills and Bible courses, designed to allow people to be involved in the center's activities throughout the year and provide input along the way. During this third stage, we hope that the church becomes more involved. Our efforts will be more focused on the process of finding resources within the community of Bathore itself, to further encourage the community to take charge of this work.

Mission Possible envisions a project that takes illiterate people, transforms them into citizens, and makes them Christian believers. This three-step process, if successful in the Bathore area, could then be transferred into other areas of Albania and beyond, where issues and problems have many commonalities. We hope to see local communities transformed into places where children are valued, nurtured, and loved with the love of Christ. We hope to see children benefiting from stable, welcoming communities where they can grow and learn.

> **The Goal**
>
> Mission Possible envisions a project that takes illiterate people, transforms them into citizens, and makes them Christian believers.

CHAPTER 3
DISCUSSION QUESTIONS

1) If children's right to thrive in stable and loving relationships is threatened by unhealthy family structures, violence, abuse, and death, then what are the implications for our attempts to see God's intent for children fulfilled?

2) As an organization (or church), in what ways are you welcoming children into decisions and planning processes that impact them? How could you give them more access?

CHAPTER 4
WELL-BEING IN SOCIETY

Society has a God-given responsibility for the well-being of children and families.

All children and families live in society and are dependent on institutions for healthcare, shelter, access to social services, safe drinking water, information and safety. The Church must collaborate with these institutions for the common good, and if they fail, the Church must speak and act with and on behalf of the vulnerable.

God intends children to flourish in a just society.

"He has told you, O mortal, what is good;
and what does the Lord require of you
but to do justice, and to love kindness,
and to walk humbly with your God?"

—Micah 6:8 NRSV

"Christian ministry to children serves to create a world that submits to God's intentions for children."

—Tri Budiardjo

"Learn to do good;
seek justice,
rescue the oppressed,
defend the orphan,
plead for the widow."

—Isaiah 1:17 NRSV

BIBLICAL REFLECTION

LET LOVE BE GENUINE AND RELATIONAL

By Wendy Sanders, with supplementary material from Tri Budiardjo
Adapted by Paul Stockley

Introduction

In his book *Words of Courage*, former U.S. President Jimmy Carter shares a story about a Cuban priest he was blessed to meet. Carter asked the priest the secret to his incredible capacity to draw people to God. The priest humbly responded, "Señor Jimmy, it is to love God and whoever happens to be standing in front of you at any given moment."[1] Carter suggests this is the message of the entire Christian Bible and for us, the priest's understanding of *relational, just love* is clearly the essence of the topic of justice.

To understand God's heart for children, we must first understand God's love and justness and then understand God's call and our response to be a just society. If *justice* is the trait of a society living in a reciprocal relationship with God,[2] then perhaps *integrity* is an accompanying trait to be spiritually transformed within individuals who are the people of God.

> Jesus is the ultimate, incarnate role model of justice with relevance in understanding God's heart for children at risk today.

God Is Just

The people of Israel knew God was just through his word and deeds. In the New Testament, Jesus builds on this view as the ultimate, incarnate role model of justice. Together, these have relevance to our understanding of God's heart for children at risk today.

Understanding God through His Word

"He is the Rock, his works are perfect, and all his ways are just. A faithful God who does no wrong, upright and just is he" (Deut. 32:4).[3] Justice may be perceived as God's love in action.[4] God's justness is described in the law, the prophets and the writings. God is the Lord of all creation. "Righteousness and justice are the foundation of [God's] throne"

---

[1] Jimmy Carter, *Sources of Strength: Meditations on Scripture for a Living Faith*.
[2] See Pamela King, "The Reciprocating Self: A Trinitarian Analogy of Being and Becoming."
[3] All Scripture quotations are taken from the New International Version unless otherwise noted.
[4] Christopher J.H. Wright, *Old Testament Ethics for the People of God*, 28.

(Ps. 89:14). "The LORD is a God of Justice" (Isa. 30:18) and God always acts justly (Gen. 18:25).

Understanding God through His Deeds

The people of Israel knew God through his deeds, beginning with his power which drew them from the depths of slavery in Egypt. The trigger for God's action was his concern for their suffering—God saw, heard, cared and went into action (Ex. 2:23–25; 3:7–10). This pattern continues later on in the role of the judges.[5]

Advocacy in the Psalms

The wisdom writings reveal profound truths and convictions of who God is, his character, and what would please him, as reflected in his handiwork, his involvement in the history of his people and the whole world, and his special interventions to the plight of the righteous throughout the ages. Amazingly, they include God's particular interests on issues affecting children.

In the Book of Psalms, God is the Almighty King who sits on the heavenly throne and reigns over the nations, judging in righteousness (Ps. 11:7; 22:28; 29:10; 47:7, 8; 67:4-5; 95:3; 97:1-6; 98:8-9; 103:19; 145:1, 13, 17). The purpose of exercising justice and righteousness is for the sake of the weak, the poor and the oppressed, who are special to God.[6] He is God who says, "Because of the oppression of the weak and the groaning of the needy, I will now arise . . . I will protect them from those who malign them" (Ps. 12:5, TNIV). And again, "He upholds the cause of the oppressed and gives food for the hungry. The LORD sets the prisoners free, the LORD gives sight to the blind, the LORD lifts up those who are bowed down, the LORD loves righteousness" (Ps. 146:7-8).

Among those who are described as the weak, the poor and the oppressed, the children seem so central. For the sake of the children, for their protection, their well-being and their interest, God exercises his justice and righteousness. They are on his heart. He claims to be "A father to the fatherless, a defender of widows" (Ps. 68:4–5), who, "hears the desire of the afflicted . . . encourages them and listens to their cry, defending the fatherless and the oppressed, in order that people, who are of the earth, may terrify no more" (Ps. 10:17–18).[7] Children are special in God's heart, especially those who are weak, poor, needy, and oppressed.

Another exciting aspect of this is seen in Psalm 82:1–4. The Psalmist describes God as a King speaking in his congress. "God presides in the great assembly; he gives judgment among the 'gods': How long will you defend the unjust and show partiality to the wicked? Defend the cause of the weak and fatherless; maintain the rights of the poor and oppressed. Rescue the weak and needy, deliver them from the hand of the wicked" (NIV). God in his

---

[5] Wright, 261.
[6] See also Psalm 9:8-9, 19.
[7] See also Psalm 146:9

heavenly meetings has an agenda for children. God's interest in children is expressed in demands for comprehensive protection for children.

God stepped into history when children were at risk. He delivered the children of the Israelites from intolerable violence, exploitation, and infanticide. He punished Agag, the king of the Amalekites, with total destruction to his people because of his sins against children as he made many women childless by his brutal policies (1 Sam. 15:33). Because of his justice and protection of children, God is known by his people as the ultimate defender of the weak and oppressed. The needy can call on the Lord to avenge and judge the wicked. Who are the wicked? The Psalmist describes them as those who "slay the widow and the alien; they murder the fatherless" and then say "The LORD does not see; the God of Jacob pays no heed" (Ps. 94:1–6).

God's Words and Deeds

God's justice and his call to justice are based upon the underlying truth that *God created the world and it was good.* He created adequate resources for all because God cares deeply about the well–being of the people he created in his own image (Gen. 1:26–31; Ps. 146). All Scripture cries of the love of God for all people (Ps. 112; 1 John 3:16–17), and God hates any injustice for it results in harm within his creation.[8]

God Speaks of Justice

Consequently, *God especially loves and cares for those in need:* "'Because of the oppression of the weak and the groaning of the needy, I will now arise,' says the LORD. 'I will protect them from those who malign them'" (Ps. 12:5).[9] God will not forget nor ignore the pleas of the needy.[10]

This leads to what is perhaps of most significance for our topic, namely that throughout the Old Testament, the theme of *God's justice for children at risk reverberates.*[11] "God executes justice for the orphan and the widow and shows his love for the alien by giving him food and clothing" (Deut. 10:18 NASB). "A father to the fatherless and a judge for the widows is God in his holy habitation" (Ps. 68:5 NASB).

God Acts in History

Throughout history, God acts for the oppressed and against the oppressor (Deut. 6:20–25; 26:1–11). These actions were based upon God's love for his people and his faithfulness to his promise to Abraham to be a light to the nations; these are the relational components of God's justice. Because of this concrete action in history, the people of Israel began a new depth to their relationship with God because they *knew* him as the Lord of liberating

---

[8] See Mary J. Evans, *1 and 2 Samuel.*
[9] See also Psalm 34:18.
[10] See Psalm 9:12, 17–18; 10:12; Isaiah 41:17. See also Millard J. Erickson, *Christian Theology.*
[11] See Exodus 22:22; Deuteronomy 16:11, 14; 24:17-21; 26:12-13; 27:19; James 1:27.

justice (cf. Ex. 6:6–8). From this experience, the people became a "community of righteousness founded on the justice of God".[12]

The people of Israel experienced God's call to be a just and righteous people through the giving of the commandments (Ex. 22).[13] The Levitical and Deuteronomic codes (Deut. 10:12–19) gave detailed ways in which this guidance was to play out in Israelite society. And God judged his people when they failed to act with justice towards others. The prophets, notably Isaiah and Amos (Isa. 1:16–17; 58; Amos 4:1–3; 5), cried out against the injustices.

The Hope of Merciful Justice

Hope must fill the people of God for he promised the remnant the salvific mercy of God and a return from exile as they turned from rebellion and injustice (Isa. 54:21–25).

This hope is extended to all the nations in Psalm 33:5: "The LORD loves righteousness and justice; the earth is full of his unfailing love" (NIV). Wright suggests that the people of God saw what he did for them, since he is the only true God: "God must be like this for all. His justice must be universal."[14]

God Calls People to Be Just

God met his people's desire for governments but calls rulers to justice and the people to draw their rulers to justice and be a light to the nations. This may begin with a personal integrity of justice.

God loves us first; God is just; and our human response to this is to act with the love which breeds justice (John 15:12; Rom. 12:1; 1 John 4:19). Justice in this world is founded on God's redeeming grace and sustained by his forgiving grace. The people of God were called not because they were perfect, but because they could model to the nations the redemptive power and mercy of God.

Child Protection in the Law

The law was given so that the people of God would live differently to the surrounding nations and thus manifest God's glory. Does the Law have a perspective on children? It surely should if God is a God who cares about children and if they are so important in his redemption plan.

The Law is holistic. It has spiritual and practical dimensions as well as individual and collective. It regulates religious and social obligations. In fact, spirituality, according to the Law of the Israelites, is not a transcendental matter only. It has practical dimensions to be reflected in the day-to-day life experiences of the people as a community.

---

[12] Wright, 261.
[13] Wright, 262–3.
[14] Wright, 264–5.

Sabbath. Take, for example, the laws covering the various types of Sabbaths. The most common one is of course the Day of Sabbath, the day of rest (Ex. 23:12), more than the day of worship. By resting, the people of God will have time to reflect God's goodness through worship. Not only did the master rest, but the slaves, the strangers, and the animals are told to rest as well. These simple regulations speak so loudly in almost every part of the world where there are poor (mostly women and children), and where people do not have time to rest, because if they rest, they will not have anything to eat that day. To rest is a luxury for the poor. Sabbath is a cruel demand if it is required only from the perspective of worship, without any ministry to meet their daily needs. The elements of protection and ministry are added to make the Sabbath a blessing, and not an act of cruelty.15

Feast of Weeks. Detailed instruction of the Feast of Weeks (Lev 23:16-21) is interrupted in verse 22, with God declaring, "do not reap to the very edges of your field or gather the gleanings of your harvest. Leave them to the poor and the alien." The instructions on celebrating the Feast of Weeks includes instructions expressing social concern to the poor.

In the parallel verses (Lev. 19:9–10; Deut 24:19–22) children in special circumstances, along with other disadvantaged groups, aliens and widows, are mentioned as the ones entitled to gather what is left in the field during the harvest. Thus, what seems to have only religious significance, actually has a dimension of child protection. In modern language, this may be some kind of social safety net or social security, to protect children especially from physical neglect.

Feast of Tabernacles. Similar instruction is given for the celebration of the Feast of Tabernacles (Lev. 23:33ff; Num. 29) When we combine these two references and examine who should participate in the celebrations (Deut. 16:13–14), we learn that the most sacred religious festival, which is commonly known to have a vertical relationship (atonement), is actually very rich with horizontal relationships, especially to care for the poor, including poor children.

Jubilee. In Exodus 23:10–11 the social dimension of this spiritual law is made explicit: "For six years you are to sow your fields and harvest the crops, but during the seventh year let the land lie unplowed and unused. Then the poor among your people may get food from it . . ."

Tithes. The integration of social responsibilities in religious obligations can also be noted in special offerings, such as tithing (Deut. 14:22–28; 26:12–13).

God Hears the Orphan's Cry. Exodus 22:22–24 says, "Do not take advantage of a widow or an orphan. If you do and they cry out to me, I will certainly hear their cry. My anger will be aroused, and I will kill you with the sword."16 God warns his people not to abuse their children, even in the name of worship or religion: "You must not worship the Lord God in their way, because in worshiping their gods, they do all kinds of detestable things the Lord hates. They even burn their sons and daughters in the fire as sacrifices to their gods" (Deut. 12:31; cf. Deut. 18:9–13).

---

[15] See Luke 14:1-6.
[16] See Deuteronomy 24:17.

Society's Responsibility

We are compelled to integrate both the Old and New Testaments as we consider the biblical call for a community response to justice.

Caring for Others. Every third year, a tithe was to be given to the priest, the traveler, the orphan, and the widow (Deut. 14:28–29), and all debts were to be remitted every seventh year (Deut. 15:1–2; Lev. 25:1ff). God's people were to lend money to the poor (Deut. 15:7–8) without interest rates (Ex. 22:25), and the people of God were called to not be too efficient in their harvests (Ex. 23:10-11; Deut. 23:25; 24:19; Lev. 19:9–10; 23:22; Ruth 2:1–3).

In the Sermon on the Mount, Jesus calls people to be merciful, have compassion for those who suffer, demonstrate integrity, act as peacemakers, and not be afraid of persecution for acting in God's name (Matt. 5:7–11). Followers of Christ should live in this world as salt, to prevent moral decay and to be light to the world (Matt. 5:13–14), to bring immorality and injustice to the attention of the world through our willingness to display the fruits of redemption within our lives. He encourages them to strive for interpersonal reconciliation, to maintain stable, covenantal family relationships, to be true to promises, to love enemies (Matt. 3:8, 23–24, 33–37, 43–48), to give with integrity, and to ground service in prayer (Matt. 6:2–15).[17]

Helping Children in Need. The people of God were called to seek justice for orphans and other oppressed people (Isa. 1:17–18), to loosen bonds of wickedness, let the oppressed go free, break every yoke, divide bread, bring homeless to their homes, clothe the scantily clad (Isa. 58). "Give justice to the weak and the fatherless; maintain the rights of the afflicted and the destitute. Rescue the weak and the needy, deliver them from the hand of the wicked" (Ps. 82:3 NRSV). Repeatedly, Jesus took time from his ministry with adults to compassionately meet the needs of children (Luke 8:40–42; 49–56; 9:37–43).

Abhorring Injustice. The people of God were commanded not to do evil, enable unjust decisions, deprive the needy of justice, or rob people of their rights (Isa. 10:1–3). They were not to turn away the poor from just governance (Amos 5:12). The self–indulgent women were ridiculed as "Cows of Bashan" for oppressing the poor and crushing the needy by their lifestyle (reclining on beds of ivory and sprawling on couches while eating their fill without regard for anyone else) (Amos 4;1; 6:4–7). People were warned against the unjust behaviors of showing anger, engaging in the slave trade and war, rejecting God's laws, and causing the righteous to fall (Amos 1–3).

Jesus called the people to turn away from anger in their hearts to avoid sexual temptation, to refrain from retaliation and self–aggrandizing fasting (Matt. 5:16–18, 21–22, 27–30, 38–42). He taught about the evils of wealth, calling the people to keep their hearts focused on God, not on worldly riches (Matt. 6:19–23). The people of God were warned against a judgmental attitude because that role belongs to God alone (Matt. 7:1–6).

The book of James, warns against showing impartiality to the wealthy of this world, conveying an image that the righteous poor are superior to the ungodly rich:[18] "Pure and

---

[17] Douglas Moo, *The Epistle to the Romans*, 106.
[18] See Erickson, *Christian Theology*.

undefiled religion in the sight of our God and Father is this: to visit orphans and widows in their distress and to keep oneself unstained by the world" (James 1:27 NASB).

Judgment

In the Old Testament, judgment is not simply punishing the wicked, but coming to the rescue of the needy. Judgment will occur (Isa. 10:3 NASB; cf. Jer. 17:11; Hab. 2:9). "The unrighteous man must forsake his ways or perish; a loving God cannot force obedience."[19]

Our courts may be fair or scandalous, but we have a responsibility to be salt and light and certainly to sharpen our Christian sisters and brothers. At our best, we should strive for this world's judicial system to emulate God's laws and God's justice as we discussed earlier. We must also be mindful that eternal judgment lies in the hands of Christ.[20]

In Matthew 25, we read of Jesus' view of social justice through compassion. The second half of the passage describes the judgment to the unjust:

> *Then he will also say to those on his left, 'Depart from me, accursed ones, into the eternal fire which has been prepared for the devil and his angels; for I was hungry, and you gave me nothing to eat; I was thirsty and you gave me nothing to drink; I was a stranger and you did not invite me in; naked and you did not clothe me; sick and you did not visit me.' Then they themselves also will answer, 'Lord, when did we see you hungry, or thirsty, or a stranger, or naked, or sick, or in prison, and did not take care of you?' Then he will answer them, 'Truly I say to you, to the extent that you did not do it to one of the least of these, you did not do it to me.' These will go away into eternal punishment, but the righteous into eternal life (Matt. 25:41–46).*

While God calls the community to be just, specific tasks relate to the governments and their roles, and to the role of the people in creating just rule.

God Calls Governments to Be Just

The people of God were called to hate evil and love good by establishing justice in the government (at the gates) and to grieve over injustice (Amos 4:10–11; 5:15). As the population grew, Moses was brought to realize that he needed assistance from others in helping settle disputes among the people, always striving to judge as God would direct (Deut. 1:10–18; 16:18–20). Judges were called to lead, to inspire, and to administer justice (1 Sam. 7:15–17; Judg. 4:5).

---

[19] J. N. Schofield, "'Righteousness' in the Old Testament," in *Bible Translator* 16 (3):114.
[20] See Gretchen Gaebelein Hull, "God's Call to Social Justice." See also J.B. Payne, "Justice."

An Ideal World in the Prophets

"The Lord loves justice" (Isa. 61:8). In Isaiah 28:17, he says, "I will make justice the measuring line and righteousness the plumb line." Jeremiah testifies the same thing: "I am the Lord, who exercises kindness, justice and righteousness on earth, for in these I delight" (Jer. 9:24). Isaiah urges the people of Israel to "learn to do what is right! Seek justice, encourage the oppressed. Defend the cause of the fatherless, plead the case of widows" (Isa. 1:17). His vision is a Kingdom of justice and righteousness (Isa. 38:1) where the king will reign in righteousness and rulers will rule in justice. Those who are against God and practice anything contrary to his justice and righteousness will be in trouble. Especially to those who oppress disadvantaged children, the prophet says, "Woe to those who make unjust laws and to those who issue oppressive decrees, to deprive the poor of their rights and rob my oppressed people of justice, making widows their prey and robbing the fatherless" (Isa. 10:1–2).

The prophets warn the people of Israel of their sins. If the people of Israel listen to their message and obey by living in righteousness and justice, God's blessing will be upon them. They and their children will live in prosperity. If they fail to live according to God's commandments, however, their children will reap the consequences of their ungodliness. This is the principle: Children will suffer the consequences of the sins of their parents. It is true at individual and family levels, as well as national and international levels.

In political conflicts that lead to physical conflicts and violence, it is the children who pay the highest costs, in the form of trauma, poor health, lack of educational opportunities, interrupted childhood, and other negative consequences. When the economic system of a country collapses, the most vulnerable group in that society are children. When a couple can no longer get along well and see a divorce as the solution to their situation, the children are those who bear the cost. Children suffer the most when something has gone wrong in society.

In this light we need to see the ministry of the prophets. Some prophets understood this truth more clearly than others, though direct references to children's issues are not common.

On a number of occasions, Lamentations mentions how greatly the children suffer because of the sins of their nation (Lam. 2:11–12; 4:4, 10). These verses are not biblical superlatives alone. They are the reality of day to day life in many developing countries and among families and communities in crisis. There are many untold stories of young girls being sold into prostitution by their very own parents, or young boys ending up in bonded labor because their parents sell them, to stop the moneylenders from taking away their meager possessions such as a goat, a piece of land, or a humble shelter. Millions more children are "sacrificed" by evil systems in places all over the world that cause them to live in different forms of bondage. The president of Compassion International once said, "Child sacrifice has been taboo in the major world religions for over 3000 years but it goes on every day. We are practicing worldwide sacrifice of

> "Our most vulnerable citizens, children in poverty, have become the most disposable commodity."
>
> —Wesley Stafford

children on all fronts. Our most vulnerable citizens, children in poverty, have become the most disposable commodity."[21]

Government and People

Influence of Cultures. People are influenced by observable cultures around them. One day, the people of Israel decided they needed a king. They were given a national responsibility, but they wanted to abdicate to a royal responsibility which was the tradition of nearby cultures.[22] They chose to adopt the neighboring cultural patterns instead of humbly seeking God's will.[23]

God warned the people through Samuel, saying that while leaders are chosen by God, they will demand taxes and service, provisions and military from the people (1 Sam. 8:1–22). Nevertheless, "God starts from where people are and provides choices that could lead them forward in his plans."[24]

We must be mindful that governments are appointed by God (Rom. 12:1–6). If the people of God "fear the LORD and serve him, and listen to his voice and do not rebel against the command of the LORD, then both you and also the king who reigns over you will follow the LORD your God. If you will not listen to the voice of the LORD but rebel against the command of the LORD, then the hand of the LORD will be against you, as it was against your fathers" (1 Sam. 12:14–15 NASB).

Leadership: Godly or Evil? Solomon was noted for his kingly wisdom (1 Kgs. 3:16–28) because his prayer to God was not for riches but for an understanding servant's heart to judge the people using godly discernment between good and evil. His humble supplication was granted by God (1 Kgs. 3:6–14). He was made king "to maintain justice and righteousness" (1 Kgs. 10:9). Kings were called to "Do what is just and right" (Jer. 22:3). They were to champion the cause of the least powerful: "Speak up for those who cannot speak for themselves, for the rights of all who are destitute. Speak up and judge fairly; defend the rights of the poor and needy" (Prov. 31:8–9).

However, none of the initial kings in the Old Testament reflected purity in God's justice. Saul, David and Solomon each fell to self–interest as did so many beyond them. Isaiah condemned the authorities of Jerusalem for the suffering, violence, robbery, corruption, and exploitation that took place (Isa. 1:21–23; 10:1–2).[25]

Josiah is recognized as one of the greatest kings because he restored the law of God in society by sharing it with all the people, great and small and making a covenant with God to walk in God's ways (2 Kgs. 23:1–3). He did what was right and just by defending the poor and needy (Jer. 22:15–16).[26]

Structures: Liberating or Oppressive? Power structures may be necessary in societies with large populations, but how they function in society determines whether they

---

[21] Wesley Stafford, "Making a Difference Together for Children in the 21st Century."
[22] See Joyce Norman, "Long Live the King."
[23] Evans, 10, 42.
[24] Evans, 14.
[25] Wright, 273.
[26] Wright, 274.

are acceptable to God, whether they liberate or oppress society. Power structures used in the service of God may be liberating, but those used for personal gain work against God.[27]

Nations are the embodiment of power structures, especially in economically disadvantaged nations and developing countries that find themselves obliged to conform to the power structures of the world's most powerful nations. Injustice is the failure to meet God's just guidance, or the putting of one's personal gain over the needs or common good of the community.[28] "Egoistic human pursuits blind reason."[29]

Hope of Heavenly Justice

The prophets also envisioned the people of the world in which God wants them to live.

Future Vision

Isaiah's vision of a new heaven and a new earth does not speak of spiritual realities alone, but of day-to-day life, and living conditions where there is justice, prosperity, and blessedness (Isa. 65:17–25). And children are included in that vision: "Never again will there be in it an infant that lives but a few days . . . They will not toil in vain or bear children doomed to misfortune, for they will be a people blessed by the LORD" (Isa. 65:20, 23).[30]

Zechariah also speaks of the new Jerusalem: "The city streets will be filled with boys and girls playing there" (Zech. 8:5). Play is the best way for children to develop many physical, emotional, and social skills. However, this vision is the complete opposite of the current reality in the world's major cities, where millions of children are forced to struggle for their survival while being exploited and oppressed. Today's streets are a place of danger, and children are often there to earn their living.

Finally Malachi speaks of restored relationships between parents and children. At the end of time, God will send his prophet who will "turn the hearts of the fathers to their children, and the heart of the children to their fathers" (Mal. 4:6). The prophet speaks of restoration of family life at a personal level.

This reconciliation continues from the personal level to the national, international, and even the cosmic level, where there will be no more enmity, violence, or threats against children. Children are an essential part of the vision of the prophets.

Jesus: God Incarnate

Jesus' servanthood was prophesied in Isaiah 40–55. Jesus was born into poverty (Luke 2:24). He came to preach the gospel to the poor, the captive, the blind, and the oppressed (Luke 4:18), and he spoke woe to those who felt rich in spirit and in this world for they will experience spiritual hunger, mourning, and weeping (Luke 6:20–26). He came to speak

---

[27] See Gnana Robinson, *1&2 Samuel: Let Us Be Like the Nations.*
[28] Robinson, 7–9, 53.
[29] Robinson, 54.
[30] See also Isaiah 11:6-8.

to the people of Israel who had forgotten, ignored, or turned away from God's ways, from God's sense of love and justice.

Jesus spoke of the new covenant, another concept of righteous mercy or social justice during the Sermon on the Mount. Jesus articulates an "inaugurated eschatology"—his Kingdom is inaugurated with Christ's embodiment on earth. However, this new world view will never be fully realized until Christ's return. These principles guide how the people of God should permeate society with these ideals in a persuasive rather than coercive fashion. The thesis statement is this:[31] "Do not think I came to abolish the Law or the Prophets; I did not come to abolish but to fulfill . . . Whoever then annuls one of the least of these commandments, and teaches others to do the same, shall be called least in the Kingdom of Heaven; but whoever teaches them and keeps them shall be called great in the Kingdom of heaven" (Matt. 5:17–20 NASB).

Jesus used the quotation from Isaiah to announce justice in his humble and compassionate ministry. Weaving compassion (Matt. 12:20) and "a correct understanding of the Torah—that God desires mercy and not sacrifice—offers freedom in the form of his lighter yoke to those who are oppressed and downtrodden."[32] Contrasting Jesus' healing action with the Pharisees' negative reaction for doing so on the Sabbath (Matt. 12:13–14) suggests that their obsession towards religious rules is unjust.[33]

Discipleship and Social Justice

Clearly, Jesus "explicitly connected discipleship with concern for social justice (Luke 6:27–36) and made it clear that compassion for the needy is one measure by which he will recognize his followers (Matt. 25:31–46)."[34] "For I was hungry and you gave me something to eat . . . Truly I say to you, to the extent that you did it to one of these brothers of mine, even the least of them, you did it to me" (NASB). Jesus, the incarnation of God's justice, draws us both to act in this world and to eagerly await the consummation, when Jesus will bring justice victoriously.[35]

Personal Integrity

While we tend to view Hebrew culture as a collectivist society with a community definition of the people of God and a more individualist world view among Greek thinkers, there are references in both testaments to individual integrity.

In Samuel's retirement, though he failed as a father, he asked the people if he had acted with integrity as a judge. They responded in unison, "You have not cheated us or oppressed us" (1 Sam. 12:4).

---

[31] Blomberg, 95.
[32] Beaton, 22.
[33] Beaton, 20–21.
[34] See Hull.
[35] Beaton, 22–23.

Jeremiah cries that three of the best individually oriented gifts of God (wisdom, strength, and wealth) are nothing in comparison to God's delight in kindness, justice and righteousness (Jer. 9:23-24).[36]

The psalmist teaches that the one (singular) who may dwell in God's sanctuary is the one who does what is just (Ps. 15:1–2). Worship from individuals who trampled on or oppressed through injustice was not only unacceptable, it was an abomination to God (Amos 5:21–24; Isa. 1:10–17; Jer. 7:1–11).[37]

Blomberg suggests the pericope in Matthew 25 refers initially to all people, but then Matthew makes the point (by substituting a personal pronoun in the Greek) that individuals and not just nations will be affected.[38] The singular pronoun makes clear that the acts of compassion were also to be individual acts. In Matthew's account of the Sermon on the Mount, individuals are clearly called to spiritual transformation, justice, and integrity. Throughout the New Testament we are challenged to spiritually transform ourselves into the merciful, just, and loving image of the incarnate Christ.

"Relational Love Justice"

In the New Testament, Romans presents insights for government and society. Paul sets up the basis of a just community by describing what Wright refers to as *"relational love justice."*[39]

Paul focuses on interpersonal relationships among Christians and between Christians and non–believers. Genuine love is the underlying motif of this section: humility, a common mindset, love and care for fellow Christians, and love towards enemies characterize the biblical concept of love. In addition, hope, endurance, and prayer are the tools of the believer (Rom. 12:9–21).[40]

Believers are to embody this love and concern for one another in the community (*koinonia*), to do what is good to all people including their enemies, and to do all this with a mindset that encompasses a Christian worldview, not being overcome by evil, but overcoming evil with good by being a peacemaker (Rom. 12:13–21). Christians are not to be vengeful but to give place to God's wrath.[41]

Paul then turns to the interrelationship of Christians and government in Romans 13. God has established authorities in the world and they have roles to play even after Jesus' inauguration of the new reign of God. Paul's theology of the Christian's role in the world becomes evident in Romans 13. Christians are to advocate for justice and live lives of integrity. They are to refrain from taking judgment into their own hands, recognizing that God is the purveyor of judgment.[42]

---

[36] Wright, 267.
[37] Wright, 267.
[38] Blomberg, 376.
[39] Wright, 266.
[40] Moo, 785.
[41] Wright, 786.
[42] Moo, 791–793.

Submit. Christians are to submit to the governing authorities because rulers live out God's purposes. They are to render to authority what is due them: taxes, customs, fear, and honor (Rom. 13:7).

Do What is Good. The people under the reign of God are to have no fear of the authorities if they do what is good, if they are people of integrity fighting for justice. Only if we do what is right and just, meeting the requirements of citizenship in our countries, will we have an opportunity to speak wisdom to ruling authorities, the very servants of God (Rom. 13:3–14).

Discern Injustice. In the Sermon on the Mount, the people are warned to be prepared to walk through the narrow gate or in the Greek concept, to experience trouble or difficulty instead of prosperity. He warns them to discern a lack of integrity in others and use Jesus' principles as a firm foundation for all of their work (Matt. 7:13–27).

> Only if we do what is right and just, meeting the requirements of citizenship in our countries, will we have an opportunity to speak wisdom to ruling authorities, the very servants of God.

Speak Against Injustice. Interestingly, Paul did not use the verb "obey" in relation to authorities. This may leave space for civil disobedience, such as Peter and John demonstrated when they responded to the Jewish leaders' demand that they stop teaching about Jesus: "We must obey God rather than people" (Acts 5:29).[43]

In the Old Testament, the prophets were called to speak out against injustice (cf. Ez. 3:18–19), and the people of God were exhorted to cry out to God for deliverance (Lam. 2:18–19 NASB).

We can, as God does, "start from where people are and provide choices that could lead them forward in God's plans."[44] Ultimately, "Our service is to reform and recreate culture as we seek new ways of faithful penultimate living with our neighbors."[45]

Until God Comes

The Sermon on the Mount closes with a call to remember God's love and that he will give generously to meet our needs (Matt. 7:7–11). Paul concludes the section in Romans 13 about the relationship of Christians to society by instilling hope, "for salvation is nearer than we believed. The night is almost gone and the day is near.

---

[43] Moo, 797, 806.
[44] Evans, 42.
[45] Charles C. West, "Culture, Power and Ideology in Third World Theologies," *Missiology: An International Review* 12, no. 4 (1984).

> "Why is it a matter of cosmic rejoicing that God is coming? Because when God comes, things will be put right."
> —Christopher J. Wright

Therefore, let us lay aside the deeds of darkness and put on the armor of light . . . Put on the Lord Jesus Christ" (Rom. 13:11–14 NASB).

Wright summarizes for us, "Why is it a matter of cosmic rejoicing that God is coming? Because when God comes, things will be put right . . . God comes to judge . . . and finally to establish justice, right relationships between God and people, among people and between people and the created order."[46]

Conclusion

One time when I faced the injustices to children in this world, I was overwhelmed with sadness and cried out to God, "Why?" I sensed two clear responses: First, it breaks the heart of God to see children suffer. Let me repeat that again to indicate the depth of God's pain: it breaks God's heart. However, the pain of this world must be so overpowered by the joy and peace of eternal life that it is almost insignificant. That is what gives us hope and a will to carry on in our work with children.

But for those suffering today, we cannot be 'blinded' by the light of heaven. Instead, we must be diligent in our work to cry out against injustice and seek as churches and individuals to rectify the injustices that others face. In 1975, Dr. Bruce Birch responded to the world hunger crisis with these words about the church which still resonate today:

> *What is demanded is not less than a renewed understanding of the church's biblical and theological resources so that we might be in the vanguard of the movement to reorder values and priorities in a suffering world. As we respond to the crisis, we must also challenge the biblical and theological assumptions which have allowed the church to participate uncritically in structures that contribute to the root causes of global hunger and poverty.*[47]

As for individuals, when I was doing some brief work in Nicaragua, I met a Costa Rican evangelical pastor who shared this story with me: One night, he awoke in the early hours of the morning. He knelt to speak with God. He felt closer to God than ever before. With boldness, he prayed, "God, I feel so close to you, could you possibly give me a hug?" He felt no response. He prayed again. "God, I feel so close to you, is it asking too much to touch your feet?" God responded: He gave the pastor the image of a Nicaraguan child's face. God spoke, "If you touch the feet of this Nicaraguan child, you touch my feet. If you hug this Nicaraguan child, you will hug me."[48]

---

[46] Wright, 278.
[47] Bruce C. Birch, "Hunger, Poverty and Biblical Religion," *The Christian Century* 11, no. 5 (1975): 593–599.
[48] Name withheld for protection. Personal conversation. June, 2001. Managua, Nicaragua.

CRITICAL ISSUES

SOCIETY HAS A GOD-GIVEN RESPONSIBILITY FOR THE WELL-BEING OF CHILDREN AND FAMILIES

By Ravi Jayakaran with Paul Stockley

> *She came through the shadows in the rain pushing a small cart, her face barely visible in the light of the street lamp. The push cart was full of things probably scrounged from rubbish bins. Perched on top of it, two little girls clung to torn umbrellas, trying desperately to protect themselves from the rain.*
>
> *Suddenly I realized what had caught my attention: it was the expression on the woman's face—it mirrored all at once the pain and determination of 'this is one more task that I have to do and I'll get it done!' As I watched, dry, from the comfort of my car, thoughts raced through my mind. Why did she have to go out on a rainy night like this? Worse still, why did she have to bring her two small children with her? Was she so bereft of any support or without access to even one person whom she could trust and leave her children behind with?*
>
> *What was wrong with society? Why had it failed this woman so badly that she was left to completely fend for herself and her children all alone? How long would she be able to keep them safe, nourished, and protected? And who would bring society to account for failing and not even bothering to apologize or even care for her and others like her?*

Society Certainly Has Failed to Fulfill God's Sacred Responsibility to Take Care of the Well-Being of Children and Families

Families who are desperately poor struggle daily to just survive, often taking drastic steps when survival becomes difficult. The parents may turn to prostitution to supplement income or even sell off their own children into prostitution. This is a serious issue in most of the countries that I am familiar with in Asia and Africa.

During one of my recent government–supported training programs in Thailand for government officials from over 20 countries, I gave an assignment to each country group to prepare Physical Quality of Life Indicators and details illustrating access to basic social care services.

When the figures were made available, it was obvious that those who needed the greatest care had the least access to it. We studied why this was happening, and realized that the ones who decided the rules of engagement were the ones who were most powerful, and always framed things in their own favor.[1]

---

[1] See Appendix 1 for statistical data on serious deprivations in access to basic services.

Globally, this same injustice is propagated. While all members of marginalized families suffer, children bear the brunt of this brutal neglect. Society has a God–given responsibility for ensuring the well-being of children and families at all levels in the community, so that all have equal access to shelter, institutions of healthcare, social services, safe drinking water, information, and safety. Society for its part has badly failed in this task.

What Children Need

What is God's mandate concerning children? He expects families to provide what is necessary, and for society at large to enable families to do so. God's first expectation is that we *provide* what children need for their care and nurture (Prov. 22:6). We must ensure that children have all that is theirs by way of their rights as human beings and also ensure that they are given adequate guidance by 'training them in the way in which they should go.'

God's second requirement is that we *include* children in our planning for the future (Matt. 19:13-15; Mark 10:13-16). This especially means ensuring their full participation in matters related to their own future because 'they are also the future in the present,' inheriting tomorrow the world we leave behind today.

The final expectation that God has is for us to *protect* children, ensuring they are kept safe as they interface with the adult world. Jesus' warning to those who might cause children to stumble in sin comes with one of the sternest warnings in scripture—that someone guilty of such an offence is better off dead![2] Jesus then elaborates on this thought, referring to the *deeds, direction,* and *desires* of society to ensure they will not cause children to stumble.

During discussions on holistic development and child participation at a community workshop,[3] I learned of the 'Deprivation–Exclusion–Vulnerability' syndrome that adversely affects children. These three facets reflect a situation in which children are subject to the exact opposite of society's responsibility toward them, as understood from Jesus' teaching—namely, that we should 'Provide–Include–Protect.' Since that time, I have expanded on this theme, and developed and field-tested a participatory tool called the 'DEV Index.' The 'DEV Index' is designed to measure the extent to which a community has failed to fulfill its God–given responsibility toward children. The index uses the 'Ten Seed Technique'[4] in which community members place seeds on a chart to indicate needs and priorities, and participatory needs assessment is the first step towards empowerment for action. The DEV Index can be used at different

DEV: Deprivation, Exclusion, Vulnerability
PIP: Provision, Inclusion, Protection

---

[2] Mark 9:42-50.
[3] "Christian Community Development Workshop and Conference" (Mosbach, Germany, March 11-15, 2005). See http://www.ccd-network.net.
[4] Ravi Jayakaran, "The Ten Seed Technique," http://www.worldvision.org.au/resources/files/Ten-Seed.pdf (accessed July 26, 2006).

levels: village, district, province, and nation. The result helps to classify how 'safe' or 'at risk' a community is.

Taking an example from Cambodia, the DEV Index was carried out with members of Thanoung Village (see Figure 1 in Appendix 3). Out of a maximum total score of 30, this particular village has a score of 16 for safety and 5 for risk. The reasons identified for risk (deprivation, exclusion, and vulnerability) were:

- family poverty, needing children to supplement family income
- widowed parents depending on children's work for financial support
- inability of parents to pay school fees
- children working in unsafe environments, such as garment factories or the construction industry
- children working a long distance from home, such as in Phnom Penh
- children being sent abroad to Thailand for work

It is easy to see and empathize with the desperate situation of families that live under such pressures, and understand why they take desperate steps when things become extremely difficult for them. However, this represents the situation of the poor in rural areas, whose circumstances, though terrible, are much better than those of the urban poor.

If we compare a profile of the status of street children from Bangalore city in India, we find a rating of 30 for risk. The salient points of the analysis identify the following:

- no access to health care, social services, or schooling for these children
- almost no care provided to them by the community
- mostly deprived of normal childhood experiences
- exposure to inherent dangers of street life

On the positive side were two mitigating factors:

- some are able to retain their sense of joy
- some learn to cope with their vulnerability to a limited extent

The status of street children is quite similar in many cities around the world. Yet society at large often turns a blind eye when it comes to taking action to protect them.

Economics of Marginalization

The economic disparity between rich and poor nations continues to grow, as does the gap between the rich and the poor within nations. Even in nations where prosperity is newly coming, the poor continue to struggle and are left to fend for themselves. Meanwhile, the rich and powerful continue to influence the 'operating principles' of society in their own favor. The poor are in desperate need of advocates who will take up their cause and enable their plea for help to be heard in the corridors of power.

I once heard a Kenyan named Dote Hallalke give a powerful definition for empowerment. "Empowerment is when the voice of the poor is heard outside of their boundaries." The irony is that the longer the poor continue to have their voice ignored or not 'loud enough' to be heard, their problems will continue to persist. They will continue to be pushed to the edge of despair where they will be forced to take desperate measures which once taken, are almost impossible to reverse.

> "Empowerment is when the voice of the poor is heard outside of their boundaries."
>
> —Dote Hallalke

What is the Way Out?

Each community must identify the area within which it can have an influence, and then aim to put a 'PIP Action Plan' in place. The PIP (Provide–Include–Protect) Action Plan involves first identifying communities that are at risk, then within the community identifying the most marginalized families. Through interactive discussions with the community focus group, the appropriate interventions are discussed and planned for ensuring that provision, inclusion and protection is given to every child. Efforts must then be made to support these families, and facilitate the plan. This will enable the creation of the opposite of the DEV syndrome, which would be a *safe and nurturing refuge for children.*

Setting Priorities

Taking a particular community in San Jose, Philippines as an example, we profiled all the households using a Rapid Food Security Assessment (RFSA) chart with the Ten Seed Technique (see Figure 3 in Appendix 3).

Households within the community were categorized into one of four groups according to their economic status: the wealthy and middle income (both living above the poverty line), the poor (below the poverty line), and the very poor (below the charity line).

The following distinctions were identified:

- the first group had an income–expenditure ratio of 7:3, indicating a considerable surplus. These are the wealthiest 20 percent.

- in the second RFSA level, the ratio changed to 6:4, still a surplus of income. 20 percent of households were in this category.

- at the third RFSA level, the ratio was 4:6, and the surplus became shortage. Again, 20 percent are in this category.

- the fourth group had the worst ratio of 2:8. Some 40 percent of households were in this category.

- in both the third and fourth groups, the deficit between income and expenditure leads to progressive debt.

While there may be variations in the actual ratios, this broad pattern is typical of many developing economies.

In order to bring about improvements in the situation of the community, external development efforts aim at increasing income and reducing expenditure. Increasing income is much easier to do, and, as a means to development, it is also validated as being in conformation to sound economic theory. Many emerging economies in Asia in recent years are benefiting from the results of this approach. They have freed up their economies and encouraged the entrepreneurial populace to increase their economic activities.

Increasing income essentially helps RFSA groups 1 and 2. However, there is not the same effort to reduce the expenditure burden made on poor households, either because it is not the priority of the rich decision-makers or because, globally, all forms of 'subsidy' and 'state sponsored social support' are looked down upon and discouraged. One only has to look again at the figures to see that efforts to reduce expenditure (on food, healthcare, schooling, and safe drinking water) benefits most the RFSA groups 3 and 4. This requires strong advocacy on behalf of the poor, which will mobilize action even though it is not what decision-makers would choose to do.

The Role of the Church in Society

Churches exist within society and have a vital role to play. Jesus' command to his followers was that they should be like salt and light in society.[5]

If society has failed in its task, then so has the Church in not speaking out and taking action to correct the situation. It often appears that the church is more concerned about debating what true evangelism is, and how to alienate and differentiate it from holistic development. This is a serious mistake.

---

[5] Matthew 5:13-16.

Are the practical actions mentioned above only catering to the physical needs of the community? No, the evidence is that spiritual well-being is linked to practical action. On a recent trip to Cambodia, for example, the greatest impact in response to the gospel was in places where the project responded with the greatest love and concern for the most marginalized sections of the community. The success of the organization, I believe, was in ensuring that they made every effort to help the poorest of the poor. This is an important lesson for the Church to learn.

> Efforts to reduce expenditure (on food, health care, schooling, and safe drinking water) require strong advocacy on behalf of the poor, which will mobilize action even though it is not what decision-makers will choose to do.

Some Important Steps that the Church Can Take to Encourage Society to Fulfill its God–Given Responsibility for the Well–Being of Children and Families

1) *Become conscious of its mandate* to collaborate with institutions for healthcare, shelter, access to social services, safe drinking water, information, and safety to ensure that all children and families (especially the poor and very poor) have proper access to them. (These have been in the past, the areas in which the Church has had its greatest impact—why has it stepped back from doing this in recent years?)

2) *Spread this awareness* to all its members and mobilize them to advocate for access on behalf of the poor.

3) *Identify places that are high risk* areas where children are deprived, excluded or vulnerable using the DEV Index, and through interaction with those communities, empower them to provide, include, and protect (PIP) every child.

4) *Play the role of being salt and light* in society to influence the people in authority to make the necessary changes on behalf of the poor and very poor.

5) *Support interventions* wherever possible, by working with local churches and organizations who are doing something about the issue.

6) *Act soon before it is too late.* The church can no longer afford to say, "It is not our responsibility."

PRACTITIONER'S RESPONSE

CARING IN SOCIETY

By Glenn Miles

"Society..."

Firstly, who do we mean by 'society'?

The Family

The smallest unit of society is the family, so the unit with the most 'responsibility' is the family. But families in every society are breaking down. Many families are far more complicated than the simple two parent/two child nuclear family of northern countries, or even the wider extended family of the south all living together in one household. Even the most complicated family structure can still be a functioning family, from grandparent-headed households to child-headed households and they must feel accepted and loved, so that they themselves can effectively function and then reach out to others.[1]

We have sometimes exported a theology from the west to children's ministries in developing countries where physical, emotional, and spiritual care are compartmentalized. Many children in all of our societies are at risk and not only of spiritual neglect. 'Well-being' can mean physical, emotional, and socio-economic wholeness, as well as spiritual wholeness.[2]

Church Sunday Schools for children are often seen as being responsible for children's spiritual education and nurturing, but it is the primary caregivers' responsibility to spiritually nurture children and bring them to the Lord. We must be careful not to disempower Christian parents and caregivers by taking over this important role. Rather, we must provide them with the resources they need. In the same way, we need to model empowerment in our organizations so that parents and other caregivers in turn do not disempower their own children as they grow into adulthood.

This also means that whilst we may need to fill the gap as advocates for children, it is the caregivers who must be the primary advocates for their own children, and we must facilitate them in this role.

Who are Children's Caregivers in Society?

Outside of the family, who are children's caregivers in society? The community in which the child lives plays an important role, but the UN Convention on the Rights of the

---

[1] For more on this topic, see the third affirmation in this volume.
[2] See also the article by Meredith Long in this volume.

Child reminds us that governments also have responsibilities, especially where there is negligence and abuse. What about the role of the United Nation bodies, NGOs, and the church itself? Following are a few comments about the way that we sometimes look at and interface with those outside of the church.

Sometimes we can take on the characteristics of different kinds of children.

Like a child who doesn't want to play with others, we sometimes forget that God uses other organizations. Though many Christians have impacted child rights issues globally, God has also used people of no faith and of other faiths. Sometimes I wonder if it is because the Church itself has not responded when it should have done so. Let's not turn our backs on opportunities where we can speak up on behalf of the vulnerable.[3]

Like an insecure child, we sometimes feel that we are too small. One very experienced Christian orphanage I visited said they only had the energy to do what they were doing and that was enough. In fact, I think they were actually acting as a role model for others and *were* being salt and light in the wider community. However, I was saddened that their lack of self-esteem and vision seemed to be limiting what more they could have been doing simply because they were not looking beyond their boundaries.

Like a child who is shy, we sometimes feel intimidated by the United Nations officials and ambassadors and the 'successful' organizations that seem so articulate. We must remember, however, that God has put each of us into the positions we are in. As faith-based organizations who are known for our long-term commitment to children and who therefore understand their context well,[4] we can be welcomed for what we offer in terms of understanding and willingness to go and be in places others may be reluctant to go. As Dr. Ravi says, the Church must "mobilize [its members] to advocate for access on behalf of the poor, when society fails."[5]

Like a child who is a 'show off,' we sometimes give the impression that we are the only ones actually doing something, and so waste many opportunities and much emotional energy. The passage in Mark 9:49-50 says, 'have salt in yourselves and be at peace with each other.' We don't have to agree with everything our brother says or does, but we must seek peace.

We are sometimes like a self-absorbed child, so heavily influenced by our own culture that we absorb the way our society and culture treat children. For example, we can overemphasize what the Bible says about children's responsibilities towards adults and underemphasize what the Bible says about adults' responsibilities towards children. In contrast, we need to take time to look for a biblical model and seek to apply it in our response as well as the Church's response.

---

[3] See the article by Ravi Jayakaran in this volume.
[4] This is based on a statement made by M. Kul C. Gautam, Deputy Executive Director of the United Nations Children's Fund (UNICEF) at the Cutting Edge IV Conference, October 15, 2002. For more information, see www.viva.org.
[5] See the article by Ravi Jayakaran in this volume; see also www.viva.org/en/articles/gods_heart/facilitation_guidelines.pdf.

" . . . Has a God-Given Responsibility . . . "

Responsibility

Responsibility is a big word. As parents and caregivers, we have a responsibility to bring up our children according to biblical instruction. In our ministries, we have a responsibility to bring justice and restoration to children living in risky environments. However, there may be several right choices. We should never put ourselves in a position where we feel paralyzed because we are afraid to make a choice or to take the next step. Perhaps, if we saw our role as being a tiny part of the body of Christ, we would feel less daunted. If we all shine our bit of light and add our tiny bit of flavor to the world, think what we could do together as the body of Christ!

> Perhaps, if we saw our role as being a tiny part of the body of Christ, we would feel less daunted.

Of course, there is a codicil here for those of us who tend to overwork. Perhaps the hardest lesson for us is learning what *not* to do.

Respecting Children's Opinions and Ability to Participate

Society, parents, and caregivers are responsible for the well-being of children, but as the child's age increases, so does their responsibility. Parents cannot completely relinquish responsibility for their children, but they must gradually let children make their own decisions from an early age, well before they leave home.

Similarly, in children's ministry, we are increasingly aware that children need to be involved in decisions that concern them. We are starting to consider how we can facilitate active participation and partnership with children and are often humbled by their insightful understandings.

Protection versus Participation

Protection of children continues to be of great importance, especially where children cannot speak up for themselves. Where possible, we can encourage and empower children and their communities. In Cambodia, Tearfund UK has empowered children to speak up for themselves through our research conducted on children's own perceptions of violence and abuse.[6]

Also in Cambodia, Tearfund helped bring together a coalition of Christian agencies to develop a karaoke video about protecting children from violence as a 12-week training program for children which can be used by schools, communities, and NGOs. Children were actively involved in developing the materials. There were insights that would not have been possible had only adults sat around discussing what children needed to know! It makes sense, doesn't it? But how often do we do it?

---

[6] Glenn Miles and Sun Varin, "Stop Violence Against Us!" www.kone-kmeng.org (accessed August 25, 2006).

Some of us may feel as if protection and participation cannot be done at the same time. But children often understand their context very well and are both willing and able to contribute to policy and program development, and to share in discussions about how they can be protected from harm.[7]

" . . . For the Well-Being of Children and Families."

What exactly do we mean by the *well-being* of children and families? As Dr. Ravi has said, "the evidence is that spiritual well-being is linked to practical action,"[8] and perhaps even the resilience we hope they inherit in the faith.

Three current trends of well-being focus on reducing poverty, addressing vulnerability, and promoting personal fulfillment and happiness.

Poverty Reduction

Is poverty reduction (this decade's most favored approach) *the* answer? Tearfund UK and many others have put much effort into collaborating on the 'Drop the Debt' campaign to lobby governments with gratifying results.[9] We know that poverty in itself is as a result (and a cause) of terrible injustices, but we must be careful not to see the relief of poverty as the *one and only answer*. Even in the wealthiest nations of the world, children are being brutalized and, sadly, sometimes in the name of Christ, such as some of the 'Christian' juvenile 'boot camps' in America where excessive brutality has been reported.[10] Reduction of poverty alone will not stop children from being violated.

> Reduction of poverty alone will not stop children from being violated.

Ascertaining Vulnerability

Ascertaining and addressing vulnerability of children and/or their communities may also be an important tool, but we must be careful not to spend all our energies in assessing the problems. In presenting our research on violence against children in Cambodia to key stakeholders at the UN Study on Children & Violence regional forum in Bangkok in June 2005,[11] we realized that the responses from the Cambodian Government about our results revealed more about their concern for feeling misrepresented than the fact that many children were being abused and violated. In any case, in policy terms, does it matter whether 20 or 50 percent of children are being abused in a certain way? Whilst there is some validity in demonstrating prevalence through statistics, something needs to be done immediately to address the injustices taking place against children every day.

---

[7] See the seventh affirmation of this volume.
[8] See the article by Ravi Jayakaran in this volume.
[9] See www.tearfund.org/News/Press+release+archive/April+2004/Tearfund+urges +MPs+to+read+the +Bible+and+drop+the+debt.htm.
[10] See www.nospank.net/boot.htm.
[11] See www.violencestudy.org/.

Personal Fulfillment

It is unlikely that those of you in the field will get swept along with the armchair theorists who feel that personal fulfillment and happiness is the ultimate goal for children. You know only too well that many children have to experience terrible things that no one should have to experience. But it is useful for us to sometimes take a step backwards and look at our goals for the children, families, and societies that we serve. How are our ministries encouraging society's God-given responsibility for the well-being of children and their families?

Conclusion

The church must support society, starting with the family, to advocate for children. But are we doing enough to ensure that their spiritual needs are also being met (without 'spiritual abuse' of children—see footnote below)?[12] Are those of us who are primarily concerned with children's spiritual needs taking into consideration the physical, emotional and socio-cultural needs of children? Are we adequately working together to achieve this goal? What are the things that block us from achieving this goal? Pride? Low self-esteem? Unrealistic goals? Insufficient vision? Cultural blindness?

In truth, "the poor will always be with us" (John 12:8), and many children will continue to be poor and/or vulnerable until Jesus returns. In the meantime, God has given us the privilege of working with him and each other to bring justice and holistic ministry to many children.

---

[12] "Spiritual abuse occurs when a spiritual leader, or someone in a position of spiritual power or authority (whether organisation, institution, church or family) misuses their power or authority, and the trust placed in them, with the intention of controlling, coercing, manipulating, or dominating a child. Spiritual abuse is always about the misuse of power within a framework of spiritual belief or practice, in order to meet the needs of the abuser (or enhance his or her position) at the expense of the needs of the child. Spiritual abuse results in spiritual harm to a child and can be linked to other abuse, such as physical, emotional and sexual abuse." Spiritual Abuse Working Group, "Protecting Children from Spiritual Abuse," (Cirencester, UK: Cutting Edge V Conference, September 29-30, 2005).

CASE STUDY

ADVOCACY: A CHALLENGING ISSUE?

BY JOANNA WATSON
VIVA NETWORK

Facing Up to the Challenge of Injustice

The Bolivian city of Potosi was dedicated to Satan when it was founded.

A poor city, Potosi is famous for its abundant minerals and silver. Often, children are involved in the mining and have to go through various satanic dedication rituals beforehand.

For centuries, these practices have gone unchallenged, but not any more! The leaders of the Evangelical churches in Potosi became increasingly concerned, particularly about the child miners and decided they wanted to see their city rededicated—this time to God. They knew it might be risky. It always is when it comes to challenging traditions. But they also knew that they had to find the courage to speak out.

Covering all that they did with prayer, they began to develop relationships with the municipal authorities, local organizations and other Christian churches in the community. Everyone agreed they wanted to help, but they were daunted by the possibility of confrontation with those in positions of power.

The Evangelical churches persisted, saying it was important for the children—and the future. Their perseverance has paid off. In 2006, the city was rededicated to God in a public ceremony. This would transform the community and particularly benefit the children involved in mining, as they would no longer have to go through oppressive and evil rituals. Instead, the churches would work with them to teach them about Jesus and his love for them.

Challenging our Excuses

This shows the power behind unity—both in terms of purpose and action.

The question is, would you, or could you, do the same?

Most of us, if we are honest, come up with excuses. "I'm really scared about saying something. It's just too risky." "What if I put myself or other people in danger?" "What difference will I make? I feel so small and insignificant." "I just don't have the resources to put into it." It is easier to get someone else to do it, to keep quiet, to avoid potential confrontation. But is that a reason to hold back? I would suggest not.

> Is the church prepared to stand in the gap between society and children?

The Evangelical churches in Potosi had concerns, yet they were prepared to face up to them, address them, and overcome them. Will we listen to God's challenge to use our voices to face up to injustice?

The Challenge Facing Society

Society is about people living interdependently within community. It is about the fabric of people's relationships and interaction. It is in our infrastructure and our surroundings; in a sense of common identity and culture. It permeates our vocabulary and yet, somehow, remains intangible.

Those who represent society are generally those in positions of power and influence and are the ones to fulfill society's mandate of responsibility for the well-being of children and families.

The question of 'well-being' is subjective, varying across different cultures and contexts. However, in relation to children, the United Nations Convention on the Rights of the Child (CRC) has been accepted almost universally.[1] The CRC places official obligations on governments, parents, caregivers, others who represent society and even on children themselves. These rights are all matters of 'basic needs' that society has a duty to provide, through provision of access and resources, and in conjunction with families.

Families and communities are meant to care for children as part of the covenant relationship between God and humanity. However, when they fail, the CRC helps address the factors involved, embodying the belief that where parents are unable to protect the rights of their children, other mechanisms are needed.

Sometimes, children themselves will speak out against injustice, utilizing one of the most fundamental rights in the CRC, namely the right to express their opinions and participate fully in society. This principle is radical because it affirms children as autonomous individuals, as well as members of families and communities. The one proviso is that their right to influence decisions made on their behalf needs to be exercised in accordance with parental guidance, age, and level of maturity.

Some Christians might argue that children should not be given this right, on the basis that it undermines parental authority. But the Bible affirms that children should be given the opportunity to express their opinions. Further, it contains examples of children used by God in their courage to speak out in this way. God sees each child as a unique individual, and families and communities are called to care for them.[2]

---

[1] Only the United States and Somalia have not yet signed the CRC. For more on this topic, see the articles by Dave Scott and Tri Budiardjo in this volume.

[2] This concept will be developed further later in this article. See also the first and third affirmations of this volume.

The Challenge Facing the Church

If God intends children to flourish in a just society, then society's responsibility towards children is God-given. Society often falls short, though, and it is then that a challenge arises for the Church. Promoting respect for the rights of children, as expressed in the CRC, is in many ways an expression of the mission of the Church in reaching out to children, and consistent with core Christian values.

Throughout the Bible, there are stories in which children and young people have been active in God's plans and purposes, and Jesus made it clear that children are not to be pushed aside or considered less important. The Bible leaves no room for doubt that children are called by God and used by God—Samuel, Esther, the boy with the loaves and fishes, Jesus as a boy in the temple . . . [3]

The Bible teaches us how to respect the unique dignity of children, how to support them in fulfilling their potential, and how to strengthen them in their contributions to society. It affirms they have the right to speak and be heard—and that God uses them when this happens.

Some Christians argue that human rights are self-centered. They would rather focus on responsibilities. But the problem seems to stem not so much from the concept of rights as from the way they are worked out in practice. "If rights are implemented within a framework of individual human autonomy, their expression can be self-centered demands. Acknowledging the dignity of every person under God counters a selfish or self-centered approach to human rights."[4] To put it another way, "Each person is not only unique with a sense of responsibility towards God (vertical), but also has a responsibility towards others (horizontal) who are equally unique."[5]

If the Church is going to hold society to account for its God-given responsibilities towards children, and uphold and affirm the dignity and uniqueness of every child,[6] it needs to understand, and engage with their rights, both in terminology and in language. This is one reason why Viva Network facilitates an email group about Christian perspectives on child rights.[7]

God is calling the Church to stand in the gap. When children are failed by society, their communities, and families, the Church must speak and act with, and on, their behalf. This challenge is Scriptural: "Speak up for those who cannot speak for themselves, for the rights of all who are destitute. Speak up and judge fairly, defend the rights of the poor and the needy" (Prov. 31:8-9).

On the whole, the Church is very good at 'acting' and this is demonstrated many times over by the projects run by Christians who are simply responding to the needs they find on their doorsteps. The harder challenge for the Church is 'speaking.'

---

[3] See 1 Samuel 3; Esther 2:7ff; John 6:1-15; Luke 2:41-52.
[4] "Here We Stand: World Vision and Child Rights."
[5] Judith Ennew and Paul Stephenson, eds., *Questioning the Basis of Our Work: Christianity, Child Rights and Development*, 41.
[6] See the article by Doug McConnell in this volume.
[7] For more details, please visit http://www.viva.org/?page_id=257.

Rising to the Challenge of Speaking Out

If children and their families are dependent on society to fulfill its God-given responsibility to uphold and implement their rights, the challenge to the Church is to speak and act on their behalf when society falls short. Society's failures break God's heart. He wants justice for his children,[8] but often, that will only come about when we find the courage to ask for it. Scripture is clear about the mandate, but the Church needs to become clearer about how to fulfill it.

> Advocacy: speaking or pleading with, or on behalf of, another to bring about justice and to challenge the causes of injustice.

What?

Speaking and acting on behalf of others who are vulnerable or oppressed is often referred to as 'advocacy'. Some seasoned advocates refer to advocacy as 'the organized influence of decision-makers.' Advocacy literally means speaking or pleading with, or on behalf of, another to bring about justice and to challenge the causes of injustice.

Why?

The paramount reason is the Biblical mandate for advocacy. God is a God of justice and he wants to use his people to bring about justice. The Bible contains many examples of ordinary people who God used as advocates—Abraham, Moses, Nehemiah, Esther and, of course, Jesus, the supreme example of an advocate, pleading with God on our behalf.[9] And God can use you and me in the same way.

Advocacy also works! David Alton, a British Parliamentarian once said, "Landslides happen when small stones start to move". When individuals speak out, change begins to take place.

How?

Advocacy work varies in complexity and urgency, but the key stages are generally the same and include: identifying the problem, gathering accurate information, developing a strategy, determining goals and objectives, and deciding how these will be monitored and evaluated.

When it comes to taking action, there are many methods to choose from including campaigning, working in coalitions and alliances, lobbying, using the media, praying, and sharing stories of successful advocacy. Whichever methods we choose, they must build the capacity of those affected by the problem, so they become agents of change and advocates in their own right.

---

[8] See Isaiah 1:17; Amos 5:24; Psalm 89:14. See also Gary Haugen, *Good News About Injustice*.
[9] See 1 John 2:1.

There are many good advocacy resources available, [10] particularly Tearfund's advocacy toolkit.[11]

Top 4 Excuses for *Not* Engaging in Advocacy

1) "It's just too risky."
2) "What difference will I make?"
3) I just don't have the resources."
4) "Someone else will do it."

Top 4 Reasons For Engaging in Advocacy

1) We have a biblical mandate—God tells us to!
2) God uses ordinary people.
3) Advocacy works!
4) Advocacy tackles the root problems in society.

Which issues?

Regarding children at risk, there are many issues about which the Church needs to find its voice—including exploitative and dangerous labor, sexual exploitation and trafficking, child soldiers, education, HIV and AIDS, malnutrition, war, and conflict. The list could go on.

Meeting the Challenge

If this is the theory, then what does it look like in practice? Viva Network has been cataloging case studies of successful advocacy for some years.[12] One such story took place in Uganda, where many babies and children are being orphaned and abandoned because of the HIV and AIDS pandemic. In Kampala, Uganda, a network of projects linked to Viva Network has worked together to bring positive change to both the social views and laws of the nation in regards to fostering and adopting children. As a result of their efforts, in 2004, the Ugandan government initiated a month-long review of the fostering and adoption process, and carried it out in full consultation with the working group.[13] The network may

---

[10] See http://www.viva.org/?page_id=237 for Viva Network's recommended advocacy resources.
[11] See http://tilz.tearfund.org/Topics/Advocacy/Advocacy+toolkit.htm.
[12] For advocacy case studies, see http://www.viva.org/?page_id=239.
[13] Rita Nkemba to Joanna Watson, January-December 2004. Phone calls and personal e-mails.

have to continue working on this issue for several years to come, but that is to be expected; effective advocacy often requires a long-term commitment.

Society has a God-given responsibility for the well-being of children and families. But where society fails them, the Church must speak and act with them and on their behalf. Unless this happens, children may not flourish in a just society, in the way that God intends.

PRACTICAL IMPLICATIONS

HUMAN TRAFFICKING: CHILDREN AND THE SEX TRADE

By Christa Foster Crawford and Mark Crawford
Just Food, Inc. /The Garden of Hope

Malee's Story

Malee will turn 17 this month. She has a high IQ, leadership aptitude, and looks like a young, Asian version of Jennifer Garner of the "Alias" TV show. In California, she might be valedictorian, or homecoming queen. But life is different for Malee. Unlike most American teenagers, Malee has been sold multiple times and been a victim of sexual slavery and torture—all for the pleasure and profit of others.

Malee was first sold at three months of age by her birth mother. She became the property of a "mother" who viewed Malee as a both a commodity and a daughter. When Malee was two, this "mother" sold her to a family in a neighboring country who loved Malee and raised her as their own. But at age six, Malee's nightmare recurred when her "mother" broke in and stole Malee back.

When Malee entered puberty at 13, her "mother" tricked her into a hotel room with a foreign tourist. Malee fought her way to escape untouched, but the forces of greed and lust continued to press against her until she was crushed. When Malee was 14, her "mother" convinced her to go work in a wealthier neighboring country where a friend promised her a job at a restaurant. A government official drove Malee across the border.

The restaurant had only one item on the menu. That first night, Malee's virginity was sold to a Chinese businessman for nearly US$1,000. He believed the investment well worth it for the luck, prosperity, and long life he would receive from sleeping with a virgin. Malee did not feel lucky. The brothel owner had to beat Malee into submission, tie her up and gag her in order to give the man a good time. But that was not Malee's final customer that night. The owner sold her to several men willing to pay extra for the "first night." Within several days, Malee's market value dropped to US$5 per customer. To make up lost profit, the owner forced her to have up to ten customers a day. In her weeks in the brothel before being rescued by Christians, Malee had over 100 customers. She received no payment, was kept in slavery-like conditions, and was beaten regularly by the owner to keep her in line.

> CSEC: commercial sexual exploitation of children

What Are "Trafficking" and the "Child Sex Trade"?

International law defines trafficking in persons as recruiting, transporting, transferring, harboring, or receiving people through force, threats, abduction, deception or fraud, abuse of power or vulnerability, or payments to others for the purpose of exploitation.[1]

> International law defines trafficking in persons as recruiting, transporting, transferring, harboring, or receiving people through force, threats, abduction, deception or fraud, abuse of power or vulnerability, or payments to others for the purpose of exploitation.
>
> —*United Nations Trafficking Protocol*

Across the world, children are trafficked for many exploitative purposes—forced and hazardous labor, slavery and slavery-like practices, domestic servitude, begging, illegal adoption, child soldiers, sexual slavery by military troops, for their organ parts, and sexual exploitation. The commercial sexual exploitation of children (CSEC), also known as the "sex trade," consists of pornography, prostitution, sex trafficking, sex tourism, and child and forced marriages.[2] However, children trafficked for non-CSEC purposes, especially domestic laborers and beggars, are also subject to sexual exploitation.

Who Is Vulnerable to Trafficking and CSEC?

All children are vulnerable to trafficking and CSEC. Trafficking takes place domestically and internationally, in both developed and developing countries. In fact, the United States may have the largest number of prostituted children in the world.

A number of societal and individual factors make some children more vulnerable to trafficking than others, whether they're runaways, homeless, refugees and internally displaced people, aliens without citizenship and language,[3] regular and irregular migrants, or members of lower class, caste, or economic levels. Individual vulnerabilities include past sexual or other abuse, lack of education (both formal and in terms of awareness of trafficking dangers), lack of marketable skills or viable job options, pressure to earn income to support families, consumerism, and desire to escape poverty. Societal factors include societal change, restrictive migration policy, criminalization of victims, gender discrimination, the low status of women and girls, family breakdown, war and conflict, political instability, and natural disaster.

---

[1] Article 3(a) of the United Nations Trafficking Protocol (Protocol to Prevent, Suppress and Punish Trafficking in Persons, especially Women and Children, which supplements the United Nations Convention against Transnational Organized Crime). This is the first internationally recognized definition of trafficking in persons.
[2] ECPAT International, "Commercial Sexual Exploitation of Children," http://www.ecpat.net/eng/CSEC/definitions/csec.htm (accessed August 22, 2005).
[3] For a further discussion on naming, see the article by Joanna Watson in this volume.

According to God's design, children are inherently vulnerable and dependent, and are therefore to be protected.[4] Society has a God-given responsibility to nurture and care for the vulnerable and to create a just and nurturing society to eliminate individual and societal vulnerabilities that result in harm.[5]

Why Does the Child Sex Trade Exist?

Trafficking of children would not exist without demand and demand is often supported locally by social attitudes and cultural practices. In Thailand and other parts of Asia, for example, the overwhelming majority of the demand for CSEC is local. This trend is not unique to any part of the world or any level of development, including America.

Sex tourism also feeds the demand for CSEC. An estimated three million children in Africa, Asia, Central Europe, and Latin America are victims of tourists who travel internationally, regionally, or domestically to sexually exploit children.[6] America is a "major source" of sex tourists,[7] along with other western countries. There are permanent or semi-permanently "sexpatriates" as well as those who go on sex tours. Regional sex tourism is also prevalent whether it is from a wealthier to a poorer Asian nation or less sophisticated establishments for day travelers.

Both victims and perpetrators come from across the globe. Internet pornography and chat rooms have increased the number of offenders.[8] Tolerance, corruption, and the lack of laws, effective law enforcement, and meaningful punishments (including extraterritorial jurisdiction which holds offenders accountable for overseas illegal acts) fuel local and foreign demand. **[INSERT TEXTBOX 4.18 ABOUT HERE]**

Children live in a broken, fallen, and unjust world which permits and encourages trafficking and CSEC to exist.[9] The church must seek to transform individuals and societies to protect children.[10]

Extent of Trafficking and the Child Sex Trade

Trafficking in persons is a billion-dollar-a-year business and is "the fastest-growing business of organized crime" and more profitable and less risky than drug trafficking.[11]

---

[4] See the second affirmation of this volume.
[5] See the first, third, and fourth affirmations of this volume.
[6] Cory Croymans-Plaghki, "Street Children are Not for Sale."
[7] The Protection Project, "United States Country Report (The Protection Project, 2002)," http://www.protectionproject.org/main1.htm (accessed August 22, 2005).
[8] ECPAT International, "Child Pornography: A Contribution of ECPAT International to the 2nd World Congress against Commercial Sexual Exploitation of Children," (Yokohama, Japan, December 17-20, 2001), 9.
[9] See the second and fourth affirmations of this volume.
[10] See the second, third, and fourth affirmations of this volume.
[11] M2PressWire, "UN Secretary-General Calls Human Trafficking 'One of the Greatest Human Rights Violations' of Today," August 2, 2002,
http://www.humantrafficking.com/humantrafficking/client/view.aspx?ResourceID=199 (accessed August 22, 2005).

Estimates are, up to 800,000 people globally each year are trafficked internationally and millions more are trafficked domestically.[12] Other estimates put the number of children trafficked worldwide at 1.2 million per year.[13]

The sex trade is also a multibillion-dollar industry. UNICEF estimates that globally "approximately one million children enter the sex trade every year."[14]

> A male with money
> \+ A female with less money
> = Prostitution

While it is impossible to know the actual number of children who are victims of trafficking and CSEC, God's love for children and our Biblical mandate to protect, rescue, and restore them from harm is unmistakable.[15] In God's eyes, the trafficking and commercial sexual exploitation of even one child is too many.

Impact of CSEC on Children

Sexual exploitation of children violates their basic human rights, dignity, and the image of God in every person.[16] CSEC involves physical abuse, assault, deprivation, and rape, which cause serious physical damage including sexually transmitted diseases, HIV and AIDS, pregnancy, forced abortions, and other injuries, including death. CSEC also causes devastating emotional damage ranging from trauma, depression, shame, and post-traumatic stress to severe psychiatric disorders, substance abuse, suicide, and sexual abuse by the children themselves.

Christians are called to minister God's compassion and to heal the brokenhearted.[17] Those who sin against children and cause them to sin will face judgment, but so will we if we do not care for children as we would care for Christ himself.

Biblical Accounts of Trafficking

While the terminology is new, human trafficking is not. We find examples throughout the Bible: Joseph's brothers trafficking him transnationally to the Ishmaelites (Gen. 37); the Canaanite army trafficking girls for rape and sexual slavery (Judg. 5:30); and creditors threatening to traffic a poor widow's children into debt bondage and slavery (2 Kings 4:1). In each of these cases God provided rescue, and even blessed the victims of the trafficking experience.

---

[12] Secretary of State Condoleezza Rice, "On the Release of the Fifth Annual Department of State Trafficking in Persons Report," June 3, 2005, http://usinfo.state.gov/gi/Archive/2005/Jun/03-82857.html (accessed August 22, 2005).
[13] UNICEF, "Trafficking and Sexual Exploitation," http://www.unicef.org/protection/index_exploitation.html (accessed August 22, 2005).
[14] UNICEF, "Profiting from Abuse," 1.
[15] See the article by Paul Stockley in this volume.
[16] See the first affirmation of this volume.
[17] See the second and fourth affirmations of this volume.

Amos 2:6-7 describes God's response to the trafficking and exploitation of the needy:

Thus says the Lord: "For three transgressions of Israel, and for four, I will not revoke the punishment; because they sell the righteous for silver, and the needy for a pair of sandals—they who trample the head of the poor into the dust of the earth, and push the afflicted out of the way; father and son go in to the same girl, so that my holy name is profaned."

Ultimately, God promises an end to trafficking. When Babylon falls, merchants will no longer find markets for the "bodies and souls of men,"[18] nor for the women and girls who are often most vulnerable to trafficking (Rev. 18:11–13 NIV).

How Christians Can Respond to the Child Sex Trade

Only the ultimate expression of the Kingdom of God will bring a complete end to the child sex trade. But Christian individuals, organizations, and churches are not only called but are also specially equipped to address the needs of children across the trafficking spectrum today.[19]

Churches are the single largest untapped resource in the fight against child sexual exploitation. They are present in every country of the world and have a mandate to protect and advocate for the abused.[20] Even governmental and secular agencies are crying out for the Church to help.[21]

Churches can raise awareness, pray, protect, and heal from sexual abuse within local churches, address sexual impurity, assist local efforts, learn good practices, and mentor other churches. Only after such preparation and study of the child exploitation situation in another country, including a comprehensive needs analysis in consultation with experienced missionaries and ministries should individuals, organizations, or churches seek to begin a work in a foreign country.[22]

Conclusion

Salvation for sexually exploited children is a long-term process involving release, healing, provision, education, access to sustainable livelihood, transformation of the spirit

---

[18] The "trafficking spectrum" includes prevention, protection, recovery, rehabilitation, reintegration, return, repatriation, and prosecution of traffickers. See United Nations, *Combating Human Trafficking in Asia: A Resource Guide to International and Regional Legal Instruments, Political Commitments and Recommended Practices*. See also http://www.unescap.org/esid/GAD/Publication/index.asp.

[19] See the articles by Paul Stockley and Ravi Jayakaran in this volume.

[20] See the articles by Glenn Miles and Joanna Watson in this volume.

[21] The Asha Forum, "Asha Forum Resource CD" (The Asha Forum, 2003). The Asha Forum is the sexual abuse forum of Viva Network. See www.viva.org and www.asha.viva.org.

[22] The Asha Forum, "Asha Team Model," http://www.ashaforum.org/involve_churches.htm (accessed August 22, 2005).

through a relationship with Christ and growth in discipleship. All are essential and only Christians can offer this ultimate hope.

As a result of her rescue, Malee now attends church, is learning to pray and trust God. We helped her start a small business and she receives counsel and love in Jesus' name. Malee is an inspiration to all who know her. But since we first met her, another 2,999,999 children have been forced into the sex trade. What would Jesus do? What will you do? The problem is complex and the solutions are not simple, but do something we must, otherwise there will be children to pay.

CHAPTER 4
DISCUSSION QUESTIONS

1) What do we mean by the "well-being of children"? What is distinctive about a Christian understanding compared to a secular or other faith viewpoint?

2) What is the scope of the Church's responsibility within society? How can the Church function as society's conscience? How should our churches promote godly values in society?

APPENDIX 4.1

GLOBAL STATISTICS ON SERIOUS DEPRIVATION IN RELATION TO BASIC SERVICES[1]

Health

- 1.1 billion people lack access to improved water sources (2004).

- 2.6 billion people lack access to basic sanitation (2004).

- Nearly 39 million people are living with HIV and AIDS, and 35 million of these live in the developing world (2005).

Education

- 1.3 billion adults are functionally illiterate, and 834 million of these are women (2004).

- 17 percent of primary school entrants do not reach grade five (2004).

Income Poverty

- 1.4 billion people live on less than US$1 a day, and 85 percent of these live in the developing world (2004).

- 3.4 billion people live on less than US$2 a day (2005)

Children

- 154 million children under age five are underweight (2005).

- 10.1 million children under five die annually, and 98 percent of these deaths occur in the developing world (2005)

---

[1] Sources: *State of the World's Children 2007; 2007 World Population Data Sheet;* World Health Organization 2007.

APPENDIX 4.2

ACCESS TO BASIC SOCIAL WELFARE FACILITIES: A COMPARATIVE PROFILE

	Ethiopia	D.R. Congo	Burundi	Luxemburg	Norway	Switzerland
Infant mortality rate 2003	112	129	114	5	3	4
Under 5 mortality rate 2003	169	205	190	5	4	5
Maternal mortality ratio 2000 (adjusted)	850	990	1000	28	16	7
Adult literacy rate &%) 2004	41.5	62.7	50.4	NA	NA	80.9
GDP per capita average annual growth rate (%) 1990/2003	+1.9	-6.4	-3.6	+3.6	+2.8	+0.4
GDP per capita (in $US) 1999	560	710	740	32,700	24,700	26,400
Life expectancy at birth (years) 2003	46	42	41	78	79	79
Child immunization rate (% of 1 yr olds) 2003	TB: 76 Polio3: 57 HepB3: NA	TB: 68 Polio3: 55 HepB3: NA	TB: 84 Polio3: 69 HepB3: NA	TB: NA Polio3: 98 HepB3: 49	TB: NA Polio3: 90 HepB3: NA	TB: NA Polio3: 95 HepB3: NA
Population access to improved drinking water (%) 2002	22	46	79	100	100	100
Under 5 malnutrition rate (%) 2003	Underwt: 47 wasting: 11 stunting: 52	Underwt: 31 wasting: 13 stunting: 38	Underwt: 45 wasting: 8 stunting: 57	Underwt: NA wasting: NA stunting: NA	Underwt: NA wasting: NA stunting: NA	Underwt: NA wasting: NA stunting: NA
Population earning less than US$1 per day (%) 2002	26	NA	58	NA	NA	NA
Total population (1000s)	70678	52771	6825	453	4533	7169

Note: These details were obtained from a combination of sources for the sake of comparison, and to show how the distribution of access to services varies, being least available to those in greatest need of it.

APPENDIX 4.3

PROFILES

The three levels at which the seeds are found under each section refer to those that are at high risk (on the periphery), those in the middle (partly safe), and those within the confluence of the three circles (safe).

Figure 1

A PROFILE FROM CAMBODIA:

THANOUNG VILLAGE

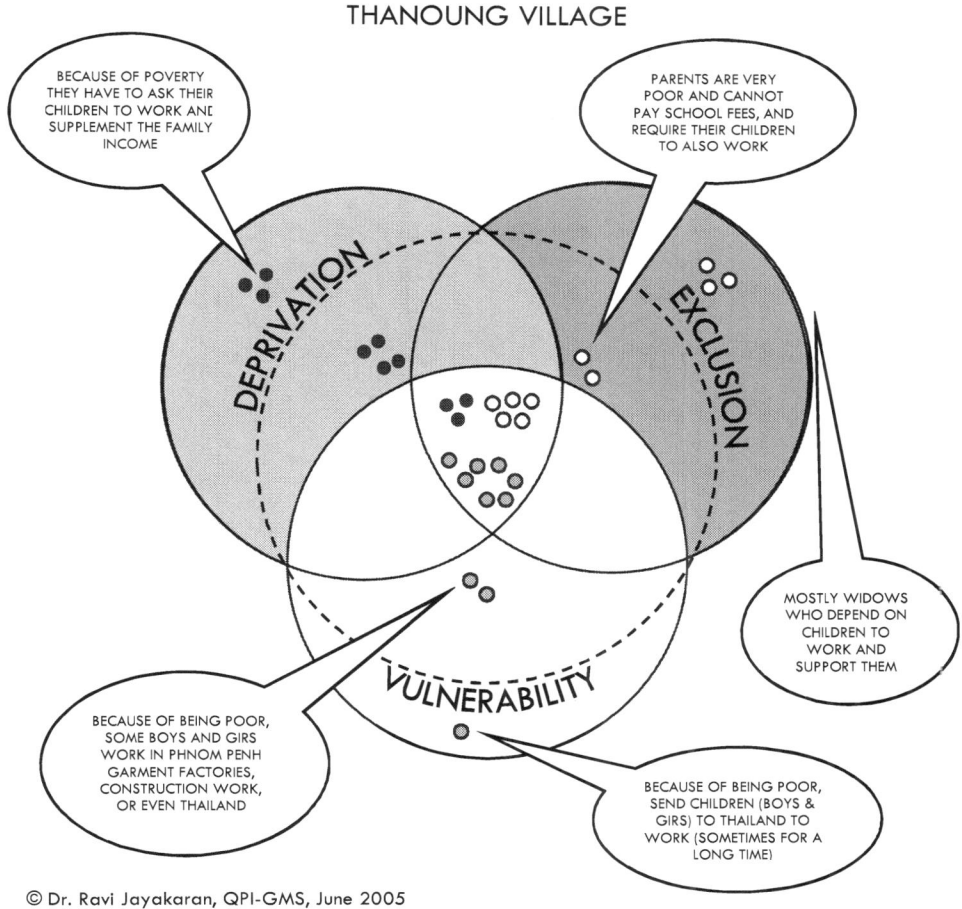

© Dr. Ravi Jayakaran, QPI-GMS, June 2005

FIGURE 2

A PROFILE FROM INDIA:

STREET CHILDREN IN BANGALORE (MAJESTIC AREA)

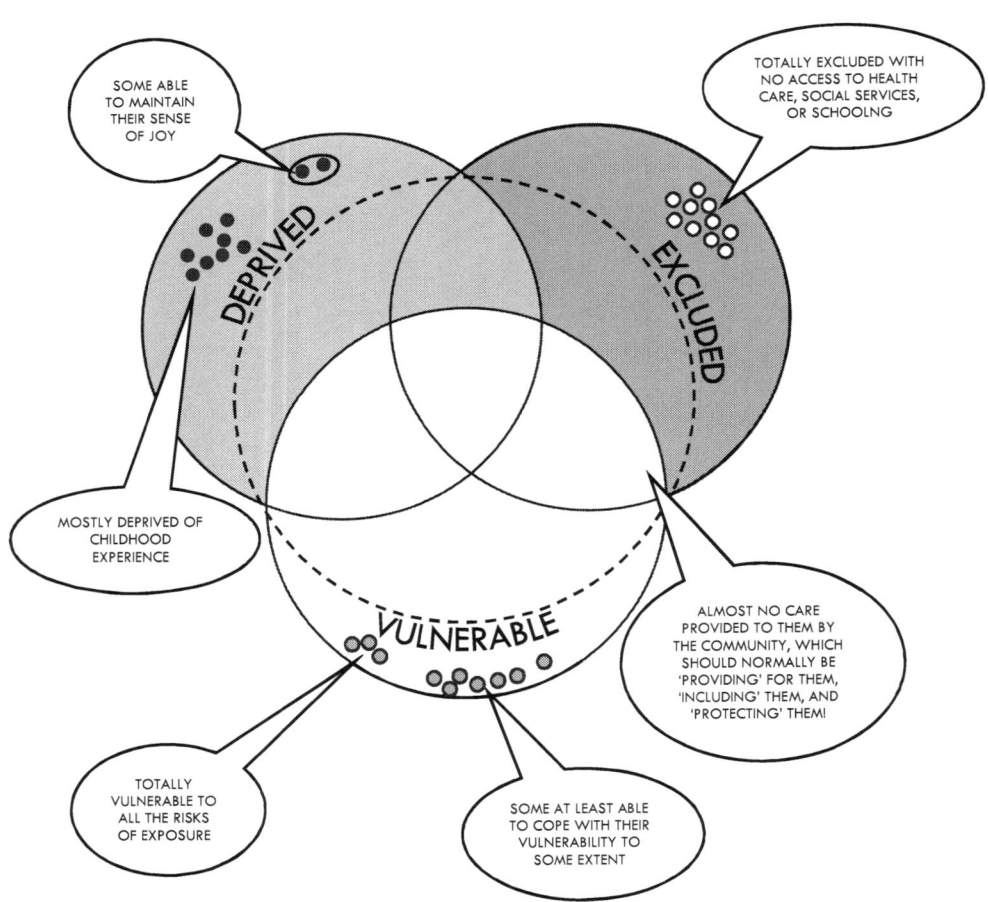

© Dr. Ravi Jayakaran, QPI-GMS, June 2005

Figure 3

Shown here is a Rapid Food Security Assessment (RFSA) profile of households in a community in the Philippines. The first column shows the ratio in which the community has these various RFSA categories distributed. The second column shows the categories and their listing as RFSA-1, 2, 3, and 4. The third column shows the name by which the different RFSA groups are called locally, while the last column shows the economic status of the group. The fourth and fifth columns are the ones that show the income to expenditure ratios for each group.

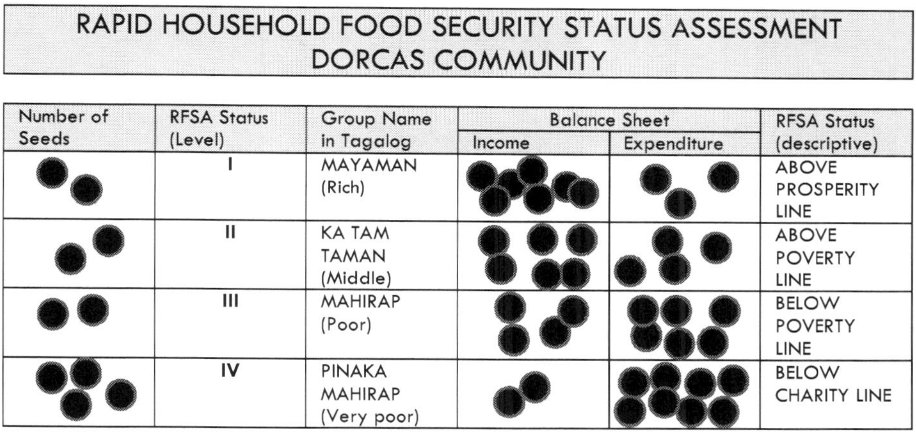

RAPID HOUSEHOLD FOOD SECURITY STATUS ASSESSMENT
DORCAS COMMUNITY

Number of Seeds	RFSA Status (Level)	Group Name in Tagalog	Balance Sheet		RFSA Status (descriptive)
			Income	Expenditure	
●●	I	MAYAMAN (Rich)	●●●●	●●●	ABOVE PROSPERITY LINE
●●●	II	KA TAM TAMAN (Middle)	●●●●●	●●●●	ABOVE POVERTY LINE
●●●	III	MAHIRAP (Poor)	●●●	●●●●●	BELOW POVERTY LINE
●●●●●	IV	PINAKA MAHIRAP (Very poor)	●●	●●●●●●	BELOW CHARITY LINE

APPENDIX 4.3

CHAPTER 5
A HOPE FOR THE GENERATIONS

Children are a promise of hope for every generation.

Each generation has a unique contribution in God's purposes for human history. Children have been shaped by the history of their community, are living fully in the present moment, and will reshape their community for the future.

God intends that each generation will extend faith and fullness of life to the next. God intends that this generation grasp the centrality of children to his purposes for our time.

"Working with children begins by hearing the cry of the generation. God said that he came to deliver the Israelites from slavery because he heard their cries and saw their suffering. God hears the cry of every child the world over."
—Alemu Beeftu

"You shall put these words of mine in your heart and soul, and you shall bind them as a sign on your hand, and fix them as an emblem on your forehead. Teach them to your children, talking about them when you are at home and when you are away, when you lie down and when you rise. Write them on the doorposts of your house and on your gates, so that your days and the days of your children may be multiplied in the land that the Lord swore to your ancestors to give them, as long as the heavens are above the earth."
—Deuteronomy 11:18-21 NRSV

"Those of us who face the tragedies that violence enacts in the lives of children are prone to losing a sense of hope. We need a theological framework that puts current events on a divine timeline. A theology of hope gives people of faith a foundation, a meta-level context for present suffering in the midst of God's future glory and past faithfulness. It gives people of faith a voice with which to cry out to God asking for change, asking for intervention."
—Sherry Walling

BIBLICAL REFLECTION

CHILDREN ARE A PROMISE OF HOPE FOR EVERY GENERATION

BY STEPHEN TOLLESTRUP
TEAR FUND NEW ZEALAND

Introduction

"There is no wealth where there are no children"

—Jabo Tribe, Liberia

Children are a promise of hope for every generation. They are the tangible hope of renewal for humanity. Of course, we are not restricting the notion of hope as something projected out into the future, assuming that when child becomes adult the fruition of that hope is realized. On the contrary, children are intrinsic to hope in the present; to the degree to which they are nurtured, empowered, and respected, hope is expressed. Children are the presence of the future.

If we are to grasp the breadth of meaning and the imaginative possibilities in the fifth affirmation of the "Understanding God's Heart for Children Biblical Framework," we have to begin by unpacking the layers of assumptions that easily get in the way and compromise our understanding. We need to 'clear the decks' so to speak about the whole notion of 'children as a promise of hope' if we are to usefully and positively address it.

Let me begin by making some qualifying statements.

First, we need to take great care in assigning children as a 'promise of hope.' While we can speak of putting our hopes for the future in children, or that their growing hopes will shape our world, we still need to keep the bigger perspective that it is Christ alone who is our 'promise of hope.'[1] If there is in any sense in which children carry an eschatological hope, it is always in subordinate relationship to God's presence and purposes.

The birth of a child is a tangible expression of God's promised and hoped for redemption to come. With the birth of Jesus, the first son of a refugee family, born in the humility of a stable, every new life is worthy of the promise of hope for our world. To otherwise emphasize children beyond this Christ-centered eschatological sense requires a degree of restraint so as not to lose the critical clarity of the issues involved.

Secondly, countering the western pre-occupation with individualism, there is the important observation that God does not look on us as detached individuals but as persons in relationship. Children are part of our world, and if there is any sense in which children

---

[1] Promise is likewise the language of eschatology and, for the Christian, shares with hope the sense of expectation. As Paul points out, all the promises find their fulfillment in Jesus Christ (2 Cor. 1:20).

are bearers of hope, it is in relationship to the adult world. Perhaps sadly, but in truth, children do not often significantly affect changes in the world, adults do. It is for this reason that there is a necessary, important, creative, and dynamic interdependence.[2]

Thirdly, I bring an integrationist perspective. We must be cautious of any assumption that places children in the pre-eminent position of God's love and concern at the expense or exclusion of every other. I believe all persons are held in the center of God's affection and concern. Jesus comes into this world for humanity in distress, including children. If we want our passionate concern to be heard, we must work together with the diverse ministries of the Church. We are the body of Christ for the redemption of humanity and creation.

Finally, it is both unhelpful and difficult to segregate children into categories of poor and wealthy, developed country or under-developed. While from time to time these distinctions leak through and the examples cited are primarily using children in oppressive or risky situations, if the title is to have meaning, it must be for all children.

Hope

For our purposes here, hope is defined as the expectation of good things to come. Each child is part of a generation, which carries into adulthood attitudes, values, and strengths, learned and experienced in childhood. Each and every generation holds the promise of the possibility that through children, our world can be improved.

Importantly, hope, as a promise for every generation, is an intergenerational enterprise. It requires reciprocity between generations where respect and hope is shared. For example, on one trip to Ethiopia, I stopped at a small village south of Addis Ababa. As usual, we were quickly surrounded by swarms of playful and inquisitive kids. With my attention elsewhere, I suddenly noticed a very small hand slip into mine and rub their cheek into the back of my hand. As I turned to look down, I saw the face of a truly beautiful child looking up at me. Our eyes caught in recognition and we smiled. Let me ask you this: At that moment, who was the promise of hope?

> Hope: the expectation of good things to come

We need each other; adults and children in dialogue and partnership for hope to emerge. In fact, we are in more than dialogue. As Christians, we recognize the Spirit of Christ who is the presence and hope of the future with us. Perhaps the idea of 'trialogue' is more correct. Our adult task is to make possible the expression of hope in children and young people who come within our sphere of influence. We are to make this expression of hope tangible through a variety of biblically based, Spirit-led and sociologically sound strategies.

Prerequisites to Hope

---

[2] See the articles by Doug McConnell and Perry Downs in this volume.

To begin, we need to make sure that we have a view of children beyond what the world offers. Children are not 'little adults' that at some point in their maturation become legitimate. That view, which I fear is far more prevalent than any of us would like to admit, distorts the reality of childhood. Wess Stafford puts the issue succinctly:

Too many of us tend to treat childhood as a preamble to actual life, a vulnerable period of time merely to be survived in order to get on with the real business of being valid, contributing members of the human family. This is the mindset that causes us to speak of children as 'tomorrow's world,' or the 'church's future.' As noble as that can sound, it is all about pushing off the value of children to the Realm of Someday. Someday they will add value.[3]

Just as in the case of minorities and the disadvantaged, stereotypes and assumptions often work to diminish the value and credibility of children's contributions. Today, children are being re-imaged to suit the marketing interests of transnational corporations, the fashion industry, the media, and other multinational groups like MTV. As a result, children all around the world are being given models of criminality and sexuality, from Ice-T to Brittany Spears.

In church and ministry, we also need to take care that we don't impose our own stereotypes. In the past the church, too, has had the tendency to view children narrowly: as holy innocents to be adored, unruly kids requiring control, or victims incapable of resistance and requiring protection.[4] There is no denying that many children appear to have a unique and wonderful spirituality or that children require adult protection and sometimes discipline. Nevertheless, we need to review how we consider children and take special care not to exploit stereotypes to elicit the generous adult sentiment of our donors.[5]

We need a fuller, more expansive picture of young people as competent, empowered and made in the image of God.

John Paul II expressed it precisely when he said,

The Son of God did not come in power and glory, as he will at the end of the world, but as a child needy and poor . . . After that decisive moment for the history of humanity, to despise childhood means to despise the one who showed the greatness of his love by humbling himself and forsaking all glory in order to redeem humanity.[6]

---

[3] Wess Stafford, *Too Small to Ignore*.
[4] See the article by Jennifer Orona in this volume.
[5] There is an interesting parallel here with aid and development images generally. At a recent conference on Africa held at UNITECH Auckland, African speakers slammed western portrayals of Africa as maintaining a stereotype that actively worked against private investment, resulting in ongoing poverty.
[6] John Paul II, "Message of his Holiness Pope John Paul II for the XXIX World Day of Peace: Let us Give Children a Future of Peace," http://www.vatican.va/holy_father/john_paul_ii/messages/peace/documents/hf_jp-ii_mes_08121995_xxix-world-day-for-peace_en.html (accessed August 18, 2006).

It is important to pause for just a moment and say that we have yet to see a really satisfactory 'Theology of Childhood' or 'Theology of the Child.'[7] The need for such a theology is urgent.

In the meantime, those of us in children's ministries are required to be advocates for a more realistic and constructive understanding of children within the Church and society.

Children's self-definition and right to express their sense of identity is critical to this task. In 1999, I handed out 20 disposable cameras to village children in South India, giving them the task of photographing 'friends, family and fun.' The candor and intimacy of these photographs taken from an altitude of three or four feet rather than five or six were deeply moving. They remain my favorite photographs of children for their honesty. Here, we touch on a point of importance—the empowerment of children to self-define.

Of course, children still need adults. Children do not live in isolation, and there are social and economic forces that in a very real sense are contending for their lives in both the developed and developing world. Melba Maggay, from the Institute for Studies in Asian Church and Culture, describes the situation this way:

> . . . of specific relevance [is] . . . the power of global media to penetrate the remotest corners of the earth, to project worldwide the dreams of its consumerist culture, and to shape the imagination of what has come to be known as the 'global child' . . . Our children are growing up, not on stories told round a fire on the great deeds of our ancestors, but on the super heroic and futuristic myths of robocops and animes that make us feel it is inferior to be human. This poses a clear and present danger to our cultural memory, to the continuity of our understanding of who we are as races and as peoples.[8]

While resisting any education whose role is simply the socializing of children into passive and submissive occupants of the adult world and its agendas, we have a responsibility to pass on the spiritual and life skills required to live confidently and successfully. From an early age, faith, justice, compassion, peacemaking, and social responsibility are all part of that curriculum. We need to demonstrate that Kingdom-centered alternatives to the 'way-things-are-world' exist. We need to equip children with the ability to identify, manage, and resist those things that are the enemy of self-respect, love, and life.

> **We have a responsibility to pass on the spiritual and life skills required to live confidently and successfully.**

---

[7] Robert Orsi, "A Crisis About the Theology of Children," *Harvard Divinity Bulletin* 30, no. 4 (2002). Robert Orsi, writing in the Harvard Divinity Bulletin, says that this absence has contributed to the inability to respond comprehensively to the scandal of clergy and caregiver abuse, a problem which has a far greater destructive influence for the Church than many realize.

[8] Melba Padilla Maggay, *Globalisation and Culture*, 1.

Hope is not the possession of all children. Today, this lack is the major source of youth suicide, crime, drug use, loneliness, and despair. The major component is alienation, and it is not just a problem in the developed world; it is a critical global challenge.[9] I doubt that this was a widely present malady in the world of ancient Israel. That is because there was a strong cultural and community cohesiveness based on common features of worship, law, and the re-telling of the salvation history. That salvation history recalled God's goodness to Israel and his judgment on its enemies in order to encourage confidence, security, and a verifiable reason to hope.[10]

> Hope is not the possession of all children

Importantly, Hebrew thinking actually believed in a future to bestow on their children and in which to exercise hope. We take this for granted in our modern world, but in the flat-earth of the ancient near east, Israel alone pointed to a future in which hope, trust, and faith could be placed. Outside the covenant community, the Canaanite nations were captive to an idolatrous belief of a never-ending cycle of seasons renewed only through ritual and sacrifice. The predictability of this worldview had tremendous influence and attraction, and for that reason we see instances of the people of Israel, even their leaders, falling back to the apparent comfort and security of worship of the Canaanite deities in the high places. It took courage and faith to live in a world with an unfolding future in which to hope.

In the world today with its terrorism and militarism, rapid change, and uneven distribution of resources and wealth, we need to point to a future that children can take a hopeful hold of. As in the Hebrew world, we need to look back with our children and acknowledge God's presence and saving acts in the history of our lives and communities. Childhood is meant for vision and action, for pushing boundaries and testing limits. We also need to help children and youth harness their energy and encourage them to dream big and have confidence to influence their world.[11]

Next, if we are going to 'empower' children and entrust them with hope, we will need to rethink our notions of children and young people's competency. Until we give them the opportunity to participate, a rich resource lies undiscovered and remains only latent.[12]

---

[9] Rita Aaron, et al., "Suicides in Young People in Rural Southern India," *The Lancet* 363, no. 9415 (2003): 1117-1118. The average global suicide rate is 14.5 deaths per 100,000 people, with suicide being the fourth leading cause of death in the 15-19 age group. A study published in the British medical journal *The Lancet* indicates that the suicide rate in the 15-19 age group living around Vellore in Tamil Nadu, India, was 148 per 100,000 for women, and 58 per 100,000 for men.

[10] This is typified in Deuteronomy 26 and repeated often in the Old Testament. The adult world recognized the centrality of its responsibility to nurture children and exercise their hope in YHWH as pivotal to the ongoing existence of the community and nation.

[11] See Acts 2:17.

[12] See the articles by Gustavo Crocker, Karissa Glanville, and Cathryn Baker in this volume.

As the ASHA Programme demonstrates,[13] kids are remarkably competent when given opportunity. We should remember too, that it was the notion of limited competency that legitimized the exclusion of women, slaves, immigrants, and countless minority groups throughout the world from full democratic and social participation. I would like to ask what our measure for competency is, who is defining it, and how much competency is required for participation in planning, managing, and democratic participation anyway? In terms of children, perhaps a simpler and less 'experienced' voice would be the contribution that

---

The ASHA Programme

The ASHA Programme in New Delhi sees the empowerment of children in planning and education as central to the success of their work, especially in health care.

As Booth and Martin state in *Lancaster Urban Health and Development*, "Children who grow up in slums take on adult responsibilities early . . . We should . . . work with them to solve their problems and those of the community that affect them."

ASHA considers children "ready to go" change agents, citing their quick learning, imagination, enthusiasm, flexibility, energy, and readiness to volunteer. An example of planning and implementation incorporating children includes independent community mapping where children identify their own community priorities. Children can act as child-to-child and even child-to-adult teachers in areas like community health through songs, drama, puppetry, or organizing small-scale events. The evidence is overwhelmingly positive when children are given the opportunity to participate.

---

brings needed insight into a problem or challenge, particularly as it impacts kids.

From a community development point of view, acknowledging children's capacity and competency is dynamic. That is, it creates positive effects by giving a sense of worth and confidence in the ability to tackle challenges that children and their communities face. When visiting projects like ASHA, where children have been empowered through real participation and a voice, the pride of accomplishment is tangible, as is the sense of hope that things can be different. On the other hand, where empowerment is absent, the sense of incompetence can become internalized. This sense of internalized worthlessness is one of the most tragic, debilitating, and anti-developmental byproducts of poverty.

Biblically

How does all that I have said sit biblically? In the Bible, children are very much agents of change. Their transformational capacity is given generous recognition. It is as if sentimentality regarding childhood is almost entirely absent in Hebrew and Semitic

---

[13] B. Booth and K. Martin, *Lancaster Urban Health and Development*, 135.

thinking. The word 'cute' does not seem to be in the Hebrew language. The reading of Proverbs 20:11 that even children are known by their actions, by whether their conduct is pure and right, invests a substantial and noteworthy degree of autonomy in children within the framework of the community.[14] In the Bible, we see children in refreshingly candid vignettes participating within the covenant community (for example, Isaac, Joseph, and Samuel).

Perhaps the most recognizable child displaying this unique autonomy is David, the shepherd boy who becomes king. In 1 Samuel 17:28ff, young David is running an errand for the big brothers. When he reaches their camp, he enters into a conversation with one of the fighters. The eldest brother Eliab considers this inappropriate and tells him to keep quiet. The New International Version captures David's response beautifully and with a contemporary nuance: Exasperated David quips, "Now what have I done? Can't I even speak?" David is shown requesting his own voice in the midst of the adult-centered world of soldiers and combatants. When he does eventually speak, he takes the opportunity to bring hope and encouragement. A little later on, through his own independent initiative and even disregarding Saul's suggested adult strategy, he slays Goliath (1 Sam. 17:38-40, 48-51).

This is more than just a simple Sunday School story, as valuable as that might be.[15] A biblical social analysis demonstrates that at its root, this story was not only about trust in God as a singular and isolated act of piety. It was also a faithful act with profound political consequences that changed the course of the nation and in doing so brought hope. Likewise, a careful reading of Esther will reveal a number of similarities.[16]

Present-Day Examples

This same competence and agency to seek a more just, Kingdom-focused future also has outstanding examples in our own times. A fascinating and exemplary chapter is that of the contribution of children in the American civil rights campaigns of the 1950's. David Halberstam's book, *The Children,* recounts the important and courageous role played by children in this period.[17]

One case that struck a chord with me was that of six-year-old Ruby Bridges who courageously crossed the segregated school picket lines of New Orleans despite the jeers and taunts of angry adult crowds. No doubt Goliaths in their own context! Ruby responded

---

[14] A grim reality of just how much responsibility and competency is assigned children in the Hebrew community can be found in the fact the children could face execution based on their actions and character. See Deuteronomy 13:6ff; 21:18ff.

[15] The transformational and social content of the David and Goliath episode is almost entirely missing in any Sunday School or children's training material. Faithfulness and obedience are stressed above the possibility of social impact. Children need to know that they can impact and change their world.

[16] Esther is an intriguing book. Some say that God is explicitly absent in the text but implicitly and tangibly sensed throughout in the background. They note that like David, her faith establishes courage and she expresses actions and voice, which brings down a tyrant of the nation. She is an agent of hope bringing spiritual and political renewal.

[17] See David Halberstam, *The Children*.

to a school counselor who was concerned about the trauma she may have experienced by saying that she had been praying for those in the angry mob just like Jesus did when he faced the same situation.

Halberstam found that these young people grew up in families, churches, and communities, that though poor were rich in nurture, identity, values, and often, Christian support. They were often mentored and encouraged, instilled with possibilities and hope for a just future.

Berry Mayall of the University of London writes that a particularly hopeful contribution is possible when children are given real access to voice and participation. Children have important lessons for moral philosophers on issues of autonomy and interdependence. While western liberal thinking has valued autonomous, independent moral agency, children have regard for relationships as the cornerstone of their lives—interconnectivity.[18]

Research bears out that children and young people have a unique view of social order and a deeply rooted and almost instinctual acknowledgement of the interdependence between people and groups. They can provide us with a unique set of ideas about the social order, which both help us to understand how it works, and also provide us with insights into ways of improving childhood. Mayall suggests that if we could acknowledge this way of seeing, we could experience fresh and hopeful opportunities for the way we approach life. From the project level right through to international policy, we could dramatically and positively re-orientate our perspective.[19]

As well as life-skills, values, and encouragement, children need what are termed 'safe spaces'—physical, social, and political—to thrive and hope. Safe spaces are not just environments that provide physical safety and security, but ones absent of ridicule, emotional bullying, and a culture dismissive of the perspectives of children and young people. Safe spaces allow questioning, emotional honesty, room for experimentation and rehearsal, and space for mistakes. In a word, they are environments of empowerment.[20]

In New Zealand, Action for Children and Youth Aotearoa (New Zealand) or ACYA has called for more genuine opportunities for meaningful participation. ACYA and others are lobbying with some success for reference groups to be established that include the participation of children for all policy decisions that impact them.[21] I would challenge all of us to ensure that the voice and aspirations of children and youth and the impact on children of decisions made by institutions and governments reaches deeply into policy frameworks. Otherwise any talk of 'Children as a promise of hope' is empty sentiment and jargon.

---

[18] Such inter-connectivity as distinct from western liberal thinking is also present in the biblical understanding of social order.
[19] See http://www.hopehousedc.org.
[20] Even in a limited degree, any improvement on security and safe space impacts hope. That includes refugee camps and street environments as well as settled communities and neighborhoods.
[21] Action for Children and Youth Aotearoa, *Children and Youth in Aotearoa 2003: The Second Non-governmental Organisations' Report from Aotearoa New Zealand to the United Nations Committee on the Rights of the Child*, 226.

For those of us in Christian community development, Mayall puts forward a final challenge. Just as gender analysis has been mainstreamed into development and helps us to understand social power between women and men, she suggests that we should consider a generational analysis to help us understand the relationship of children to adults.[22] I may be straying at this point over to the practitioner side of this discussion, but I have for a long time been disquieted by the emphasis on gender analysis at the expense of wider social analysis, particularly in regards to children. It is refreshing to have Mayall remind us of this. As in all social analysis, it requires the active and direct participation of those concerned as well as their involvement in monitoring and evaluation. Likewise, special issues arise for girls as distinct from boys, children with disabilities, and those in the context of conflict or disaster.

While it is almost proverbial that the thing parents want most is for the welfare of their children, it is equally true that what children want most is the best for their families and communities. Steve Bradbury of Tear Fund Australia once remarked to me that the single possession of the poor that should never be diminished or compromised by any external imposition is solidarity. Children, families, and communities are part of an organic whole. We cannot really build children of hope without building communities of hope.[23]

Countless studies demonstrate that children thrive in the context of healthy families or caregivers and in secure communities, including the Church. An extremely important point in this discussion is the need for the adults who are the primary caregivers to be provided with the support, dignity, and recognition required to lovingly and effectively parent. No external agency should ever usurp that role or become surrogate except under the most extreme situations or the absence of loving natural caregivers. We must recognize the need to support poor families and their communities holistically in poverty reduction through food security, cessation of conflict and peace-building strategies, micro-credit and enterprise, shelter, literacy, and education to name but a few.[24] Holistic Christian development acknowledges and celebrates the role of an empowering faith. As Francis Yeboah, an educator and field worker from Ghana, stated, "to deny the Gospel is only to add to oppression."

Finally, a challenge for us all. Throughout this paper, we have been developing a case for building environments and contexts for hope to be birthed in, to be expressed by, and to thrive in children. Success will vary from situation to situation, but the essential principles remain. Herein lies the big question: Christian hope has the capacity to carry a prophetic voice. When our children and youth speak, will we as adults be able—that is, will we have the competence and capacity ourselves—to hear their prophetic voice? Our world needs the answer to be yes.

When Jesus called the children to himself and remarked with the imperative, "Let the little children come to me, and do not hinder them, for the Kingdom of God belongs to such as these" (Luke 18:16 NIV),

> We cannot really build children of hope without building communities of hope.

---

[22] Action for Children and Youth Aotearoa, 134.
[23] See the third affirmation in this volume.
[24] See James 2:14-17. For a further discussion, see the fourth affirmation in this volume.

along with conveying his tender heart and mercy for children, he was also expressing an invitation of access to the resources of the Kingdom in all its radicalness and power to change our lives and the world around us. To 'hinder not' was the command to remove every obstacle to that hope and encourage every opportunity for its expression and celebration.[25]

The realization that 'children are a promise of hope for every generation' will not happen passively as something out of the blue. It is a latent truth waiting for the opportunity of expression. It will require an intergenerational enterprise under the guidance of the Holy Spirit. Pierre Teilhard de Chardin profoundly remarked, "The future belongs to those who offer hope." In truth, each generation, offers it in part to every other.

---

[25] Note: "*kwluvete*" (hinder, prevent, forbid) ⬜ is the imperative case.

CRITICAL ISSUES

HOPE FOR EVERY GENERATION

By Linda Wagener
Fuller Theological Seminary

Introduction

From its beginning, Israel was given hope by God in the promise that generations of Abraham's descendants would make a great nation.

Go from your country and your kindred and your father's house to the land that I will show you. I will make of you a great nation and I will bless you, and make your name great so that you will be a blessing (Gen. 12:1-3).

The covenant between God and Abraham shaped the tradition that children are carriers of hope and reminders of the promise that God has made. This promise brought into history an attitude of orientation toward the future that reaches fulfillment in the birth of the Messiah and his reign of peace (Isa. 9:6). Hope here is conceptualized as the expectation that God will keep his promises to us. Importantly, hope is embedded in a process that binds the generations together. Adults can experience hope that the generation that follows them will receive God's promised blessings, yet children need adults in order to be prepared to receive that promise.

> With each baby, a unique new life begins that is different from any that has existed previously. Because of this, the future is open to new possibilities. With new possibility comes another chance for peace and justice.

The birth of each child is a symbol of life's possibilities. God promises that his historical purposes will endure beyond our own time into future generations. Whether in baptism or dedication, a child's arrival is celebrated as a gift from God, entrusted to parents and the community.

Theologian Jürgen Moltmann explains that children are metaphors of hope for all of God's people.[1] With each baby, a unique new life begins that is different from any that has existed previously. Because of this, the future is open to new possibilities. Future generations are not compelled to repeat the patterns of previous generations but will have a chance to transcend old ways of violence and oppression. Children are not only a realization of our own hopes, but Moltmann points out that they "also are metaphors of God's hope for us; God wants us, expects us . . . and welcomes us as God's great love." Of course, as Stephen

---

[1] Jürgen Moltmann, "Child and Childhood as Metaphors of Hope," *Theology Today* 56, no. 4 (2000): 592-603.

Tollestrup has clarified, we must not confuse the hope that is brought by the birth of a new child with the supreme hope for salvation that only Christ can bring.[2] Children must be seen realistically as limited and interdependent, as are all people.

Responding to God requires that we enter seriously into a covenantal relationship with children, taking God's word to heart, and preparing the next generation to receive God's promise. Every child can receive God's promise. With this hope, however, comes a responsibility for adults to provide children with the opportunities and resources that will nourish their hope.

In God's perfect plan, children should be formed under God's loving and watchful eye. They are born vulnerable and dependent to parents within the covenant of marriage. Communities are meant to encircle the family, providing support, opportunities for meaningful contribution, and patterns of righteous living that ensure the safety of all its members. Children are to be received as full members in God's global church, joining with other believers in worship that honors God and God's creation.

Yet too often, hopelessness intervenes when the developmental context meant to support and nurture children is broken. Too often, children are left without the support of loving and committed parents, without the safety net of a committed marriage between their parents and without a caring attentive community.[3] Even worse, children are often exposed to unwholesome influences and neglect. Throughout this volume are stories of children orphaned by war or epidemic, abducted into slavery as soldiers or sex workers, or defeated by poverty and lack of opportunity. In Amos 4 we read of a world similar to ours in which the poor and the needy have been oppressed and crushed.

What does it mean to say that these children are symbols of God's promise?

How also can we respond to men and women whose hopes for their children have been destroyed? Those who have remained barren despite prayer, those whose children have been lost to violence, disease, drugs, or prison? How can we maintain our hope when we see generations turning away from God, destroying creation and oppressing God's people?

When we turn to God's Word, we are reminded that God's promise breaks through in unexpected and unpredicted ways, even violating the laws of nature. Hannah, Sarah, Elizabeth and the Virgin Mary are given children in impossible situations.[4] In today's world, we can also see evidence of God's promise breaking through in impossible situations. Children are born and loved in even the most desperate of circumstances.

Three decades ago, in my own field of developmental psychology, researchers were fascinated by a particular group of children, originally dubbed as "invulnerable" and later "resilient". These children were considered to have been born into situations in which they were predicted to develop severe pathology. Yet, despite the predictions, they developed into healthy, productive, and functional adults. Now "resiliency" is considered to be the "ordinary magic" of development.[5] In the most overwhelming of situations, children have

---

[2] See the article by Stephen Tollestrup in this volume.
[3] For a further discussion on this topic, see the second and third affirmations of this volume.
[4] For more on this topic, see the article by Judith Ennew in this volume.
[5] A. Masten, "Ordinary Magic: Resilience Processes in Development," *American Psychologist* 56 (2001): 227-238.

the ready potential to adapt and achieve. This is in contrast to the expectation that resilience is a rare or exceptional response in development. Children are apparently created to seek out those elements within their environment that will help them to grow.

Faithfulness to God requires us to do all that we can to ensure that environments have those elements that will allow children to respond resiliently. It was found, for example, that if children living in difficult circumstances had even one consistent adult such as a grandma or auntie who loved and nurtured them, they were likely to be able to overcome the trauma they experienced.

Ten-year-old Rebekah lost both of her parents to AIDS. She was left orphaned but not alone as she was raised by her grandmother in a devout Christian home. The local church supported Rebekah and her grandmother who were well-known to many in the congregation. Rebekah's birthday was celebrated by neighbors and friends. She received help to buy her school uniforms and many were proud of her when she graduated from high school. Rebekah was able to maintain her hope in God because she was able to experience love and commitment.

Specific resources or assets have been identified that help to strengthen children's natural tendency to respond resiliently. Search Institute, a private, non-profit organization founded to help communities promote the positive development of kids, has identified 40 assets that fall into eight categories.[6] Four of these categories identify personal assets of resilient children. These include positive values, positive identity, social competency, and commitment to learning. A second group of assets refer to those elements of community that support resiliency in children. These include supportive relationships, consistent boundaries, opportunities for empowerment, and constructive activities. The more that we can surround children with a developmental infrastructure that provides these resources, the more likely it is that they will be able to hold on to the hope that God will keep his promises to them, even under devastating circumstances.

In this framework, our care for children goes beyond simply being good and kind people. It is a response to God himself. Jesus made this connection explicit in this well-known passage: "Whoever welcomes one such child in my name welcomes me" (Matt. 18:5). Therefore, we must nurture children by providing them with food, shelter, and medical care so that they can become adults who will labor in God's fields. It means that we must care for the earth and preserve its resources so that future generations may enjoy and steward all creation.[7] It also requires that we prepare children to be the instruments of God's purpose by inviting them to become followers of Christ. For this, children must be given the resources that they need to be whole physically, psychologically, socially, and spiritually.

> Children are significantly poised in the hinge between the past and the future.

Children are significantly poised in the hinge between the past and the future. From the past, they must glean wisdom as the tradition of lessons learned over generations of

---

[6] P.L. Benson, *All Kids are Our Kids: What Communities Must Do to Raise Caring and Responsible Children and Adolescents.*
[7] See the article by Doug McConnell in this volume.

human history and experience. In order to meet the future, they must develop skills that allow them to solve problems in new ways. It is the responsibility of the community of adults to provide the tools and opportunities for young people to be educated and mentored in ways that allow them to creatively move into the future, using their gifts for God's Kingdom.

Neither is new wine put into old wineskins; otherwise, the skins burst, and the wine is spilled, and the skins are destroyed; but new wine is put into fresh wineskins, and so both are preserved (Matt. 9:17).

Resources

From the beginning, God created earth with sufficient resources for the well-being of humankind (Gen. 1:29). As caretakers of God's earthly Kingdom, we must develop an attitude of stewardship so that future generations will have the material resources they need to thrive (Gen. 1:28). Principles of sustainable development must be integrated into policies and programs. The degradation and loss of environmental resources must be curtailed. Like their elders, young people need to develop attitudes of respect for the environment and a desire to protect natural resources. Together, we need to develop harmonic lifestyles so that future generations will not face irremediable resource deprivation. We must safeguard our natural environment, with its diversity of life, its beauty, and its resources, all of which enhance the quality of life, for present and future.[8]

Education

All children, regardless of gender, ethnicity, religious affiliation, or socioeconomic status must have access to and complete high quality primary education that is free and compulsory. Disparities in secondary education must be eliminated so that all young people have equal opportunity to develop their God-given gifts. God has demonstrated that women and men, young and old, the weak, the powerless, and the disenfranchised are often those that are chosen to participate in God's Kingdom. Therefore, education should aim to develop each child's personality, talents, and mental and physical abilities to the fullest extent Young people across the globe need access to socially and culturally beneficial information from diverse sources. As Keith White suggests, education of the young often reflects cultural values and practices that are not in line with God's plan for children and we should critique educational practices that are directed toward primarily consumerist and

---

[8] United Nations, "UN Millennium Development Goal 7," http://www.un.org/millenniumgoals/ (accessed September 8, 2005); UNICEF, "A World Fit For Children, Declaration 7.10," http://www.unicef.org/specialsession/docs_new/documents/A-RES-S27-2E.pdf (accessed September 8, 2005).

oppressive ends. Likewise, steps should be taken to protect children from materials that have been demonstrated to be harmful such as violence and pornography.[9]

Mentoring

In addition to ensuring that children develop the skills and competencies that are needed to approach the future, it is essential that this generation pass on values and principles consistent with God's Word. Children should be fully prepared to live in relationship with God and each other in society. They should be brought up in the spirit of peace, dignity, tolerance, freedom, equality and solidarity. Values are transmitted in the context of caring and committed mentoring relationships with adults. Children need adults who can be readily available to them and serve as their advocates. Adults need to give of their time, getting to know and care for children deeply, modeling respect for the child's parents, their own cultural identity, language, and values, and for the cultural background and values of others. Children of minority communities and indigenous populations have the right to enjoy their own culture and to practice their own traditions and language. They need adult role models who can pass on the cultural traditions that have sustained their people for generations. Finally, children must have time and opportunity to engage in leisure, play and participation in cultural and artistic activities.[10]

Healing

For I know the thoughts that I think toward you, says the Lord, thoughts of peace and not of evil, to give you a future and a hope (Jer. 29:11).

The insidious nature of sin is passed from generation to generation.[11] Children who bear wounds from trauma need special care and attention so that they may be healed. This care includes the devoted daily attention and affection of adults who value each child because of their own intrinsic worth as a child of God. Adults must model God's love to children whose primary experiences have been contrary. Without such care, it is almost certain that children will carry the sin that has been done to them into the future. Of special concern are children who have been victims of war, violence, and sexual assault. Children who live in impoverished circumstances without access to basic necessities may be forced to turn to illicit and illegal forms of economic support. Jesus has made it clear that those who tempt children into sin are cursed. Without intervention, such children may not

---

[9] See Matthew 18:6; United Nations, "UN Millennium Development Goal 2, 3," http://www.un.org/millenniumgoals/ (accessed September 8, 2005); UNICEF, "A World Fit For Children, Declaration 7.5," http://www.unicef.org/specialsession/docs_new/documents/A-RES-S27-2E.pdf (accessed September 8, 2005); United Nations, *Convention on the Rights of the Child*, "Articles 17 and 28."

[10] United Nations, *Convention on the Rights of the Child*, "Articles 29, 30, and 31." See also the article by Dave Scott in this volume.

[11] For more on this topic, see the second affirmation of this volume.

recognize themselves as children of God, bearers of hope, and recipients of God's promise. Children need to hear about God's promise to fill their future with hope. They need to understand that God will restore power where there is none and return order where there is only chaos. Children need to know that God promises that good lies ahead and that the future is bright because of his Lordship.

Full Members of the Christian Community

You shall put these words of mine in your heart and soul, and you shall bind them as a sign on your hand, and fix them as an emblem on your forehead. Teach them to your children, talking about them when you are at home and when you are away, when you lie down and when you rise. Write them on the doorposts of your house and on your gates, so that your days and the days of your children may be multiplied in the land that the Lord swore to your ancestors to give them, as long as the heavens are above the earth (Deut. 11:18-21).

A vital aspect of preparing young children to become participants in the next generation of God's people is to invite them to become followers of Jesus. Adults must spend time and effort by going to young people with the agenda of inviting them to become disciples of Christ, grounded in his life and teachings. Adults must also communicate to young people that to be truly Christian, they must have both a personal and a corporate faith. The local church must be a welcoming community committed to bringing children fully into the life of the body. Children need to be participants who have a reciprocal relationship to the community in which they receive, giving according to their gifts (Prov. 20:29). Wherever possible, children should be given responsibility that is developmentally appropriate. Jesus also teaches that children are to be role models to us of the way to receive God's Kingdom (Matt. 18:3-5).[12] We are not given the opportunity to serve God because of our knowledge, power, or status. Rather, we are given the opportunity to enter the Kingdom simply because we are God's beloved children.

> We are not given the opportunity to serve God because of our knowledge, power, or status. Rather, we are given the opportunity to enter the Kingdom simply because we are God's beloved children..

Building Blocks of Development

In order for children to thrive, they need more than food, water, and medical care. While these are absolutely critical to sustain life, they are not enough. Young people also need essential social and emotional resources in order to be prepared to contribute to God's purposes for their lives. They need first and foremost to be embedded in relationships with

---

[12] For more on this topic, see the third and sixth affirmations of this volume.

adults who consistently care about them. Adults must provide care and affection as a model of God's love. The same community of caring adults must also pass along the rules and boundaries that God has provided to his people as a means for them to understand how they are to live. Adults must also get to know children well so that they can identify the gifts and talents of each child. Finally, adults can help children find the support and opportunities that they need in order to fully develop these gifts. For one child, it may be that God has gifted her with abilities that will allow her to solve complex medical problems. Another may be able to bless and soothe his community with gifts of music and storytelling, and still another may harbor the ability to help others solve conflicts. God's people require the continual input of new members, each with the gift that they bring to the body as a whole (Rom. 12:6). Each child has something to bring, but each child needs the adults who know them best to help them discover and nurture their gifts in accordance with God's purpose.

Conclusion

God's promises extend beyond the present into future generations. Because of this, children are the hope of God and of humankind. Without resources, education, mentoring, healing, and opportunity to participate in the community of God's people, children will be ill-prepared to receive, understand, and act on God's promises. For the church to effectively respond to children, they need to be viewed in the light of their role in God's Kingdom. Even those children who have been subject to trauma, abuse, or other devastating circumstances need to be seen through the lens of hope. We recall that our God has the power to break through into the world in the most unlikely of circumstances. He can be born into a stable in Bethlehem to a teenage mother who is a virgin. He can make the barren fertile, he can tame the violent, he can heal the sick and he can save the wicked. While we need to pay attention to the vulnerabilities and brokenness of children, we must also see that they are capable of thriving and receiving the promise that God has made.

PRACTITIONER'S RESPONSE

A CHILD SPELLS HOPE IN THE WAKE OF THE TSUNAMI

BY KEITH J. WHITE
MILL GROVE

Introduction

Our heavenly Father is ultimately concerned not with what schemes, policies, plans, legislation, charters of rights, or campaigns we have designed and fought for, but with which particular children, families, and groups we have shared a cup of the water of good news, hope, justice, and forgiveness. He knows each by name.

With Stephen Tollestrup's cautions firmly in place,[1] we can with confidence affirm that children should be valued as gifts and social agents, and that one way in which we can do this is to create safe and secure spaces in which they can speak and we can hear them.

We need to go beyond generalizations and clichés. So here is a check list of practical issues we must never lose sight of:

1) We must reckon with gender issues. The girl-child in many parts of the world has very different hopes and expectations from her brother.

2) Children (that means both boys and girls) are like litmus paper or barometers of the world in which they live:[2] some are full of promise and hope; some despair and die. We must reckon with these differences.

3) We must also reckon with the matter of age. In relation to age, it may be that we tend to agree with Jürgen Moltmann that theologically it is babies (rather than "children in general") who are the real metaphors of hope. By this the Bible means suckling babes or babies in a parent's arms, before negative social, political, and cultural forces have eaten their way into the soul of the child.[3]

4) If so, our primary task is to hold the space open for this hope to grow into maturity by creating and maintaining spaces in which children can experience the fullness of God's love with every fiber of their being and soul.

If this promise of hope is to be fulfilled, then in practice there are profound obstacles to be overcome and challenges to be faced. These are not only the obvious forms of sin as

---

[1] See the article by Stephen Tollestrup in this volume.
[2] Kathy Vandergrift, "A Little Child Shall Lead Them: Seeking Justice with a Focus on Children."
[3] Jürgen Moltmann, "Child and Childhood as Metaphors of Hope" *Theology Today* 56, no. 4 (2000): 592-603. See also the article by Linda Wagener in this volume.

it takes ugly shape and form in famine, war, greed, and injustice, but also other forces that marginalize or render children invisible.

Obstacles that Bar the Realization of Hope

Our *language and philosophy, cultures and traditions* unconsciously shape everything that we do, and they are the most stubbornly resistant to the change and reformation that Jesus called for when he placed a child in the midst of his disciples and warned them that unless they repented, they would not enter the Kingdom of heaven.

Liberal theory and democracy often render children invisible or virtually powerless.[4]

> **Obstacles that Bar the Realization of Hope**
> - Language and Philosophy, Cultures and Traditions
> - Liberal Theory and Democracy
> - The Market
> - Education
> - Church
> - Theology
> - Christian Children's Organizations

A close companion, *the market,* refuses to see children as anything other than consumers or potential consumers.

Education is taken to be a good thing in nearly every charter, constitution and mission statement, but it is one of the universal ways in which adults achieve their purposes and squeeze children in their mold (as distinct from creating the space in which they grow into God's mold).

Learning has become inextricably linked with hard work and labor, production and industry. All the time the obvious truth that children are created to play, dance, sing, and laugh seems to be marginalized by the adult determination to shape children for future roles at the expense of their enjoyment and spontaneous learning in the present moment.

Church is a major obstacle in the way of growth; denominations possibly more so, and sadly, child abuse occurs within both.[5] *Theology* needs reformation with a child in the midst. *Christian children's organizations* can reinforce existing ways of seeing children. Yes, that's you and me!

Examples from History

One of the things we must do is seek out, study, learn from, be inspired by, and follow some of the great pioneers who understood the significance of hope in the lives of children. Each practitioner in the following examples has demonstrated extraordinary, incarnational, radical, and practical expressions of hope.

Pandita Ramabai (1858-1922) founded *Mukti*, a residential community for child widows, orphans, and destitute girls in India. *Mukti* means freedom. Ramabai placed

---

[4] J. ONeill, "The Missing Child in Liberal Theory."
[5] See R. Orsi, "A Crisis About the Theology of Children," *Harvard Divinity Bulletin* 30, no. 4 (2002): 1-2; see also www.childtheology.org.

inestimable value on the life and life-story of every girl-child in her care; she developed an indigenous philosophy, curriculum, and method of education and learning applicable to the whole of India; she saw the impossibility of any genuine relationship and intervention without contextualization; she offered the Bible to her people in their own tongue, printed on her own presses and translated herself; she knew that for hope to flourish it needed a village to parent; she unmasked powers and ideologies of her time whether Indian, British, or international. She gave to all of her children because the hope of Christ inspired her, and she never despaired.[6]

The story of *Janusz Korczak's* heroic sacrifice of his own life in order that he might walk through the shadow of death with the Jewish orphans as they boarded a train to Nazi death camps is well known. What is less well known is the radical nature of Korczak's residential communities, informed by substantial theological and philosophical reflection and insight. He called his homes "children's republics"; he called for a Magna Carta of the rights of the child; established children's parliaments and newspapers run by the children; and his own writings are imaginative and profound. He refused to accept the prevailing ideologies, traditions, and despair that eventually infused the Warsaw ghetto.[7]

Both Ramabai and Korczak faced impossible situations of famine, disease, war, and death, but they refused to despair. They were prepared to put their own careers, projects, and even lives at risk to encourage the hope of the children around them.

Hope Expressed and Nurtured in Current Processes and Practice

What are the present signs that the seeds of hope in children worldwide are finding space in which to grow?

The Pavement Project empowers thousands of street children and others to discover a sense of worth, identity, community, and hope in and through Jesus Christ.[8]

The histories of world movements are being rewritten as children have been foregrounded. So we have Harry Sprange's study, *Children in Revival*, along with David Halberstam's *The Children*,[9] on the contribution of children to the American Civil Rights campaign. As we are given to understand from the Scriptures that children are agents of *missio Dei*,[10] so we will re-explore the content and dynamics of history ready to discover the distinctive and often pivotal role of children in transcending the ideologies and necessities of their time and place and ushering in new eras and processes of hope.

> missio Dei:
> mission of God

---

[6] Keith J. White, "Pandita Ramabai: A Re-Evaluation of her Life and Work."
[7] S. Joseph, ed., *A Voice for the Child: the Inspirational words of Janusz Korczak*.
[8] See http://www.lifewords.info/uk/global_action/pavement_project/. The PEPE Project, with its roots in the *favelas* of São Paulo, is another model that is transforming the lives of destitute children and families. It is opening up new insights into the meaning, origins, nature, and dynamics of "church." See www.PEPE-Network.org, along with the article by Stuart and Georgie Christine in this volume.
[9] H. Sprange, *Children in Revival: 300 Years of God's Work in Scotland*; David Halberstam, *The Children*.
[10] Keith J. White, "Rediscovering Children at the Heart of Mission," 189-199.

My wife and I recently experienced a church school, camp, service, and prayer day for children living in difficult circumstances in Kuala Lumpur, in which children from both rich and poor Christian and Muslim families were at the very heart of things, serving, leading the way, and opening the minds of adults to the possibilities of prayer and mission where there is a child's trust and hope in Jesus.

Many of you know that I live in a household and extended family called *Mill Grove*. Since 1899, it has been a place where children from broken or fragile families and communities of many varied traditions, cultures, and backgrounds have come for care, love, and support. Over 1,200 children have lived with us since Mill Grove's beginning, and well over that number have come for informal support. It is the hub of a worldwide network of members in this family or community. Mill Grove is rooted in faith in God and the belief that hope is never extinguished in the eyes and heart of God, however bleak things seem to the human eye and soul.

In addition, the *Child Theology Movement* has given me the great blessing of seeing how the actions and teaching of Jesus placing a child in the midst of his disciples has begun to transform Christian thinking and practice around the world.

Various training course are also now available, including the Master's Course in Holistic Child Development and a Child Theology International Learning and Development Resource Centre in Malaysia, multiple Child Theology resources, the *Celebrating Children* course, and more.[11]

Conclusion

Soon after the Tsunami that hit Southeast Asia in December 2004, I was invited to facilitate a Child Theology consultation in my adopted home of Maharashtra, West India. At the end of the day, I asked everyone present to imagine a child standing on the shore having lost everyone and everything—family, neighborhood, possessions, and friends. In light of our study of the Scriptures, participants were asked to crystallize into one word what that child (a stranger on the shore) meant for them. The common result was the word "hope." We know that this is how God sees every situation; pregnant with opportunities for the advancement of the Kingdom of heaven. The life, death, and resurrection of Jesus are the foundation and guarantee of that hope. Children are born with the seeds of that hope within them. It is our calling to offer to the world, whether through church, Christian organizations, or social reform, models that demonstrate that this hope is well founded. By God's grace, he has left us with such examples from every part of the world, past and present, where children are in the midst, active participants in every part of the process.

---

[11] Reports of four Child Theology Consultations (Penang, Cape Town, Houston and Penang 2), along with leaflets in English and Spanish are available from ChILD Resource Centre MBTS, Batu Ferringi, Penang or CTM, 10 Crescent Road, London E18 1JB.

CASE STUDY

GENERATION 2 GENERATION

By Daphne Kirk with Paul Stockley
Generation 2 Generation

Vision and Mission

"Our passion is Jesus. Our heart is for unreached people and persecuted nations."[1] Our task is to mobilize this generation to see the great commission fulfilled.

Our mission is to reconnect the generations and release children and young people to have an uncompromising passion for Christ, with a heart for mission and evangelism.

This is the vision that *Generation 2 Generation* holds as we face the challenge of this biblical edict.

Our purpose and *raison d'être* is founded on two biblical mandates for raising the next generation. These are:

1) that each generation is responsible for the next; and

2) that parents are responsible for their children.

These two statements provide the underlying motivational values for all the work of this organization.

People and Resources

Generation 2 Generation comprises a family–based leadership team who offer their expertise to pastors and leaders, train children from the age of seven years for mission, and take teams to Asia to give them a vision for the harvest. Our vision is to raise a generation which will walk through the end times of this earth and, overcoming to the end, shout to the nations that the King is coming. Our team has worked with church pastors and leaders in every continent. We provide training through conferences, preaching and teaching, and through making disciples.

Typically, a foundation conference for pastors and leaders would be three or four days in length, structured as follows:

Aims: to assist with strategy for child and youth discipleship
Method: sharing information and experience through teaching
Content: each conference includes a selection of:

---

[1] Daphne Kirk, "Our Vision," http://www.gnation2gnation.com/Group/Group.aspx?id=9014 (accessed September 5, 2006).

- biblical foundations for the generations
- the prophetic mandate for every generation
- family, parenting, and the discipleship of children
- models for children's cell groups and for intergenerational cell groups
- guidelines for implementing and evaluating church policies
- equipping children and young people to share their faith with others
- ideas for prayer with children and young people
- tools for writing materials
- information on cultural engagement

For parents, a one-day conference is also offered, focused specifically on equipping them to disciple their own children. Each conference is supplemented by a spectrum of self-published resources (books and tapes) covering the same themes.

Generation 2 Generation also provides materials to assist cell groups with ongoing discipleship.

Empowering Others Sustainably

Our desire is to promote the biblical values of intergenerational ministry within the church, inspiring more intentional and effective discipleship of children and young people.

Church leaders are not expected simply to replicate a formulaic pattern or model, but are encouraged to evaluate their own ministries against the biblical values of protecting and discipling young people, as well as challenging parents to take their parental responsibilities seriously.

As we do this, a process of repentance and reconciliation between the generations takes place as the Holy Spirit brings healing to the generations. Where children have been neglected and depreciated, they need to be accepted fully within the family of the church, and where they have despised the older generation, they need to see that they can stand on the foundations of generations past.

Each church is responsible to design and implement their own pastoral support system and discipleship program for the parents and young people within their care, or within their chosen outreach community. In this they demonstrate commitment to their God-given calling to train a generation that knows its God.[2]

---

[2] See Judges 2:10.

> **Theological Approaches to Hope**
>
> 1) This moment is not permanent. There is a future, there was a past. This pain, like other pains, will someday shift to the past, leaving the future open for other experiences.
>
> 2) The world can be changed. The present evil is not the final word. God desires his people to be agents of change and to call on him to bring justice and correction on their behalf.
>
> 3) God is not a stranger to suffering. He has intervened in the suffering of others and he has endured his own suffering. his mightiest, most hopeful action on earth occurred in a moment of extreme suffering.
>
> —Sherry Walling

Consultancy

In this respect, *Generation 2 Generation* is not working directly with children, but is empowering others to disciple children and young people within the sustainable environment of the local church.

Our team is initially available to train, and then to provide further consultancy and advice to the church leaders.

Example: Taiwan

In Taiwan, one church decided to put the principles they had learned from *Generation 2 Generation* into practice, and take seriously the biblical mandates that each generation is responsible for the next, and that parents are responsible for their children.

They began to reach out to the single-parent families they found begging on the streets around the city, many of whom had come from mainland China. With the two elements of the biblical mandate in mind, every member of the church assumed responsibility for one of these families on the street. As a result, this church now impacts over one thousand families, demonstrating a long–term commitment that is now being replicated by fifteen more churches. Seeing the value of children in God's purposes, they are also rising to the challenge of extending faith and fullness of life to the next generation.

Where a few staff in a local NGO could not possibly have such a wide impact, these churches are sustainably serving thousands of families.

A leader from the church pioneering the outreach explained the vision: "We are going to make the most dishonored people the most honored in our nation. These children will be missionaries to Asia. They will be future pastors. They will be in the government, and they will transform our nation and Asia."

> Building Hope in Traumatized Children
>
> 1) Foster hope by helping children develop a strong future orientation, along with realistic future goals and ideas of how to concretely attain those goals. Listen carefully for hints of "futurelessness" and address those beliefs gently and sensitively.
> 2) Affirm a child's capacity to "get through" the trauma. If nothing else, affirm the fact that they survived the event. Gently increase their hope for themselves, their hope in their ability to face difficulties in life.
> 3) Another way to build hope is to provide positive distracters that allow the child a temporary release. Moments of happiness, laughter, and fun may help the child to establish hope in the fact that life will not always feel so painful and hard.
>
> —*Sherry Walling*

Example: Ukraine

In Kiev, Ukraine, children are being rescued from the streets, receiving healing and deliverance, and being placed with family units for their care and nurture.

The children then go back to visit the communities from which they were rescued, many of whom are still living in the sewers of the city. They share the good news of Jesus.

They also go into the prisons, hospitals, and schools around the city, sharing their own Christian testimony, and evangelizing and discipling others.

These young people are already changing their nation.

Conclusion

At *Generation 2 Generation*, we see these as examples of God at work, using the call of God to reach these children, and to turn families, communities, and even nations towards Jesus.

PRACTICAL IMPLICATIONS

HIV AND AIDS: CARE FOR ORPHANS AND VULNERABLE CHILDREN

By Paul Stephenson, Bard Luippold, Mark Lorey et al.
World Vision International

Theoretical Context

The rapid spread of HIV in developing countries is devastating an entire generation of children, along with their families, communities, and societies. In many countries, unless HIV is addressed specifically, all progress on reducing poverty will be undermined.

The response of this generation to the centrality of children affected by HIV and AIDS to God's purpose for our time is critical. These children are not only being shaped by this unfolding tragedy, but will reshape their communities for the future. How they do this largely depends on the nature of the compassion, care, and hope in Christ incarnated in the Church's response.

The sheer size and consequences of the HIV and AIDS pandemic forces the Church to act. Members of its own congregations face sickness and death, whilst the decimation of populations in villages and towns in countries like Uganda gathers pace.

The HIV pandemic is orphaning children in unprecedented numbers. Globally, it is estimated that more than 15 million children under the age of 18 have lost either one or both parents to AIDS, and about 30 million more children have become highly vulnerable. The number of orphans due to AIDS in sub-Saharan Africa is projected to surpass 18 million by 2010, with 36 million more children highly vulnerable due to AIDS. When combined with all other causes of orphaning in Africa, including conflict, hunger, and others, it is estimated that over one in five children in Africa (87 million children) will be orphaned or highly vulnerable by 2010. While the crisis is most acute in Africa, where 90 percent of the pandemic's orphans live, the situation is worsening in Asia and Eastern Europe. The proportion of children orphaned in most countries will not peak until well after 2010.[1]

This chapter will describe the impact of HIV and AIDS on the lives and futures of children, as well as addressing the role of the Church, and the children themselves, as bearers of hope.

---

[1] UNICEF, *Fighting HIV and AIDS: Strategies for Success 2002 – 2005*.

The Impact

The HIV and AIDS pandemic is having a devastating impact on children, on the systems designed to educate them and enable them to be productive adults, and on the societies in which they live.

... on Children

Children bear the brunt of the impact of HIV and AIDS. They face challenges for survival as they lose parents and extended family members. The loss of loved ones, increased responsibility for siblings, the need to take on the role of provider and carer for sick parents, stigma, and social isolation can also lead to distress, trauma, and depression. Despite their resilience and ingenuity, children are ill-equipped to cope with these demands.

Psychosocial trauma can be caused by the sickness and death of a parent, a deteriorating and vulnerable living situation, separation from siblings, and more. These challenges, in turn, can cause children to internalize negative feelings, suffer from depression, engage in anti-social behavior, abuse substances, and live at higher risk of contracting HIV.[2]

Orphans and vulnerable children are also more likely to live in poverty, be exploited, and suffer from stigma and discrimination. Households affected by HIV and AIDS, or which are fostering orphans, may experience a drop in consumption of almost 20 percent.[3] Orphans are more likely to be the subject of discrimination and abuse in extended and foster family units than in their birth families, some even having their land or inheritance taken away.[4] They are less likely to attend school and more likely to have to do excessive household chores and work for people in the community.[5]

Orphans and children living in the most vulnerable situations are often subject to physical, sexual, and psychological abuse, and may be driven by necessity into prostitution and "survival sex," scarring them for life.[6] A UNICEF study in Zimbabwe found that orphaned girls are three times more likely to be infected with HIV than age-matched non-orphans, resulting from a combination of rape, survival sex, and other factors.

---

[2] Barnett and Whiteside, as quoted in M.J. Kelly. *Children in Distress: The AIDS Legacy of Orphans and Vulnerable Children*; James Sengendo and J. Nambi, *The Psychological Effect of Orphanhood: A Study of Orphans in the Rakai District;* UNICEF, *Africa's Orphaned Generation*; Minki Chatterji, et al., *The Well-Being of Children Affected by HIV and AIDS in Lusaka, Zambia, and Gitarama Province, Rwanda: Findings from a Study*.

[3] Corinne Siaens, K. Subbarao and Quentin Wodon, *Are Orphans Especially Vulnerable? Evidence from Rwanda*.

[4] Anne C. Case, C. Paxson, and J. Ableidinger, *Orphans in Africa*.

[5] Leanne McGaw and Amboka Wameyo, *Violence Against Children Affected by HIV and AIDS: A Case Study of Uganda*; Mbulawa Mugabe, Mark Stirling, and Alan Whiteside, *Future Imperfect: Protecting Children on the Brink*.

[6] Laurie Garrett, *HIV and National Security: Where are the Links?*

Psychological abuse can come from both caregivers and other children in the community. Examples of words used to abuse orphans and vulnerable children include:[7]

- "You orphan, we are suffering with you. Your mother gave us nothing; now we are stuck with you."

- "Your mother brought AIDS and shame to our family."

- "You are lazy. Why don't you leave our family and go away."

... on Education

Schooling can act as a 'social vaccine' to prevent HIV infection, as well as helping heal the psychosocial wounds experienced by OVC.[8] However, school systems across the developing world are in crisis: governments cannot train teachers fast enough to replace those who are sick or dying.[9] Furthermore, orphans are less likely to be enrolled in school than other children, and they are often less able to learn and develop skills due to poverty, malnutrition, pervasive psychological trauma, stigma, and, for orphaned children, the absence of the psychological support and guidance of their parents.[10]

> OVC: Orphans and Vulnerable Children

... on the Social Fabric

HIV and AIDS are having a disastrous impact on families and communities. Within communities, HIV and AIDS claims the lives of the very people who can best protect and provide for children, including doctors, nurses, and teachers.[11] Also, the extended family system, which has traditionally cared for orphaned children in Africa, is at the breaking point. In Uganda, a recent DHS survey estimates that every fourth family is hosting an orphan.[12] The sheer number of orphans means that children are increasingly forced to fend for themselves, either living in child-headed households or on the street. Indeed, in some heavily affected communities more than 10 percent of homesteads are

---

[7] McGaw and Wameyo, *Violence Against Children Affected by HIV and AIDS*.
[8] Kelly, *Children in Distress;* Oxfam, *Learning How to Survive: How Education for All Would Save Millions of Young People from HIV and AIDS*.
[9] World Vision, "Hope Alert Newsletter."
[10] World Food Programme, *Widening the 'Window of Hope:' Using Food Aid to Improve Access to Education for Orphans and Vulnerable Children in Sub-Saharan Africa*, 10; Clive Bell, Shantayanan Devarajan, and Hans Gersbach, *The Long-Run Economic Costs of AIDS: Theory and an Application to South Africa*; Deininger, Garcia, and Subbarao, *AIDS-induced Orphanhood as a Systemic Shock;* HelpAge International, *The Cost of Love: Older People in the fight against AIDS in Tanzania*; C. Coombe, "Mitigating the Impact of HIV and AIDS on Education Supply, Demand and Quality."
[11] M.J. Kelly, *Planning for Education in the Context of HIV and AIDS*.
[12] Deininger, Garcia, and Subbarao, *AIDS-induced Orphanhood as a Systemic Shock*.

headed by children.[13] They are at higher risk for drug and alcohol addiction, and for becoming HIV positive.

Economies and governance are also affected. HIV and AIDS cause a drastic reduction in the supply of labor and capital in affected economies. Seven African countries—Botswana, Zimbabwe, Swaziland, Lesotho, Namibia, Zambia, and South Africa—are currently losing 10 to 18 percent of their working age populations every five years, compared to roughly 1 percent every five years in developed countries.[14] Fewer adults must care for more children, and more children are not developing the life-skills that they need to become productive members of society.[15]

In addition, HIV and OVC offer serious challenges for the international and domestic security of heavily affected states. AIDS weakens military, police, and judicial infrastructures. High infection rates in the military, a population structure (or "youth bulge") that is conducive to violence, and the presence of a large cohort of OVC can lead to increased political instability and conflict.[16] Even more troubling, in the 25 countries that have the most demographic risk of conflict, there will be 37.7 million orphans and vulnerable children by 2010—*15.5 percent of their total child populations.*[17]

> HIV and OVC offer serious challenges for the international and domestic security of heavily affected states.

Challenges Based on the Contextual Realities

Overall, the growing devastation wrought by HIV and AIDS, when coupled with the massive group of orphans and vulnerable children left by AIDS, conflict, and other causes, points to serious consequences for affected societies and for the increasingly interdependent international community as a whole. In a chilling analogy, Laurie Garrett, of the Council on Foreign Relations, writes of AIDS and society that: "Striking similarities between HIV and AIDS and the Black Death can be seen . . . *No event in documented world history, before or since, has had as dramatic an impact on the human population—until the arrival of HIV.*"[18]

These challenges seem insurmountable given the shrinking economies, corruption and lack of basic services within developing countries. New approaches and commitment will be needed to care for even a small portion of the children affected.

---

[13] Kelly, *Children in Distress.*
[14] Richard Cincotta, Robert Engelman, and Daniele Anastasion, *The Security Demographic: Population and Civil Conflict After the Cold War.*
[15] Bell, Devarajan, and Gersbach, *The Long-Run Economic Costs of AIDS.*
[16] Lee Nah Hsu, *HIV Subverts National Security*; Mark Schneider and Michael Moodie, *The Destabilizing Impacts of HIV/AIDS: First Wave Hits Eastern and Southern Africa; Second Wave Threatens India, China, Russia, Ethiopia, Nigeria;* Garrett, *HIV and National Security;* USAID, *Sub-National Distribution and Situation of Orphans: An Analysis of the President's Emergency Plan for AIDS Relief Focus Countries.*
[17] Cincotta, Engelman, and Anastasion,*The Security Demographic*; UNICEF, *Children on the Brink.*
[18] Garrett, *HIV and National Security.*

Approaches to Supporting Orphans and Vulnerable Children

Non-governmental agencies working for prevention, intervention, and advocacy for OVC believe that addressing the needs of OVC is essential in order to tackle the long-term nature of the problem. This can be done by:

- *Prolonging the lives of their HIV positive parents and caregivers by improving their access to care and treatment.* This will help preserve families and ensure that children continue to receive parental love, care, and guidance for as long as possible;[19]

- *Strengthening family and community care for orphans and other vulnerable children* rather than resorting to institutional care;

- *Ensuring that orphans and other vulnerable children have equal access to essential* services such as primary and secondary education, shelter, good nutrition, and health and social services;

- *Protecting orphans and other vulnerable children from all forms of abuse*, violence, exploitation, discrimination, trafficking, and loss of inheritance;

- *Providing orphans and other vulnerable children with spiritual counseling* and other forms of psychosocial support;

- *Ensuring that orphans and other vulnerable children participate in planning,* implementing, and evaluating HIV and AIDS prevention and care programs;

- *Equipping orphans and other vulnerable children with the knowledge and skills* necessary to protect themselves from HIV infection and to support themselves when they become adults.[20]

---

[19] The World Health Organization (WHO) reports that of the six million people living with HIV and AIDS who are in urgent need of antiretroviral therapy, only 400,000 people, or 7 percent, are receiving it. In sub-Saharan Africa, only a mere 100,000, or 2 percent of those who need it, are receiving it. Antiretroviral therapy and treatments for opportunistic infections must be made available and accessible to adults and children living with HIV and AIDS, especially women.

[20] A call to action on behalf of orphans and other vulnerable children living in a world with HIV and AIDS, HACI and other civil society organizations committed to the well-being of orphans and other vulnerable children at the Bangkok HIV and AIDS World Conference in July, 2004.

Support to Faith-Based Organizations: The Church's Role and Capacity to Respond

Amid the statistics and bleak forecasts, the Church, though often under-resourced and itself strained by HIV and AIDS, is a beacon of hope. AIDS presents the church with arguably its greatest opportunity and challenge: to overcome its own lack of capacity and divisive theologies, its tendency to cast judgment and discriminate against those who are living with HIV, and act out its mission to bring the hope and healing of Jesus Christ.

The Church is the primary vehicle through which God works to share the Good News of the Kingdom. Sider argues that it is both a "reconciled and reconciling community whose visible life is a powerful sign of the Kingdom."[21]

As it awakens to the AIDS crisis, the Church can preach and live out the whole Gospel in simple and compelling ways: by speaking out against discrimination and for inclusion, bringing hope to families and children through the redemptive power of Christ, and also through ministering to their immediate physical, social, and emotional needs. It can, as Tollestrup states, become instrumental in "building environments and contexts for hope to be birthed, thrive, and be expressed by children."[22]

Children affected by HIV and AIDS can become part of this redemptive community, with God using their talents, creativity, energy, and courage to drive change and rebirth in their societies.

Service to children extends the hope of faith and fullness of life from this generation to the next. A recent study commissioned by the World Conference of Religions and Peace found a massive response—reaching almost 140,000 OVC—among churches and FBOs (82 percent of them Christian) in six countries in east and southern Africa, and this report barely skimmed the surface of the size of the actual response across the African continent, representing only 0.25 percent of the estimated 150,000 plus congregations in the study countries alone. Most of these initiatives are small-scale projects combining material, spiritual, educational, and psychosocial support to OVC.

> FBO: Faith-Based Organization

Despite the small and difficult-to-measure nature of many grassroots FBOs, donors and large development organizations should equip these locally connected and self-reliant organizations to strengthen their work in the following ways:

- Encourage religious leaders to dispel myths and judgmental attitudes

- Raise awareness about HIV and AIDS in their communities, and mobilize congregations and communities to reach out to OVC

- Listen to OVC and build effective responses based on their perspectives

---

[21] R.J. Sider, *Good News and Good Works*.
[22] See the article by Stephen Tollestrup in this volume.

- Build networks to gain leverage for funding and share best practices

- Partner with agencies who can strengthen organizational capacity

- Participate in national policy processes and advocacy

Listening to OVC

In the rush to help children, caregivers often neglect to listen to what the children feel is important to them. Despite their vulnerability, OVC have clear views on what their needs are. In a recent workshop in Zimbabwe, OVC made several recommendations to caregivers including:

- Involving children in day-to-day decision making in the home

- Creating a group of children to act as representatives in their communities who will help to make decisions that affect children

- Training children in care of the home, helping sick relatives, budgeting and financial responsibility, and other life skills to equip them if responsibility comes upon them before they become adults

Conclusions

The future looks very dark for Africa's children and societies: Children without care, love, hope, and the fulfillment of their basic rights; grandparents and extended families in survival mode; communities and churches stretched severely to bridge the gap. Where can we look for hope amid the suffering and despair caused by a vicious cycle of HIV, war, and poverty?

First, we can look for inspiration to the children, families, and communities who are confronting this crisis. Children and adults are facing tremendous hardship with grace, determination, and remarkable resilience. We see extraordinary strength emerging in these families, with children and the elderly caring for and supporting each other. Nearby, neighbors are giving up their food for tomorrow so that the orphans next door can eat today. Across Africa, many thousands of caring women and men reach out to provide help and hope as they visit the homes of people living with AIDS and the orphans they leave behind. As is so often the case in God's Kingdom, the worst of times brings out some of the best in people.

> In the rush to help children, caregivers often neglect to listen to what the children feel is important to them.

Hope also comes from knowing that God is working, from knowing that he uses all things for the good of those who love him, and from not knowing what he is doing.

We can be hopeful because God is working. While the Israelites were suffering in exile in Babylon, the Lord sent the prophet Zechariah to paint vivid pictures for them of his promised future. In Zechariah 8, the Lord says: "Old men and old women shall again sit in the streets of Jerusalem, each with staff in hand because of their great age. And the streets of the city shall be full of boys and girls playing in its streets . . . *I will save my people . . .* the vine shall yield its fruit, the ground shall give its produce, and the skies shall give their dew; and I will cause the remnant of this people to possess all these things" (Zech. 8: 4-5, 7, 12, emphasis added). The truth is that amid the devastation, God is planting seeds of peace and prosperity, of a beautiful and bountiful future.

We can also be hopeful because, as Paul describes in 2 Corinthians 1, God uses all things to fulfill his good purposes. God may be planning to raise up this generation through unimaginable suffering in order to fulfill purposes of unimaginable beauty in their lives and for his Kingdom.

God's promise is transformational, affirming the dignity and value of this generation and involving its members—and the Church globally—in the process. Both Tollestrup and White draw our attention to the remarkable work of individuals who, motivated by Christ's redemptive power, serve children sacrificially. He promises to make all of us who are involved "symbols and sources of blessing."[23]

Peace, prosperity, and purpose may seem distant and unrealizable dreams for orphans and vulnerable children—as distant as those of a powerless and captive people longing for a good life in their homeland. But God goes on to say: "All this may seem impossible to you now, a small and discouraged remnant of God's people. But do you think this is impossible for me, the LORD Almighty?" (Zech. 8:6). God's call must reach our ears as well—compelling us to reach out, walk alongside those who face these difficulties, and do what we can to support their truly heroic efforts.

---

[23] See Zechariah 8:13.

CHAPTER 4
DISCUSSION QUESTIONS

1) What do we understand by "fullness of life" in all its aspects? How can we be open to give it, and to ensure that children receive it?
2) How can we break the cycles of dysfunction in society, and so guard against dysfunctional ways of relating being passed from one generation to the next?

CHAPTER 6

MEMBERS IN GOD'S CHURCH

God welcomes children fully into the family of faith.

Children are essential to the life and ministry of the church, bringing spiritual gifts and abilities and fulfilling definite roles. The church needs to be a place where children may dynamically connect with God and engage in meaningful participation: discipled, equipped and empowered for life and ministry. As members of the family of God, children are to be cared for as sons and daughters. They are part of the admonition to love and serve one another.

God intends for churches to provide children with opportunities to know him and fulfill their calling in the body of Christ.

"God, the framer of our very being, knows that the earlier values and beliefs are imparted on the human being, the more lasting they become. God also knows that from a receptivity point of view, the early years are by far better and unmatchable and should therefore be captured to sow the seeds of faith and discipleship. I think these are some of the underlying causes why children (childhood), the tender years of life, are the focus of God. He who taught us to sow on the "good" soil knows full well that the early years of life are the best sowing season. This makes it clear to us that children are on the radar screen of God's mission like adults are."

—Shiferaw Michael

"People were bringing even infants to him that he might touch them; and when the disciples saw it, they sternly ordered them not to do it. But Jesus called for them and said, 'Let the little children come to me, and do not stop them; for it is to such as these that the Kingdom of God belongs. Truly I tell you, whoever does not receive the Kingdom of God as a little child will never enter it.'"

—Luke 18:15-17 NRSV

"Part of my responsibility as a parent and as a member of the community of faith is to expose young children to the history, the expectations and the ways of God. During their formative years, children develop their decision-making perspectives and patterns. Helping them in that process is one of the most important responsibilities we have as humans; engaging them at a young age is a critical strategic choice."

—George Barna

BIBLICAL REFLECTION

GOD WELCOMES CHILDREN FULLY INTO THE FAMILY OF FAITH

By Kara Powell
Center for Youth and Family Ministry, Fuller Theological Seminary

Introduction

"Time for dinner."

I love saying those three words because I love what dinner means for our family.

More than just a time to eat, it is a time for my five-year-old son, my three-year-old daughter, my husband, and me to enjoy being together. As we eat, we often talk about our favorite parts of our days. My son usually talks about the friends he played with, my daughter tends to talk about the food she ate, and my husband and I share about people we spent time with at work or church. The four of us tell funny stories, laugh, giggle, and simply enjoy being together. I admit that sometimes it's a bit chaotic, but it's always fun.

Our neighbors do it a little differently. They have three sons, all younger than five years old. They've decided that it is too much work to try to eat together. Instead, they eat in separate shifts. The kids eat dinner first. Once the kids go to bed, the parents have dinner on their own. Faced with the challenge of getting everyone gathered at the same time, our neighbors have decided to eat different food at different times in different places.

Every once in a while, due to a meeting or event that evening, our family ends up eating separately, too. But that is the exception, not the norm.

I look at the way our neighbors have dinner and I can't help but wonder: what are they missing out on when they eat separately? What stories go untold, what memories go unshared, and what hopes go unspoken because they don't gather every night to share life together? When the kids grow up and move out of the house, will our neighbors regret that they didn't make the effort to connect with each other over dinner?

We could probably ask the same questions not just about dinner, but about our churches, too. Many churches and Christian communities in various cultures have made similar decisions to segregate children from adults, at least to some degree. I realize that there are developmental differences between three-year-olds, thirteen-year-olds, and forty-three-year-olds. I also acknowledge that the questions that those three age groups are wrestling with are different and merit separate times for discussion. But perhaps in our well-intentioned efforts to meet various age groups' specific needs, we miss out on the richness that comes from being together. If your community fails to include and appreciate children in the midst of your life together, what will you be missing? What special gifts will be absent from your community that only children can bring? What memories of the past remain untold because adults and children aren't spending enough time together? What dreams for the future remain unspoken because you're not together to share them?

This paper explores some of these questions in its effort to better understand the meaning and power of intergenerational community. My goals are twofold: (1) to discuss Jesus' teachings about the role of children in faith communities, and (2) to provide snapshots of how children can be better appreciated and integrated. It's quite possible that we miss out on opportunities far more rich than gathering together for meals when we fail to welcome and embrace children in our communities.

An Exploration of Select Gospel Texts

Because of the multiple accounts of Jesus' interactions with children, this paper will focus the bulk of its attention on those gospel accounts. While many of us are somewhat familiar with the most often quoted passages describing Jesus' interactions with children, a closer examination of their context and their complexity makes Jesus' teachings all the more revolutionary.

The View of Children in the Old Testament

To better understand the context underlying these New Testament texts, we need to start by examining the Old Testament view of children. According to Dr. Judith Gundry-Volf of Yale University, in the Old Testament Jewish tradition, children were viewed as a divine gift and sign of God's blessing. An abundance of children was equated with an abundance of blessing and joy (Ps. 127:3-5; Ps. 128:3-6). Childlessness was wretched and Old Testament Jews took drastic and unusual measures to overcome it.[1] Children were a central component of God's promise to Abraham to bless him and make him a "great nation" by providing him with descendants as numerous as the dust of the earth and the stars of the heavens.[2]

There are some negative references toward children in the Old Testament, such as Elisha's calling down a curse on children who were jeering at him (2 Kings 2:23-24) and the reference to the "folly" which is "bound up in the heart of child" (Prov. 22:15a).[3] In general, however, children were esteemed positively, so much so that Jews could fathom that the long-awaited Messiah would be born as a baby (Isa. 7:14).[4]

The View of Children in the First Century

At the time of the writing of the gospels, in many ways the cultural pendulum had swung toward a more negative view of children. In the Greco-Roman world, children were

---

[1] See Genesis 30:1-22; 1 Samuel 1; Deuteronomy 25:5-10. Also see the articles by Jennifer Orona and Judith Ennew in this volume.
[2] Judith Gundry-Volf, "To Such as These Belongs the Reign of God," *Theology Today*, 2000, 56(4), 470. See Genesis 12:2; 13:16; 15:5.
[3] Gundry-Volf, "To Such as These Belongs the Reign of God," 2000. All Scripture quotations are taken from the New International Version unless otherwise noted.
[4] Robin Mass, "Christ as the *Logos* of Childhood: Reflections on the Meaning and the Mission of the Child," *Theology Today*, 2000, 56(4), 458-459.

not viewed as equal persons. Instead, they were among the least valued members of society. Harsh discipline, abandonment, and infanticide were allowable practices if they were the wishes of the child's father.[5] According to Dionysius of Halicarnassus, "The law-giver of the Romans gave virtually full power to the father over his son, whether he thought proper to imprison him, to scourge him, to put him in chains, and keep him at work in the fields, or to put him to death."[6] Likely more common than this type of extreme treatment of children as some sort of property was simply the view that childhood was a training ground for adult life, not a significant stage of life in itself.[7]

Jesus' Entry as an Infant

In the midst of these mixed messages about the value of children, the Messiah entered the world as a newborn. Perhaps twenty centuries later, the radical nature of Jesus' entry as a baby has been somewhat obscured. Yet the provocative nature of this entry should not escape us. The fifth century patriarch of Constantinople, Nestorius, was so struck by the implications of this that he wrote, "I deny that God is two or three months old."[8] The twentieth century theologian Karl Barth wrote of the helpless baby Jesus, "This is your God!"[9] Indeed, it is difficult to imagine the fullness of the Creator God contained in the small body of a newborn. It becomes even more unfathomable given how children were viewed in the culture into which Jesus was born. Jesus' revolutionary teachings about childhood parallel his revolutionary entry into the world as a child himself.

Jesus' Link Between "Greatness" and Children

The radical nature of Jesus' birth is echoed in his radical perspective on greatness. In Luke 9:46, an argument breaks out among Jesus' disciples about who is the greatest. The timing of this dispute makes sense in the overall context of Luke 9:28-43. In Luke 9:28-36, Jesus takes three disciples (Peter, James, and John, often referred to as the three closest to Jesus) onto a mountain to pray. Perhaps the selection of those three and the exclusion of the others fueled feelings of jealousy and insecurity in the nine left behind. The fact that those who were left behind were unable to heal a demon-possessed boy likely made them feel even more inferior and resentful (Luke 9:37-43).

> Indeed it is difficult to imagine the fullness of the Creator God contained n the small body of a newborn.

Knowing about the disciples' argument over greatness, Jesus takes a little child and has the child stand beside Him. Then he teaches, "Whoever welcomes this little child in

---

[5] Bonnie J. Miller-McLemore, *Let the Children Come*, 96-98.
[6] Dionysius of Halicarnassus *Rom. Ant.* 2.26.4, as quoted in Judith M. Gundry-Volf, "The Least and the Greatest," 33.
[7] Gundry-Volf, "The Least and the Greatest," 34.
[8] Keith White, "Rediscovering Children at the Heart of Mission," 192.
[9] White, 192.

my name welcomes me; and whoever welcomes me welcomes the one who sent me. For he who is the least among you all—he is the greatest" (Luke 9:48).

Thus Jesus has placed two figures before the disciples: himself, who they greatly respect, and a child, who would probably hold little intrinsic value in their eyes. Yet Jesus shows the inestimable but hidden value of children by linking them to greatness. The good news for the disciples is that greatness can be pursued and possessed. The bad news for the disciples is that greatness does not come in a manner familiar to them. It does not come from comparison with others, as they had assumed. It comes by welcoming a child, who in being the least somehow becomes the greatest. As Jesus often did, he shows that the Kingdom of God is an upside-down Kingdom with upside-down values.[10]

> "Whoever welcomes this little child in my name welcomes me; and whoever welcomes me welcomes the one who sent me. For he who is the least among you all—he is the greatest."
> —Luke 9:48 NIV

In Greek, the verb Jesus uses here for "welcome" is *dechomai*, which was often used in the context of showing hospitality to guests. Thus, it carries a certain connotation of servanthood. What makes this teaching all the more remarkable is that in the first century, taking care of children was a task generally fulfilled by members of the culture who were viewed as different, and even inferior, to the male disciples: women and slaves.[11] Jesus was asking the disciples who had just been arguing about their individual greatness to take on a role requiring utmost humility.

Jesus' Link Between Receiving the Kingdom and Children

It seems that the news of Jesus' goodwill toward children had spread, for in Luke 18:15 people bring babies to Jesus to have him touch them. Parents probably equated Jesus' touch with an act of blessing and they were eager for their children to receive that favor.

Apparently the disciples did not approve of this, as evidenced by their rebuke of those who brought children to Jesus. Jesus, however, saw the situation quite differently. He calls the children to him and says, "Let the little children come to me, and do not hinder them, for the Kingdom of God belongs to such as these. I tell you the truth, anyone who will not receive the Kingdom of God like a little child will never enter it" (Luke 18:15-17).

In Jesus' response to the disciples, he makes two important points. First, children are eligible to receive the Kingdom. Second, they are not only eligible, but they are *models* of what it means to receive the Kingdom. Of course, that begs an important question that Jesus doesn't explicitly answer: what does it mean to receive the Kingdom of God like a little child? Some possibilities include a child's openness, willingness to trust, freedom from hypocrisy or pretension, conscious weakness, and

> Children are not only eligible to receive the Kingdom, but they are models of what it means to receive the Kingdom.

---

[10] See the article by Joni Middleton in this volume.
[11] Gundry-Volf, "To Such as These Belongs the Reign of God," 475-476.

readiness for dependence.[12] While the exact answer cannot be pinpointed, what is most relevant for the purposes of this paper is that children were most certainly an example for others who want to grow in their faith.

Jesus' Link Between Worship and Children

While not generally as well known as the previous two Lukan texts, Matthew's account of Jesus at the temple sheds light on one reason to involve children in our faith communities. When Jesus enters the temple area, he drives out all who were trying to make a profit from temple worship and sacrifices. He overturns the tables of the money changers and the benches of those who were selling doves (Matt. 21:12). He warns them, "It is written, 'My house will be called a house of prayer,' but you are making it a 'den of robbers'" (Matt. 21:13). As Jesus heals the blind and the lame who have come to him, some children in the temple area start shouting, "Hosanna to the Son of David" (Matt. 21:15). The chief priests and teachers become indignant about the children's cries, possibly because they deny that Jesus deserved such acclaim.

The religious leaders ask Jesus, "Do you hear what these children are saying?" (Matt. 21:16a). Jesus answers by quoting Psalm 8:2, "Yes, have you never read, 'From the lips of children and infants you have ordained praise'?" (Matt. 21:16b). While it's possible that the children gathered did not fully understand the meaning of their shouts of praise, they are nonetheless validated and encouraged by Jesus' affirmation of the value of children's worship. Those who had great religious training failed to see what children ably recognized: Jesus was the Son of David and thus deserved great praise.

Snapshots of How to Fully Welcome Children Into Faith Communities

We have seen a consistent theme in Jesus' words: children are important in our faith communities. Whether children are viewed as a way to welcome Jesus, as models of receiving the Kingdom, or as valuable contributors to our worship, we cannot escape the underlying message of all three texts: Jesus values children and therefore we should, too. In order to understand practical ways that we can begin to embody and communicate the importance of children in our community, we will turn to several sources including Scripture, the relevant insights of other child-friendly organizations, and the contemporary experiences of churches worldwide.

Children are Ministers Too

Scripture is bursting with examples of the important ministry of children and youth including David in his battle with Goliath, Esther's courage on behalf of the Jews, the prophet Jeremiah who took God's message to the people, Josiah who became king when he was eight years old, and even young Mary giving birth to Jesus.[13] While these are

---

[12] John Nolland, *Word Bible Commentary*, vol. 35B.
[13] See the articles by Stephen Tollestrup, Gustavo Crocker, and Karissa Glanville in this volume.

important illustrations of the powerful ministry of children, few of the children you and I know will be kings, queens, or parents of the Savior. So is it possible for the children in more "ordinary" circumstances and positions to have a powerful impact in our communities?

We can answer that question with a resounding "yes" because of the doctrine of the priesthood of all believers. The doctrine of the priesthood of all believers stems largely from Paul's writings about first-century church community. In his letters, Paul uses the Greek term *ekklesia* for "church." Many of us today equate an *ekklesia* or a "church" with a physical location or building in which we gather for worship services. That concept was foreign to Paul's view of *ekklesia*. First, there were no church buildings in the first century. Typically, churches met in large homes that could hold up to forty or more people.[14] Second, the very word *ekklesia* actually means "called out ones." When Paul writes of a church, he's thinking of *people*, not a location.

An important element of these gatherings of people was their mutual ministry to each other through their spiritual gifts. These gifts are described in Romans 12:1-8, 1 Corinthians 12:1-31, and Ephesians 4:1-13 and include gifts of faith, prophecy, serving, and teaching. While Scripture makes it clear that all believers have spiritual gifts and talents, some communities tend to over-emphasize and even rely on the gifts of certain designated leaders (i.e., pastors, deacons, and teachers) while the gifts of other believers remain hidden and undeveloped.

A crucial truth is that Paul does not limit the spiritual gifts to a certain group of "leaders." In fact, he never limits them to believers of a certain age or maturity level, either. Therefore, it is reasonable to assume that children possess spiritual gifts. The gifts may be nascent, they may be undeveloped, and they may be blocked by the position of children in a society, but since children possess these gifts, they can (and should) make valuable ministry contributions in our community. As the Consultative Group on Ministry Among Children explains, "[Children] can have a distinctive teaching ministry in which they ask apparently innocent questions, voicing the doubts and questions which adults are too self-conscious to raise and enabling answers to be found for all. They can have a distinctive prophetic ministry when they notice our failure to live by the gospel we proclaim and ask us why."[15]

---

[14] Robert Banks, *Paul's Idea of Community*, 35.
[15] Consultative Group on Ministry Among Children, *Unfinished Business: Children and the Churches*, 52.

In many cultures it seems that the teachings that are more explicitly related to children in their immediate family context have been emphasized instead of Paul's doctrine of the priesthood of all believers. These include his admonition in Ephesians 6:1 that children should "obey your parents in the Lord, for this is right" and similarly in Colossians 3:20 that children should "obey your parents in everything, for this pleases the Lord." While these commands are important and should be followed, perhaps our communities and families would be more balanced if we also embraced Paul's teachings about the use of spiritual gifts in the community.

> Inviting children to share their experiences, help with various projects, and even play roles in worship experiences can provide unintimidating ways for children to test out the nature of Christian community even before deciding to follow Jesus as Lord and Savior..

Practitioners in many cultures often invite children to make contributions to the community as an effective first step in welcoming them into Christian community. Inviting children to share their experiences, help with various projects, and even play roles in worship experiences can provide unintimidating ways for children to test out the nature of Christian community even before deciding to follow Jesus as Lord and Savior. While many leaders' evangelistic efforts are focused on adults and integrate children as an afterthought, it seems logical that an increase in commitment, energy, and funding dedicated to children could benefit not just those children, but their parents, and the entire Christian community as a whole.[16]

Children Minister through Their Actions

This paper presents two practical ways for children to minister in and to their community. The first is through their actions. One way we've already seen that children's actions are an example of ministry is through their worship. Whether it is by worshiping the Lord in song, or worshiping him in other ways including art, dance, or music, the way that children praise the Lord is an important part of the way a community praises the Lord.

In addition to worship, children's prayers are another important way that they minister through their actions. According to C. Fuller, children's prayers are characterized by the following:

- A childlike faith that views the impossible as possible.

- Hearts of incredible grace, compassion, and care.

- Trust in God's faithful provision.

- Forgiving hearts that keep short accounts.

---

[16] For more on this topic, see George Barna, *Transforming Children into Spiritual Champions*.

- Simple prayers that are direct and honest.

- A desire to be a participant in effecting positive change.

- Hearing God speak without the barriers of spiritual jargon or adult rationalizations.[17]

In addition to their prayers and worship, children also help guide our faith communities by their advice and input. Whether it is through informal discussion with children, or the formal inclusion of children on committees and leadership groups, children have a unique perspective that often goes unsolicited and unheard.[18] One particular method of involving children is to seek their input while communities are designing, monitoring, and evaluating their programs and ministries.[19] Since children will be affected by this work, they undoubtedly have input that could greatly maximize its effectiveness and impact.

Children also minister to the community by sharing their stories. Opportunities to process their experiences and observations are important not only for the community, but for the children themselves. Telling stories appears to be an important element of healing for children with traumatic backgrounds, as evident by a survey conducted by Mooli Lahad. Lahad surveyed four hundred children who had been traumatized by war and other similar events and found that the quality that children most needed in those who cared for them was that of being a "witness." This "witness" was most helpful to children when he or she saw their pain and their joy, heard their stories, and stood with them.[20] In referring to this study, Josephine Joy-Wright concludes, "Whether we are called to be therapists or carers in different ways, we are called fundamentally to be witnesses."[21]

Finally, children minister to the church community by expanding its vision to reach out to those who are not yet part of the community. As described in *Unfinished Business*, "Many parents have been drawn to Christian commitment through their children. Children may have an apostolic ministry in being sent out to the places where children are making Christ present in the world. Within the playground they may work against bullying and racism, befriend the lonely, or show a generosity of spirit, all of which make the Spirit of Christ evident to other children."[22]

---

[17] C. Fuller, *When Children Pray*, as quoted in Josephine-Joy Wright, "Exploring and Releasing Children's Strengths, Gifts and Potential," 137-138; see Laurence Gray, "The 'Right' of the Child to Speak and Be Heard," 85.
[18] Save the Children, "Three Models of Child Participation in Community Based OVC Care," *The Chris-Caba Journal* 3, no. 1 (2005): 13-15.
[19] "Guidelines for Children's Participation in HIV/AIDS Programs," *The Chris-Caba Journal* 3, no. 1 (2005): 25.
[20] Mooli Lahad, "Story Making in Assessment Method for Coping with Stress," *Drama Therapy Theory and Practice II*, 92, as quoted by Josephine-Joy Wright, "Listening to Children and Enabling Their Involvement," 66.
[21] Josephine-Joy Wright, "Listening to Children and Enabling Their Involvement," 66.
[22] Consultative Group on Ministry Among Children, 52-53.

Children Minister through Their Being

Not only do children minister through their actions, they also minister by their very being. Merely including them can transform the tone of any community. For example, the United Nations General Assembly Special Session on Children (UNGASS) in 2002 included large numbers of children as official members of various delegations. Kofi Annan described the effects:

The children's presence transformed the atmosphere of the United Nations. Into our usually measured and diplomatic discussions, they introduced their passions, questions, fears, challenges, enthusiasm and optimism. They brought us their ideas, hopes and dreams . . . And they contributed something only they could know: the experience of being young in the 21st century—in a time when HIV and AIDS continues to grow at a devastating rate; in a time when unprecedented wealth coexists with extreme poverty; in a time when the rights of children, while almost universally recognized, are abused systematically and daily throughout the world.[23]

Perhaps part of what changed the United Nations is described by the German preacher and theologian Freidrich Schleiermacher as children's "pure revelation of the divine." According to Schleiermacher, a child is "altogether in the moment . . . the past disappears for him, and of the future he knows nothing—each moment exists only for itself."[24] Maybe the power of children's being also relates to what Roman Catholic theologian Karl Rahner calls children's "infinite openness."[25] Or perhaps it's due to what the Consultative Group on Ministry Among Children calls their "gift of visible growth and change, helping everyone to remember that all are on the journey."[26] While these theologians and leaders have different interpretations of what children uniquely bring to the community's pursuit of God, they agree that children's intrinsic attitudes are a source of powerful growth and change.

Finally, a child's being ministers to the community because of the many ways we can learn deep theological truths as we observe and engage with them. We gain a better picture of our divine Father's unconditional love as we interact paternally and maternally with children in our contexts. We get a glimpse of the allure of sin as we watch children wrestle with whether or not to obey the adults who care for and nurture them. We understand more about our deep dependence on God as we realize how dependent children are upon others for their very survival. In addition, when we choose to adopt children, we gain a greater appreciation for what it means to be adopted by God into his family.

---

[23] UNICEF, 2003, vii, as quoted in "An Introduction to this Child Participation Issue," *The Chris-Caba Journal* 3, no. 1 (2005): 4.
[24] Friedrich Schleiermacher, *Sammtliche Werke* (Verklin: Georg Reimer) 2, no. 6 (1834-1864): 71-72.
[25] Mary Ann Hinsdale, "'Infinite Openness to the Infinite': Karl Rahner's Contributions to Modern Catholic Thought on the Child," 428.
[26] Consultative Group on Ministry Among Children, 57.

Conclusion

Having researched Jesus' teachings on the inclusion of children as well as explored snapshots of ways children can be involved in communities, I have become even more grateful for the time that our family gathers together every evening for dinner. I believe that now, God is extending an invitation to his entire family so that all who are his sons and daughters can gather and minister to each other in the midst of sharing life together. While at times it will be necessary, and maybe even recommended, for children and adults to be separate, many communities may want to consider greater cross-generational communication and integration. Just like when we eat dinner, at times it might be a bit more chaotic, but it's likely that we'll all walk away feeling more full and satisfied.

CRITICAL ISSUES

NURTURE AND THE FAMILY OF FAITH

By Ndaba Mazabane with Doug McConnell
Rosebank Union Church, South Africa; World Evangelical Alliance

Introduction

The critical challenge facing the contemporary church is how it takes up seriously the notion of being "the family of faith" for all who belong to it, especially children. When Jesus Christ died on the cross, he paid a price through his blood to redeem and save all who had missed the mark. When, by faith, they turned to him and believed in his name, he gave them a new lease on life. He gave them "the right to become children of God—children born not of natural descent, nor of human decision or a husband's will, but born of God" (John 1:12-13 NIV). Out of the people, he created a forceful and dynamic community we now know as the church. This community is comprised of the young and old, the rich and poor. It cuts across the racial and gender divide, making us "all one in Christ Jesus" (Gal. 3:28 NIV).

> The Church has unique gifts to offer that others do not: the power of transformation in the Lord Jesus Christ and the hope of the coming kingdom of God. Children are essential in the realization of this kingdom, and for this reason, the Church should be in the forefront of the struggle for the sake of children.
>
> —*Tri Budiardjo*

There are several images that are employed to help us understand clearly the nature of the church and its significant role in equipping all of its members. Let's examine the following examples:

- The assembly—As Kara Powell explains, the word *ekklesia* means "called out ones" and was used by the Greeks for a gathering of people called out from their homes into a public square for the purpose of discussion. The church is a collective group, called out for a special purpose of doing God's work (1 Peter 2:9-10).

- The people of God—This term is used to refer to a fellowship of those who live under the lordship of Christ, regardless of their status (1 Cor. 15:9). God's people represent and reflect his image and reproduce generations that honor and serve his purposes.

- The body of Christ—of which Jesus is the head. This is fittingly designed in order to accommodate and give space for every member to exercise "gifts" and talents given by God (1 Cor. 12:12ff).[1] The body functions better and at its maximum when there is unity as well as diversity.

- The family—Next to the family, the church is one of the few places where the spiritual life of the individual can be nurtured. In faithfully training its members and teaching the word of God, the church affirms that Scripture was written to help children, young people, and fathers (1 John 2:12-14).

Given these images, we can better see the significance of Affirmation 6 in the "Biblical Framework for Understanding God's Heart for Children."

Children as part of the family of faith are essential to the life and ministry of the church, bringing spiritual gifts and abilities and fulfilling definite roles. The church needs to be a place where children may dynamically connect with God and engage in meaningful participation; discipled, equipped and empowered for life and ministry. As members of the family of God, children are to be cared for as sons and daughters. They are part of the admonition to love and serve one another.

Biblical Teachings Concerning Children

Let me advance the following truths about children, which promote the biblical practice of welcoming them to participate fully into the family of faith. In the context of Israel, children were not merely included in religious activities, but they were also assimilated and incorporated with a deep sense of belonging into the family of God's covenant people. In the early church, homes (Acts 4:46) were used as centers of worship and instruction.

1) The theological importance of children gave them a place of value and prominence to God's people.

Because God was regarded as the "giver" (Ps. 127:3) of children, their births were acknowledged as having divine implications. Therefore, each child was given a divine value and could not be disregarded. In addition, parents were given an important responsibility. God was the ultimate possessor of children. Thus, it seemed only natural to regard children as God's possession as well as a reminder of the imperative to treat them with utmost care and never "causes one of these little ones . . . to sin" (Matt. 18:6 NIV). We will recall a practice in the Old Testament family in which parents would symbolically give their firstborn son back to God and, in turn, receive the child as a sacred trust from Him.

---

[1] See the article by Kara Powell in this volume.

Children were to grow up with a sense of belonging to their immediate family, their nation, and the family of God. The Old Testament intimate household of faith gave rise to the New Testament family of God.[2]

2) The belief that children were able to experience worship and praise of God afforded them an important place in the religious life of his people.

As a result, children participated meaningfully in the Sabbath celebrations, the joys of thanksgiving, and the national festivals. At home during meals, especially at the Passover, God's faithfulness would be remembered and recounted and faith lessons drawn and applied. Children would ask questions of which parents would provide answers (cf. Ex. 12:25-28).

3) The importance of children as the future of Israel forced a close and intimate relationship between the young and the old.

The people of God clearly saw that their future was intimately wrapped up in their children. Children were regarded as the future bearers of Yahweh's name, and they were to be the ones who were to perpetuate their parents' faith and values. This relationship of respect for parents' faith and values assumed that children would receive the baton of faith, run with it into the future and hand it on to their own children. In so doing, generations would be impacted and faithful living would continue on and on.[3] Essential to this process was an ideal imperative of transmitting faith from parent to child (Deut. 6:4-6).

> There is room for children in the house of the Lord. Yes, there is room for the child Jesus in the Temple.
>
> —Tri Budiardjo

4) The corporate nature of childhood demanded a belonging and caring environment.

Human nature, as created in the image of God, is corporate, requiring from the time of creation a developed family environment. This is what has made the family the basic and essential unit of society. Similarly, the life of faith must be nurtured in the context of life in community. Strong relationships in the church community are essential if faith is to be shared and passed on from one generation to the other.

5) Adults can learn from children.

When Jesus "called a little child and had him stand among them" (Matt. 18:2-4 NIV), he made a profound statement and lesson. What were some of the childlike qualities that the Master wanted them to learn? What about innocence, the ability to wonder, the capacity

---

[2] For a further discussion of this concept and its ethical implications, see C.J.H. Wright, *Old Testament Ethics for the People of God*.
[3] See the articles in Chapter 5 of this volume.

to forgive and fully forget? The willingness to learn, the eagerness to do, the contentment to simply be who they are without needing to impress, are some of the qualities worth acquiring.

The Priority to Nurture Children

When Jesus said, "Let the little children come to me, and do not hinder them" (Matt. 19:14 NIV), he was also inviting them to "learn from me" (Matt. 11:28ff NIV). It is becoming clearer that the most important segment of the population towards which churches should focus their energies and resources is children. With all the dangers and risks facing children, the church has to create an environment conducive to and fitting for children. By investing time and resources now in educating them, we will be ensuring a bright future filled with possibilities.[4] What must be considered when we nurture children? The nurture of young children:

- is the primary responsibility of parents.[5]

- is a 24 hour-a-day, seven-day-per-week process that continues from birth until maturity.[6]

- must have as its primary goals the salvation of and discipleship of the next generation.[7]

- must be based on the Word of God, holding Christ as pre-eminent in all of life.[8]

- if and when delegated to others by parents, must be done with utmost care to ensure that all teachers follow these principles.[9]

- results in the formation of a belief system or worldview that will be patterned after the belief systems or worldviews of their teachers.[10]

The Benefits of Welcoming Children into the Community of Faith

Welcoming children, especially those who are living in risky environments, to participate fully in the family of faith is like welcoming one of the least among us all—

---

[4] See the article by Marcia Bunge in this volume.
[5] See Deuteronomy 6:4-9; 11:18-21; Psalms 78:1-7; 127:3; Proverbs 22:6; Malachi 2:13-16; Ephesians 6:4.
[6] See Deuteronomy 6:7; 11:19; Proverbs 22:6.
[7] See Psalm 78:6-7; Matthew 18:6, 28:19-20.
[8] See Matthew 24:35; Psalm 119; Colossians 2:3, 6-10.
[9] See Exodus 18:21; 1 Samuel 1:27-28; 3:1-10.
[10] See Luke 6:40.

indeed, these children are among the greatest. To welcome them in our lives is to welcome the Lord, so close are they to his heart. Invariably, this brings benefits not only to them but to their extended family of believers. A whole network of family members may also find the church as a place of refuge. This would then give the church an opportunity to offer its resources to assist and open its children's program and sanctuary for worship, support, and counseling or for participation in the life of the church in other ways.

Christ demonstrated his love and service to others by offering himself voluntarily on the cross. He humbled himself before his disciples, washing their feet in one of his final gestures. In that moment, Jesus said, "Now that I, your Lord and Teacher, have washed your feet, you also should wash one another's feet" (John 13:14 NIV). An open ministry to children in difficult circumstances provides a multitude of opportunities to follow Jesus' example. The honorable work of serving children in love generates a deeper understanding of God's devotion to his people. Sacrificial service is the catalyst for growing spiritually robust disciples of Christ.

Welcoming children at risk goes with the reminder of Christ's affirmation, ". . . whatever you did for one of the least of these brothers of mine, you did it for me" (Matt. 25:40 NIV). When the Apostle Paul was exhorting fellow believers to "Submit to one another out of reverence for Christ" (Eph. 5:21 NIV), he had in mind children too. Growing closer to God is the ultimate motivation for serving children in his name. To incorporate them into the life of the church and to see that they are nurtured in the context of lasting relationships would strengthen the bonds of Christian love. This would set them on a path of growing in Christ and in relationship with one another as all follow Christ's example of service.

A local church ministry that is focused on reaching children in this way holds a promise of changing the community it is serving. How often have our churches pondered taking the Gospel to distant mission fields, hoping to help others with more significant ministry concerns, while overlooking children with needs in our immediate spheres of influence?

Children play a vital role in the church. They teach us by their example about compassion, commitment, unconditional love, and forgiveness.

> Growing closer to God is the ultimate motivation for serving children in his name.

Churches are uniquely positioned as welcoming agents of transformation, to train children in the ways of the Lord by "[making] disciples . . . baptizing . . . and teaching them" and so to fulfill the Great Commission (Matt. 28:19-20 NIV). The church is also capable of demonstrating to children how "to love him with all your heart . . . and to love your neighbor as yourself" (Mark 12:33 NIV).

Strategic Guidelines to Inform a Potential Model of Welcoming Children in the Church

It is one thing to *say* that children are welcome and free to participate in the life and ministry of the church. In reality, however, this is far removed from the actual practices of most churches. Traditionally, children are relegated to Sunday school, which often is a stand alone service, excluding the rest of the gathered people of God—offering no integrated approach to corporate worship and missing the need to model the true functional family of faith.[11] Even the children's church model does not adequately address the concern of how children really feel as a part of the whole assembly of God's people. I submit in this paper a model that attempts to ensure that children are fully welcomed into the family of faith. The Church must consider the following guiding principles:

1) Acknowledge the theological importance of children and their rightful place as members of the church of God.

2) Fit and integrate the learning process, effectively achieved in the family environment, within which the interflow of Christian experience takes place naturally.

3) Provide a maximum opportunity and effectiveness of faith practice for children and together with them, rather than merely processing them through a formal teaching procedure. The focus is on children having faith in God as opposed to a lesson delivered.

4) Effectively incorporate children into the heart of worshiping God with love, acceptance and a joyful sense of belonging and celebration. In an environment of loving and caring relationships, faith is easily nurtured and is most effectively passed on to children.

5) Enable parents to fulfill their obligation for the spiritual well-being of their children and the responsibility they have to pass on their legacy of faith.

6) Promote awareness amongst all members, young and old, of their functional worth and responsibility for the continual building up of their faith in God and the importance of sharing it with others.

7) Encourage the development of responsible leadership from an early age through participation in worship and service.

What is it that we are likely to see as a result of implementing the above-mentioned principles and practices? Here are eight likely outcomes.

- Children will be afforded a maximum exposure to people of faith and given the chance to develop trusting relationships in the process of moving towards a faith of their own.

- Children will develop open minds by asking questions; they will develop a desire to know what faith is all about. This will provide a context for powerful learning.

---

[11] See the article by Kara Powell in this volume.

- Children will begin to detect and exemplify the cherished values of God's people.

- Children will sense their value to God and the church and come to an understanding of their functional values as they participate in worship and take on other responsibilities.

- Children will develop a sense of ownership and belonging to the church and its members from an early age as they interact, worship, and are accepted.

- Children entrenched in a sense of belonging to the church will be less inclined to break out and be influenced by outside group pressure.

- Children will begin to realize their responsibility to serve God and will begin to look for opportunities to share their experiences with their peers, aiming to draw them into this welcoming "world" fit for children.

- Children entrusted with responsibilities at an early age will naturally develop in leadership and become useful members of the body of Christ.

The challenge is for the community of faith to accept the responsibility for children in its midst and become models of a living faith. May God help us as we welcome them.

PRACTITIONER'S RESPONSE

BEING THE FAMILY OF FAITH

By Douglas McConnell
Fuller Theological Seminary

From the pulpit of the sanctuary, a pastor has the unique vantage point of seeing the entire congregation. At least that is the common understanding. However, from the vantage point in the back row of the sanctuary recently, a large number of children were barely noticeable as they played in the dirt not far from the open doors. Apparently the Sunday school classes had dismissed their young charges before the pastor concluded the sermon. Reflecting on this typical Sunday morning scenario, one wonders if anyone seriously considered them part of the actual congregation.

This scene took place in a small city in Kerala, India. While the setting is unique, the situation is not. Indeed, it could be in Accra, Cochabamba, or Melbourne. In this sixth point we affirm that children are an important part of the Church. Clearly this is the biblical understanding of God's heart for children. So as we respond to our affirmation, we must also consider how this touches the children we are called to serve.

Belonging

A theme that emerged from our study is that children should fully belong to the family of faith. Whether born into the family and confirmed as part of the covenant or born again through the witness of the Gospel, every child who has faith in Christ is a member of the family of God. Along with other believers, children should find the local congregation a place that feels like home.[1] In the case of many children, it must be a home unlike those they have known. Security replaces threat, stability replaces uncertainty, and hope for the future resides in the family of those adopted as children of God. For belonging to be realized, the needs of children must be met in a relational manner that helps them to identify with this new family.

In his presentation, Ndaba Mazabane reminds us of the way Jesus connects care for the weak and marginalized with service to the Lord (Matt. 25:40). This is a powerful motivation for anyone who desires to serve the Lord. Caring for children and welcoming them into the family of faith is caring for Jesus himself. To achieve this means a conscious effort to reach out to those on the margins, especially the littlest ones. Thus, welcoming children will inevitably change the way churches approach their ministries.

The most common approach to developing a sense of belonging is to group children according to age and/or stage of development. Programs such as Sunday school, children's

---

[1] Andrew Walls, *The Missionary Movement in Christian History: Studies in the Transmission of the Faith*, 7.

clubs, and youth groups are found in most churches. This approach recognizes the differences between adults and children, often building on the educational models within the broader cultural setting. Children form friendships among their peers in a setting in which they begin learning about the Christian faith. Assuming that the child's family or support network continues to facilitate their attendance, this can have a lasting impact in shaping their commitment.

Among the effective movements that strengthen Sunday programs in local churches with more disciplined approaches are the Boys' Brigade, Girls' Brigade, and Awana.[2] The introduction of a strong sense of belonging with a commitment to the group and clear rewards for achievement are important motivators, particularly for children who have few positive experiences with which to identify in their daily routines.

Being Family

As we consider belonging to the family of faith, moving beyond these age-related programs is important. One of the weaknesses of children's programs is the lack of intergenerational involvement. As Kara Powell reminds us, there are older leaders in most programs for children, but they lack integration with the life of the church. When we use the family metaphor for the church, we must remember that families, by their very nature, embrace young and old with significant roles for all.[3]

To illustrate the family approach, let us consider the following example about a church that was planted in the eastern suburbs of Melbourne, Australia in the mid-1980s. Initially, the children and youth programs followed the typical age and stage approach. In time a group of parents and elders decided to try to bring together the children and youth involved in a weekly group followed by attendance at the Sunday evening church service. Dinner was prepared by adults while another group of adults was involved in discipleship groups divided into age groups. After the discipleship groups, everyone would eat the meal together. While they experienced a moderate degree of resistance, the leaders persisted and in time, the youth began to choose to attend, even inviting their friends. After securing a core group in the "Alive at Five" group, the leaders began to involve the youth in the evening service. At first it was taking up an offering, reading Scripture, and the more task-oriented activities. Soon, however, a number of the talents and gifts of the youth were identified and the entire service, apart from the sermon, was assigned to them. Looking back on this group of young people, it is not surprising to see the commitment of the participants 15 or more years later.[4]

---

[2] For more information please see the following websites: Boys' Brigade, www.boys-brigade.org.uk; Girls' Brigade, www.girlsbrigadeew.org.uk; AWANA, www.awana.org.
[3] See the article by Kara Powell in this volume.
[4] Among the youth who were active in that group during their secondary school years are Reuben & Sarah Morgan, internationally known for their leadership in the worship community at Hillsong Church near Sydney, Australia. For more information on the ministry of the Morgans, please visit www.hillsong.com/music/bin/view.pl?sitename=music&page=index.

Where families are dysfunctional or non-existent, this element of the church's ministry takes on even more significance. An illustration of this greater involvement comes from the city of Cochabamba, Bolivia. Upon retirement from their work in the United States, a couple joined a church planting team of missionaries. They spent time in language study and practical assistance for the team. Much to their surprise, the search for ministry led to an open door to visit the prison for women. Even more surprising was the discovery of children incarcerated with their mothers. After the initial shock, they requested permission to take some of the children during the school hours to provide emotional and spiritual care, nutritional meals, and opportunities for education. Permission was given, leading to a vibrant ministry with children of prisoners as part of their work with the church. In addition to care from the couple, others on the team and in the church provide an extended family that models strong, loving relationships. Doors continued to open to this isolated group of children as the team earned the trust of both mothers and officials.

In both of these examples, the programs and participants draw children and youth into the family of God with a strong sense of belonging. Ndaba Mazabane rightly asserted, "To welcome [children] . . . into our lives is to welcome the Lord so close are they to his heart."[5] Whatever the hurdles, the benefits to the fellowship of the family and to the children are worthy of our greatest efforts. As psychologist Pam King notes, the gain for at-risk youth may be measured in their increased social and spiritual assets to move beyond surviving to thriving.[6]

Nurturing

As children are accepted into the life of the church, they must also be encouraged to discover their gifts and the contribution they can make to the ministries of the church. When children are viewed as part of the ministry team of the church, they are nurtured in the context of doing ministry. Learning by doing is a vital part of the process of maturing spiritually.[7] Children should be viewed as part of the laity of the church among whom the ministry grows and expands (Eph. 4:7-16; Rom. 12:1-8). Children as disciples also share the mandate to be witnesses in the world beyond the boundaries of the congregation. In this way the role of children in the church will embrace the words of Jesus, "It is to such as these that the kingdom of God belongs" (Mk. 10:14).

---

[5] Ndaba Mazabane, "God Welcomes Children Fully Into the Family of Faith," 5.
[6] Pamela E. King, "The Hopeful Lens of Positive Youth Development," *Theology News & Notes*, Fuller Theological Seminary (Fall 2005):11-13.
[7] See the articles by Karissa Glanville, Cathryn Baker, and Daphne Kirk in this volume.

To adequately nurture children and youth, the ministry of a congregation must also engage in their lives outside of the church services. Due to the wide range of challenges this raises for the church, particularly smaller churches, many specialized ministry movements have emerged to help broaden their capacity to nurture. One of the earliest movements was Scripture Union (SU) founded in 1867 as Children's Special Service Mission.[8] The impact of SU, particularly in the British Commonwealth countries has been a great asset to churches. Their engagement in schools, camps, and other types of meetings along with the distribution of daily reading materials that teach the Bible have raised a clear standard for nurturing faith. So effective is their ministry in Ghana, for example, that a leader of SU observed that often when a young person wants to say he or she is a believer, they will say, "I'm SU."[9]

Groups like SU model an important part of welcoming children fully into the family of faith: embracing the gifts that children bring into the ministries of the church. To nurture those gifts means that opportunities for ministry accompanied by wise oversight must be an integral part of church life. In Awana Clubs, Boys' and Girls' Brigades, and SU, children are given responsibility for ministries from their earliest involvement. As they are mentored, their gifts are recognized and affirmed, providing a broader base for ministry. Nurture that actively engages children in areas of ministry has the added benefit of strengthening not only the children, but also the church as a whole. As children learn to minister as a regular part of the church, they must also be empowered for witness outside of church life.

> Nurture that actively engages children in areas of ministry has the added benefit of strengthening not only the children, but also the church as a whole.

Whether through partnership with larger movements like SU or individual local church programs, to fully nurture young people into the family of faith, churches must take responsibility for impact beyond the congregational gatherings. For many, the biggest hurdle is overcoming the concentration on programs and moving toward a greater emphasis on nurturing as a family engaging all aspects of life. From observation, this is a major challenge to ministries and projects working with children living in risky environments. There are simply too many needs and too few workers. Yet we cannot depart from the fact that the church is called to be a community of God's people. As point one of the Lausanne Covenant states,

---

[8] For more information on Scripture Union, visit their website at www.scriptureunion.org.uk.
[9] In the U.S., Young Life founded in 1938 has a broad impact on many lives and is an excellent means of engaging with lay leaders in local churches. Their focus on nurturing young people in the faith and cultivating leaders produces leaders for both church and para-church ministries. For more information on Young Life, visit their website at www.younglife.org.

[God] has been calling out from the world a people for himself, and sending his people back into the world to be his servants and his witnesses, for the extension of his Kingdom, the building up of Christ's body, and the glory of his name.[10]

Conclusion

The difficulty we face in trying to identify our congregations, either from the pulpit or from any other point, is that we all too often miss the children who stand at the margins of the church's activities. To adequately embrace the sixth point of the *Biblical Framework for Understanding God's Heart for Children*, we must adjust both our vision and our practice to ensure that the truth of the statement is reflected in the reality of our church life. The mandate is clear: children from every people group on earth must be found and loved with the love of Jesus Christ. In so doing, the Gospel message may be spoken through our actions, our lives, and our words. As this takes place, the service of welcoming children into the church by offering a place to belong, a family to accept them, and the nurture that goes beyond the gatherings of the congregation can bring hope to those who face the overwhelming risks of life.

> The mandate is clear: children from every people group on earth must be found and loved with the love of Jesus Christ.

---

[10] Lausanne Committee for World Evangelization, *The Lausanne Covenant*, 1974, http://www.lausanne.org/Brix?pageID=12891 (accessed September 2, 2005).

CASE STUDY

FAITH-BASED ORGANIZATIONS AND EVANGELICAL CHURCHES IN ROMANIA: PARTNERSHIP, THEOLOGY, AND CHILDREN AT RISK

BY BILL PREVETTE WITH JENNIFER ORONA
ASSEMBLIES OF GOD WORLD MISSION, ROMANIA

Since the fall of communism in 1989, hundreds of individuals, churches, and organizations have sought to help children in Romania. Nevertheless, thousands of children are still living in risky environments. Overcrowded and under-funded institutions have lost all state funding, and three problematic ideas about institutionalized children have come into focus:[1]

1) Institutionalized children were separated out, devalued, and stigmatized.
2) Children with special needs faced the most discrimination because they were seen as unproductive members of society.[2]
3) Parents were encouraged to place all disabled children in institutions at birth and to "forget about them."[3]

Children were branded as a social problem instead of being welcomed as a precious gift and resource. Instead of assisting families and communities, the State took over the care of unwanted children. This created a decreased sense of personal accountability for children, and an increased amount of labeling, even to the point of placing children in different institutions based on their perceived levels of ability.

Also since 1989, many new, dynamic partnerships have been formed between local churches, local FBOs, and western FBOs to minister to children. Some organizations have taken this opportunity to work with local churches, but many others have not. To build relationships, enhance effectiveness, and provide a more holistic ministry, I would like to make several suggestions for ministry in the future.

First, faith-based organizations and churches should take time to discuss a biblical framework for addressing children's needs. Most FBOs have focused on physical, educational, and psychosocial interventions for children. Most churches, on the other hand, are concerned with spiritual questions, such as sin and salvation for children. If these

---

[1] For more information, see World Bank, *Romania at a Glance*, http://siteresources.worldbank.org/ROMANIAINROMANIANEXTN/Resources/anexe_I.pdf (accessed August 14, 2004); http://www.oci.ro/Directory/idframe.htm; and www.prochild.ro.
[2] Michael Burke, *Child Institutionalization and Child Protection in Central and Eastern Europe.*
[3] George Lansdown, *Disabled Children in Romania: Progress in Implementing the Convention on the Rights of the Child, 2002.*

groups can share information and wisdom through dialogue, they will develop a richer, more holistic theology for doing ministry. Furthermore, children should be encouraged to participate in this dialogue. As Doug McConnell states, "every child who has faith in Christ is a member of the family of God."[4] Their membership in God's family extends to all areas of church life. "Children are essential to the life and ministry of the church,"[5] and just as Jesus demonstrated, they are not just an outcome of missions; they are part of the theology of doing missions.

Second, we must consider the characteristics of local churches and FBOs when working with children. FBOs often have more flexibility, mobility, education, and finances. Local churches often have more long-term relationships and consistency in the local community. Each may be able to provide some elements of ministry that the other cannot. What is more, partnership and teamwork between various groups provides a better environment for children, "a place where children may dynamically connect with God and engage in meaningful participation."[6] An understanding of God's design for children can help both local churches and FBOs learn to work together, and to provide better ministry to children in difficult circumstances.

> Children were branded as a social problem instead of being welcomed as a precious gift and resource.

When caring for children, we also need to think about the human resources that are available in the local church. Churches were forbidden to engage in social work under communism, but now, many vibrant and growing churches are ready to take on the challenge of ministering to the children in their communities. Children themselves possess spiritual gifts and abilities, and welcoming them fully into the family of faith also means including them in and empowering them for ministry.[7] This method may take more time and effort, but the benefits (cultural awareness, peer discipleship, long-term ministry opportunities, and more) far outweigh the challenges.

Finally, we must plan wisely for the future. It has been fifteen years since the fall of communism, but child abuse, abandonment, poverty, and corruption are still current issues in Romania. Despite the mistakes that have been made, the situation for children has changed for the better. By 2007, Romania may have less than 5,000 children in institutional care (less than 5 percent of the 100,000 living in institutions in 1992). In addition, Romanian Christians who have worked for various western organizations are now beginning to pastor Romanian churches and lead new indigenous Romanian organizations to minister to children and youth. Evangelical churches have grown in number, and although embracing change is difficult for many, the possibility of a moral awakening among Romanian Evangelical youth could help to reshape the larger society, especially if the younger generations are channeled toward a Kingdom understanding of social concern. In order to plan wisely for the future, then, churches and other organizations must seek to understand the subculture of the younger generations, discipling, equipping, and

---

[4] See the article by Doug McConnell in this volume.
[5] Affirmation #6. See Matthew 18:1-11.
[6] Affirmation #6.
[7] See the articles by Kara Powell and Ndaba Mazabane in this volume.

empowering them, and providing them with opportunities to know Christ and fulfill their calling in his churches across the globe.

PRACTICAL IMPLICATIONS

BACK TO BASICS: CARE FOR CHILDREN AFFECTED BY HIV AND AIDS

By Susie Howe with Jennifer Orona
The Bethany Children's Trust

HIV Disease and The Bethany Children's Trust

In countries most affected, HIV and AIDS are relentlessly 'tearing the very fabric of childhood.' As we have seen in the article by Stephenson, Lorey, and Luippold, et al, never before have we so needed a Church that will not only hear the word, but put it into practice.

The Bethany Children's Trust (BCT) is a small organization based in the United Kingdom whose goal is to be a prophetic voice to the Church, calling it to live out an authentic, counter-cultural, biblical lifestyle that expresses its worship of God by acting justly and compassionately—particularly in response to children and families affected by HIV disease.

> "If the Church of Jesus Christ rises to the challenge of HIV and AIDS, it will be the greatest apologetic the world has ever seen."
> —Ravi Zacharias
> *Prescription for Hope Conference*

HIV Care: What Stops the Church from Getting Involved?

It is not easy to get churches involved. The delegates that attend our Training, Equipping, and Mobilising (TEAM) Project workshops learn about how to develop child-focused, community-centered care that emphasizes the centrality of prayer, God's Word, and the cross.

Still, they need to discover truths for themselves rather than being told them. Throughout our workshop activities, we try to 'hold up a mirror' that participants can look into in order to see their heart attitudes for what they really are.

In the past, one challenge has been the fact that the delegates have not always had the authority needed to put the training into action. To deal with this issue, we encourage the local agencies to think strategically when issuing invitations to the workshop, and to ensure that participants either have a leadership role or the full endorsement of their church leaders, who need to have a commitment to implementing action related to HIV and AIDS. In addition, participants are informed when they are invited that they will be required to set goals, work toward their fulfillment after the workshop, and participate in follow-up and evaluation activities. We encourage local partners to offer ongoing opportunities for further learning, and participants are encouraged to network with other local and regional agencies so that mutual learning and relationship-building takes place.

> Steps of Progress in the Workshop
> 1) See examples of children in the Bible.
> 2) Describe role of children in own community.
> 3) Identify "fruit" desired in children's lives.
> 4) Identify "roots" to be nourished
> 5) Note effect of withholding care
> 6) Recognize neglect of vulnerable children.

Sometimes, churches simply focus on the spiritual well-being of those in need and neglect other important areas such as mental, emotional, and social needs. Using Jesus as our example, we act out stories in the gospels. Through them, participants discover how he brought *holistic* healing and restoration to individuals. Participants also role-play common scenarios involving families affected by HIV, and then they analyze the holistic needs of the characters in the plays through group work and brainstorming.

To further help participants think more deeply about the root causes of HIV and its effects on families, communities, and nations, we ask them to draw a 'Problem Tree' and list the causes of HIV at the roots and the effects and outcomes of the disease as the fruit. In this way, they discover the cultural, social, economic, and political beliefs and practices that help to propagate HIV, and they start to explore how the Church may act to bring about positive change.

All too often, vehement contention over condom use precludes rational debate. Participants are happy to contemplate abstinence and being faithful to a married partner for life, as well as the use of condoms within the context of a married relationship. In contexts outside of marriage, however, participants often suggest ideal (but very unrealistic) solutions such as "we will preach to these people and they will get saved, and then they will change their lifestyles and accept the A and B approach."[1] Even with real-life scenarios and small group discussions, the sessions seem to inevitably end in (very loud!) disagreements and a refusal to explore the issue further.

When we ask the participants to explore what hinders the Church from getting involved in HIV care, prevention, and orphan care, we often use the story of the Good Samaritan. Delegates are asked to role-play the story, while imagining that the person mugged by the robbers is someone who is HIV positive. They are then asked to discuss in groups why the religious leaders walked over to the other side of the road and why the Church is still doing that today in relation to people living with HIV or AIDS. Having identified what obstructs the Church, participants are then asked to discuss in groups how

---

[1] "Abstinence and Being Faithful" approach.

these fears, prejudices and assumptions can be overcome and how the Church can be motivated to respond positively.

At the end of each workshop, we ask the participants to re-enact the role-plays mentioned previously, showing how they as the local church can help to practically meet the holistic needs of the families in the plays using their existing skills, talents, resources, and love. This is always a time of revelation, as participants see the situations they are enacting being visually transformed, and they begin to realize how much they can do to transform their own neighborhoods. We call this approach 'Hands and Heart Ministry,' in which Christians are encouraged to simply use their hands and hearts in ways that are natural and achievable in order to make a difference in the lives of the people in their communities. They are also enabled to see the strengths children possess and how their resilience can be enhanced in very practical ways. Usually, participants show signs of relief that they don't have to set up large projects, take special training, or have certain qualifications—that between them, they have all they need to get started in reaching out to people living with HIV.

A Case Study

In 2002, The Bethany Children's Trust was approached by AIDS Prevention Care Ministry (APRECOM) in Kigali, Rwanda, and asked to run a TEAM workshop for local churches. APRECOM was involved in running a home-based care project for families living with HIV disease. They wanted to mobilize local Christians to give holistic care and support to these families and to teach HIV prevention, but they had little experience in running training workshops. BCT agreed to run the workshops, as long as the APRECOM team was prepared to help lead. Another Christian agency, Judah Trust, ran several of the workshops with us. As a consequence, local churches formed groups of volunteer workers who now go into the homes of people in Kigali to give care and support.

APRECOM then connected with the Episcopalian Church in Kigeme, near the Burundi border. The Bishop asked them to train his pastors. APRECOM asked BCT and Judah Trust to facilitate a couple of workshops with them. APRECOM led the workshops, and BCT and Judah Trust provided support.

As a consequence, the church birthed a significant project called *Abisunzimana*, (He whose Hope is in the Lord). In this project, members of the church and 22 volunteers from the local community visit 100 families to offer practical care and spiritual support. The church works in partnership with local people living with HIV to run an adult support group and a children's club for children affected by HIV disease. They have started kitchen gardens, animal breeding projects, and a prevention program, and they give food, school fees, and medicines to the neediest children. They also share the Gospel and pray for the families. As a result of this biblical, holistic ministry, many community members have come to Christ, and now, several other churches in the diocese have come to visit the project, wanting to start a similar work. As one member said, "Life has now come to Kigeme."

> Our team workshops start with the question, "What is our raison d'être—our purpose—as God's people?" Through studying key Bible texts we help them to see that:
>
> - Jesus is our King, and we are citizens of his Kingdom (Luke 22:29; I Pet. 2:9-10; Rev. 17:14).
> - God's Kingdom is not like the world's kingdoms. We are to be upholders of Kingdom culture, not the world's culture. (John 18:36).
> - Children, the poor, the marginalized, and the vulnerable are priorities for God (Mark 9:33-37; Matt. 25:31-45)
> - As God's people, we are to share his priorities (Eph. 5:1; 1John 2:6).
> - We are to "shine like stars in the universe as [we] hold out the word of life" (Phil. 2:14-16 NIV).
> - We are to do good works and bring healing and restoration in a broken world (Isa. 58:6-12; Eph. 2:10).
> - As we do so, we bring glory to Jesus, show others what he is like, take ground from the enemy, and prepare the way for Christ to come again.

Finally

The Church is overwhelmed in areas where HIV prevalence is at its highest. This, coupled with fear and ignorance, can lead to apathy and inertia in relation to HIV and AIDS and children affected by the disease. Through our 'back to basics' approach, however, we help churches to see that they have all they need to transform lives: by doing what they are good at with the power and help of a mighty God who has mandated them to take action, this ministry can become a vehicle by which they can help their communities, demonstrate the love of Christ, and gain a deeper understanding of the heart of God.

In his report, "The Contribution of Christian Congregations to the Battle with HIV/AIDS at the Community Level," Stan Nussbaum wrote, "A crisis often has an opportunity hidden on the underside, and a massive crisis can hide a massive opportunity."[2]

This is the day of massive opportunity for the global Body of Christ to impact the world as never before as we bring hope in the face of despair and life in the face of death. Through our 'training of trainers' approach, participants are enabled to go back to their faith communities and to train others to put what they have learned into action. In this way there is a ripple effect, whereby more and more Christians come on board and more and more children and their families are touched by the 'hands and heart' of Jesus.

---

[2] Stan Nussbaum, ed., *The Contribution of Christian Congregations to the battle with HIV/AIDS at the Community Level: A Seven-Country Research Report Prepared for the Summer Mission Briefing at the Oxford Centre for Mission Studies 7-9 June 2005*, 9.

CHAPTER 6
DISCUSSION QUESTIONS

1) Are children truly an integral part of the church, its life and work? Do we give children real responsibility, letting them share in church life in ways that make a difference? While we hold onto this, how do we provide nurture that is appropriate to ability and stage of development?

2) Using different models of understanding church (as pilgrim community, body of Christ, school of faith, hospitable space, new creation, and so on) which are most helpful for us and the children we serve? Which models are not helpful?

CHAPTER 7
PARTICIPANTS IN GOD'S MISSION

Children are essential to the mission of God.

God desires every child in every generation across the world to know him and make him known. Through his death and resurrection, Jesus calls the whole Church (including children) to reconcile relationships: with God, with family, with community and with society.

God intends that his Church be a witness in every community of his transforming power, so that his purpose for each one of his children can be accomplished.

"Children are the storm center in the battle between the forces of God and those of the evil one."

"Children are not only the mission of God, but they are also instruments of profound importance for the mission of God."

— *Shiferaw Michael*

"So if anyone is in Christ, there is a new creation: everything old has passed away; see, everything has become new! All this is from God, who reconciled us to himself through Christ, and has given us the ministry of reconciliation. So we are ambassadors for Christ, since God is making his appeal through us; we entreat you on behalf of Christ, be reconciled to God."

—*2 Cor. 5:17-18, 20* NRSV

BIBLICAL REFLECTION

CHILDREN AND GOD'S MISSION

By Gustavo Crocker with Karissa Glanville
Church of the Nazarene, Eurasia

Introduction

We see their pictures in almost every mission agency's propaganda. Their faces vary—they are sad, happy, clean, dirty, well-fed, malnourished. They represent the kaleidoscope of God's creation. It almost seems as if children are at the center of every missionary enterprise in the world. The reality is, however, that children have just been utilized by mission agencies and charities as promotional materials that attract donors with their picture-ready faces, while very few of these institutions truly have children in mind as central to God's mission. On the one hand, mission agencies and charities understand that children have the ability to move even the most insensitive heart. On the other hand, these same agencies do not seem to understand or care about the role that children have in God's missionary plan. This paper explores some of the biblical premises that place children at the center of God's mission both as the object of his mission and as the carriers of the mission themselves by presenting a biblical survey of children *as* God's mission and *in* God's mission. Finally, we will examine the practical implications for ministry for and with children in God's mission.

Children *as* God's Mission

In his book "Children of Promise,"[1] Bromiley argues that, according to the New Testament, "the Lord Jesus Christ has a concern for children, not merely as living parables but as they are themselves." This clear concern is evidenced not only by the way in which Jesus used children to illustrate the Kingdom of God (the mission of reconciliation), but also by the way in which he directly cared for and protected them (the object of his mission). Bromiley goes on to say, "we may surely say with confidence that Christ himself did not envisage an exclusion of children from salvation or an impossibility of childlike faith in him."[2]

Children are at the heart of God's redemptive mission, which reaches their lives and, through them, their families, their communities, and their societies. In God's mission, children represent a key link in breaking the cycle of poverty, oppression, and sin.

---

[1] Geoffrey Bromiley, *Children of Promise: The Case for Baptizing Infants*.
[2] Bromiley, 92-93.

When Christ gave the disciples the Great Commission, he instructed them to "go and make disciples," teaching them all things that they had seen him doing (Matt. 28:19-20). He also gave the Great Commandment (Matt. 22:37-40) on which to base how this is done. The disciples they were to make included those who, like children, were vulnerable, harassed, and helpless.

In a case for missionary involvement to a well-known Christian relief and development agency in the United States, I stated,

> *It is a tragic fact that millions of children suffer in relentless poverty and misery. They are hungry, sick and hurting. They are the helpless victims of disease, war, and ignorance. Their lives are an endless struggle to survive. In fact, in a given day in the world, tens of thousands of children die of preventable causes and, in a world where more than half of the population are children and youth, a vast majority of them suffer from sin, malnutrition, abuse, neglect, and poverty.*[3]

Seeing children hungry, naked, sick, and abused, the call for Christ's church is to respond as if responding to Christ himself. "Truly I tell you, just as you did it to one of the least of these who are members of my family, you did it to me" (Matt. 25:40). Scripture goes on to suggest that vulnerable children and widows are the object of true religion (James 1:27).

In missiological terms, understanding God's heart for the last, the least, and the lost is the first step to understanding the missiological imperative for a given culture, people group, or segment of the population. This alone should be enough for mission agencies, churches, and charities to redesign their ministry strategy and focus on children, not as publicity magnets, but as the object of God's redeeming mission.

> Understanding God's heart for the last, the least, and the lost, is the first step to understanding the missiological imperative for a given culture, people group, or segment of the population.

To further prove the value of children in God's missionary enterprise, I would like to submit to you some strategic factors suggesting that engaging in work with children is one of the most fundamentally sound missionary strategies.

- Ministry to children has the potential to bring unity among ministries across denominations.[4]

- In the U.S. it has been "discovered that the probability of someone embracing Jesus as his or her Savior was 32 percent for those between the ages of five and twelve; 4 percent for those in the 13- to 18-year-old age range; and 6 percent for people 19 or older. In other words, if people do not embrace Jesus Christ as their

---

[3] Gustavo Crocker, *Why Children? A Case for Involvement.*

[4] Crocker.

Savior before they reach their teenage years, the chance of their doing so at all is slim."[5]

- We are instructed in Proverbs 22:6 to "Train children in the right way and when old, they will not stray." It is key for the shaping of a life, to start when they are young.

- In the context of helping the world's children, UNICEF points out that "participation of religious leaders and organizations is vital to addressing sensitive issues related to children. Religion plays a central role in social and cultural life in most developing countries, and religious leaders and faith-based organizations are greatly respected and listened to."[6]

- Viva Network believes "that children and young people should be the single greatest priority for Christian work in the coming decade. Their needs are enormous, their numbers are exploding, and their age group could not be more strategic—spiritually, biologically and educationally . . . Yet it remains true that less than 15 percent of our budgets and personnel are directed to ministry amongst children and young people. This is a perilous oversight that needs urgent correction."[7]

- "Children are a priority for the King and his Kingdom: They are many, they are strategic, they suffer and God's unambiguous mandate in their favor shouts for urgent action right across the pages of Scripture. They are both key to the Great Commission and an essential expression of the Great Commandment."[8]

What would happen, then, if churches, mission agencies, and communities would seriously consider children at the heart of the Great Commission instead of the cover pages of their promotional materials? Let me suggest a picture of our society in which the church seriously places children at the heart of the Great Commission:

---

[5] George Barna, *Transforming Children into Spiritual Champions,* 34.
[6] The United Nations Children's Fund (UNICEF), *The State of the World's Children 2006,* http://www.unicef.org/publications/index_30398.html (accessed , September 12, 2007), 73.
[7] Dan Brewster and Patrick McDonald, "Children—The Great Omission?" 2.
[8] Dan Brewster, *Child, Church and Mission: A Resource Book for Christian Child Development Workers,* 15.

Pay close attention now: I am creating new heavens and a new earth. All the earlier troubles, chaos, and pain are things for the past, to be forgotten. Look ahead with joy. Anticipate what I am creating. I will create Jerusalem as sheer joy, create my people as sheer delight. I will take joy in Jerusalem, take delight in my people: No more sounds of weeping in the city, no cries of anguish; no more babies dying in the cradle, or old people who don't enjoy a full lifetime... They will build houses and move in. They will plant fields and eat what they grow ... They won't work and have nothing come of it, they won't have children snatched out from under them. For they themselves are plantings blessed by God, with their children and grandchildren likewise God-blessed" (Isa. 65:17-23 MSG).

> **Children at the Heart of the Great Commission**
>
> "I have a dream that one day all people would volunteer to help others."
> —Brendan (age 6)
>
> "One day, there will be no poor people and all children will be happy."
> —Beth (age 10)

This is God's desire, God's promise for the future. This future hope is what sets us apart from all other groups working with children around the world. We do not simply have a temporary or present-day solution, or no solution at all. God's mission extends beyond this temporal life span, and children are essential to it.

Children *in* God's Mission

But children are not just objects of God's mission. Children are more than a people group that mission agencies must strategically target in order to achieve the Great Commission. Many times in the Bible and today, children have actually been the carriers of God's mission.

The Child as an Agent of God's Provision: Joseph

Genesis records how Joseph, when still a teenager, was given the vision of being the intercessor on behalf of his family and his people. While enduring hatred from his own family, being sold as a slave, and ending up in prison because of evil scheming, the young Joseph remained faithful to God's plan and mission, saying, "You intended to do harm to me, God intended it for good, in order to preserve a numerous people ... So have no fear; I myself will provide for you and your little ones" (Gen. 50:19-21).

In this narrative, God's plan was for the young Joseph to grow into the intermediary between the economic power of his time, Egypt, and a needy people who were to face hardship in the years to come. Joseph was trained in the most reputable schools and the most sophisticated management and production systems of his time, not for his own sake, but for the good of his family and his people.

Joseph's story has become a key biblical parable for ministries to children that focus primarily on the individual child. The "Joseph principle" is widely used by child sponsorship ministries that believe that by bringing one child out of their context of poverty, and by educating them, the child will eventually become God's tool to lead the way for their family and community to leave conditions of poverty and sin.

Some may argue that perhaps Joseph was chosen because of his faithfulness to God in the face of adversity and not simply because God wanted one member of his family. Of course, a "call and response" dynamic must be considered as we call children to be part of God's mission. We may call out a child, but they also have to respond with a heart of faith. And this faith will be tested repeatedly, just as Joseph's was.

> **Children in God's Mission**
> 1) Agent of God's Provision: Joseph
> 2) Prophet: Samuel
> 3) Liberator: David
> 4) Community Resource: Feeding of the 5,000
> 5) Messiah: Christ

Also, when one person is selected out of a group, as Joseph was from among his brothers, bitterness and jealousy can become a poisoning factor that will need to be dealt with. Joseph remained faithful, but a rift had been created in his family. The pain and betrayal in Joseph's story demonstrate the need for family restoration. Still, God was able to use these circumstances for the good of the entire family.

In spite of the problems Joseph faced and the cautions which should be noted, the principle of God choosing to bless an entire family or community through one person can still be seen. In fact, there are many leaders in the church today, who are where they are, because of its application in their own lives.

Victor is one of such cases. He was a small child of a very poor family in the barrios of Rio de Janeiro when he found refuge in a pastor's home that cared for him. He was headed for the same future that millions of children in the barriadas of Rio have to endure. Most likely, Victor was destined to be another street child joining the statistics of poverty, crime, and sin in the city. But God used a local pastor to minister to Victor. The pastor took Victor under his care, trained him, loved him, and taught him the value of education, work, and above all, the love of Christ. Today, Victor is a medical doctor. He still lives in the barriadas of Rio (his own choice) where he has built one of the largest Christian healthcare systems in the city as well as one of the most effective church-based ministries in the area.

The Child as a Prophet: Samuel

The book of Samuel narrates the way in which God used the child Samuel in bringing the prophecy of redemption and victory for the people of Israel, especially in times of spiritual and political hardship. An obedient disciple, Samuel was instructed since his childhood to listen to God's voice and to serve him in whatever capacity God asked. 1 Samuel 3:1 narrates the Lord's call to Samuel, a boy serving in the temple in times when "the word of the Lord was rare; when there were not many visions." Samuel grew up in the presence of God and his prophetic record was flawless. Everyone in Israel, from Dan in the north to Beersheba in the south, recognized that Samuel was the real thing—a true prophet of God.

When children are exposed to the word of God at an early age, they become sensitive to God's mission for his people. Children *do* have the capacity to understand and explain God's plan of redemption so that people can be transformed, and the "Samuel Principle" empowers children to share their God-given words and testimonies when they have the anointing of the Holy Spirit to prophesy, evangelize, and witness.

Sofia is one of such cases. Sofia was the oldest daughter of an alcoholic father in the countryside of Guatemala when she received Christ in a mission-based Vacation Bible School. At age thirteen, she was so enamored with the redeeming grace of the Gospel that she decided to spend most of her time at church, learning from the missionaries and the Scripture. Several months later, Sofia received the mandate of evangelizing her entire family and her community. Nearly forty years after she committed her life as an agent of grace, Sofia continues evangelizing children through radio programs, community-based child evangelism programs, and personal evangelism among working children in the open market. Thousands of children have received Christ because of Sofia's obedience when she said early on, "speak, for your servant is listening" (1 Sam. 3:10 NIV).

The Child as a Liberator: David

The story of the boy David and the giant Goliath is among the best-known child-related stories in the Bible. The Bible describes how Samuel had the task of selecting Saul's successor to fight the Philistines and to bring the people of Israel to freedom and victory (1 Sam. 16). While traditional human standards of leadership suggested (as they still do today) that the liberator had to be an experienced adult, a person with knowledge, expertise, and strength to fight the battle, God anointed a child, a shepherd boy, to go in his strength and liberate the people of Israel. This event, crucial in the life of God's chosen people, challenged the leadership standards of the time just as they challenge the leadership standards of today. The requirements were not (and still are not) stature, experience, and dexterity in handling the tools of war. God's requirements were (and still are) summarized in the person of a child "for the Lord does not see as mortals see; they look on the outward appearance, but the Lord looks on the heart" (1 Sam. 16:7).

As with today's society, this sheep-tending boy is again overlooked by his brothers (even though they had witnessed as he was anointed king of Israel). Being overlooked by adults, however, does not diminish David's liberating spirit.[9] In an exchange between the current king and the child David, he is again told, "you are just a boy, and he has been a warrior from his youth" (1 Sam. 17:33). David's reply, however, is the reply that we still hear from children and youth across the world whom the Lord has anointed to be symbols and agents of liberation in their communities: "The Lord, who saved me from the paw of the lion and from the paw of the bear will save me from the hand of this Philistine." (1 Sam. 17:37).

The Lord continues protecting, saving, and anointing children for his redeeming mission. Many ministers, who today bring *shalom* and liberation to their communities,

---

[9] See Glanville's discussion on the challenge Samuel faced in not overlooking a youth, even though he himself was used by God during his youth.

were preserved by God from the hand of disease, hunger, and abuse when they were infants. Many of them, survivors of the paws of poverty, were called as children to mobilize their schools, their parents, and their churches so that abundant life could come to their households, their villages, and even their nations. And the calling still continues.

The Child as a Community Resource: The Feeding of the Five Thousand

All four gospels record one of the most fascinating feeding programs ever witnessed by humankind. Five thousand men, plus women and children, were fed by Jesus, who performed the miracle of multiplying five small barley loaves of bread and two small fish (John 6:9). While there are many elements to the miracle, one cannot overlook the fact that it was an anonymous boy who had the physical resources for the miracle. These meager physical resources, in the hands of Jesus, became the endless resource that people needed.

The same is true in community work. Children and youth are some of the most effective resources in community development (not just the excuse for community programs).[10] Filled with creativity and energy, children and youth have the ability to network, mobilize, and multiply resources, which in the hands of Christ can bring *shalom* to their communities. Furthermore, children, unlike adults, do this for the sake of the community and the fellowship that it brings, not necessarily to get their names in the inauguration plaques or the history books. Just like the anonymous child in the story, every day thousands of children and youth flavor their communities with the vitality and hope that Christ gives them, and they are sharing such flavor with "experienced" community and mission workers.

Many secular agencies seem to understand and maximize the potential of children and youth in community transformation. Unfortunately, in spite of the biblical evidence that highlights the value of children and youth as a community resource, churches and mission agencies seem to have "professionalized" ministry to extremes and badly overlooked the tremendous potential of anonymous children in our midst.

The Child as the Messiah: Christ

God only had one child, and he was a missionary. God's ultimate act of redemption was incarnated in the life of a child. "For God so loved the world that he gave his one and only Son, that whoever believes in him shall not perish but have eternal life" (John 3:16 NIV). It was God himself who chose to take the form of a child and dwell among us. "The Word became flesh and made his dwelling among us. We have seen his glory, the glory of the One and Only, who came from the Father, full of grace and truth" (John 1:14 NIV).

God accomplished his redemptive plan by fulfilling one of the most tremendous prophecies of the Old Testament: "For a child has been born for us, a son given to us; authority rests upon his shoulders; and he is named Wonderful Counselor, Mighty God, Everlasting Father, Prince of Peace. His authority shall grow continually" (Isa. 9:6-7).

Bromiley suggests that:

---

[10] See the article by Judith Ennew in this volume.

Christ in his humanity was to become an infant, the babe of Bethlehem, with no more self awareness than other infants, yet not on that account deprived of his fellowship with the Father and the Holy Spirit. The second-century writer Ireneaeus was not altogether fanciful when he suggested that Christ identified himself with all the stages of human life from infancy to maturity in order that there might be salvation and identification with Christ at every stage.[11]

This assertion is critical for understanding God's plan of redemption for people of all ages and through people of all ages. The same God incarnate faced and lived in the environments that children, youth, and adults live so that we can, with his guidance, live out his redeeming mandate as children, as youth, and as mature adults in the soils where we are planted. Luke 2:52 describes that the child "Jesus increased in wisdom and in years, and in divine and human favor," a model that most experienced Christian child development agencies use as the pattern for holistic human and social transformation.

Jesus further expressed God's mission by quoting Isaiah's promise and declaring its fulfillment:

He unrolled the scroll and found the place where it was written: 'The Spirit of the Lord is upon me, because he has anointed me to bring good news to the poor. He has sent me to proclaim release to the captives and recovery of sight to the blind, to let the oppressed go free, to proclaim the year of the Lord's favor.' And he rolled up the scroll, gave it back to the attendant, and sat down. The eyes of all in the synagogue were fixed on him. Then he began to say to them, 'Today this scripture has been fulfilled in your hearing' (Luke 4:16-21; cf. Isa. 61:1-4).

We are reminded that our work also has a greater end. Jesus worked to bring the Kingdom into the present circumstances where he was. He saw fulfillment when he walked the earth, and recognized that there is also a day of greater fulfillment to come.

Practical Implications for Engaging Children in the Great Commission

3) Children are an essential part of God's mission in that they represent one of the largest missiological segments in today's world.

4) Not only are children a key missiological people group, children are key actors in implementing the Great Commission.

5) By employing the "Joseph principle," mission agencies can educate, disciple, and mobilize children (while managing interpersonal relationships with care) so that children can become the agents of social transformation for their families and their communities.

---

[11] Bromiley, 93. See the article by Keith White in this volume.

6) The "Samuel principle" calls for mission agencies to intentionally evangelize and involve children as bearers of the good news of salvation.

7) While armies and political systems have manipulated children and youth to become the innocent casualties of the wars which those systems support, ministries must understand the value that spirit-filled children and youth have in leading their communities to justice, righteousness, and liberation.

8) Children and youth are some of the most valuable resources in the community. Because of their energy, boldness, creativity, and ingenuity, children have the capacity to mobilize immeasurable resources for the holistic transformation of their communities.

9) Children are the epitome of the Kingdom incarnated by the Messiah. Christ came as a child and grew into the Rabbi of Nazareth so that people of all ages could experience and carry the redeeming mission of our loving father.

10) Finally, children should be considered as partners in mission. When filled by the Spirit of God, children can and will discuss with "experienced" ministers the matters of the Kingdom. They, too, will respond to us, "Why were you looking for me? Didn't you know that I had to be here dealing with the things of my Father?" (Luke 2:49, MSG).

Conclusion

Pictures of children have been used to motivate giving, whether or not children are the main target of the organization. It is no accident that these pictures of children can tug at our hearts and move us into action. We instinctively know that they are significant, and important enough to pay crucial attention to. Through the biblical examples of children *as* God's mission, as well as children *in* God's mission presented in this chapter, you have seen the nature of God's heart towards involving children as both a necessary target of mission, as well as a significant partner in the mission of God. May your steps from here forward be ones of intention that remember the fundamental connection of children and God's mission.

CRITICAL ISSUES

RAISING KIDS OF MISSION IN THE 21ST CENTURY

By Karissa Glanville
Fuller Theological Seminary

Depending on where one is in the world today, different expectations could be placed on a 13-year-old youth. In one place, they may have the sole responsibility of going to school and having fun and yet be expected to be rebellious and distant from adults. Elsewhere, they play a significant role in bringing income to their family, or leading a church cell group. And in yet other settings, they might find themselves the head of the family after parents have died from AIDS.

When looking at views of children and childhood, we need to understand that our views vary across the globe and even differ from views held in the past.[1] Concepts and perceptions of childhood have changed throughout history.[2] For example, the more western concept of 'adolescence' can be seen as a "historically shaped social 'product.'"[3] To some degree, the beginnings and endings of phases of life are determined and fostered by social structures and attitudes.

To understand how much can and should be expected from children and youth and how to help them get there, we must first, disengage from our preconceptions and expectations of children and youth and then try to discern how God sees them.

We get hints of their potential in Biblical stories. As a youth, Moses' sister, Miriam, helped to further the plans of God in Moses' life and all of the people of Israel (Ex. 2). David was a young man when he was chosen as the next king (1 Sam. 16). A young slave girl helped Naaman find out about the prophet Elisha (2 Kings 5). When God called Jeremiah to be a prophet, he protested that he was only a youth. God told him not to use this as an excuse and not to be afraid (Jer. 1:5-8). It didn't matter to God how old Jeremiah was, God gave him authority to affect the nations (Jer. 1:9-10).

Repeatedly in the Bible, we see God believing it is worth calling out children and youth, giving them the opportunity to choose to fulfill his will, even occasionally through positions of authority (2 Chron. 34:1-3). God took youth seriously, called them out, began their training and used them to impact those around them. Why haven't we seen this happening on a wider scale? And how can we?

Could it be possible that because we have not taken the ability of young people to participate in the mission of God seriously, we have reaped the consequences and not seen many young people carry on the faith of their parents, or seen them simply drift aimlessly

---

[1] W. A. Strange, *Children in the Early Church*, vii. See also Powell's chapter for a discussion on first century views of children.
[2] Marcia J. Bunge, "Introduction," 3.
[3] Klaus Hurrelmann, "The Social World of Adolescents: A Sociological Perspective," 3.

for years before returning to the faith of their parents? Among Christian families, perhaps the societal disconnect between generations that God never intended has seeped into our way of living.[4] This disconnect between generations can be seen especially in western nations and places where western culture has influenced the societal views of teenagers. In the case of children from non-Christian homes, could it be said they have simply not been challenged or shown the opportunity by Christians to live up to the fullness of their spiritual potential?

If we truly see God's purpose in the natural and church family, there should be no disconnect between the generations.[5] If youth are challenged to participate in the mission of God, by those who are loving and caring for them like family members, they will often rise to the occasion. If we do not raise the challenge in the context of love, they will most likely not rise to it. We can raise the challenge for our own children and those we enfold into the family of faith. The following are some successful examples that I have seen personally.

- When a group of ten- and eleven-year-olds were told about the situation of genocide in Sudan they were appalled. But it wasn't until they were asked by their teacher "What do you want to do about it?" that they came up with ideas beyond what the teacher expected. The teacher thought they'd just write letters to government leaders, but instead, they started an informational and awareness website, invited Sudanese refugees to come and share with them, and sent two students and teachers to the nation's capital to speak with government officials.

- Four Chinese youth who came from troubled families and Buddhist backgrounds were discipled weekly by an adult who believed God had purposes for their lives. They hung out, ate together, were shown love and taught about the ways of God. Over six years, they built a loving and trusting relationship with their mentor and with each other, becoming, in a sense, a surrogate family. Now ages 17 and 18, they can hear God's voice, have seen God heal others through their prayers, challenge adults and each other with their faith and words from God.

- A group of teenage students at a Christian school started a movement called Youth Quake with the help of their school chaplain. They held conferences for youth, led by youth, focusing on prayer and evangelism for their communities. Their chaplain had inspired them with stories of God working among students and in revivals throughout history. They envisioned a future in which their school and community could be transformed.

---

[4] See also Tollestrup's discussion of the importance of "hope, as a promise for every generation . . . an intergenerational enterprise . . . [requiring] reciprocity between generations where respect and hope is shared."
[5] See the second and sixth affirmations of this volume for an in-depth discussion on the role of family and the family of God.

- A 13-year-old girl was being drawn away by her peers and disconnecting from the Christian beliefs of her family. Her parents began spending more time with her, were more intent on discipling her and involved her in ministry opportunities. Over the next few years she became a passionate Christian who taught other children about God and dedicated her entire life to living for God.

Each of the above examples shows what can happen when an adult takes the spirituality and potential of a young person seriously.

We find a key biblical example of an adult's influence upon a child in the story of Samuel and Eli. Samuel was not even a teenager when he began to hear God's voice and have words from the Lord to speak to his leader, Eli, and take part in priestly duties (1 Sam 3; 2:18). It was Eli's instruction however, that allowed him to begin to converse with God.[6]

What would have happened if Eli had not told Samuel that he was hearing God's voice and did not instruct him how to respond to God's voice? Perhaps Samuel would have learned to ignore God's voice. Perhaps he would have missed the opportunity to participate in what God was doing.

Samuel may have been the one called, but he still needed the assistance of Eli. Even though Eli was incompetent in other areas, he could still explain what was happening and teach Samuel how to respond. Because of Eli's coaching, Samuel was able to participate in the mission of God before he grew into full adulthood (1 Sam. 3:19).

We have the opportunity and responsibility to teach and challenge the young people around us. We can teach children and youth how to hear God's voice and how to respond to His pursuing them. We can play the role of facilitator, helping young people to enter in to all the training God has for them, encouraging them to participate in God's purposes, and nurturing their growth in relationship with God. Not all children and youth will be prominently visible leaders like Josiah or Samuel. A child may not 'seem' to be called or chosen for a significant role in God's mission, but this does not mean that they cannot or will not influence others greatly. A young slave girl simply knowing about Elisha significantly impacted the life of Naaman. All children can participate in the mission of God; all are called to be participants in God's missional family.

Even younger children want to, and can, make a difference in the world around them. They only need to be given opportunity and assistance.

The following are examples from around the world of kids involved in the mission of God.

Street boys in King's Kids, YWAM, in Delhi, India, return to visit their parents and pray for them as well as do outreaches at local churches sharing their testimonies.[7]

> We have the opportunity to challenge the young people around us and look with expectation for those who have a heart for God and a calling to advance his Kingdom.

---

[6] See Crocker's discussion of "The Child as Prophet: Samuel" for another angle on Samuel as an example.
[7] Barbara Ruegger, personal email, June 28, 2005. See also the article by Barbara Ruegger in this volume for further examples within the context of YWAM's King's Kids.

In a church in Nuremberg, Germany, students aged eight to fourteen were trained to be involved in prophetic prayer ministry. They enjoyed ministering alongside the adults and seeing people deeply moved.[8]

At a Southern California church outreach, a seven-year-old Latin American girl became a Christian while a church member painted a picture of a rainbow on her cheek and shared the Gospel. In the following weeks, the young girl witnessed to all her friends in her apartment building, many of whom became Christians and started attending church.

In Mozambique, Iris Ministries has taken in over 2,000 orphans and abandoned children. The day they are brought in, even as young as three, they are introduced to Jesus and taught the Holy Spirit can live and work through them. From day one, they participate in the mission of God.

The Mozambican children are placed in family groups (similar to cell groups) of 12-15 children. The group leaders are youth of around twelve years old. There are also discipleship classes taught by older youth and young adults who were brought up in Iris Ministries. Youth are promoted and given more responsibility as they mature and jobs become available. Decisions relating to major issues however, are left to the adults.[9]

The Mozambican children, of all ages, go out on missions into outlying areas with adults and testify, pray for the sick, and preach with amazing results seen. When Heidi Baker (of Iris Ministries) travels to other countries and calls people up for prayer, she also asks for the children twelve and under to come up to be her prayer team. She knows they are likely to have more faith, and that the Kingdom of God belongs to those with childlike faith. She believes children have to be taught *not* to believe.[10]

In Argentina, a children's congregation went out into the parks and offered to pray for businesspeople during their lunch breaks. The adult congregation grew as a result of their work.[11]

A CD of songs was produced, inspired and sung by children from Rwanda. These same children, who had been witnesses to terrible atrocities, performed their songs of hope in front of their government leaders who were moved to tears. One eight-year-old boldly prayed Isaiah 11:6.[12]

How To

It is easy to discount young people simply because of their size or age, as Samuel did initially when looking at David and his brothers for the next king. Samuel listened to God, however, and was able to anoint God's choice for the next king. This should be a warning to us that even if we have seen God work through youth in the past, even in our own lives,

---

[8] Ursula Schmidt, personal email, June 29, 2005.
[9] Heidi Baker, phone interview, July 20, 2005.
[10] Baker, 2005.
[11] Nelson, 2005.
[12] Robert Rice, personal email, June 29, 2005.

we must not lose sight of the potential of the youth God places before us.[13] We need to do this even though it is often easier to look to the older and seemingly stronger people in our midst to accomplish God's mission.

We must watch with the eyes of our hearts for those youth and children that have a heart after him and who are responding to God's call. We need to pour into the little ones the training and truth we have received so that they might know how to better respond. We need to allow for the expression of the ministry gifts, just as David was asked to play his harp for the king. Not only did he chase a distressing spirit away from the king (1 Sam 16:23), but he went on to surprise the entire nation by taking down Israel's greatest enemy of the day.[14]

We must also be careful not to read motives into their hearts that are not there, as David's brothers did (1 Sam. 17). We need to allow room for the expression of their youthful faith and zeal, and even learn from it. David believed more than any other man at his time that God wanted Goliath defeated and that Goliath could be defeated. He had an unpolluted faith and trust in God. The children in Mozambique mentioned above are simply told to put their hands on a blind person, pray, and the person will be healed, and they are healed.[15]

Mary is another example of unwavering faith and trust. She found the favor of God (Luke 1:30), most likely, as a teenager.[16] She had a heart that was obedient to God (Luke 1:38). She trusted God implicitly though what He asked of her was beyond all reason and would most likely provide social stigma (Luke 1:45). God found a place he could reside, in a youth, with a heart of faith and obedience.

Family

As has been mentioned already throughout this book and chapter, God has designed a wonderful context in which children can be mentored, taught, and gradually given more and more responsibilities and opportunities—the family.[17]

In the New Testament, we find the church growing in the context of households and likened even to a family (1 Tim. 3:15).[18] This family is to be the "pillar and bulwark of the

---

[13] See Gustavo's section on "The Child as Liberator: David" for a discussion on how David, even though he was often overlooked, was still able to overcome and become a liberator.

[14] Gustavo Crocker discusses this further in the context of David being raised by God as a liberator for his people.

[15] Baker, 2005.

[16] T.D. Alexander and B.S. Rosner, *New Dictionary of Biblical Theology*. "Mary is 'pledged' (*mnēsteuein*, Matt. 1:18; Luke 2:5), which means that she and Joseph have publicly exchanged consent, the first step in Jewish marriage. Often the bride was under fifteen."

[17] See Bunge's chapter on the concept of parenting from a biblical perspective and Powell's chapter on children being welcomed into the family of faith.

[18] D. R. W. Wood and I.H. Marshall, *New Bible Dictionary*, 3rd ed. The term for household, "*oikos* has both literal and figurative meanings, with 'household, family, race' in addition to 'house' . . . A most important development of the idea of 'God's house' was its application to the church . . . whose communal character was emphasized in the concepts of the 'spiritual house'" See the article by Jennifer Orona for more on the concept of *oikos*.

truth." If we truly capture this image of the body of Christ as family and the family as an extension of the body of Christ,[19] one where children are developed into the fullness of their potential, the church will surely become a pillar upholding the truth to the nations.

In Ephesians, we find instruction for how the church is to live out the life of Christ in the context of being family. Children are exhorted to obey their parents, 'in the Lord' (Eph. 6:1). 'In the Lord' modifies *how* they are to obey, and is not referring to the state of their parents. This is significant in that it shows children are able to operate 'in the Lord' without a moderator at a young age.[20] Children can respond in godly ways within the family context. They can be obedient to their parents and honor them through the grace given to them by God. Children have access to God's strength for living out their lives; they do not have to wait until they are older to experience God at work in their lives.[21]

As we participate in the family of God, we are called to see with the eyes of God. We will thus hopefully find ourselves expanding our 'family' to incorporate the youth around us. The very nature of the family implies that we are to be raising the young to follow in our footsteps. If the family we are a part of is God's, we should naturally be training the youth around us to be a part of God's work here on earth. God's missional family should continue to grow and expand as a matter of course. The work of God should be done as a family, just as a child works with their parents in a family business, learning the trade and stepping into more and more responsibility as they are able.

> God's missional family should continue to grow and expand as a matter of course, done as a family.

It is important to note that young children were not expected to have adult roles, but were brought up in the context of family.[22] Jewish male infants were to be circumcised as a sign of being a member of God's covenant people. Even as infants, they were not excluded from the covenant with God.[23] Children were taught the ways of God and expected to live them out.[24] Deuteronomy 6:7-9 shows that children were to be surrounded by their families teaching them the ways of God.

Many do not have the blessing of growing up in a Christian family or the family of faith. How are we to mentor these children into the place where God is calling them? We are to be a *missional* family, one that reaches out as a family and incorporates others. Referring to orphans and widows, the Bible states God places the solitary in families (Ps. 68:56). As representatives of God's family on earth, we have the privilege and responsibility to be family for those who do not have it so they too may enter into the fullness of God's plans for their lives.

---

[19] See Bunge's analysis of the historical views of family by Chrysostom, Bushnell, and Luther.
[20] Judith M. Gundry-Volf, "The Least and the Greatest," 55-58.
[21] See Powell's discussion on the assumption that children can have spiritual gifts.
[22] Strange, 64.
[23] Gundry-Volf, 35.
[24] Strange, 13.

Steps

Apart from what has been previously mentioned through Scriptures and the examples, the following are a few practical thoughts on helping children and youth become participants in God's mission.

First, young people need to feel loved, and time is one of the greatest ways to show this. It is amazing how young people want to grow up and be like someone who has shown them love and care through time spent with them. Simply spending a few hours each week with a young person, can draw them closer to their potential. As you show them you value them, they will in turn begin to value what you believe, how you live, and what you have to say.

Second, young people need to be respected for their opinions and inherent worth. If they are not expected to be able to contribute something of worth, they most likely will live up to this expectation. On the other hand, if adults believe that young people have something to contribute and can hear from God, these expectations will cause the young people to rise to the occasion. Related to this, wounds that children bear must also be taken seriously and healing must be sought, whether it is through counseling, the ministry of God's Spirit, prayer, or simply by being surrounded by loving people.

Third, model how you want young people to minister, take them with you as you minister to others and use the following pattern: 1) watch me 2) do it with me 3) you do it while I watch. You can also take children and youth along with you when learning new things about God yourself. They will pick up your value on learning. My parents took me everywhere they went, holding before me modern day heroes of the faith that they themselves were encouraged by. It was from going with my parents to hear missionaries share their stories, that as a young girl, I knew God was challenging me to be a missionary.

Fourth, young people need to be taught to expect what is read in the Bible to be possible in their own lives. Encourage their purer, more innocent faith even if you yourself have not experienced the miraculous that is written of in the Bible. Just because you may not have seen someone healed by your prayers, or may not have led many to Christ, you do not need to squelch their faith. The word of God was rare in Eli's day (1 Sam. 3:1), yet Eli still encouraged Samuel that God could be speaking to him. This took faith on the part of Eli, and risk. He trusted that God could use a boy to be a messenger (1 Sam. 3:17, 18).

Fifth, do not limit the areas in which young people can express their desires for service. Find out what interests them and seek opportunities for them to be mentored, and express themselves in those areas. They may notice a need in the community for which you can help them think through ways of meeting it. Or you can expose them to areas of need. They may be drawn towards issues of injustice and poverty. They may desire to express their hearts through intercession, prayer ministry, worship, art, media, preaching, dance, drama, helps, or other ministries. You can help them find channels of expression. Remember their interests may grow and change. Do not limit them to areas only you are comfortable with. If you

> There are young people that are waiting to be nurtured, loved, and given a reason for living. They are longing for purpose and someone to take them seriously.

are not able to mentor them where their interests and gifts are, find someone who can. Last, but definitely not least, invest a sacrifice of your time through prayer into the futures of the young people around you. Pray for their protection and deliverance from things that may hinder them from entering their full potential. Pray for the Spirit of God to fill them from the time of their childhood and lead them into all He has for them.

Conclusion

There are young people that are waiting to be nurtured, loved and given a reason for living. They are longing for purpose and someone to take them seriously. We must take our part in the larger family of God, train the children around us, and help them to participate in the mission of God that they were destined to be a part of.

Children can be an example of a life of faith; they can bear testimony to others and participate in the mission of God on earth. Children are not meant to be only the targets of mission, but missionaries as well.

PRACTITIONER'S RESPONSE

WE HAVE FORGOTTEN THAT WE BELONG TO EACH OTHER

By Jude Tiersma Watson
CRM/InnerCHANGE

I never planned to live in a Los Angeles barrio for over 15 years, sharing my life with youth and families who live in high-risk situations.[1] Los Angeles was the "never" of my life—"anywhere but L.A.," I thought. I had my heart set on going to one of the world's great cities—Bangkok, Manila, Mexico City—where compelling stories of need ooze out of statistics. Instead, I live in Los Angeles, where kids go to school in a district with a high school drop out rate of 50 percent (70 percent in our local high school); where families of six live in one-room apartments with no place to play; where the threat of violence hangs like a heavy shadow in some neighborhoods; where being a young Latino or Black youth carries the liability of being mistaken for a gang member either by a gang or by the police; and where some of the kids living in the most risky situations are homeboys covered in gang tattoos, packing guns, and recruiting younger kids into gangs.

We Belong to Each Other

On April 20, 1999 in Columbine, Colorado, two students went on a shooting rampage at their quiet suburban high school, killing twelve fellow students and teachers before killing themselves. Suddenly, many students, parents, and communities had their sense of security deeply shaken. Yet kids have been killing kids for years in some urban neighborhoods, and our society has paid little attention.

Although it was perhaps not intended this way, many urban youth felt that within our society, a young life in the middle class suburbia of Columbine, Colorado, was worth more than a young life in Compton, California, (a poor and largely African American and Latino city just south of Los Angeles). Many children and their families have never had the luxury of feeling safe and secure.

---

[1] This article originally appeared in "We Have Forgotten that We Belong to Each Other," *Theology News and Notes* 52, no. 3 (2005): 24-27. Reprinted by permission. To read other articles in this edition of *Theology, News, and Notes* entitled "The Church's Mission to Children at Risk," please visit http://www.fuller.edu/news/pubs/tnn/2005_fall/index.htm.

> "If we have no peace, it is because we have forgotten that we belong to each other."
>
> —Mother Teresa

Perhaps, as Mother Teresa believed, "we have forgotten that we belong to each other." Yes, the high school students at Columbine were our kids, but so are the kids living in our inner cities, attending our over-crowded schools, being killed and killing each other. Compassion comes easily when we think of innocent young children on their own in a cold, harsh world, victims of poverty and war, or victims of the bad choices of their families or their society. But what if that youth is "Diablo," the homeboy wearing $100 Nike tennis shoes, covered in tattoos, packing a gun, recruiting younger kids into the gang? What do we do with Diablo?

This is not a new question. In the 19th century, the debate centered around the worthy and unworthy poor. Everyone wanted to help the "worthy" poor, the "worthy" child at risk, the hardworking and chaste widow. Still today we all prefer to work with those who face challenges due to no fault of their own, who will show their gratitude and respond to the work of God in their lives. But who of us is truly worthy? Since when has the Gospel been for the worthy?[2]

> Who of us is truly worthy? Since when has the Gospel been for the worthy?

Losing a child to violence is a great tragedy. But what a tragedy also is that youth who initiated the violence, who cares so little for life that he can take the life of another!

Beyond the Single 'Youth at Risk' to Youth in their Context

Children and youth exist not as individuals in a vacuum, but within a particular context. They are part of families, schools, communities, cities, and nations. Developmental psychology guru and Head Start founder Urie Bronfenbrenner pioneered the concept of understanding a child not only as an individual, but also within his or her ecological context. He likened it to a set of Russian *matrushka* dolls, "Like a set of nested structures, each inside the next."[3] Using Bronfenbrenner's interlocking systems approach, we begin to see how complex and interdependent life is. We need to look within each system (called microsystems, mesosystems, exosystems, and macrosystems), as well as looking beyond to the next system.[4]

To understand these, let us look at the life of one adolescent named Joey. Joey lives with his mom and siblings in a one-bedroom apartment. Joey's microsystems are his family, school, peers, and neighborhood. After three recent deaths in her family, the mom is mentally unstable. The extended family and the father live in another state, and Joey rarely sees them. Joey's school ranks at the bottom of performing schools in the state. His home is one block from the "hood" of the local gang, and they actively work on recruiting

---

[2] See the article written by Doug McConnell in this volume.
[3] Urie Bronfenbrenner, *The Ecology of Human Development*, 22-26.
[4] In an article this length, it is not possible to do justice to these concepts. For a more in-depth explanation, see J. Garbarino et al., *Children and Families in the Social Environment*, 2nd ed.

him. Looking only at the microsystems in Joey's life might lead us to conclude that Joey is seriously at risk of entering the local gang.

Now let us look at the mesosystems in Joey's life. These are the connections between the microsystems. The more positive connections there are between the microsystems, the healthier the child's development. There are not many connections between Joey's family

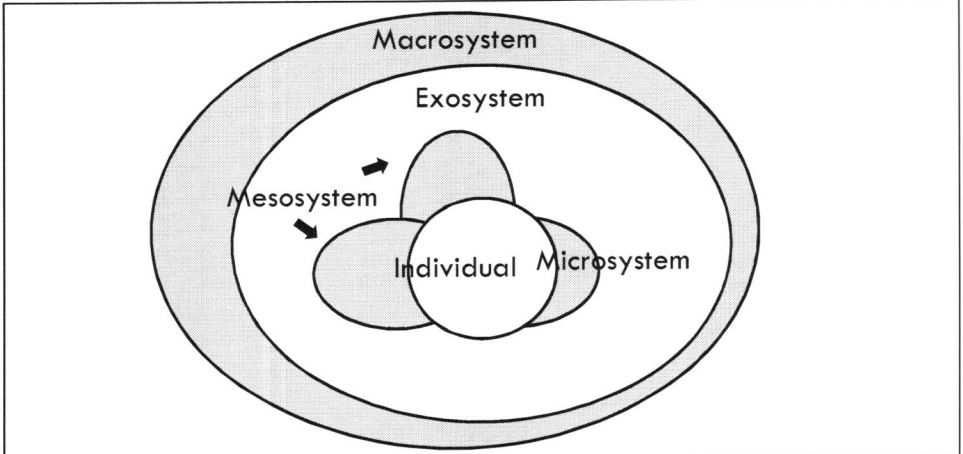

and his school, but Joey's neighborhood is a cohesive one, and neighbors look out for each other. When Joey's family forgot his birthday, neighbors gathered and made a cake for him. Every day after school, he goes home with his friend and neighbor Jesse, and this has become a second home to him. When Joey's mom is hospitalized, the neighbors rally to provide meals and childcare so that the family can stay together until she returns. In Joey's life, we see how a community can ameliorate some of the other risk factors in his life. Without the strength of the surrounding neighborhood, and the many connections between Joey, his family, and the neighbors, the family might not have survived intact during this crisis.

The next layer of systems in Joey's life is the exosystem. The exosystem greatly impacts a youth, but the impact is indirect. An example of an exosystem is a job that does not produce adequate income for the family, or a school board that makes budget cuts and eliminates an after-school program. This greatly impacts the quality of life and potential development of the youth, but is beyond his or her realm of influence. At this exosystem level, community organizations can have a great impact, coming together to organize for neighborhood improvements—churches, neighbors, and schools come together to bring changes that cannot happen through individuals or individual ministries.[5]

The next level, the macrosystem, occurs at the societal level. Racism is one example of a macrosystem. The influence of the globalizing media is another. Youth are subjected daily to images of what they cannot have, yet the media sends messages of what they must wear and drive in order to be valued in this society. Even children and youth who grow up

---

[5] For a further discussion of the role of the community, see the third affirmation of this volume.

in poor neighborhoods, can be influenced by these messages. The youth who will be most impacted, however, are those who are not hearing other messages about who they truly are. Thus Joey feels he needs to wear certain brands to form an identity and be valued as a part of society.

To be involved with Joey, we need to see that Joey lives embedded in these systems that impact his life in both positive and negative ways. This ecological approach is a serious critique of some traditional evangelical approaches to ministry. In his history of *The American City and the Evangelical Church*, Harvie Conn notes that in the past, even when the evangelical church responded to the needs of the poor, it was generally done in an individualistic manner. Those of us who are evangelicals have been better at saving souls than redeeming communities.[6]

> "So in Christ we, though many, form one body, and each member belongs to all the others."
> —Rom. 12:5 NASB

How will we see these communities transformed? God desires to use the Joeys, the youth living there. Those of us who seek to be missional workers must always remember that the best we can do is to empower children, youth, and their families to be the agents of transformation in their own communities. In John 3:30, John states, "[Jesus] must increase, but I must decrease." How true this needs to be of us as well.

Together, We Belong to God

Every year, several students from our local high school are given scholarships to attend an elite summer school for the arts. At first they have fears about going to be with "rich white kids." By the time the summer is over, they return with a new perspective, realizing that there is a richness to their lives and in their neighborhood relationships that the suburban youth envy. One said, "You have a neighborhood and community, we only have a mall." The neighborhood youth return with a new sense of pride in their communities.

When I first moved into my neighborhood, I came with the idea of serving children, youth, and their families. Far more compelling to me now is knowing we belong to each other, and that together we belong to God. For in serving and ministering to people, we can still keep a distance between them and us. When we belong to each other, a prophetic community is formed that begins to erase the lines between 'them' and 'us', and we understand that there is no platform at the cross of Jesus that elevates me above Diablo. We stand together in our need for God's grace to redeem and transform us.

---

[6] Harvie Conn, *The American City and the Evangelical Church*.

CASE STUDY

CASE STUDY: KING'S KIDS

By Barbara Ruegger with Paul Stockley
King's Kids

Vision and Mission

Many children's ministries or Sunday schools seem to simply evangelize children over and over again, or just tell them good Bible stories. While it is good to share with children the message of the Gospel, this is only the beginning. Indeed, the same should be true in the church, too! We need to move beyond a conversion message to disciple those to whom we are reaching out, and then lead them out into mission.

King's Kids is established to do just this. The values and principles on which *King's Kids* ministry is founded can be grouped under six broad themes:

1) Relationship with God: Knowing God intimately and bringing him joy.

2) Discipleship Training: Seeking godly motivation and servanthood, in the context of everyday living.

3) Spiritual Capacity: Understanding young people's destiny and spiritual capacity, appropriate to their age and stage of development.

4) Linking Generations: Restoring the place of family as important for intergenerational ministry.

5) Team Leadership: Building on unity in plurality, with balance and accountability through servant leadership and godly counsel.

6) Reaching Out: Making Jesus known to all people, extending his Kingdom together in all spheres of society, worldwide.

In short, the mission of *King's Kids* is to lead children, young people, and families worldwide into a proven knowledge of God, bring him joy, and together make him known to all peoples.

Expressions of Faith

Knowing God and making God known are at the heart of *King's Kids* ministry activities, which provide many opportunities for children and young people to grow in their Christian life and to share their faith with others through witness and service.

For many years, King's Kids has organized outreaches such as celebration teams (including choreography and drama), HANDS teams (who bring practical help to people in need), sports teams, and Daniel prayer groups[1] for children, teenagers, and families on six different continents.

Compassion Ethiopia and Tanzania

John the apostle of love says that he shares what he has heard, what he has seen and what he has touched. I want to follow John's footsteps and share how children have been greatly used by God to bring about transformation of immense proportions in the body of Christ in Ethiopia and Tanzania as Compassion carries out its ministry to children.

- In Tanzania, children became the single most important factor in building church unity. In northern Tanzania where Compassion started its ministry to children, the leaders of different denominations had serious difficulties to worship, discuss Kingdom issues, and even meet together. God used the agenda of ministry to children to break this problem. Today, the church leaders of different denominations in northern Tanzania hold quarterly meetings to pray, worship, and strategize to enlarge God's Kingdom in their country.
- In Compassion Ethiopia, over one thousand children received Jesus Christ as a result of the testimonies and prayers of children in Compassion-assisted projects.
- Several thousand parents and caregivers have also joined the family of God because of the witnessing and prayers of children in Compassion-assisted projects in Ethiopia.
- Many people have been released of evil spirits and healed from different types of diseases as a result of the fervent prayers of children.[1]

—*Shiferaw Michael*
Compassion International, Africa

---

[1] Mr. Kebebew Daka, interview by Shiferaw W. Michael, August 15, 2005; Mrs. Tesera Kebede, interview by Shiferaw W. Michael, August 13, 2005.

Strategy

King's Kids employs a four-phase approach in their ministry. Taken together, these resonate with the values expressed in the biblical affirmation that "children are essential to the mission of God", and demonstrate how such an affirmation might be worked out in reality.

These phases cover a variety of approaches, from mobilizing children and young people who have a living Christian faith through camps and outreaches, to providing year-

---

[1] See Daniel 1:3-2:49.

round discipleship programs to strengthen their relationships with God and live in a way that brings joy to his heart, to reaching out to children and teens who have little or no contact with a Christian witness through clubs, youth activity centers, and streetside church programs, to caring for the practical needs of children living in slums or on the streets, orphans, children with AIDS, children affected by warfare (including child soldiers) or by commercial sexual exploitation.

Only the four together show the fullness of what God has for our children—namely, to care for them, reach them with the Gospel, disciple them, and show them the way into mission. It is absolutely important then, that when we reach out to children and youth, we do not just form shallow relationships, but that we disciple the children and teenagers and train them to become missionaries to their own people, their own country, and to the ends of the world.[2]

Example: India

As adults, we need to find and provide opportunities where the children can put their faith into practice.

In Delhi, India *King's Kids* are working with children in a daycare center and a preschool. The *King's Kids* team has twice organized a camp for these children. The one-week camps are always full of fun and love and many hours of worship and teaching. Children and teenagers learn what it means to be a disciple, and the camp finishes with an outreach where the participants apply what they have learned.

Two children, Pavan and Dilip from Navjeeven camp have attended one of our boot camps and are now in one of our pre-schools. They met a boy from the same community, who was paralyzed in half of his body. These two boys took oil and anointed him, praying that he would be healed. Amazingly, the boy was healed, and he came to our church walking perfectly and sharing his testimony. His mother also came later and testified about what had happened.

Here we can see that children share in being a witness in their community to the transforming power of God, knowing God for themselves and making God known to others.

The *King's Kids* team in Delhi has vision for these children and is providing opportunities for them to learn. Likewise, we all need to be available as mentors, leading children into mission, teaching them God's plan for their lives, and then encouraging them to go.

---

[2] See Matthew 28:19-20 and Acts 1:8.

Conclusion

Many examples throughout history show God using children to further his purposes, including or perhaps especially children in high-risk situations. Many today in forgotten corners of the world bear witness to this in their own lives.

If we are to believe the prophetic words spoken of today's generation, many of these children and young people will go much further than we have ever been, and serve the purposes of God in ways we could not have imagined. Can we let them go? Are we ready to set them free?

www.hikidz.org:
A Unique and Strategic Website in Child Evangelism Worldwide

Children's websites should aim to be:
- Fun: child-friendly, attractive, humorous, interactive, and updated daily
- Relevant: clearly communicating the Christian message in appropriate ways for today's children
- Biblical: providing Christian teaching and a Christian perspective on current issues and contemporary culture
- Safe: where a child can navigate within a wholesome and secure infrastructure
- Pastoral: a source of help and counsel with input from trained and screened personnel
- Positive: nurturing self-esteem and personal value; giving a positive and constructive influence
- Resource-packed: featuring selected content from interdenominational organizations; providing links with other good sites

Unlike many other ministry websites, the www.hikidz.org website project presents an exciting opportunity for a dynamic children's Internet site based on the collaboration of many large and small Christian ministries which share a vision to reach out to today's generation in a relevant and engaging way. For such a site to be extensive and effective across countries and languages, it requires many ministries and the wider church throughout the nations to share in this Kingdom Project together.

Providing an ambitious, high-quality, global scale evangelistic children's website is an overwhelming task for any one ministry or even a few together. In this new age of easy global communication, this is a challenge to the whole Church throughout the world to go beyond ministry and denominational boundaries. This is a project for the Kingdom of God, the whole Church!

The HiKidz Website Project aims to engage
- Children: to grow in faith; to discover new resources, information, and entertainment.
- Pre-Teenagers/Teenagers: to continue using the links and resources they discovered as a child using the site.
- Parents: to get help for their children; to promote healthy values and find good parenting links and resources.
- Teachers: to get help to reinforce their teaching based on Christian values; to promote their school and its special projects.
- Pastors: to reinforce their church's teaching program; to communicate information about events for children and families in their city, region, or country.
- Children's Workers: to get ideas, tools and encouragement; to obtain a resource which they can creatively tie in with their program of weekly teaching, activities, and follow-up.

—*Harry Bryans*
HiKidz Website Project

PRACTICAL IMPLICATIONS

UNDERSTANDING GOD'S HEART FOR CHILDREN

By Cathryn Baker
Viva Network

Children are Essential to the Mission of God

In the global Church today, the importance of prayer in children's lives is often neglected. Sunday School or children's church sessions very rarely feature any kind of prayer time apart from the briefest prayers spoken by the children's leader. Church prayer meetings tend to be in the evenings, when younger children are unable to attend. Prayers in church services are overwhelmingly led by adults.

Mindsets and practices need to change. If the little children are to come to Jesus, knowing him and making him known, then surely one of the major elements of this should be in prayer, where relationship is developed through communication. In prayer, children learn to speak to God and listen to his voice. They recognize his greatness, his ability and desire to change lives, and his personal interest in them as individuals. Foundations are built which can last a lifetime as they come to know God personally.

When children are denied the chance to approach God for themselves in prayer, adults are also denied the example that Jesus wants to make through them. The simple faith of "such as these" is a picture of the way we should all be coming to God.

Biblical Foundations

God's plan is for all his people, regardless of their age, to come before him in prayer. The call to prayer in the book of Joel tells the Israelites to gather all the generations: "Bring together the elders, gather the children, those nursing at the breast" (Joel 2:16).[1] Even the very youngest are to be involved, no matter what their stage of development—God wants his whole Church to seek him, and that puts elders and infants on an equal level.

Throughout the Bible, we hear stories of children used by God. When his people turned away from him, God entrusted his message to Jeremiah, who at first protested against this calling, saying "I am only a child" (Jer. 1:6). Instead of waiting until Jeremiah saw himself as mature enough to take on this responsibility, God responded by assuring him of his presence and equipping: "Do not be afraid of them, for I am with you and will rescue you ... today I appoint you over nations and kingdoms" (Jer. 1:8, 10).

---

[1] All Scripture quotations are taken from the New International Version. See also the fifth affirmation of this volume.

We need to move away from the mindset that only adults can be trusted with serious responsibilities. In Jeremiah's time, the adult priests, leaders, and prophets had rebelled and dishonored God (Jer. 2:8), yet a young boy listened, obeyed, and faithfully spoke God's word.[2]

We should encourage children in prayer and expect God to respond! Childhood is not simply a preparation for adulthood, but a precious period of life that can be lived out in relationship with God, serving him in prayer and actions.

Children need to learn about what God says in the Bible about prayer, and how to apply it to their lives. Paul wrote to Timothy reminding him "how from infancy you have known the holy Scriptures" (2 Tim. 3:15). Evidently, Timothy's ministry as a young man was influenced to a great extent by his childhood awareness of God and his Word.

Matthew 6:6 can open up to them the importance of personal, private prayer: "When you pray, go into your room, close the door, and pray to your Father, who is unseen." This picture of a loving, listening Father is something that many children can identify with through their experience of parental love. For others who do not live in a secure family environment, we need to help them come to know God as the perfect Father, who can be relied on and will not abandon them.

We might think that prayer is an abstract concept for children to understand, but Jesus' teaching is visual and based on story, which children can easily engage with. For example, the story of the man who goes to borrow bread from his neighbor at night illustrates boldness in prayer (Luke 11:5-8), and this persistence and confidence is underlined by Jesus' picture of prayer as knocking on a door which will be opened (Luke 11:9-10).

Prayers in the Bible—the Lord's Prayer (Luke 11:2-4), the Psalms, or Daniel's prayer (Dan. 2:20-23), for example—can also be used as models for children's prayer. Passages of the Bible can be chosen to pray through, rooting prayer in Scripture and giving children a starting point for their prayers. **[INSERT TEXTBOX 7.14 ABOUT HERE]**

The Need to Model Prayer to Children

Children learn by example, by watching and imitating the people around them and picking up patterns of behavior from their families and friends. When children see adults making prayer a priority in their lives, they begin to understand its importance, and can start to take their part in God's mission through prayer.

Prayer within the family is deeply important. As Christians live out the exhortations of Deuteronomy 6:6-7 with their families, their children will understand that faith is not just one aspect of life, but that it affects every moment and every situation. Children can become "much-needed participants in intercession. Partnerships start at home by asking our children to participate with us in conversations with God."[3]

---

[2] See the articles by Gustavo Crocker and Karissa Glanville in this volume. See also Cheri Fuller, *When Children Pray*, 40.
[3] Fuller, 47.

Prayer needs to be integral to all church activities, including children's church sessions and nursery times. In this way, children learn to pray, and see this constant communication with God as a natural and necessary part of life. If prayer surrounds every part of church life, children will come to understand the importance of dependence on God in every area. Prayers of praise to God help children to appreciate his greatness. When they witness faith-filled intercession, they are reminded that "our God can meet all [their] needs according to his glorious riches in Christ Jesus" (Phil. 4:19). When prayers declare God's attributes, children learn more of who he is.

> **Biblical Examples of Prayer**
> - Psalms
> - Daniel 2:20-23
> - Luke 11:2-10
> - John 17
> - Nehemiah 1:5-11

Just as Samuel needed Eli to tell him how to respond when he heard the voice of God, we need to teach children how to pray, living out a prayer-filled life as an example to them.

Practical Ways of Engaging Children in Prayer

There are many ways of getting children involved in prayer, and some will suit particular contexts and cultures more than others. We need to take time to discover the best ways of connecting with the children we are responsible for, recognizing that God has purposes for them and desires them to come to him in prayer. Prayer networks, church prayer times, special events, and ongoing prayer in the family can all help children to engage in prayer and draw close to God.

> **Practical Ways of Engaging Children in Prayer**
> - Prayer networks
> - Church prayer times
> - Special events
> - Ongoing family prayer

Generally, children respond well to practical rather than abstract ideas. This might mean that creative, experiential activities are useful in helping them pray. If they are praying for a particular area of your town, for example, why not take them there for a prayer walk? Or if they are praying for a nation, why not lay out a big map of the world and have them lay hands on that place? Using a variety of media can also help them engage with issues to pray about. Drama, games, songs, and stories can all help to facilitate prayer amongst children.

Below are just a few examples of events and networks that are mobilizing children in prayer, enabling them to step out and serve God in this way.

Each year, Viva Network facilitates the *World Weekend of Prayer for Children at Risk*. In 2005, an estimated 1.2 million people took part—and half of those participants were children. People join in prayer in over 90 countries, so it is not surprising that types of prayer events vary! We have had reports of prayer marches in El Salvador and Uganda, stadium rallies in the Philippines and Madagascar, interactive prayer activities in Bangladesh and Canada, and a "Compassion Day" of prayer and practical action for children at risk in South Africa.

This kind of focused event often acts as a catalyst for further prayer in children. Their experience of prayer and unity with a large group can spark an enthusiasm which lasts much longer than the event itself. Following the World Wide Day of Prayer for Children at Risk in recent years, regular children's prayer groups have begun in nations including Papua New Guinea, the United States, and India.[4]

One successful children's prayer network is in Indonesia, a country that is 80 percent Muslim, yet is seeing amazing growth in churches and the prayer movement. *Jaringan Doa Anak* (JDA) is a network with prayer groups in fifty cities across the nation. Its vision is to pray for children (particularly those who live in risky environments), to mobilize children to pray, and to bring unity in the church, leading to transformation in the nation.

JDA was only launched three years ago, but already, thousands of children are involved. As a local group becomes established, it 'adopts' a neighboring town and prays for it. The group then approaches the town's church leaders to suggest setting up a children's prayer group there. This process creates a 'mushrooming' of groups, made possible by the links already in place through Indonesia's adult National Prayer Network. The focus on interdenominational unity is one reason why the movement is growing—churches come together to form children's prayer groups, building trust and relationships in the process.

Children's prayer leaders, pastors, and parents need to invest time in showing children who God is, teaching them to pray and listen to him, and releasing them in ministry. Thousands of children worldwide have now heard the message that children can pray and children can minister, that they don't have to wait until they are grown up to have a meaningful relationship with God, and that he wants them to use the gifts he has given them to pray, worship, and serve him.

"His Purpose for Every Child . . ."

As adults, we all accept that in order to make a difference in the world for God, and bring his Kingdom, we need to pray. If children are essential to this mission, then they too must pray! Who knows what might happen as churches, networks, and families around the world begin to equip and release children in prayer?

By showing children that their prayers are valued and heard by God, they begin to understand their identity in him and the ways that he can use them. Their prayers are powerful—it was not by chance that Jesus chose them as the example of inheritors of the Kingdom of heaven (Matt. 19:14).

We need to encourage Christians worldwide to break away from the mindset that prayer is for adults, and enable children to live out the potential God has put in them to fully take part in his mission as witnesses for him in their generation.

---

[4] "World Wide Day of Prayer for Children at Risk Feedback Reports 2004 and 2005," http://www.viva.org/?page_id=97 (accessed May 8, 2006).

CHAPTER 7
DISCUSSION QUESTIONS

1) What would happen if churches, mission agencies, and communities would seriously consider children at the heart of the Great Commandment and the Great Commission?

2) How can we partner with children as agents of change, rather than excluding them, or simply seeing them as passive recipients of our action?

CONCLUSION

By Paul Stockley
Development Worker, Oxford

In this volume we have begun to explore seven themes which are broad, but closely interrelated. These are: the child's uniqueness, need for parental care, gift to family and community, flourishing in society, a hope for one generation to another, participating in the family of faith, and partnering in the mission of God.

Why Are We Exploring These Themes?

As Christians in childcare it is vital that we learn to articulate why we do what we do. We need to reflect on our own motivation and understand what drives us. Our goal is to have a broader and deeper rationale for our work that is rooted in the values of our Christian life and faith. Without this we simply remain grounded in the human philosophies of modern and post–modern society.

It is possible, even easy, to go about our life and work as Christians without pausing to consider these things. But this will not get us very far, particularly in our work with children where the overwhelming demands and challenges we face everyday easily lead to high stress levels and burnout. Our anger at the denial of children's rights and our pity at the neglect of their needs will ultimately prove inadequate as a driving force. We need to reconnect with the defining principle behind who we are and what we do: the God in whom and for whom we live. More than this—the God who comes to us in the children we encounter, and the God who would reach out to those children with us and through us. Christ Jesus makes this unambiguously clear when he tells his followers "Whoever welcomes this child in my name welcomes me, and whoever welcomes me welcomes the one who sent me" (Luke 9:48), and also ". . . their angels in heaven always see the face of my Father" (Matt. 18:10). In other words, we respond not merely because we see that children have needs or believe that they have rights, but because only in this encounter can we discover God's way of doing things. And God's way of doing things is not merely a matter of what Jesus says and does (though that is plain enough), but in Jesus' very being as the one who comes from heaven in the power of the Spirit as a naked infant, to live and to laugh and to love. Our encounter with children takes us beyond the call and questions that their presence raises, to God's doing and God's being. It takes us back to Christ–like living in the power of the Spirit for the glory of the Father. The more deeply rooted we are in this God, the clearer we are about our own identity and purpose. And hence the less likely we are to become discouraged, to find ourselves overstretched, and ultimately to lose hope.

Nor is this pause for reflection merely for our own benefit. Clarity and focus in our own identity and purpose enables us more easily and effectively to interface with others working in the field of childcare, even (or perhaps especially) if their faith or philosophy differs from our own, be they Muslim, Hindu, Buddhist, atheist, or humanist. Working together with others towards a common goal (better child health, access to education, improved family life) becomes possible, even if we don't agree about why these goals are a good thing. We are not threatened by other's answers (or lack of answers) to the "why?" question if we have already thought it through for ourselves. This is essential for two reasons. Firstly on a theological level, God's kingdom is bigger than the Church. We need to recognize that God is at work in the world through many agencies that may not carry a Christian or evangelical label. Secondly from a practical viewpoint, the challenges we face are immense. We would be naïve to think we can go it alone.

Hence, this volume has been an attempt to give some expression to our motivation. Please note that this book is not in any sense a definitive answer to the "why?" question.[1] Nor is it intended to be! It is merely one contribution to the conversation, a kind of snapshot of where we are now, and some of the discussions and debates that have arisen.

What Contribution Have We Made?

Since the early days of the process at the Cutting Edge symposium of 1999, through the draft framework that emerged in 2004, the symposium in 2005, up until now with the publication of this volume: all have helped with the unpacking of the phrase "God's heart for children" which we have been seeking to grasp. Exploring these seven themes has enriched our understanding, and opened out the conversation.

It has also enabled us to move away from rights–based and needs–based approaches (or even others based on economic paradigms or social models) as our starting point. This is crucial for us if we are to move beyond our natural limitations and human perspective. Naturally, we must continue to attend to needs, offering generous provision to fulfill what children lack through deprivation and neglect, the essentials for children to live and grow, to flourish and thrive. And we must continue to make use of rights language (and the legal leverage that comes with it), engaging with governments and authorities in terms they can understand. But there is always more need than we can meet with our limited resources. And there are always systems and structures more powerful than our limited influence.

So we need to step back and see these (and our work) within a much broader and richer perspective of God at work in human history, and the place of children and childhood within the divine purpose. Several papers and case studies in this volume have demonstrated what is possible once we grasp this bigger picture.

In the first instance we have seen clearly how lost dignity is reborn when the image of God is fully respected in each child and they are welcomed and accepted for their inherent worth, not judged for their problematic past, nor loaded with future expectations. This is as true in the slums of Calcutta (in Premila Pavamani's case study) as in the favelas of São Paulo (in the study by Stuart and George Christine). And the resulting life transformation for the child can send strong ripples of God's beautiful grace into the child's family and

---

[1] Why do we do what we do? Why work with "children at risk"? In other words: What is our motivation?

community. In chapter two the links between sin in society and the quality of life that children experience have been clearly spelled out (by Katherine Putman), and earthed in Greg Burch's study with reference to children living on the streets.

For some of the most challenging issues, such as children in the sex trade and child soldiers, we have learnt that there are very practical responses that bring real hope (Crawford in chapter 4 and McGill in chapter 2). Effective approaches such as these arise out of a deeper understanding of "God's heart for children", going beyond a superficial view of the structural issues which impact upon the child's life. The same can be said for meaningful engagement with the challenges faced by HIV and AIDS (Susie Howe in Chapter 6). It is possible to encounter a tangible living hope through these practical measures, in situations that otherwise would offer no hope.

Furthermore, we have seen clear instances of how an appreciation of the true worth of children opens the door to wider engagement with the problems faced by a community. Besa Shapllo's study from Albania on literacy and civic education is a fine example here. And we have heard once again the call to work inter-generationally (chapter 5), and to include children at the heart of missional initiatives (chapter 7), not merely as subjects (or rather, objects), but as agents of change.

Crucially, we have drawn breath and paused to consider more closely the multi-faceted blessing of the child as God's gift to us. In chapter 3, Judith Ennew has attentively enabled us to explore what this might mean for us, when so many children are seen as an inconvenience to be eliminated, a burden to be cast aside, a curse to be exorcised. And Stephen Tollestrup (in chapter 5) has encouraged us to wrestle with the nature of promise in today's world as expressed through the children of our communities, so helping us to unlock the enigma of hope.

These are just a few examples of the wealth of contributions from authors in this volume. And many others have given insight to the conversation along the way.

What Areas Need More Serious Work?

In the process of drawing out the themes of Cutting Edge 2005 and the ensuing dialogue that has led to this volume, several crucial questions have been voiced. Not that these questions are necessarily new, but the need to find empowering answers in the context of our work with children makes the task all the more urgent.

Firstly, it is evident that we need to revisit the narrative of the biblical text, and ask ourselves some tough questions. To begin with: how do we handle Scripture in relation to our work with children? It is not a book of children's stories, though some may treat it as such, for example when writing a curriculum for a Sunday Club. Rather than limiting its power as we package it in simplified language, we must allow the Spirit to unleash the transforming grace of God's Word in a way which radically impacts the children we work with, their families, and their communities. How can we do this?

Another crucial question arises that is related to the first point: how do we respond to the problematic texts we encounter? It is easy to point to violence in other religions and its adverse effect on children, but Scripture has a fair share of infanticide and slaughter of children, much of which appears to be sanctioned by God. Skirting around these texts might look like an easy option, but actually it is an abdication of our responsibility towards children in today's world. If we are to avoid accusations of being naïve in our faith, then we have to engage with these texts and come up with some honest answers.[2]

In this respect we are reminded to always keep in balance the counter-narratives that inform the events as they unfold, the prophets and seers that speak out against the ungodly actions of leaders and the people. Also, as we read Scripture, we must not neglect to hold in mind the progression of God's self revelation. Christ and the Spirit are not absent in the ancient texts, but clearly, the narrators of the Old Testament did not understand God in the same way as the narrators of the New. Having a biblical response does not mean simply picking a few proof texts. We need to be more thorough and rigorous in our engagement of the full story (narrative and meta-narrative) if we are to be credible in our critique of the ever-pervasive mythologies of the world around us. Even keeping all this in mind, there are no easy answers to give to a world half full of children, many of whom suffer.

In talking about the meta-narratives of the biblical text, we refer not only to the over-arching cosmic story, but also to the hidden paradigms which the text brings with it. In exploring Scripture for understanding "God's heart for children" we must also look for these. If in asking "what does the bible say about children?" we simply scan a concordance for the word child (or infant, or youth, etc.) we will miss much of the insight into children and childhood issues that Scripture has for us. For example: in relation to affirmation 2, have we considered what the history of the Israelites tells us about parenting, with God as perfect parent and Ephraim (Israel) as rebellious child? Or for affirmation 6, how may the Exodus story inform our paradigms of faith development? Or for affirmation 5, what do the recurring dysfunctions in Abraham's family line tell us about intergenerational nurture? And for affirmation 7, looking at their whole life story (rather than just an instant), do the stories of characters such as Josiah or Samuel or Moses tell us anything about God's call on young lives? Much rich treasure lies undiscovered here.

A second area that needs more serious reflection is in the stories of our work, the details of our failures and successes as organizations working with children. Macro-level accounts of the number of children rescued, fed, immunized, and such may have their place, but we need to refocus on the local human story, to make the connection with the names and faces of those we seek to serve. We need to ask again: what difference have we made in the life of this child, and the child's family and community? If we don't ask this question, we risk doing a world of good, but neglecting to offer the best. Hopefully a framework such as the one posited here will open us to a more holistic perspective, and prompt us to ask questions of our work.

These are just a few of the challenges that we need to address. There are questions yet to be explored, whether through the symposia of Cutting Edge, or in the collectives of the Child Theology Movement, or in our own work with children, or in seminaries and academic institutions, or elsewhere in other contexts.

---

[2] See Bunge, Fretheim, Gaventa, eds., *Children and Childhood: Biblical Perspectives*.

Are These Affirmations Helpful? If So, To What Extent?

Certainly these seven affirmations have been helpful. They have been a useful stepping stone for the process to move forward, providing a solid framework for the 2005 symposium, and have enabled us to get to where we are in the conversation.

Such a framework as this can also help us in assessing the impact of our work. We can (and should) ask questions such as: How is our work with children enabling them to experience all that God intends? We can be more specific: In what ways is our work enabling children to thrive in stable relationships and receive the loving committed parenting they need? Where is our collaboration with government and institutions creating a more just society in which children can flourish? Are we creating opportunities for each child to discover and fulfill their unique calling within the community of faith and the wider world? Each affirmation in the framework can provoke useful questions for deeper reflection, practical outworking, and assessing impact. Doing this exercise enables us to view our organizations and work on a much broader basis than we would perhaps naturally do, particularly if our work has a quite legitimate focus on just one aspect, such as parenting and family life, for example. Such questions set the failures and successes within a more holistic context.

From some of the debates that have arisen as a result of this process, it seems evident that the affirmations cannot stand as they are. No suggestion is being made that such a framework should be discarded altogether. Nonetheless, at the very least these affirmations will need to be revisited, if they are to prove useful beyond the present.

Any affirmations such as these need to be earthed in the meta–narrative of divine history and the human story—that is to say: Creation, the Fall, the Christ–event (incarnation, life, crucifixion, resurrection, ascension), Pentecost, the Parousia. While this was considered when the affirmations were drafted, it has not been written explicitly into the framework. This has been an acknowledged limitation all along. While present implicitly to some extent, each affirmation needs to reflect the tensions between the ideal of Eden and the reality of today's world, or the now and not yet of the coming Kingdom. At the very least, the addition of an explanatory introduction to the framework would help to situate these affirmations. Clarity here would resolve some of the debates about wording.

Little words carry much more than their weight in letters. Recalling dialogues over wording of the third article in the Convention on the Rights of the Child, the best interests of the child became "a" primary consideration rather than "the" primary consideration. (In the original Polish draft it was "the paramount consideration".) Awareness of the need for care in drafting the seven affirmations, little words were not taken lightly. Nevertheless, it was not possible to anticipate the problems arising through mistaken misreadings of the text. For example, affirmation 5 was misread by some to say that "children are the promise of hope . . . " usurping the hope we as Christians have in Christ, and provoking some unnecessarily heated debate over a word that isn't there! Not helpful.

Once again, it must be stressed that the whole framework stands together. These are not seven separate affirmations. Another example may help here: you cannot read the Convention on the Rights of the Child—the whole of it, including the preamble—and imagine it is anti–family. It contains several paragraphs and articles which clearly put the family at the heart of child nurture. Likewise this framework should not be read as saying that single parent families (or even isolated two–parent families) are the ideal. It clearly does not say that. To take a phrase from affirmation 2 out of the context of the whole (with its clear reference to a fallen world and damaged relationships) would distort the meaning.

These seven affirmations have proven to be a helpful reference point. If they are to continue to be useful, the affirmations should be read carefully, together, and without neglecting the context.

Where Do We Go From Here?

Moving from a draft framework to anything definitive will not happen overnight. As it stands the framework already serves a practical purpose of inviting broader and deeper consideration of our own care for children—an invitation to which we can and should respond. While there is scope for much further reflection on the various nuances of the affirmations, how profitable this would prove is open to question. Agreeing on words and agreeing on meanings are equally problematic. Enhancing the framework with a supplementary explanation that situates the affirmations in a theological and historical context would undoubtedly help avoid some of the adverse reactions, and would serve its purpose well. Now that people have copies of the draft framework in their hands, however, making any changes might not be a simple process.

One important challenge for the future will be to keep the conversation connected! With any discussion out in the public domain, there is no telling where people will take it. As Eglantyne Jebb first penned her Children's Charter in 1923, she could not have imagined it would lead to the most widely ratified International Convention, albeit some decades later.

Our task may be somewhat less ambitious, but as different parties explore facets of child theology and rationale for work with "children at risk", it will be crucial to find ways of sharing our discoveries with each other, and so to enrich and encourage each other's insights.

The many contributions to this volume are offered willingly to your comment and critique. It is an open conversation to which all are welcome to share.

BIBLIOGRAPHY

Introduction

Bunge, Marcia J., ed. *The Child in Christian Thought.* Grand Rapids, MI: William B. Eerdmans Publishing Company, 2001.

Himes, Judith, and Angelique Olmo. "Executive Summary: International Youth." 2002. www.prcdc.org/summaries/intlyouth/intlyouth.html (accessed April 20, 2004).

Ibiblio. "World Population." www.ibiblio.org/lunarbin/worldpop/index.html (accessed October 15, 2005).

McConnell, Douglas. "A Missional Response to Children at Risk." *Theology News and Notes* 52, no. 3 (2005): 8–10. http://www.fuller.edu/news/pubs/tnn/2005_fall/index.htm.

McConnell, Douglas. "Children and the Kingdom: Missiological Reflections on Children at Risk." In *Changing Our Response: Mission in the Era of HIV/AIDS*, edited by Jonathan J. Bonk, 20-26. New Haven, CT: OMSC Publications, 2005.

Myers, Bryant. Annual missiology lectures at Fuller Seminary, Pasadena, CA, November 8, 2006.

UNAIDS. *What Religious Leaders Can Do About HIV/AIDS: Action for Children and Young People.* Geneva: UNAIDS, 2003.

UNAIDS/WHO. *AIDS Epidemic Update 2004.* Geneva: UNAIDS, 2004.

Viva Network. "Understanding God's Heart Biblical Framework." Working paper, Oxford, 2004.

Wright, Christopher J. H. *Old Testament Ethics for the People of God.* Downers Grove, IL: InterVarsity Press, 2004.

Chapter 1

"A Pobreza do Debate." *Exame*, October 6, 1999. http://portalexame.abril.com.br/busca/resultado/index.html?d1=938764800&d2=941443140&qu=escolar&ao=0&dia1=1&mes1=10&ano1=1999&dia2=31&mes2=10&ano2=1999&rd=1&num=10&x=29&y=8 (accessed August 22, 2006).

Balswick, Jack O., Pamela E. King, and Kevin S. Reimer. *The Reciprocating Self: Human Development in Theological Perspective.* Downers Grove, IL: InterVarsity Press, 2005.

Banks, R. *Paul's Idea of Community*. Rev. ed. Peabody, MA: Hendrickson Publishers, 1994.

Barth, Karl. *Church Dogmatics*. Vol. III.1. Translated by G. W. Bromiley and T. F. Torrance. Edinburgh: T & T Clark, 1957-1975..

Beeftu, Alemu. "Biblical Basis for Recognizing Uniqueness and Dignity." In *Cutting Edge 2005: Conference Papers*, 2-6. Cirencester, UK: Viva Network, 2005.

Brewster, Dan. "The 4/14 Window: Child Ministries and Mission Strategy." In *Children in Crisis: A New Commitment,* edited by Phyllis Kilbourn, 125-139. Monrovia, CA: MARC, 1996.

Brink, Paul. "Debating International Human Rights: The 'Middle Ground' for Religious Participants." *The Brandywine Review of Faith and International Affairs*, Fall (2003).

Bunge, Marcia J., ed. *The Child in Christian Thought*. Grand Rapids, MI: William B. Eerdmans Publishing Company, 2001.

Castro, Maria Helena. "Education for All: Evaluation of the Year 2000: National Report – Brazil." http://www2.unesco.org/wef/countryreports/brazil/contents.html (accessed August 22, 2006).

Consortium for Street Children. "India." http://www.streetchildren.org.uk/resources/details/?type=country&country=64 (accessed May 26, 2006).

Ennew, Judith and Paul Stephenson, eds. *Questioning the Basis of our Work: Christianity, Children's Rights, and Development*. London: Tearfund, 2004.

Grogan, G. W. *New Dictionary of Christian Ethics and Pastoral Theology*. Edited by David J. Atkinson and David H. Field. S.v. "Image of God." Downers Grove, IL: InterVarsity Press, 1995.

Gunton, C. E. *The Triune Creator: A Historical and Systematic Study*. Grand Rapids, MI: William B. Eerdmans Publishing Co., 1998.

Guroian, Vigen. "The Ecclesial Family: John Chrysostom on Parenthood and Children." In *The Child in Christian Thought*, edited by Marcia Bunge, 66-69. Grand Rapids, MI: William B. Eerdmans, 2001.

Hoekema, A. A. *Created in God's Image*. Grand Rapids, MI: William B. Eerdmans Publishing Co., 1986.

Human Rights Watch. "Police Abuse and Killings of Street Children in India." http://www.hrw.org/reports/1996/India4.htm (accessed May 26, 2006).

Isbister, J. *Promises Not Kept: Poverty and the Betrayal of Third World Development*. 7th ed. Bloomfield, CT: Kumarian Press, 2006.

Janssen and De Kievith. "Janssen and De Kievith Fotografie/Philippines." http://www.jkfoto.nl/manilla/manilla.html (accessed July 28, 2006).

Jeffrey, P. "The Gospel on Smokey Mountain: A United Methodist Congregation in Ministry." *New World Outlook*, September/October 2005. http://gbgm-umc.org/global_news/full_article.cfm?articleid=3470 (accessed July 28, 2006).

McConnell, Doug. "God Creates Every Unique Person as a Child with Dignity." *Restore: Pursuing God's Standards for Children* 1 (2005): 6-8.

Maritain, Jacques. "Introduction." In *Human Rights: Comments and Interpretations*, edited by UNESCO. London & New York: Allan Wingate, 1949.

Moltmann, Jürgen. *On Human Dignity: Political Theology and Ethics.* Translated by M. Douglas Meeks. Philadelphia: Fortress Press, 1984.

Mother Teresa. "Mother Teresa Quotes." http://www.brainyquote.com/quotes/authors/m/mother_teresa.html (accessed November 22, 2006).

Miramax. "City of God." http://www.miramax.com/cityofgod/ (accessed November 27, 2006).

Mydans, S. "Sifting for a Living on a Trash Mountain." *International Herald Tribune*, May 21, 2006. http://www.iht.com/articles/2006/05/21/news/city7.php (accessed July 28, 2006).

Myers, Bryant. *Walking With The Poor: Principles and Practices of Transformational Development.* Maryknoll, NY: Orbis Books, 1999.

PEPE Network. www.PEPE-Network.org (accessed November 27, 2006).

Stassen, Glen H. *Just Peacemaking: Transforming Initiatives for Justice and Peace.* Louisville, KY: Westminster/John Knox Press, 1992.

"The Nicene Creed." 381. http://www.creeds.net/ancient/nicene.htm (accessed July 24, 2006).

UNICEF. "At a Glance: Indonesia." http://www.unicef.org/infobycountry/indonesia.html (accessed June 20, 2006).

UNICEF. "Child Protection from Violence, Exploitation, and Abuse." http://www.unicef.org/protection/index_25228.html (accessed June 20, 2006).

UNICEF. "India." http://www.unicef.org/infobycountry/india_india_statistics.html (accessed November 27, 2006).

"Urban Crime: From Rio . . . " *The Economist* 337, no. 7943 (1995): 37.

Westminster Assembly. "The Westminster Shorter Catechism, 1647." http://www.reformed.org/documents/wsc/index.html (accessed June 4, 2005).

Wright, C. J. H. *Old Testament Ethics for the People of God.* Downers Grove, IL: InterVarsity Press, 2004.

Chapter 2

Arroyo, William and Spencer Eth. "Assessment Following Violence-Witnessing Trauma." In *Ending the Cycle of Violence: Community Responses to Children of Battered Women,* edited by E. Peled, P.G. Jaffe and J.L. Edleson, 29. Thousand Oaks, CA: Sage Publications, 1995.

Balswick, Jack O., Pamela E. King, and Kevin S. Reimer. *The Reciprocating Self: Human Development in Theological Perspective.* Downers Grove, IL: InterVarsity Press, 2005.

Becker, Jo. *Uganda, Stolen Children: Abduction and Recruitment in Northern Uganda.* Vol.15, no. 7 (A). Human Rights Watch, 2003.

Becker, Jo, and Tejshree Thapa. *Sri Lanka: Living in Fear, Child Soldiers and the Tamil Tigers in Sri Lanka.* Vol. 16, no. 13 (C). Human Rights Watch, 2004.

Bendroth, Margaret. "Horace Bushnell's Christian Nurture." In *The Child in Christian Thought*, edited by Marcia Bunge, 350-364. Grand Rapids, MI: William B. Eerdmans Publishing Company, 2001.

Berkhof, Hendrik. *Christ and the Powers.* Ontario: Herald Press, 1977.

Boyden, Jo, and Joanna de Berry. *Children and Youth on the Front Line: Ethnography, Armed Conflict and Displacement (Studies in Forced Migration).* Berghahn Books, 2005.

Bracken, Patrick J., and Celia Petty. *Rethinking the Trauma of War.* Translated by P. Stephenson. London: Free Association Books, 1998.

Bronfenbrenner, Urie. *The Ecology of Human Development: Experiments by Nature and Design.* Cambridge, MA: Harvard University Press, 1979.

Brown, William J. *Biblical Perspectives on Children and Childhood.* Edited by Marcia J. Bunge, Terence Fretheim, and Beverly Gaventa. Grand Rapids, MI: William B. Eerdmans Publishing Company, forthcoming 2007.

Browning, Don, Bonnie J. Miller-McLemore, Pamela D. Couture, K. Brynolf Lyon, and Robert M. Franklin. *From Culture Wars to Common Ground: Religion and the American Family Debate.* Louisville, KY: Westminster/John Knox Press, 1997.

Bunge, Marcia J. "A More Vibrant Theology of Children." *Christian Reflection: A Series in Faith and Ethics* (Summer 2003): 11-19.

------. "Education and the Child in Eighteenth-Century German Pietism: Perspectives from the Work of A. H. Francke." In *The Child in Christian Thought*, edited by

Marcia J. Bunge, 247-278. Grand Rapids, MI: William B. Eerdmans Publishing Company, 2001.

------. "Retrieving a Biblically Informed View of Children: Implications for Religious Education, a Theology of Childhood, and Social Justice." *Lutheran Education* 139, (Winter 2003): 72-87.

------. *The Child in Christian Thought.* Grand Rapids: William B. Eerdmans Publishing Company, 2001.

------. "The Dignity and Complexity of Children: Constructing Christian Theologies of Childhood." In *Nurturing Child and Adolescent Spirituality: Perspectives from the World's Religious Traditions,* edited by K.-M. Yust, A. N. Johnson, S. E. Sasso, and E. C. Roehlkepartain. Lanham: Rowman & Littlefield, 2006.

Burch, Greg W. *Community Children.* Miami: LAM, 2005.

Bushnell, Horace. *Christian Nurture.* New York: Charles Scribner, 1861. Reprint, Cleveland, OH: Pilgrim Press, 1994.

------. "Living to God in Small Things." In *Sermons for the New Life.* New York: Charles Scribner's Sons, 1904.

Campbell, Susan. "Spare the Rod." *Psychology Today* (Sept/Oct 2002).

Costas, Orlando E. *Christ Outside the Gate: Mission Beyond Christendom.* Maryknoll: Orbis Books, 1982.

Division for Gender Equality. *Prostitution and Trafficking in Human Beings: Fact Sheet.* Translated by M. McGill - mac. Article no. N5029. Stockholm: Swedish Ministry of Industry, Employment and Communications, Division for Gender Equality, 2005.

Dorning, Karl. *Crying Out: Children and Communities Speak on Abuse and Neglect.* Milton Keynes: World Vision International, 2002.

Emmons, Karen. *Adult Wars, Child Soldiers: Voices of Children Involved in Armed Conflict in East Asia and Pacific Region.* Translated by M. McGill - mac. Bangkok: UNICEF, 2002.

Erickson, Millard. *Christian Theology.* Grand Rapids, MI: Baker Books, 1985.

Freire, Paulo. *Pedagogy of the Oppressed.* New York: Continuum, 1993.

Friedmann, John. *Empowerment: The Politics of Alternative Development.* Cambridge, MA: Blackwell, 1992.

Garbarino, James, Nancy Dubrow, Kathleen Kostelny, and Carole Pardo. *Children in Danger: Coping with the Consequences of Community Violence.* San Francisco: Jossey-Bass, 1992.

Gelles, Richard J. and Claire Pedrick Cornell. *Intimate Violence in Families.* 2nd ed. Newbury Park, CA: Sage Publications, 1985.

Green, Duncan. *Hidden Lives: Voices of Children in Latin America and the Caribbean.* Translated by P. Stephenson. London: Cassell, 1998.

Grenz, Stanley J. *Theology for the Community of God.* Grand Rapids: William B. Eerdmans Publishing Company, 1994.

Griffiths, Paul. *Religious Reading: The Place of Reading in the Practice of Religion.* Oxford: Oxford University Press, 1999.

Guroian, Vigen. "The Ecclesial Family: John Chrysostom on Parenthood and Children." In *The Child in Christian Thought*, edited by Marcia J. Bunge, 61-77. Grand Rapids, MI: William B. Eerdmans Publishing Company, 2001.

Heppner, Kevin, and Jo Becker. *My Gun Was as Tall as Me: Child Soldiers in Burma.* New York: Human Rights Watch, 2002.

Hughes, Nonna M. and Claire Roche, eds. *Making the Harm Visible: Global Sexual Exploitation of Women and Girls, Speaking Out and Providing Services.* Kingston, RI: Coalition Against Trafficking in Women, 1999.

James, Allison and Alan Prout, eds. *Constructing and Reconstructing Childhood: Contemporary Issues in the Sociological Study of Childhood.* Translated by P. Stephenson. London: Falmer Press, 1997.

Johnson, Jeanette L. and Michelle Leff. "Children of Substance Abusers: Overview of Research Findings." *Pediatrics* 103 (1999): 1085-1099.

Johnston, Robert K. *The Christian at Play.* Eugene, OR: William B. Eerdmans Publishing Company, 1997.

Hilton, Ayesha. *No Childhood at All.* Quaker United Nations Office: Images Asia Ltd., 1997.

Kilbourn, Phyllis, and Marjorie McDermid, eds. *Sexually Exploited Children: Working to Protect and Heal.* Monrovia, CA: MARC, 1998.

Lazareth, William. *Luther on the Christian Home: An Application of the Social Ethics of the Reformation.* Philadelphia: Muhlenberg Press, 1969.

Linthicum, Robert C. *Empowering the Poor.* Monrovia, CA: MARC, 1991.

Long, W. Meredith. *Health, Healing and God's Kingdom.* Oxford: Regnum Books International, 2000.

Luther, Martin. *Luther's Works.* Vols. 44, 45, and 53. Edited by Jaroslav Pelikan and Helmut Lehmann. St. Louis: Concordia Publishing House, 1955-1986.

------. *Martin Luther's Basic Theological Writings.* Edited by Timothy F. Lull. Minneapolis: Fortress, 1989.

------. "Sermon on Keeping Children in School." 1530.

------. "To the Councilmen of All Cities in Germany That They Establish and Maintain Christian Schools." 1524.

May, Scottie, Beth Posterski, Catherine Stonehouse, and Linda Cannell. *Children Matter: Celebrating Their Place in the Church, Family, and Community.* Grand Rapids, MI: William B. Eerdmans Publishing Company, 2005.

Miles, Glenn and Paul Stephenson, "Children and Family Breakdown." *Children at Risk Guidelines.* Vol. 1. Shropshire, UK: TEARFund, 2000.

Moltmann, Jürgen. *God in Creation.* Minneapolis: Fortress Press, 1985.

Moorehead, Alex, Jemera Rone, Peter Bouckaert, and Eric Stover. *Uganda: Uprooted and Forgotten: Impunity and Human Rights Abuses in Northern Uganda.* Vol. 17, no. 12 (A). Human Rights Watch, 2005.

Nouwen, Henri J. M. *¡Gracias!* New York: Orbis Books, 1993.

Pitkin, Barbara. "'The Heritage of the Lord': Children in the Theology of John Calvin." In *The Child in Christian Thought,* edited by Marcia J. Bunge, 134-193. Grand Rapids, MI: William B. Eerdmans Publishing Company, 2001.

Putman, Katharine Meese. "Report to the Christian Ministry in the Dump Community." Unpublished report. Guatemala, February 2006.

Rakita, Sara. *Forgotten Children of War: Sierra Leonean Refugee Children in Guinea.* Vol. 11, no. 5 (5). Human Rights Watch, 1999.

Reis, Chen. *Children in Combat.* Vol.8, no.1 (G), edited by Lois Whitman and Michael McClintock. New York: Human Rights Watch, 1996.

Schuurman, Douglas. *Vocation: Discerning Our Callings in Life.* Grand Rapids, MI: William B. Eerdmans Publishing Company, 2004.

Sorajjakool, Siroj. *Child Prostitution in Thailand: Listening to Rahab.* New York: The Haworth Press, 2003.

Strauss, Gerald. *Luther's House of Learning: Indoctrination of the Young in the German Reformation.* Baltimore: Johns Hopkins University Press, 1978.

Strohl, Jane E. "The Child in Luther's Theology: 'For What Purpose Do We Older Folks Exist, Other Than to Care for…the Young.'" In *The Child in Christian Thought,* edited by Marcia J. Bunge, 134-159. Grand Rapids, MI: William B. Eerdmans Publishing Company, 2001.

Strommen, Merton. "A Family's Faith, A Child's Faith." *Dialog* (Summer 1998): 177-178.

Strommen, Merton P. and Richard Hardel. *Passing on the Faith: A Radical New Model for Youth and Family Ministry*. Winona: St. Mary's Press, 2000.

Tate, Tony. *How to Fight, How to Kill: Child Soldiers in Liberia*. Vol. 16, no. 2 (A), edited by Lois Whitman and Jo Becker. Human Rights Watch, 2004.

Tiersma Watson, Jude. "Faces of Evil in the City." Unpublished Paper. Fuller Theological Seminary, n.d.

UNAIDS. *2004 Report on the Global AIDS Epidemic*. Geneva: UNAIDS, 2004.

Wagner, C. Peter. "Territorial Spirits and World Missions." *Evangelical Missions Quarterly* 25, no. 3 (1989): 278.

Weber, Annette. *Uganda, Abducted and Abused: Renewed Conflict in Northern Uganda (Human Rights Watch)*. Human Rights Watch, 2003.

White, Keith and Haddon Willmer. *Child Theology—The Child in the Midst*. Forthcoming.

Wink, Walter. *Naming the Powers: The Language of Power in the New Testament*. Philadelphia: Fortress Press, 1984.

Chapter 3

Anderson, Ray S. *On Being Human: Essays in Theological Anthropology*. Grand Rapids, MI: William B. Eerdmans Publishing Company, 1982.

Aries, Philippe. *Centuries of Childhood: A Social History of Family Life*. New York, NY: Vintage, 1962.

Banks, Robert. *Paul's Idea of Community*. Peabody, MA: Hendrickson Publishers, Inc. 1994.

Bluebond-Langner, Myra. *The Private Worlds of Dying Children*. Princeton: Princeton University Press, 1978.

Bovon, Francois. "Family and Community in the New Testament." *Sewanee Theological Review* 45, no. 2 (2002): 127-134. http://proquest.umi.com/pqdweb?index=1&did=11021 5242&SrchMode=1&sid=2&Fmt=3&VInst=PROD&VType=PQD&RQT=309&VN ame=PQD&TS=1170275020&clientId=29876 (accessed January 31, 2007).

Brown, Colin. *That You May Believe: Miracles and Faith Then and Now*. Grand Rapids, MI: William B. Eerdmans Publishing Company, 1985.

Byrne, Iain. *The Human Rights of Street and Working Children*. London, UK: Intermediate Technology Publications, 1998.

Coles, Richard. *The Moral Intelligence of Children*. London: Bloomsbury Publishing, 1997.

Compassion International. "Child's Family." http://www.compassion.com/about/how/childsfamily.htm (accessed May 23, 2006).

Compassion International. "Church Partnership." http://www.compassion.com/about/how/churchpartnership.htm (accessed May 23, 2006).

Compassion International. "How We Work." http://www.compassion.com/about/how/default.htm (accessed May 23, 2006).

Compassion International. "India". http://www.compassion.com/about/where/india.htm (accessed February 21, 2006).

Copsey, Kathryn. *From the Ground Up: Understanding the Spiritual World of the Child*. Oxford: Barnabas, 2005.

Couture, Pamela D. *Seeing Children, Seeing God: A Practical Theology of Children and Poverty*. Nashville, TN: Abingdon Press, 2000.

Devries, Dawn. "Toward a Theology of Childhood." *Interpretation* 55, no. 2 (2001): 161-173.

Elkind, David. *The Hurried Child: Growing Up Too Fast Too Soon*. Reading, MA: Addison-Wesley, 1981.

Ennew, Judith. *Questioning the Basis of our Work*. Bangkok: Black on White Publishing, 2004.

European Society of Human Reproduction and Embryology. http://uk.news.yahoo.com/18062008/325/new-test-detecting-genetic-effects-embryos (accessed June 19, 2006).

Grenz, Stanley J. *Theology for the Community of God*. Grand Rapids, MI: William B. Eerdmans Publishing Company, 1994.

Gundry-Volf, Judith. "To Such as These Belongs the Reign of God: Jesus and Children." *Theology Today* 56, no. 4 (2000): 469.

Gundry-Volf, Judith, and Miroslav Volf. *A Spacious Heart: Essays on Identity and Belonging*. Harrisburg, PA: Trinity Press International, 1997.

Haugen, Gary A. *Good News About Injustice: A Witness of Courage in a Hurting World*. Downer's Grove, IL: InterVarsity Press, 1999.

Hay, David, and Rebecca Nye. *The Spirit of the Child*. London: Fount Paperbacks, 1998.

Hecht, Tobias. *At Home in the Street: Street Children of Northeast Brazil*. Cambridge, UK: Cambridge University Press, 1998.

Heitzenrater, Richard P. "John Wesley and Children." In *The Child in Christian Thought*, edited by Marcia J. Bunge, 279-299. Grand Rapids, MI: William B. Eerdmans Publishing Company, 2001.

Hinsdale, Mary Ann. "Infinite Openness to the Infinite." In *The Child in Christian Thought*, edited by Marcia J. Bunge, 406-445. Grand Rapids, MI: William B. Eerdmans Publishing Company, 2001.

Martin, Samuel. *Thy Rod Does Not Comfort Me: Christians and the Spanking Dilemma*. Jerusalem: Samuel Martin, 2003.

Mauss, Marcel. *The Gift: The Form and Reason for Exchange in Archaic Societies*. London: Routledge and Kegan Paul, 1974.

Miles, Glenn, and Josephine-Joy Wright, eds. *Celebrating Children!* Carlisle, Cumbria, UK: Paternoster Press, 2003.

Miller-McLemore, Bonnie J. *Let the Children Come: Reimagining Childhood from a Christian Perspective*. San Francisco, CA: Jossey-Bass, 2003.

Moltmann, Jürgen. *On Human Dignity: Political Theology and Ethics*. London, UK: Fortress Press, 1984.

Myers, Bryant L. "Strategic Trends Affecting Children." In *Celebrating Children!*, edited by Glenn Miles and Josephine-Joy Wright, 108, 114. Carlisle, Cumbria, UK: Paternoster Press, 2003.

Osmer, Richard R. "The Christian Education of Children in the Protestant Tradition." *Theology Today* 56, no. 4 (2000): 507, 513, 516.

Srinivasan, Sharada. "Development, Discrimination and Survival: Daughter Elimination in Tamil Nadu, India." PhD diss., Institute of Social Studies, The Hague, The Netherlands, 2006.

Stortz, Martha Ellen. "'Where or When Was Your Servant Innocent?.'" In *The Child in Christian Thought*, edited by Marcia J. Bunge, 78-102. Grand Rapids, MI: William B. Eerdmans Publishing Company, 2001.

Strohl, Jane E. "The Child in Luther's Theology." In *The Child in Christian Thought*, edited by Marcia J. Bunge, 134-159. Grand Rapids, MI: William B. Eerdmans Publishing Company, 2001.

Sturm, Douglas. "On the Suffering and Rights of Children: Toward a Theology of Childhood Liberation." *Cross Currents* 42, no. 2 (1992): 149-150, 157-160.

Traina, Cristina L.H. "A Person in the Making." In *The Child in Christian Thought*, edited by Marcia J. Bunge, 103-133. Grand Rapids, MI: William B. Eerdmans Publishing Company, 2001.

22nd Annual Meeting of the European Society of Human Reproduction and Embryology, June 18-21, 2006. http://humrep.oxfordjournals.org/content/vol21/suppl_1/index.dtl (accessed August 17, 2006).

United Nations. "Convention on the Rights of the Child." Geneva: Office of the High Commissioner for Human Rights, 1989.

Van Geest, Fred. "Deepening and Broadening Christian Citizenship: Going Beyond the Basics without Succumbing to Liberal and Communitarian Ideals." *Christian Scholar's Review* 34, no. 1 (2004): 91-118.

Vaughan Roberts. *God's Big Picture: Tracing the Story-line of the Bible*. Leicester, England: InterVarsity Press, 2002.

Vujicic, Nick. *From Life without Limbs to Life without LIMITS!*. http://www.lifewithoutlimbs.org/minister.htm (accessed July 2, 2006).

White, Keith. "A Little Child Will Lead Them: Rediscovering Children at the Heart of Mission." In *Cutting Edge 2001: Conference Papers*. DeBron, the Netherlands. http://www.viva.org/?page_id=296 (accessed May 31, 2006).

Williams, Rowan. In *Celtic Daily Prayer: A Northumbrian Office*, compiled by Andy Raine and John T. Skinner of the Northumbria Community. London: Marshall Pickering, 1994, 27.

Willmer, Haddon. "Child Theology." In *Cutting Edge 2002: Conference Papers*. DeBron, the Netherlands. http://www.viva.org/?page_id=147 (accessed May 31, 2006).

The Wisdom of Solomon: New Revised Standard Version. http://www.anova.org/sev/htm/ap/04_wisdomofsolomon.htm (accessed August 17, 2006).

Chapter 4

Asha Forum Resource CD. CD-ROM. The Asha Forum, 2003.

The Asha Forum. "Asha Team Model." http://www.ashaforum.org/involve_churches.htm (accessed August 22, 2005).

Beaton, Richard. "Messiah and Justice: A Key to Matthew's Use of Isaiah 42:1–4." *Journal for the Study of the New Testament* 75 (1999): 5–23.

Birch, Bruce C. "Hunger, Poverty and Biblical Religion." *The Christian Century* 11, no. 5 (1975): 593–599.

Blomberg, Craig. *Matthew*. Nashville, TN: Broadman Press, 1992.

Carter, Jimmy. *Sources of Strength: Meditations on Scripture for a Living Faith*. New York: Crown, 1997.

"Christian Community Development Workshop and Conference." Mosbach, Germany, March 11-15, 2005 http://www.ccd-network.net.

Croymans-Plaghki, Cory. "Street Children are Not for Sale." *Chiang Mai Mail*, June 11, 2005.

Dow, Allan. "UNIAP Meeting." Bangkok, Thailand, August 24, 2006.

ECPAT International. *Child Pornography: A Contribution of ECPAT International to the 2nd World Congress against Commercial Sexual Exploitation of Children*. Yokohama, Japan, December 17-20, 2001, 9.

ECPAT International. "Commercial Sexual Exploitation of Children." http://www.ecpat.net/eng/CSEC/definitions/csec.htm (accessed August 22, 2005).

Ennew, J., and Stephenson, P., eds. *Questioning the Basis of Our Work: Christianity, Child Rights and Development*. Teddington, UK: Tearfund, 2004.

Erickson, Millard J. *Christian Theology*. 2nd ed. Grand Rapids, MI: Baker Books, 1993.

Evans, Mary J. *1 and 2 Samuel*. Peabody, MA: Hendrickson, 2000.

Gautam, M. Kul C. Cutting Edge IV Conference, 2002.

Haugen, Gary. *Good News About Injustice*. Downer's Grove, IL: InterVarsity Press, 1999.

Hull, Gretchen Gaebelein. "God's Call to Social Justice." In *The IVP Women's Bible Commentary*, edited by Kroeger and Evans, Downers Grove, IL: InterVarsity Press, 2002.

Jayakaran, Ravi. "The Ten Seed Technique." http://www.worldvision.org.au/resources/files/Ten-Seed.pdf (accessed July 26, 2006).

King, Pamela. "The Reciprocating Self: A Trinitarian Analogy of Being and Becoming." In *The Handbook of Spiritual Development in Childhood and Adolescence: Moving to the Scientific Mainstream,* edited by Roehlkepartain et. al. Thousand Oaks: Sage Publications, 2005.

Kittel, G. et al. *Theological Dictionary of the New Testament*. Grand Rapids, MI: W.B. Eerdmans, 1995.

Miles, Glenn, and Sun Varin. "Stop Violence Against Us!" www.kone-kmeng.org (accessed August 25, 2006).

Moo, Douglas. *The Epistle to the Romans*. Grand Rapids, MI: Eerdmans, 1996.

M2PressWire. "UN Secretary-General Calls Human Trafficking 'One of the Greatest Human Rights Violations' of Today." http://www.humantrafficking.com/humantrafficking/client/view.aspx?ResourceID=199 (accessed August 22, 2005).

Norman, Joyce. *Long Live the King*. Bethel Theological Seminary, 2002.

Payne, J. B. "Justice." In *New Bible Dictionary*, edited by Marshall et al. Downers Grove, IL: InterVarsity Press, 1996.

The Protection Project. "United States Country Report." http://www.protectionproject.org/main1.htm (accessed August 22, 2005).

Rice, Condoleezza. "On the Release of the Fifth Annual Department of State Trafficking in Persons Report." June 3, 2005. http://usinfo.state.gov/gi/Archive/2005/Jun/03-82857.html (accessed 22 August 2005).

Robinson, Gnana. *1&2 Samuel: Let Us Be Like the Nations*. Grand Rapids, MI: Eerdmans, 1993.

Schofield, J.N. "'Righteousness' in the Old Testament." *Bible Translator* 16, no. 3 (1965): 114.

Spiritual Abuse Working Group. "Protecting Children from Spiritual Abuse." In *Cutting Edge V: Conference*, 29-30. Cirencester, UK: Viva Network, 2005.

Stafford, Wesley. "Making a Difference Together for Children in the 21st Century." Paper presented at the Cutting Edge 2 Conference, Battle, UK, 1998.

UNICEF. *Profiting from Abuse: An Investigation into the Sexual Exploitation of Our Children*. New York: UNICEF, 2001.

UNICEF. "Trafficking and Sexual Exploitation." http://www.unicef.org/protection/index_exploitation.html (accessed August 22, 2005).

United Nations. *Combating Human Trafficking in Asia: A Resource Guide to International and Regional Legal Instruments, Political Commitments and Recommended Practices*. United Nations, 2003.

United Nations. *Convention against Transnational Organized Crime*.

Viva Network. *Viva Network Annual Report 2004/2005*. December 2005.

West, Charles C. "Culture, Power and Ideology in Third World Theologies." *Missiology: An International Review* 12, no. 4 (1984).

World Vision. "Here We Stand: World Vision and Child Rights." http://www.child-rights.org/PolicyAdvocacy/pahome2.5.nsf/allreports/2034760573B7452888256E46008361D5/$file/HereWeStand.pdf (accessed January 31, 2007).

Wright, Christopher J.H. *Old Testament Ethics for the People of God.* Downers Grove, IL: InterVarsity Press, 2004.

Chapter 5

Aaron, Rita, et al. "Suicides in Young People in Rural Southern India." *The Lancet* 363, no. 9415 (2003): 1117-1118.

Action for Children and Youth Aotearoa. *Children and Youth in Aotearoa 2003: The Second Non-Governmental Organisations' Report from Aotearoa New Zealand to the United Nations Committee on the Rights of the Child.* Auckland, 2003.

Barnett, and Whiteside. In *Children in Distress: The AIDS Legacy of Orphans and Vulnerable Children*, by M.J. Kelly. University of Zambia, 2002.

Bell, Clive, Shantayanan Devarajan, and Hans Gersbach. *The Long-Run Economic Costs of AIDS: Theory and an Application to South Africa.* World Bank, 2003.

Benson, P.L. *All Kids are Our Kids: What Communities Must Do to Raise Caring and Responsible Children and Adolescents.* San Francisco: Jossey-Bass, 1997.

Booth, B., and K. Martin. *Lancaster Urban Health and Development.* London: Macmillan, 2001.

Bunge, Marcia, ed. *The Child in Christian Thought.* Grand Rapids, MI: William B. Eerdmans Publishing Co., 2001.

Case, Anne C., C. Paxson, and J. Ableidinger. *Orphans in Africa.* Princeton University, Center for Health and Wellbeing, Research Program in Development Studies, October 2003.

Chatterji, Minki, et al. *The Well-Being of Children Affected by HIV and AIDS in Lusaka, Zambia, and Gitarama Province, Rwanda: Findings from a Study.* USAID, 2005.

Cincotta, Richard, Robert Engelman, and Daniele Anastasion. *The Security Demographic: Population and Civil Conflict After the Cold War.* Population Action International, 2003.

Coombe, C. "Mitigating the Impact of HIV and AIDS on Education Supply, Demand and Quality." In *AIDS, Policy and Child Well-Being,* edited by A. Cornia. UNICEF, 2002.

Deininger, Klaus, Marito Garcia, and K. Subbarao. *AIDS-induced Orphanhood as a Systemic Shock: Magnitude, Impact and Program Interventions in Africa.* World Bank, 2003.

Garrett, Laurie. *HIV and National Security: Where are the Links?* New York: Council on Foreign Relations, 2005.

Halberstam, David. *The Children.* New York: Random House, 1998.

HelpAge International. *The Cost of Love: Older People in the fight against AIDS in Tanzania.* HelpAge International, 2004.

Hsu, Lee Nah. *HIV Subverts National Security.* UN Development Program, August 2001.

John Paul II (pope). "Message of his Holiness Pope John Paul II for the XXIX World Day of Peace: Let us Give Children a Future of Peace." http://www.vatican.va/holy_father/john_paul_ii/messages/peace/documents/hf_jp-ii_mes_08121995_xxix-world-day-for-peace_en.html (accessed August 18, 2006).

Joseph, S., ed. *A Voice for the Child: the Inspirational words of Janusz Korczak.* New York: Harper Collins, 1999.

Kelly, M.J. *Children in Distress: The AIDS Legacy of Orphans and Vulnerable Children.* University of Zambia, 2002.

------. *Planning for Education in the Context of HIV and AIDS.* UNESCO, 2000.

Kirk, Daphne. "Our Vision." http://www.gnation2gnation.com/Group/Group.aspx?id=9014 (accessed September 5, 2006).

Maggay, Melba Padilla. "Globalisation and Culture." Micah Network Conference, Queretaro, Mexico, 2003.

Masten, A. "Ordinary Magic: Resilience Processes in Development." *American Psychologist* 56 (2001): 227-238.

McGaw, Leanne, and Amboka Wameyo. *Violence Against Children Affected by HIV and AIDS: A Case Study of Uganda.* World Vision International – Africa Office, 2005.

Miles, Glenn, and Josephine-Joy Wright, eds. *Celebrating Children!* Carlisle, Cumbria, UK: Paternoster Press, 2003.

Moltmann, Jürgen. "Child and Childhood as Metaphors of Hope." *Theology Today* 56, no. 4 (2000): 592-603.

Mugabe, Mbulawa, Mark Stirling, and Alan Whiteside. *Future Imperfect: Protecting Children on the Brink.* Africa Leadership Consultation – Acting for Children on the Brink, Johannesburg, September 10, 2002.

Nolen-Hoeksema, Susan. "Children Coping with Uncontrollable Stressors." *Applied Preventive Psychology* (1992): 183-189.

ONeill, J. "The Missing Child in Liberal Theory." In *Covenant Society in a Culture of Reciprocity.* Toronto: University of Toronto Press, 1994.

Orsi, Robert. "A Crisis About the Theology of Children." *Harvard Divinity Bulletin* 30, no. 4 (2002): 1-2.

Oxfam. *Learning How to Survive: How Education for All Would Save Millions of Young People from HIV and AIDS.* Oxfam, 2004.

Sachs, J. *Investing In Development.* UN MDG Project, 2005.

Schneider, Mark, and Michael Moodie. *The Destabilizing Impact of HIV/AIDS: First Wave Hits Eastern and Southern Africa; Second Wave Threatens India, China, Russia, Ethiopia, Nigeria.* CSIS, 2002.

Sengendo, James, and J. Nambi. "The Psychological Effect of Orphanhood: A Study of Orphans in the Rakai District." *Health Transition Review,* Supplement to Volume 7, 1997.

Siaens, Corinne, K. Subbarao, and Quentin Wodon. *Are Orphans Especially Vulnerable? Evidence from Rwanda.* World Bank, 2003.

Sider, R.J. *Good News and Good Works.* Grand Rapids, MI: Baker Books, 1993.

Sprange, H. *Children in Revival: 300 Years of God's Work in Scotland.* Ross-shire, Scotland, UK: Christian Focus Publications Ltd., 2002.

Stafford, Wess. *Too Small to Ignore.* Colorado Springs, CO: Waterbrook Press, 2005.

UNICEF. *Africa's Orphaned Generation.* UNICEF, 2003.

UNICEF. *Children on the Brink.* UNICEF, 2004.

UNICEF. *Fighting HIV and AIDS: Strategies for Success 2002 – 2005.* UNICEF, 2004.

UNICEF. "A World Fit For Children" http://www.unicef.org/specialsession/docs_new/documents/A-RES-S27-2E.pdf (accessed September 8, 2005).

United Nations. "Convention on the Rights of the Child." Geneva: Office of the High Commissioner for Human Rights, 1989.

United Nations. "UN Millennium Development Goal" http://www.un.org/millenniumgoals/ (accessed September 8, 2005).

USAID. *Sub-National Distribution and Situation of Orphans: An Analysis of the President's Emergency Plan for AIDS Relief Focus Countries.* USAID, 2004.

Vandergrift, Kathy. "A Little Child Shall Lead Them: Seeking Justice with a Focus on Children." In *Cutting Edge IV Conference.* DeBron, The Netherlands: Viva Network, 2002.

White, Keith J. "Pandita Ramabai: A Re-Evaluation of her Life and Work." PhD diss., University of Wales, 2003.

------. "Rediscovering Children at the Heart of Mission." In *Celebrating Children!,* edited by Glenn Miles and Josephine-Joy Wright, 189-199. Carlisle, Cumbria, UK: Paternoster Press, 2003.

World Food Programme. *Widening the 'Window of Hope:' Using Food Aid to Improve Access to Education for Orphans and Vulnerable Children in Sub-Saharan Africa.* Word Food Programme, 2003.

World Vision. "Hope Alert April 2005." *Hope Alert* 2, no. 3 (2005). www.worldvision.org/help/aids-lib.nsf/12F3BB8E2BCC872788256888007E4DD4/92FC4A66FAB363A788256FDC005DC2B1.

Chapter 6

Asociatia OCI. Directory of the Network of Christian Ministries in Romania. Bucuresti, 2004.

Banks, Robert. Paul's Idea of Community. Massachusetts: Hendrickson Publishers, Inc., 1994.

Barna, George. Transforming Children into Spiritual Champions. Ventura, CA: Regal Books, 2003.

Burke, Michael. Child Institutionalization and Child Protection in Central and Eastern Europe. UNICEF International Child Development Centre. Florence, Italy: Economic Policy Series (1995).

Consultative Group on Ministry Among Children. Unfinished Business: Children and the Churches. London: CCBI Publications.

Fuller, C. When Children Pray. Portland, OR: Multnomah Press, 1998.

Gray, Laurence. "The 'Right' of the Child to Speak and Be Heard." In Celebrating Children, edited by Glenn Miles, and Josephine-Joy Wright, 85. Carlisle, Cumbria, UK: Paternoster Press, 2003.

Groza, Victor, et al. A Peacock or a Crow? Stories, Interviews and Commentaries on Romanian Adoptions. Euclid, OH: Williams Custom Publishing, 1999.

Gundry-Volf, Judith. "To Such as These Belongs the Reign of God." Theology Today 56, no. 4 (2000): 470, 475-476.

------."The Least and the Greatest." In The Child in Christian Thought, edited by Marcia J. Bunge, 33-34. Grand Rapids, MI: William B. Eerdmans Publishing Co., 2001.

Hammond, Sue Annis. The Thin Book of Appreciative Inquiry. 2nd ed. Plano, TX: The Thin Book Publishing Co., 1998.

Hinsdale, Mary Ann. "'Infinite Openness to the Infinite': Karl Rahner's Contributions to Modern Catholic Thought on the Child." In The Child in Christian Thought, edited by Marcia J. Bunge, 428. Grand Rapids, MI: William B. Eerdmans Publishing Co., 2001.

King, Pamela E. "The Hopeful Lens of Positive Youth Development." Theology News & Notes (2005):11-13.

Lansdown, George. Disabled Children in Romania: Progress in Implementing the Convention on the Rights of the Child, 2002. London: Disability Awareness in Action, 2003.

Lausanne Committee for World Evangelization. "The Lausanne Covenant, 1974." http://www.lausanne.org/Brix?pageID=12891 (accessed September 2, 2005).

Mass, Robin. "Christ as the Logos of Childhood: Reflections on the Meaning and the Mission of the Child." Theology Today 56, no. 4 (2000): 458-459.

Mazabane, Ndaba. "God Welcomes Children Fully Into the Family of Faith." Paper presented at the Cutting Edge Conference, Cirencester, UK, 2005.

Miller-McLemore, Bonnie J. Let the Children Come. San Francisco: Jossey Bass, 2003.

Mooli, Lahad. "Story Making in Assessment Method for Coping with Stress." In Drama Therapy Theory and Practice II, edited by S. Jennings, 92. London: Routledge.

Myers, Bryant L. "Africa and HIV/AIDS: Who is My Sister, My Brother?." MARC Newsletter 2-4 (2002): 4. http://www.worldvisionresources.com/newsletters/marc02-4.pdf (accessed June 13, 2006).

Nolland, John. Word Bible Commentary. vol. 35B. Dallas: Word Books, 1993.

Nussbaum, Stan, ed. The Contribution of Christian Congregations to the battle with HIV/AIDS at the Community Level: A Seven-Country Research Report Prepared for the Summer Mission Briefing at the Oxford Centre for Mission Studies 7-9 June 2005. Colorado Springs, CO: Global Mapping International, 2005.

Rosapepe, James. "Half Way Home: Romania's Abandoned Children Ten Years After the Revolution, a Report to Americans from the US Embassy Bucharest, Romania, Feb 2001." http://www.usembassy.ro/USAID/Documents/10YearsRetrospective.pdf (accessed August 14, 2004).

Save the Children. "Three Models of Child Participation in Community Based OVC Care." The Chris-Caba Journal 3, no. 1 (2005): 13-15.

Schleiermacher, Friedrich. Sammtliche Werke (Verklin: Georg Reimer) 2, no. 6 (1834-1864): 71-72.

------. "Guidelines for Children's Participation in HIV/AIDS Programs." The Chris-Caba Journal 3, no. 1 (2005): 25.

UNICEF. "Romania." http://www.unicef.org/infobycountry/romania.html (accessed June 8, 2006).

UNICEF. The State of the World's Children 2005: Childhood Under Threat. New York: UNICEF, 2005.

UNICEF, 2003. In "An Introduction to this Child Participation Issue." The Chris-Caba Journal 3, no. 1 (2005): 4.

Walls, Andrew. The Missionary Movement in Christian History: Studies in the Transmission of the Faith. Maryknoll: Orbis Books, 1996.

White, Keith. "Rediscovering Children at the Heart of Mission." In Celebrating Children, edited by Glenn Miles, and Josephine-Joy Wright, 192. Carlisle, Cumbria, UK: Paternoster Press, 2003.

World Bank. "Romania at a Glance." http://siteresources.worldbank.org/ROMANIAINROMANIANEXTN/Resources/anexe_I.pdf (accessed August 14, 2004).

Wright, C.J.H. Old Testament Ethics for the People of God. Downers Grove, IL: InterVarsity Press, 2004.

Wright, Josephine-Joy. "Listening to Children and Enabling Their Involvement." In Celebrating Children, edited by Glenn Miles, and Josephine-Joy Wright, 66. Carlisle, Cumbria, UK: Paternoster Press, 2003.

Zacharias, Ravi. "Prescription for Hope Conference." Washington, D.C.: Samaritan's Purse, 2002. In Lausanne Committee for World Evangelization ENewsletter. http://community.gospelcom.net/Brix?pageID=13569 (accessed June 13, 2006).

Zamfir, Catalin, and Elena Zamfir. Children at Risk in Romania: Problems Old and New. UNICEF International Child Development Centre. Florence, Italy: Economic Policy Series, no. 56 (1996).

Chapter 7 & Conclusion

Alexander, T.D., and B.S. Rosner, eds. *New Dictionary of Biblical Theology*. Downer's Grove, IL: Intervarsity Press, 2000.

Barna, George. *Transforming Children into Spiritual Champions*. Ventura: Regal Books, 2003.

Brewster, Dan. *Child, Church and Mission: A Resource book for Christian Child Development Workers*. Compassion International, 2005.

Brewster, Dan, and Patrick McDonald. *Children-The Great Omission?* Viva Network, 2004.

Bromiley, Geoffrey. *Children of Promise: The Case for Baptizing Infants.* William B. Eerdmans Publishing Co., 1979.

Bronfenbrenner, Urie. *The Ecology of Human Development.* Cambridge, MA: Harvard University Press, 1979.

Bunge, Marcia J. "Introduction." In *The Child in Christian Thought*, edited by Marcia Bunge, 3. Grand Rapids: William B. Eerdmans Publishing Co., 2001.

Bunge, Fretheim, Gaventa, eds. *Children and Childhood: Biblical Perspectives.* Grand Rapids, MI: William B. Eerdmans Publishing Company, 2008.

Conn, Harvie. *The American City and the Evangelical Church.* Grand Rapids, MI: Baker, 1994.

The Consultative Group on Ministry among Children. *Unfinished Business: Children and the Churches.* London: CCBI Publications.

Crocker, Gustavo. *Why children? A case for involvement.* World Relief strategic document, 2002.

Daka, Kebebew. Interview by Shiferaw W. Michael. August 15, 2005.

Fuller, Cheri. *When Children Pray.* Oregon, USA: Multnomah Publishers, 1998.

Garbarino, J. et al. *Children and Families in the Social Environment*, 2nd ed. New York: Aldine de Gruyter, 1992.

Gundry-Volf, Judith M. "The Least and the Greatest." In *The Child in Christian Thought*, edited by Marcia J. Bunge, 35, 55-58. Grand Rapids: William B. Eerdmans Publishing Co., 2001.

Hurrelmann, Klaus. "The Social World of Adolescents: A Sociological Perspective." In *The Social World of Adolescents: International Perspectives*, edited by Klaus Hurrelmann, and Uwe Engel, 3. Berlin: Walter de Gruyter & Co., 1989.

Internet Evangelism Coalition. "December 2004." *Web Evangelism Newsletter* (December 2004): 1. http://community.gospelcom.net/iec/assets/iecnewsletter_1204.pdf (accessed September 12, 2006).

Kebede, Tesera. Interview by Shiferaw W. Michael. August 13, 2005.

"Lausanne Covenant." http://www.lausanne.org/Brix?pageID=12891 (accessed May 1, 2006).

"Mother Teresa Quotes." http://www.brainyquote.com/quotes/authors/m/mother_teresa.html (accessed August 31, 2006).

Strange, W. A. *Children in the Early Church.* Cumbria, UK: Paternoster Press, 1996.

Sutcliffe, John. *Learning and Teaching Together.* London: Chester House, 1980.

------. "We Have Forgotten that We Belong to Each Other." *Theology News and Notes* 52, no. 3 (2005): 24-27. http://www.fuller.edu/news/pubs/tnn/2005_fall/index.htm.

UNICEF. "The State of the World's Children 2006." UNICEF: New York, 2005. http://www.unicef.org/publications/index_30398.html.

Whittaker, Tony. "Online Evangelism: A Guide to Web Outreach." http://guide.gospelcom.net/ (accessed May 1, 2006).

Wood, D. R. W., and I.H. Marshall. *New Bible Dictionary*, 3rd ed. Downer's Grove, IL: InterVarsity Press, 1996.

"World Wide Day of Prayer for Children at Risk Feedback Reports 2004 and 2005." http://www.viva.org/?page_id=97 (accessed May 8, 2006).

FOR FURTHER READING

"Advocacy Toolkit." Teddington: Tearfund, 2002. http://tilz.tearfund.org/Topics/Advocacy/Advocacy+toolkit.htm (accessed September 14, 2007).

Brueggemann, Walter. *Hope Within History.* Atlanta, GA: John Knox Press, 1987.

Chapman, J. and Mancini, A., eds. *Critical Webs of Power and Change: Planning, Reflection and Learning in People-Centred Advocacy.* Johannesburg: Action Aid International, 2005.

"Christian Perspectives on Child Rights – Resources and Email Forum." Oxford: Viva Network. http://www.viva.org/?page_id=257 (accessed September 14, 2007).

Dixon, Patrick. *AIDS and You.* 3rd ed. Reading, UK: Acet, 2003.

Dodd, Carley H. *Dynamics of Intercultural Communication.* Boston, MA: McGraw Hill, 1998.

Gordon, G. *What if You Got Involved? Taking a Stand Against Social Injustice.* Carlisle, Cumbria, UK: Paternoster Press, 2002.

Kilbourn, Phyllis. *Children Affected by HIV/AIDS: Compassionate Care.* Monrovia, CA: MARC, 2002.

McDonald, Patrick with Emma Garrow. *Reaching Children in Need.* Eastbourne, UK: Kingsway Publications, 2000.

Meeks, M. Douglas. *Origins of the Theology of Hope.* Philadelphia, PA: Fortress Press, 1974.

Moltmann, Jürgen. *Theology of Hope: On the Ground and the Implications of a Christian Eschatology.* London, UK: SCM Press, 1967.

Ratcliff, Donald. *Children's Spirituality: Christian Perspectives, Research, and Application.* Eugene, OR: Cascade Books, 2004.

Viva Network. "Recommended Advocacy Resources." http://www.viva.org/?page_id=237 (accessed September 14, 2007).

Viva Network. "Advocacy Case Studies." http://www.viva.org/?page_id=239 (accessed September 14, 2007).

Yamamori, Tetsunao, David Dageforde, and Tina Bruner, eds. *The Hope Factor: Engaging the Church in the HIV/AIDS Crisis.* Tyrone, GA: Authentic Media, 2004.

ABOUT THE EDITORS

Doug McConnell, Ph.D.—Associate Professor of Leadership and Dean of the School of Intercultural Studies, Fuller Theological Seminary

With experience in education, missions, and administration, Doug brings a solid foundation of theory and practice to this work. After serving as the International Director for Pioneers, Doug became the Dean of the School of Intercultural Studies and established the Children at Risk concentration as one of the fastest growing concentrations at Fuller. His written works include publications in the *Evangelical Dictionary of World Mission* (2000), *Evangelical Missions Quarterly*, and *Missiology*. He has written various articles for journals and dictionaries, and he jointly authored the book *The Changing Face of World Missions* (2005).[1]

Jennifer Orona, M.A.—Children at Risk Program Coordinator, Fuller Theological Seminary

Jennifer has recently completed her Master's Degree in Crosscultural Studies at Fuller Theological Seminary, specializing in Children at Risk. She has worked with children in various countries, including Mexico, Guatemala, Costa Rica, and the Philippines. She desires to help children by providing accessible and practical training materials to caregivers around the world.

Paul Stockley, M.A.—Development Worker, Oxford

Paul is freelance in development with a focus on children in especially difficult circumstances. His current portfolio includes strategic planning and facilitator training for Youth Partnership International, and technical aspects of resource integration for Viva Network's *Quality Improvement Scheme.* For three years, Paul served as Publishing Facilitator for the partnership journal *Reaching Children at Risk.* He also does volunteer relational support work for young people in his locality of St. Clements, East Oxford.

---

[1] Most of this biography is taken from Charles H. Kraft, *SWM/SIS at Forty: A Participant/Observer's View of Our History* (Pasadena, CA: William Carey Library, 2005), 227.

ABOUT THE AUTHORS

IN ALPHABETICAL ORDER

Cathryn Baker works as Prayer Mobiliser for Viva Network. Her role includes coordinating the World Weekend of Prayer for Children at Risk, and partnering with many other ministries to wake up the church to the need to pray for vulnerable children. She is married to Rob and lives in Oxford, UK.

Dr. Alemu Beeftu, founder and president of Gospel of Glory, trains pastors, businesspeople, and politicians in developing countries to make the most of God's call on their lives. Beeftu grew up on an isolated farm in the Ethiopian countryside, not learning to read or write until, at age twelve, his desire to read caused him to run away to a missionary school. Once there, he learned to read and write—and found a Savior. Now, God has called him into full time ministry with Gospel of Glory, a ministry that is fully devoted to Christian leadership development through curriculum, books, teaching tapes, and seminars. Dr. Beeftu and his wife Genet make their home in Colorado Springs, Colorado, with their children Keah and Amman.

Harry Bryans is originally from Northern Ireland and has worked in Belgium as a missionary for 23 years, mainly in children's ministry. He is married to Catherine and they have two children, Laura and Timothée. He pioneered the development of the www.hikidz.org children's website and continues to do research, writing, and webmastering for the project. He also has a heart for networking ministries that work to bring the Gospel to children around the world. Harry helped set up the European and Francophone Children's Ministry Forums in 2003.

Tri Budiardjo currently serves with Jaringan Peduli Anak Bangsa, a network of over 450 organizations in ministry to children in especially difficult circumstances in Indonesia. He has worked with World Vision in Indonesia and Cambodia for 17 years, and with Christian Children's Fund for 7 years. Tri is the author of *Sorotan Alkitab Tentang Anak* (What the Bible Says About Children). His passion is to see a transformed society where children are the priority. Tri is married to Leonora and has 3 grown up boys: Yosua (27), Yohanes (27) and Yosia (24).

Dr. Marcia J. Bunge is Professor of Theology and Humanities at Christ College, the Honors College of Valparaiso University, and Director of the Child in Religion and Ethics Project. She edited *The Child in Christian Thought* (Eerdmans, 2001) and has written several articles on children. Her current project was funded by a generous grant of $538,000 from the Lilly Endowment, Inc. and aims to strengthen theological and ethical understandings of children and childhood. She is also the co-chair of the "Childhood Studies and Religion Consultation" of the American Academy of Religion; a co-director of the international "Child Theology Movement"; and a consultant for the "Center for the Theology of Childhood." She has spoken widely on issues regarding children and is presently co-editing a book on *Biblical Perspectives on Children and Childhood* (Eerdmans, forthcoming).

Greg W. Burch is currently studying for his Ph.D. at Fuller Theological Seminary. He is a husband and a father of two children, and he authored *Community Children: A Ministry of Hope and Restoration for the Street Dwelling Child* (Latin America Mission, 2005).

Georgie Christine, OBE is founder and curriculum consultant to the PEPE Program. The Christines have served in Brazil along with their four children since 1977.

BMS World Mission's Regional Secretary for Latin America is **Stuart Christine.** He acts as a mission consultant to the Program of Preschool Education (PEPE) with his wife Georgie in Brazil.

Mark Crawford and **Christa Foster Crawford** have worked in Thailand for four years addressing issues of trafficking and sexual exploitation of women and girls in the Mekong subregion. Mark is a graduate of the School of Intercultural Studies at Fuller Seminary, where he began his study of effective ministry to people in prostitution. Christa is a Harvard Law School graduate and authored/edited the publication, *Combating Human Trafficking in Asia: A Resource Guide to International and Regional Legal Instruments, Political Commitments and Recommended Practices* while working for the United Nations in Bangkok. They are founders of Just Food, Inc./The Garden of Hope, a holistic ministry addressing the spiritual, psychological, and physical needs of people at risk of or rescued from trafficking and prostitution.[1]

Dr. Gustavo Crocker is currently the Regional Director for the Church of the Nazarene in Eurasia. He has also served as the Senior Vice-President for Programs at World Relief Corporation and the Director of Field Management for Compassion International. His ministry included several years as the Administrative Director of Nazarene Compassionate Ministries International out of Kansas City, Missouri, and two years as Regional Coordinator of Nazarene Compassionate Ministries out of Quito, Ecuador. A Guatemalan by birth, Dr. Crocker has taught in the areas of Global Missions, Evangelism and Church Planting, Cross-cultural Ministry, International Development, International Business, and Social Development in various universities in Latin America, Europe, and the United States. He and his wife Rachel have two daughters, Raquel and Elizabeth, and they currently reside in Buesingen, Germany.

---

[1] Mark Crawford and Christa Foster Crawford, "Human Trafficking: Children and the Sex Trade," *Theology News & Notes*, Fuller Theological Seminary (Fall 2005):17.

Professor and Associate Dean of Trinity Evangelical Divinity School, **Dr. Perry Downs** authored *Teaching for Spiritual Growth* (Zondervan, 1994) and edited the *Christian Education Journal*.

A Senior Research Associate at the Centre for Family Research, University of Cambridge, **Judith Ennew** has been an activist and researcher in children's rights since 1979. Possibly best-known for her work with street children, her more recent publications include *Questioning the Basis of our Work: Christianity, Children's Rights and Development* (Tearfund, 2004, with Paul Stephenson). She lives in Bangkok and is studying theology through an online postgraduate diploma at the University of Melbourne.

Karissa Glanville has an M.Div. from Fuller Theological Seminary and is currently working there on her Ph.D. with a focus on discipling at-risk youth. She has taught and discipled children for over fifteen years; formally, informally, and as a public school teacher. She also writes fiction for children and youth and is part of a small film production company.

Since 1983, **Susie Howe** has specialized in the hospital and community-based nursing care of those living with HIV and AIDS. In 1995, she founded The Bethany Project, a ministry in Zimbabwe that gives community-based support to children affected by HIV disease. In 1998, she became the Founding Director of the Pavement Project and set up The Bethany Children's Trust. Since 2001, she has been full-time Director of The Bethany Children's Trust in the UK, and frequently travels to Africa in the course of her work. Susie was part of the steering group that set up the Christian HIV/AIDS Alliance, and is now on the Executive Committee. She is married to Jeremy.

Dr. Ravi Jayakaran is Chief Consultant for Quality Professional Interfaces-GMS and has more than 28 years of development experience, primarily in Asia. He specializes in poverty reduction strategies and programming for the Greater Mekong Sub-Region in Southeast Asia, and has also written over 17 books on issues related to development. The final draft for his latest book, *Mobilizing Child Participation in the Development Process* has just been completed. Dr Jayakaran and his wife Vimla are based in Phnom Penh, where Vimla teaches at an international school. Their older son Amit is a research scientist with GE's Global Research center, while their younger son Rohit has an exciting career as a media specialist.

Daphne Kirk serves as the director for Generation 2 Generation, a ministry focused on generational healing, discipleship, and mission. Daphne is the author of over 21 books including *Reconnecting the Generations* (Generation 2 Generation, 2006) and *Born for Such a Time as This* (Generation 2 Generation, 2006). Daphne's leadership team includes Andrew (23 years of age) and Daniella (21 years) who have traveled with her and been an integral part of the ministry for about 12 years. They are now committed to the vision and minister and travel in their own right.

Dr. Meredith Long has led ministry teams in integral Christian ministry since 1986 with fourteen years of international service in Bangladesh and East Africa. As Vice-President for Planning and Integration with World Relief, he presently guides planning and ministry integration for all of World Relief's programs. *Health, Healing and God's Kingdom* (Regnum Books, 2000) captures his reflections on the biblical integration of health and healing ministries into the task of missions in Africa and *The AIDS Crisis: What We Can Do*, co-authored with Debbie Dortzbach (InterVarsity Press, forthcoming). Meredith's three children have so far yielded four incomparable grandchildren and his wife, Kendra, is the Director of Spiritual Formation at Church of the Ascension in Westminster, Maryland.

Mark Lorey leads program research, learning, and development for World Vision's global HIV and AIDS response.

Bard Luippold is Resource and Project Associate for World Vision's HIV/AIDS Hope Initiative. He lives with his wife, Kristin, in Tacoma, WA.

Ndaba Mazabane serves as a Missions and Outreach Pastor at Rosebank Union Church in Johannesburg, South Africa. He is the president of the Association of Evangelicals in Africa and the chairman of the International Council of the World Evangelical Alliance.

Associate Professor of Leadership and Dean of the School of Intercultural Studies at Fuller Theological Seminary, **Dr. Doug McConnell** co-authored *The Changing Face of World Missions* (Baker, 2005) and has written various articles for journals and dictionaries.

Patrick McDonald is the Founding Director of Viva Network. He wrote *Children at Risk: Networks in Action* (World Vision International, 2000) and *Reaching Children in Need: What's Being Done—What You Can Do* (Kingsway Communications, 2000).

Michael McGill served as the founder and Director of Viva Network's Asha Forum for six years. He practiced as a master's level therapist at a residential treatment facility for children in Chicago and is currently pursuing a Ph.D. in intercultural studies at Fuller Theological Seminary, researching how to equip children to help bring peace in violent developing nations.

Shiferaw Michael has served as the Child Advocacy Director for Compassion International in Africa since 2003. Shiferaw has written several books in Amharic (the Ethiopian language), and his book, *Handbook on Children's Ministry: Vision Casting and Partner Development* will soon be published by Compassion East Africa Area.

Shiferaw loves to mobilize the church and theological schools for ministry to children. He and his wife Seble have three children

In 1997, God called **Joni Middleton** out of Africa to work with "girls in trouble." Not knowing who these girls were, she soon realized that God was calling her to bring new life to girls scattered around the world, and especially in South Asia, who had been sexually exploited and abused. Having seen God work His beautiful designs in their lives, she says she works with "the world's best women and girls." She presently works as a training and network consultant with Project Rescue (A/G). She is based in Calcutta where she learns how to be "Joni Auntie" to girls from the local red-light areas.

Glenn Miles has worked with children for 20 years in various areas such as child health nursing, child public health, and other issues that affect children, including violence, abuse, trafficking, HIV and AIDS, and disability. He co-edited *Celebrating Children: Equipping People Working with Children and Young People Living in Difficult Circumstances around the World* (Paternoster Press, 2003) and co-wrote TEARFund's *Child Development Study Pack* and *Children at Risk Guidelines* (TEARFund, 2000). Glenn is passionate to see the church passionate about children. He and his wife Siobhan have three children.

Jennifer Orona serves as the Children at Risk Program Coordinator at Fuller Theological Seminary. She has worked with children in Mexico, Guatemala, Costa Rica, and the United States, and she is passionate about helping children who have been neglected, abandoned, and orphaned.

Premila Pavamani is the Executive Secretary for Emmanuel Ministries Calcutta based in India. She is also the director of the Calcutta Emmanuel School and is actively involved with street children, community development, and advocacy.

Dr. Kara Powell serves as the Executive Director at Fuller Theological Seminary's Center for Youth and Family Ministry. She is also an Assistant Professor in Youth and Family Ministries and has written a number of books including *Deep Ministry in a Shallow World* (Zondervan, 2006) and *Mirror Mirror* (Zondervan, 2002).

Bill Prevette with his wife Ky and son Daniel live in Bucharest, Romania and are missionaries with the Assemblies of God World Missions. For the past 24 years, they have been involved in training emerging leaders and working with children and youth at risk. They have lived in Los Angeles, Thailand, Cambodia, and have worked throughout Southeast Asia and Eastern Europe. Bill is currently studying for his Ph.D. at the Oxford Centre for Mission Studies. His research and interest is in equipping churches to care for children, youth, and the poor.

Dr. Katharine Meese Putman is an Assistant Professor of Psychology at the Fuller Graduate School of Psychology. She participates in the Headington Program in International Trauma, which studies the impact of chronic stress and trauma on humanitarian aid workers. She has conducted training, consultations, and research in Africa, Guatemala, Trinidad, China, Holland, and Sweden. Currently, Katharine studies spirituality and trauma among aid workers in Guatemala, particularly those who minister to at-risk youth. She teaches courses on play therapy, family therapy, cross-cultural integration of psychology and theology in Guatemala, community care for children at risk, program evaluation, and consultation. She lives in Pasadena, California, and is married to Keith, a filmmaker.

Barbara Ruegger has served as the South Asia Coordinator for King's Kids International for the past seven years. She is a trained nurse and has worked with children and youth both in the church, children's homes, and the streets in Switzerland and South Asia for the past 17 years. She has a passion for training workers in ministries to children and for that reason travels widely, mainly speaking in Youth with a Mission schools and seminars and doing member care for people in children's ministry.

Wendy Sanders is currently studying for her Ph.D. at Fuller Theological Seminary. She teaches courses on early childhood and child development.

Dave Scott has served on a part-time basis as the Facilitator for Tertiary Training Programs for Viva Network for seven years. He is currently an adjunct instructor, academic advisor, Ph.D. student, and Children at Risk research fellow at Fuller Theological Seminary.

Besa Shapllo has served as the director of Mission Possible in Albania since 1991, the year when Albania opened up to the world and Besa received Jesus Christ into her life. She is married but has no children. God has blessed her with hundreds of children all over Albania with whom she and her team work with so much love.

The Director of Children in Development for World Vision International, **Paul Stephenson** has written and edited numerous works, including *Questioning the Basis of Our Work: Christianity, Children's Rights and Development* (TEARFund, 2004, with Judith Ennew) and *Child Participation* (TEARFund, 2004). Paul has worked in international relief and development for 20 years, specializing in education, child rights and community development. He is married to Lisa, an ordained minister and actor, and has two children.

Paul Stockley is freelance in development with a focus on children in especially difficult circumstances. His current portfolio includes strategic planning and facilitator training for Youth Partnership International, and technical aspects of resource integration for Viva Network's *Quality Improvement Scheme*. For three years, Paul served as Publishing

Facilitator for the partnership journal *Reaching Children at Risk*. He also does volunteer relational support work for young people in his locality of St. Clements, East Oxford.

Thomas Swaroop serves as the Manager of Programs for Compassion International in India. He has more than 25 years of experience in Christian relief and community development in the Indian context. He is a visiting faculty member at Malaysia Baptist Theological Seminary in Penang. Thomas has compiled comprehensive readers on *The Asian Context of Children at Risk* and *Project Management & Facilitation* and has contributed several articles for Christian journals on development issues.

Dr. Jude Tiersma Watson and her husband, John, serve as missionary team leaders for the Los Angeles team of CRM/InnerCHANGE, a Christian Order Among the Poor. Tiersma Watson is an associate professor of Urban Mission in the School of Intercultural Studies at Fuller, and serves on the Executive Committee for the Center for Youth and Family Ministry. She co-edited, with Charles Van Engen, *God So Loves the City: Toward a Biblical Theology for the City* (MARC, 1994).

Stephen Tollestrup has been the Executive Director of TEARFund New Zealand since 1995. His special interests include children's rights and their inclusion and participation in community development. Stephen has an honors degree in theology and post-graduate qualifications in organizational development and labor studies from the University of Auckland. He speaks and runs seminars on justice and development throughout New Zealand and is a contributor to numerous journals and magazines. He is married to Deirdre and has one daughter and three sons.

Linda Wagener, Ph.D. is Associate Dean and Associate Professor of Psychology on the faculty of Fuller Theological Seminary. She is a clinical psychologist with 30 years of experience in research, teaching, and practice with high risk children and adolescents. Her special interest is in the moral, religious, and spiritual development of youth as reflected in her recent co-edited volume, *The Handbook of Spiritual Development in Childhood and Adolescence* (Sage, 2006). She is currently working in the area of adolescent violence prevention supported by a grant from the U.S. Office of Juvenile Justice and Delinquency Prevention. She and her husband have four children.

Sherry Walling is a doctoral student in clinical psychology at Fuller Seminary's Graduate School of Psychology. She is pursuing specializations in traumatic stress and cross cultural therapy. She has spent time working with street children and refugees in West Africa as well as young veterans returning from the Gulf War. Sherry plans to continue researching and writing about the impact of trauma on the cultural identity and spirituality of children.

Joanna Watson works for Viva Network, supporting Southern networks in their advocacy work for children at risk. She regularly speaks and trains on advocacy-related issues, including child rights and child protection. She contributed to "Keeping Children Safe" (2006), co-edited "Achieving Our Dreams for 2015" (2005) by the Grow Up Free From Poverty Coalition, and has written a variety of articles for *The Christian Herald*, *Release*, and other UK magazines. Prior to joining Viva Network, Joanna was a UK lawyer, specializing in children's law. Passionate about social justice, she is studying part-time for a Master's Degree in International Development. She enjoys travel and meeting new people.

Keith White and his wife, Ruth, serve as the leaders of Mill Grove, a Christian residential community caring for children in the United Kingdom. Keith, Chair of the Child Theology Movement and Trustee of the Christian Child Care Forum, lectures in sociology, theology and child development, and has authored and edited many books, including *Caring for Deprived Children* (Palgrave MacMillan, 1979), *A Place for Us* (Mill Grove, 1981), *The Art of Faith* (Baker, 1997), *Children and Social Exclusion* (National Council of Voluntary Child Care Organisations, 1999), and *Changing Child Care* (2000). He has recently edited an international version of The Bible.

Made in the USA
Lexington, KY
23 May 2019